THE BOOK ®

Honda
CBR600F1 & 1000F Fours
Service and Repair Manual

by Mark Coombs and Penny Cox

(1730-240-1Z4)

Models covered

CBR600F1. 598 cc. UK January 1987 to December 1991
CBR600F1 (Hurricane). 598 cc. US February 1987 through 1990
CBR1000F. 998 cc. UK January 1987 onwards
CBR1000F (Hurricane). 998 cc. US March 1987 onwards

Refer to manual No. 2070 for the 599cc CBR600F2 model.

© Haynes Publishing 2000

ABCDE
F

A book in the **Haynes Service and Repair Manual Series**

ISBN **1 85960 228 2**

British Library Cataloguing in Publication Data
A catalogue record for this book is available from the British Library

Printed in the USA

Haynes Publishing
Sparkford, Yeovil, Somerset BA22 7JJ, England

Haynes North America, Inc
861 Lawrence Drive, Newbury Park, California 91320, USA

Editions Haynes
4, Rue de l'Abreuvoir
92415 COURBEVOIE CEDEX, France

Haynes Publishing Nordiska AB
Box 1504, 751 45 UPPSALA, Sweden

Contents

LIVING WITH YOUR HONDA CBR

Introduction

Daily (pre-ride) checks

MAINTENANCE

Routine maintenance and servicing

Contents

REPAIRS AND OVERHAUL

Engine, transmission and associated systems

Chassis components

Electrical system

Wiring diagrams

REFERENCE

Index

The Birth of a Dream

by Julian Ryder

There is no better example of the Japanese post-War industrial miracle than Honda. Like other companies which have become household names, it started with one man's vision. In this case the man was the 40-year old Soichiro Honda who had sold his piston-ring manufacturing business to Toyota in 1945 and was happily spending the proceeds on prolonged parties for his friends. However, the difficulties of getting around in the chaos of post-War Japan irked Honda, so when he came across a job lot of generator engines he realised that here was a way of getting people mobile again at low cost.

A 12 by 18-foot shack in Hamamatsu became his first bike factory, fitting the

Honda C70 and C90 OHV-engined models

generator motors into pushbikes. Before long he'd used up all 500 generator motors and started manufacturing his own engine, known as the 'chimney', either because of the elongated cylinder head or the smoky exhaust or perhaps both. The chimney made all of half a horsepower from its 50 cc engine but it was a major success and became the Honda A-type. Less than two years after he'd set up in Hamamatsu, Soichiro Honda founded the Honda Motor Company in September 1948. By then, the A-type had been developed into the 90 cc B-type engine, which Mr Honda decided deserved its own chassis not a bicycle frame. Honda was about to become Japan's first post-War manufacturer of complete motorcycles. In August 1949 the first prototype was ready. With an output of three horsepower, the 98 cc D-type was still a

simple two-stroke but it had a two-speed transmission and most importantly a pressed steel frame with telescopic forks and hard tail rear end. The frame was almost triangular in profile with the top rail going in a straight line from the massively braced steering head to the rear axle. Legend has it that after the D-type's first tests the entire workforce went for a drink to celebrate and try and think of a name for the bike. One man broke one of those silences you get when people are thinking, exclaiming 'This is like a dream!' 'That's it!' shouted Honda, and so the Honda Dream was christened.

'This is like a dream!' 'That's it' shouted Honda

Mr Honda was a brilliant, intuitive engineer and designer but he did not bother himself with the marketing side of his business. With hindsight, it is possible to see that employing Takeo Fujisawa who would both sort out the home market and plan the eventual expansion into overseas markets was a masterstroke. He arrived in October 1949 and in 1950 was made Sales Director. Another vital new name was Kiyoshi Kawashima, who along with Honda himself, designed the company's first four-stroke after Kawashima had told them that the four-stroke opposition to Honda's two-strokes sounded nicer and therefore sold better. The result of that statement was the overhead-valve 148 cc E-type which first ran in July 1951 just two months after the first drawings were made. Kawashima was made a director of the Honda Company at 34 years old.

The E-type was a massive success, over 32,000 were made in 1953 alone, but Honda's lifelong pursuit of technical innovation sometimes distracted him from commercial reality. Fujisawa pointed out that they were in danger of ignoring their core business, the motorised bicycles that still formed Japan's main means of transport. In May 1952 the F-type Cub appeared, another two-stroke despite the top men's reservations. You could buy a complete machine or just the motor to attach to your own bicycle. The result was certainly distinctive, a white fuel tank with a circular profile went just below and behind the saddle on the left of the bike, and the motor with its horizontal cylinder and bright red cover just below the rear axle on the same side of the bike. This was the machine that turned Honda into the biggest bike maker in Japan

ready for the TT. In 1959 the factory entered five riders in the 125. They did not have a massive impact on the event being benevolently regarded as a curiosity, but sixth, seventh and eighth were good enough for the team prize. The bikes were off the pace but they were well engineered and very reliable.

The TT was the only time the West saw the Hondas in '59, but they came back for more the following year with the first of a generation of bikes which shaped the future of motorcycling - the double-overhead-cam four-cylinder 250. It was fast and reliable - it revved to 14,000 rpm - but didn't handle anywhere near as well as the opposition. However, Honda had now signed up non-Japanese riders to lead their challenge. The first win didn't come until 1962 (Aussie Tom Phillis in the Spanish 125 GP) and was followed up with

with 70% of the market for bolt-on bicycle motors, the F-type was also the first Honda to be exported. Next came the machine that would turn Honda into the biggest motorcycle manufacturer in the world.

The C100 Super Cub was a typically audacious piece of Honda engineering and marketing. For the first time, but not the last, Honda invented a completely new type of motorcycle, although the term 'scooterette' was coined to describe the new bike which had many of the characteristics of a scooter but the large wheels, and therefore stability, of a motorcycle. The first one was sold in August 1958, fifteen years later over nine-million of them were on the roads of the world. If ever a machine can be said to have brought mobility to the masses it is the Super Cub. If you add in the electric starter that was added for the C102 model of 1961, the design of the Super Cub has remained substantially unchanged ever since, testament to how right Honda got it first time. The Super Cub made Honda the world's biggest manufacturer after just two years of production.

Honda's export drive started in earnest in 1957 when Britain and Holland got their first bikes, America got just two bikes the next year. By 1962 Honda had half the American market with 65,000 sales. But Soichiro Honda had already travelled abroad to Europe and the USA, making a special point of going to the Isle of Man TT, then the most important race in the GP calendar. He realised that no matter how

advanced his products were, only racing success would convince overseas markets for whom 'Made in Japan' still meant cheap and nasty. It took five years from Soichiro Honda's first visit to the Island before his bikes were

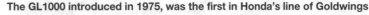

The GL1000 introduced in 1975, was the first in Honda's line of Goldwings

a world-shaking performance at the TT. Twenty-one year old Mike Hailwood won both 125 and 250 cc TTs and Hondas filled the top five positions in both races. Soichiro Honda's master plan was starting to come to fruition, Hailwood and Honda won the 1961 250 cc World Championship. Next year Honda won three titles. The other Japanese factories fought back and inspired Honda to produce some of the most fascinating racers ever seen: the awesome six-cylinder 250, the five-cylinder 125, and the 500 four with which the immortal Hailwood battled Agostini and the MV Agusta.

When Honda pulled out of racing in '67 they had won sixteen rider's titles, eighteen manufacturer's titles, and 137 GPs, including 18 TTs, and introduced the concept of the modern works team to

Carl Fogarty in action at the Suzuka 8 Hour on the RC45

Photo courtesy of Kel Edge

motorcycle racing. Sales success followed racing victory as Soichiro Honda had predicted, but only because the products advanced as rapidly as the racing machinery. The Hondas that came to Britain in the early '60s were incredibly sophisticated. They had overhead

An early CB750 Four

cams where the British bikes had pushrods, they had electric starters when the Brits relied on the kickstart, they had 12V electrics when even the biggest British bike used a 6V system. There seemed no end to the technical wizardry and when in 1968 the first four-cylinder

CB750 road bike arrived the world changed for ever. They even had to invent a new word for it: superbike. Honda raced again with the CB750 at Daytona and won the World Endurance title with a prototype DOHC version that became the CB900 roadster. There was the six-cylinder CBX, the first turbocharged production bike, they invented the full-dress tourer with the Goldwing and came back to GPs with the revolutionary oval-pistoned NR500 four-stroke, a much-misunderstood bike that was more rolling experiment than racer. It was true, though, that Mr Honda was not keen on two-strokes - early motocross engines had to be explained away to him as lawnmower motors! However, in 1982 Honda raced the NS500, an agile three-cylinder lightweight against the big four-cylinder opposition in 500 GPs. The bike won in the first year and in '83 took the world title for Freddie Spencer. In four-stroke racing the V4 layout took over from the straight four, dominating TT, F1 and Endurance championships and when Superbike arrived Honda were ready with the RC30. On the roads the VFR V4 became an instant classic while the CBR600 invented another new class of bike on its way to becoming a best-seller.

And then there was the NR750. This limited-edition technological tour-de-force embodied many of Soichiro Honda's ideals. It used the latest techniques and materials in every component, from the oval-piston, 32-valve V4 motor to the titanium coating on the windscreen, it was - as Mr Honda would have wanted - the best it could possibly be. A fitting memorial to the man who has shaped the motorcycle industry and motorcycles as we know them today.

The Honda CBRs

The CBRs continued the Honda tradition of DOHC four-valves-per cylinder across-the-frame fours, but added water cooling for the first time. This was in line with industry trends, but eschewing expensive aluminium frames in favour of good old steel wasn't. Neither was the all-enclosing bodywork and big, flared front mudguard which some observers found a little bulbous for their tastes. Those air intake scoops either side of the headlight showed that the designers had spent a lot of time on the problem of feeding the motor with a supply of slightly pressurised, still air - internal aerodynamics they called it.

Aesthetics aside, there was no doubt that Honda achieved their design aims of over 130 bhp per litre from both the 600 and 1000 yet still managed to shrink the dimension of the motor compared to the air-cooled fours in all directions. Valves were waisted, camshafts were hollow, piston rings thinned down, a typical inventory of Honda attention to detail. The valve gear consisted of rocker arms pivoting on ball-and-pillow joints in the head thus liberating room for a straight inlet tract with a good degree of downdraught. The layout bore a very close resemblance to the arrangement on the VFR750 which was launched a year before the CBRs.

The only internal differences between the 600 and 1000 were that the 600 had a balance shaft gear-driven directly off the crankshaft and the 1000 had its alternator mounted piggy-back behind the cylinders to keep its engine width acceptable. Both bikes avoided the fashionable pitfall of 16-inch front wheels and used 17-inch front wheels that gave quick steering without compromising stability.

The DCBS (Dual Combined Braking System) CBR1000F model

There wasn't anything startling about the spec sheet of the CBRs when they were new and in many ways there still isn't. It is therefore remarkable that the 600 effectively invented the Supersport 600 class and then continued to dominate it and fill the best-seller slot in countries all over the world. The first 600, the F-H stayed basically unchanged for four years until the F-M arrived in 1991. In that time, initial suspicion engendered mainly by its looks, disappeared as the CBR600 dominated the new Supersport 600 racing class and revealed itself as the best road-going all-rounder in its sector of the market. When the Supersport 600 class got its own TT in 1989, Steve Hislop won it on a CBR600 averaging over 112 mph for the 150-mile race. But unlike some other bikes in the class, the private owner could load his CBR600 up with luggage and a passenger and go touring in comfort.

Up to the time of writing, the 600 had been comprehensively revamped twice but the 1000 has remained largely unchanged save for the suspension and bodywork being updated for the F-K model in 1989. The P-model that appeared in late '92 was used to showcase a mechanical linked-braking system that Honda hoped would give some of the advantages of electronic ABS without the cost.

But where the 1000 was a perfectly good bike in the big sports tourer class, stuffed full of exceptional bikes, the CBR600 was a remarkable bike in a class that was at the cutting edge of both technology and sales. To achieve that with what at first sight looks like a conservative design is a remarkable feat.

Acknowledgements

Our thanks are due to APS Motorcycles of Wells, Bridge Motorcycle World of Exeter, and Paul Branson Motorcycles of Yeovil who supplied the motorcycles featured in the photographs throughout this manual. We would also like to thank the Avon Rubber Company, who kindly supplied information and technical assistance on tyre fitting, and NGK Spark plugs (UK) Ltd for information on spark plug maintenance and electrode conditions.

Thanks are also due to Honda (UK) and Kel Edge for supplying the cover transparencies.

About this Manual

The aim of this manual is to help you get the best value from your motorcycle. It can do so in several ways. It can help you decide what work must be done, even if you choose to have it done by a dealer; it provides information and procedures for routine maintenance and servicing; and it offers diagnostic and repair procedures to follow when trouble occurs.

We hope you use the manual to tackle the work yourself. For many simpler jobs, doing it yourself may be quicker than arranging an appointment to get the motorcycle into a dealer and making the trips to leave it and pick it up. More importantly, a lot of money can be saved by avoiding the expense the shop must pass on to you to cover its labour and overhead costs. An added benefit is the sense of satisfaction and accomplishment that you feel after doing the job yourself.

References to the left or right side of the motorcycle assume you are sitting on the seat, facing forward.

We take great pride in the accuracy of information given in this manual, but motorcycle manufacturers make alterations and design changes during the production run of a particular motorcycle of which they do not inform us. No liability can be accepted by the authors or publishers for loss, damage or injury caused by any errors in, or omissions from, the information given.

Professional mechanics are trained in safe working procedures. However enthusiastic you may be about getting on with the job at hand, take the time to ensure that your safety is not put at risk. A moment's lack of attention can result in an accident, as can failure to observe simple precautions.

There will always be new ways of having accidents, and the following is not a comprehensive list of all dangers; it is intended rather to make you aware of the risks and to encourage a safe approach to all work you carry out on your bike.

Asbestos

● Certain friction, insulating, sealing and other products - such as brake pads, clutch linings, gaskets, etc. - contain asbestos. Extreme care must be taken to avoid inhalation of dust from such products since it is hazardous to health. If in doubt, assume that they do contain asbestos.

Fire

● Remember at all times that petrol is highly flammable. Never smoke or have any kind of naked flame around, when working on the vehicle. But the risk does not end there - a spark caused by an electrical short-circuit, by two metal surfaces contacting each other, by careless use of tools, or even by static electricity built up in your body under certain conditions, can ignite petrol vapour, which in a confined space is highly explosive. Never use petrol as a cleaning solvent. Use an approved safety solvent.

● Always disconnect the battery earth terminal before working on any part of the fuel or electrical system, and never risk spilling fuel on to a hot engine or exhaust.

● It is recommended that a fire extinguisher of a type suitable for fuel and electrical fires is kept handy in the garage or workplace at all times. Never try to extinguish a fuel or electrical fire with water.

Fumes

● Certain fumes are highly toxic and can quickly cause unconsciousness and even death if inhaled to any extent. Petrol vapour comes into this category, as do the vapours from certain solvents such as trichloro-ethylene. Any draining or pouring of such volatile fluids should be done in a well ventilated area.

● When using cleaning fluids and solvents, read the instructions carefully. Never use materials from unmarked containers - they may give off poisonous vapours.

● Never run the engine of a motor vehicle in an enclosed space such as a garage. Exhaust fumes contain carbon monoxide which is extremely poisonous; if you need to run the engine, always do so in the open air or at least have the rear of the vehicle outside the workplace.

The battery

● Never cause a spark, or allow a naked light near the vehicle's battery. It will normally be giving off a certain amount of hydrogen gas, which is highly explosive.

● Always disconnect the battery ground (earth) terminal before working on the fuel or electrical systems (except where noted).

● If possible, loosen the filler plugs or cover when charging the battery from an external source. Do not charge at an excessive rate or the battery may burst.

● Take care when topping up, cleaning or carrying the battery. The acid electrolyte, evenwhen diluted, is very corrosive and should not be allowed to contact the eyes or skin. Always wear rubber gloves and goggles or a face shield. If you ever need to prepare electrolyte yourself, always add the acid slowly to the water; never add the water to the acid.

Electricity

● When using an electric power tool, inspection light etc., always ensure that the appliance is correctly connected to its plug and that, where necessary, it is properly grounded (earthed). Do not use such appliances in damp conditions and, again, beware of creating a spark or applying excessive heat in the vicinity of fuel or fuel vapour. Also ensure that the appliances meet national safety standards.

● A severe electric shock can result from touching certain parts of the electrical system, such as the spark plug wires (HT leads), when the engine is running or being cranked, particularly if components are damp or the insulation is defective. Where an electronic ignition system is used, the secondary (HT) voltage is much higher and could prove fatal.

Remember...

✗ **Don't** start the engine without first ascertaining that the transmission is in neutral.

✗ **Don't** suddenly remove the pressure cap from a hot cooling system - cover it with a cloth and release the pressure gradually first, or you may get scalded by escaping coolant.

✗ **Don't** attempt to drain oil until you are sure it has cooled sufficiently to avoid scalding you.

✗ **Don't** grasp any part of the engine or exhaust system without first ascertaining that it is cool enough not to burn you.

✗ **Don't** allow brake fluid or antifreeze to contact the machine's paintwork or plastic components.

✗ **Don't** siphon toxic liquids such as fuel, hydraulic fluid or antifreeze by mouth, or allow them to remain on your skin.

✗ **Don't** inhale dust - it may be injurious to health (see Asbestos heading).

✗ **Don't** allow any spilled oil or grease to remain on the floor - wipe it up right away, before someone slips on it.

✗ **Don't** use ill-fitting spanners or other tools which may slip and cause injury.

✗ **Don't** lift a heavy component which may be beyond your capability - get assistance.

✗ **Don't** rush to finish a job or take unverified short cuts.

✗ **Don't** allow children or animals in or around an unattended vehicle.

✗ **Don't** inflate a tyre above the recommended pressure. Apart from overstressing the carcass, in extreme cases the tyre may blow off forcibly.

✔ **Do** ensure that the machine is supported securely at all times. This is especially important when the machine is blocked up to aid wheel or fork removal.

✔ **Do** take care when attempting to loosen a stubborn nut or bolt. It is generally better to pull on a spanner, rather than push, so that if you slip, you fall away from the machine rather than onto it.

✔ **Do** wear eye protection when using power tools such as drill, sander, bench grinder etc.

✔ **Do** use a barrier cream on your hands prior to undertaking dirty jobs - it will protect your skin from infection as well as making the dirt easier to remove afterwards; but make sure your hands aren't left slippery. Note that long-term contact with used engine oil can be a health hazard.

✔ **Do** keep loose clothing (cuffs, ties etc. and long hair) well out of the way of moving mechanical parts.

✔ **Do** remove rings, wristwatch etc., before working on the vehicle - especially the electrical system.

✔ **Do** keep your work area tidy - it is only too easy to fall over articles left lying around.

✔ **Do** exercise caution when compressing springs for removal or installation. Ensure that the tension is applied and released in a controlled manner, using suitable tools which preclude the possibility of the spring escaping violently.

✔ **Do** ensure that any lifting tackle used has a safe working load rating adequate for the job.

✔ **Do** get someone to check periodically that all is well, when working alone on the vehicle.

✔ **Do** carry out work in a logical sequence and check that everything is correctly assembled and tightened afterwards.

✔ **Do** remember that your vehicle's safety affects that of yourself and others. If in doubt on any point, get professional advice.

● If in spite of following these precautions, you are unfortunate enough to injure yourself, seek medical attention as soon as possible.

VIN (Vehicle Identification Number)

The frame Vehicle Identification Number (VIN) is stamped into the frame on the right side of the steering head. This is duplicated on a metal plate, riveted to the frame just behind the steering head.

The engine VIN is stamped into the crankcase. On 600 models it is on the right upper side of the crankcase, just behind the clutch operating arm, and on 1000 models it is situated on the front edge of the crankcase next to the crankcase mating surfaces. The VIN is made up of a model code, a serial code, the model year and the manufacturer's identification.

The VIN should be recorded and kept in a safe place so it can be quoted to law enforcement officials in the event of theft. The VIN should also be stated when purchasing or ordering parts for the machine. It is a good idea to write it on a card and keep tucked away with your drivers licence, then it will be handy when you need it.

The VIN can be used to identify the actual model of machine using the accompanying list. *Note that the dates given refer to the year of production by Honda - this is not necessarily the same as the date of sale or registration.*

Buying spare parts

Once you have located all the VIN numbers, record them for reference when buying parts. Since the manufacturers change specifications, parts and vendors (companies that manufacture various components on the machine), providing the VIN numbers is the only way to be sure you are buying the correct parts.

Whenever possible, take the worn component to the dealer so direct comparison can be made with the new component. Along the trail from the manufacturer to the parts shelf, there are numerous places the part can ond up with the wrong number or be incorrectly listed.

The two places to purchase new motorcycle parts - franchised dealers and independent accessory stores - differ in the type of parts they carry. While a dealer can obtain virtually every stock part on the motorcycle, as well as aftermarket items, the accessory dealer is usually - not always - limited to such items such as shock absorbers, tune up parts, engine gaskets, cables, brake parts, etc. Often, however, an accessory outlet will sell aftermarket suspension components, cylinders, transmission gears and other major components.

Used parts can be obtained for roughly half the price of new ones, but you can't always be sure of what you are getting. Once again, take the worn part to the salvage yard (breaker) for direct comparison.

Whether buying new, used or rebuilt parts, it is a good idea to deal directly with someone who specialises in parts for Honda motorcycles.

Model year	Model code	Engine VIN	Frame VIN
UK CBR600 F:			
1987	CBR600F-H	PC19E-2000081 to 2019843	PC19-2000017 to 2008955
1988	CBR600F-J	PC19E-2102061 to 2114053	PC19-2100101 to 2108645
1989	CBR600F-K	PC23E-2000049 on	PC23-2000144 on
1990/1	CBR600F-L	PC23E-2100677 on	PC23-2100659 on
US CBR600 F (*Hurricane) 49-state model:			
1987	CBR600F-H*	PC19E-2000032 to 2019534	PC190*HM000014 to 008281
1988	CBR600F-J*	PC19E-2100006 to 2019020	PC190*JM100004 to 105415
1989	CBR600F-K	PC19E-2200001 to 2206643	PC190*KM200001 to 204860
1990	CBR600F-L	PC23E-2100015 on	PC230*LM000004 on
US CBR600 F (*Hurricane) California model:			
1987	CBR600F-H*	PC19E-2000022 to 2019020	PC191*HM000002 to 002523
1988	CBR600F-J*	PC19E-2100365 to 2113305	PC191*JM100003 to 101632
1989	CBR600F-K	PC19E-2202101 to 2206333	PC191*KM200001 to 201434
1990	CBR600F-L	PC23E-2100022 on	PC231*LM000005 on
UK CBR1000 F:			
1987	CBR1000F-H	SC21E-2000033 to 2017564	SC21-2000021 to 2012950
1988	CBR1000F-J	SC21E-2105332 to 2114793	SC21-2100865 to 2110310
1989	CBR1000F-K	SC09E-2000035 on	SC24-2000028 on
1990	CBR1000F-L	SC09E-2100696 to 2106547	SC24-2100706 to 2105980
1991	CBR1000F-M	SC09E-2200803 to 2205358	SC24-2200765 to 2205070
1992	CBR1000F-N	Not available	Not available
1993	CBR1000F-P	SC09E-2400017 to 2403062	SC24-2400033 to 2402908
1994	CBR1000F-R	SC09E-2500179 to 2503368	SC24-2500177 to 2502859
1995	CBR1000F-S	SC24E-2600529 on	SC24-2600420 on
1996	CBR1000F-T	SC24E-2700001 on	SC24A-TM000001 on
US CBR1000 F (*Hurricane) 49-state model:			
1987	CBR1000F-H*	SC21E-2000041 to 2016805	SC210*HA001001 to 004855
1988	CBR1000F-J*	SC21E-2100001 to 2103504	SC210*JA100001 to 100480
1989	No model produced		
1990	CBR1000F-L	SC24E-2000001 on	SC240*LM000001 on
1991	CBR1000F-M	SC24E-2100001 to 2101985	SC240*MM100001 to MM101643
1992	No model produced		
1993	CBR1000F-P	Details not available	
1994	CBR1000F-R	Details not available	
1995	CBR1000F-S	Details not available	
1996	CBR1000F-T	Details not available	
US CBR1000 F (*Hurricane) California model:			
1987	CBR1000F-H*	SC21E-2000064 to 2014846	SC211*HA001003 to 004975
1988	CBR1000F-J*	SC21E-2102301 to 2104018	SC211*JA100001 to 100722
1989	No model produced		
1990	CBR1000F-L	SC24E-2000001 on	SC241*LM000001 on
1991	CBR1000F-M	SC24E-2100001 to 2101112	SC241*MM100001 to MM100341
1992	No model produced		
1993	CBR1000F-P	Details not available	
1994	CBR1000F-R	Details not available	
1995	CBR1000F-S	Details not available	
1996	CBR1000F-T	Details not available	

Frame VIN location

Engine VIN location - 600 models

Note: *The daily (pre-ride) checks outlined in the owner's manual covers those items which should be inspected on a daily basis.*

1 Engine/transmission oil level

1 Unscrew the filler cap/dipstick from the right crankcase cover and wipe it clean.

2 Insert the dipstick so that the filler cap threads are just resting on the crankcase cover - do not screw it in.

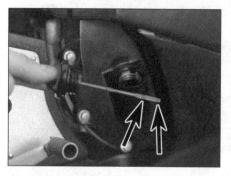

3 The oil level should lie between the marks on the end of the dipstick.

4 Add the specified oil to restore the oil level.

Before you start:

✔ Start the engine and let it idle for a few minutes, allowing it to reach normal operating temperature. ***Do not run the engine in an enclosed space such as a garage or workshop.***
✔ Stop the engine and place the motorcycle on its centrestand. Allow it to stand undisturbed for about five minutes to allow the oil level to stabilise. Make sure the motorcycle is on level ground.

Bike care:

● If you have to add oil frequently, you should check whether you have any oil leaks. If there is no sign of oil leakage from the joints and gaskets the engine could be burning oil (see ***Fault Finding***).

The correct oil

● Modern, high-revving engines place great demands on their oil. It is very important that the correct oil for your bike is used.
● Always top up with a good quality motor oil of the specified type and viscosity and do not overfill the engine. If the engine is inadvertently overfilled, excess oil can be removed using an empty plastic squeeze pack such as that used for gear oils.

Oil type	API grade SF or SG
Oil viscosity	SAE 10W40

2 Coolant level

⚠ **Warning: DO NOT remove the radiator pressure cap to add coolant. Topping up is done via the coolant reservoir tank filler. DO NOT leave open containers of coolant about, as it is poisonous.**

Before you start:

✔ Make sure you have a supply of coolant available (a mixture of 50% distilled water and 50% corrosion inhibited ethylene glycol antifreeze is needed).
✔ Place the motorcycle on its centre stand whilst checking the level. Make sure the motorcycle is on level ground.
✔ Remove the right sidepanel and on 1000 models also remove the seat. Start the engine - the coolant level check is made with the engine running.

Bike care:

● Use only the specified coolant mixture. It is important that antifreeze is used in the cooling system all year round, not just during the winter months. Don't top-up with water alone, as the antifreeze will become too diluted.
● Do not overfill the reservoir tank. If the coolant is significantly above the upper line at any time, the surplus coolant should be siphoned off to prevent it from being expelled out of the breather hose when the engine is running.
● If the coolant level falls steadily, check the system for leaks as described in Chapter 1. If no leaks are found and the level still continues to fall, it is recommended that the machine be taken to a Honda dealer who will pressure test the system.

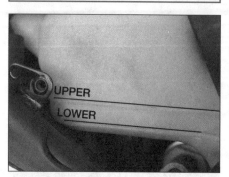

1 Coolant level must lie between upper and lower marks on reservoir with engine running - 1000 model shown.

2 Stop the engine. If the level is low, remove the filler cap and top up to the upper level mark using only the specified coolant.

3 Brake fluid levels

> ⚠️ **Warning: Hydraulic fluid can harm your eyes and damage painted surfaces, so use extreme caution when handling and pouring it. Do not use fluid that has been standing open for some time, as it absorbs moisture from the air which can cause a dangerous loss of braking effectiveness.**

Before you start:

✔ Position the motorcycle on its centrestand and turn the handlebars until the top of the master cylinder is as level as possible.

✔ On 1000 models, remove the right sidepanel for access to the rear brake fluid reservoir. This isn't necessary on 600 models due to the inspection slot in the panel.

✔ Make sure you have the correct hydraulic fluid. DOT 4 is recommended.

Bike care:

● The fluid in the master cylinder reservoirs will drop slightly as the brake pads wear down.
● If either fluid reservoir requires repeated topping-up this is an indication of an hydraulic leak somewhere in the system, which should be investigated immediately.

● Check for signs of fluid leakage from the hydraulic hoses and components - if found, rectify immediately.

● Check the operation of both brakes; if there is evidence of air in the system (spongy feel to lever or pedal), it must be bled as described in Chapter 7.

1 Front brake fluid level is checked via sightglass - it must be above lower level line (arrow).

2 Remove the two screws (arrows) to free the front brake reservoir cap.

3 Top up with new clean hydraulic fluid of the recommended type to the upper mark cast on the front inside face of the reservoir. Take care to avoid spills (see **Warning** above).

4 Ensure that the diaphragm is correctly folded before installing the float (where fitted) diaphragm, plate and cover.

5 Some models have a span adjuster on the brake lever - check that the adjuster wheel notch aligns with the arrow on the lever (arrow).

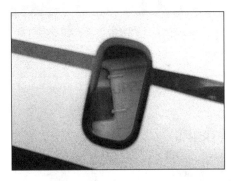

6 On 600 models, the rear brake fluid level can be seen through slot in right sidepanel. Fluid must lie between upper and lower lines.

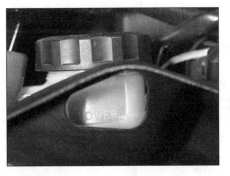

7 On 1000 models, remove the right sidepanel to view the rear brake fluid level. Fluid must lie between upper and lower lines.

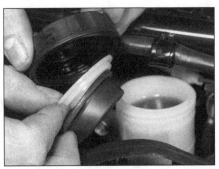

8 Unscrew the cap and lift out the plate and diaphragm to add fluid on 1000 models.

4 Clutch fluid level (1000 models)

⚠️ **Warning:** Hydraulic fluid can harm your eyes and damage painted surfaces, so use extreme caution when handling and pouring it. Do not use fluid that has been standing open for some time, as it absorbs moisture from the air which can cause a loss of clutch effectiveness.

Before you start:

✔ Position the motorcycle on its centrestand and turn the handlebars until the top of the master cylinder is as level as possible.

✔ Make sure you have the correct hydraulic fluid. DOT 4 is recommended.

Bike care:

● If the fluid reservoir requires repeated topping-up this is an indication of an hydraulic leak somewhere in the system, which should be investigated immediately.

● Check for signs of fluid leakage from the hydraulic hoses and components - if found, rectify immediately.

● Check the operation of the clutch; if there is evidence of air in the system (spongy feel to lever), it must be bled as described in Chapter 7.

1 Clutch fluid level is checked via sightglass - it must be above lower level

2 Remove the two screws (arrows) to free the reservoir cap.

3 Top up with new clean hydraulic fluid of the recommended type to the upper mark cast on the front inside face of the reservoir.

4 Ensure that the diaphragm is correctly folded before installing the plate and cover.

5 Suspension, steering and final drive

Suspension and Steering:

● Check that the front and rear suspension operates smoothly without binding.
● Check that the suspension adjustment settings are as required.
● Check that the steering moves smoothly from lock-to-lock.

Drive chain:

● Check that drive chain slack isn't excessive.
● If the chain looks dry, lubricate it - See Chapter 1.

1 Check the drive chain for correct tension.

6 Legal and safety checks

Lighting and signalling:

● Take a minute to check that the headlamp, taillamp, brake stop lamp and turn signals all work correctly.
● Check that the horn sounds when the switch is operated.
● A working speedometer is a statutory requirement in the UK.

Safety:

● Check that the throttle grip rotates smoothly and snaps shut when released.
● Check that the engine shuts off when the kill switch is operated.
● Check that sidestand return spring holds the stand securely up when retracted. The same applies to the centrestand.

Fuel:

● This may seem obvious, but check that you have enough fuel to complete your journey. If you notice signs of fuel leakage - rectify the cause immediately.
● Ensure you use the correct grade unleaded fuel - see Chapter 1 Specifications.

7 Tyres

The correct pressures:

● The tyre pressures must be checked when **cold**, not immediately after riding. If the motorcycle has just been ridden the tyres will be warm and their pressures will have increased. Note that extremely low tyre pressures may cause the tyre to slip on the rim or come off. High tyre pressures will cause abnormal tread wear and unsafe handling.

● Use an accurate pressure gauge.

● Proper air pressure will increase tyre life and provide maximum stability and ride comfort.

Tyre care:

● Check the tyres carefully for cuts, tears, embedded nails or other sharp objects and excessive wear. Operation of the motorcycle with excessively worn tyres is extremely hazardous, as traction and handling are directly affected.

● Check the condition of the tyre valve and ensure the dust cap is in place.

● Pick out any stones or nails which may have become embedded in the tyre tread. If left, they will eventually penetrate through the casing and cause a puncture.

● If tyre damage is apparent, or unexplained loss of pressure is experienced, seek the advice of a tyre fitting specialist without delay.

Tyre tread depth:

● At the time of writing UK law requires that tread depth must be at least 1 mm over 3/4 of the tread breadth all the way around the tyre, with no bald patches. Many riders, however, consider 2 mm tread depth minimum to be a safer limit. Honda recommend a minimum tread depth of 1.5 mm (0.06 in) for the front tyre, and 2.0 mm (0.08 in) for the rear.

● Many tyres now incorporate wear indicators in the tread. Identify the triangular pointer or TWI mark on the tyre sidewall to locate the indicator bars and replace the tyre if the tread has worn down to the bar.

1 Check the tyre pressures when the tyres are **cold** and keep them properly inflated.

2 Measure tread depth at the centre of the tyre using a tread depth gauge.

3 Tyre tread wear indicator bars (A) and location marking on sidewall (B).

Loading/speed	Front	Rear
All 600 models and 1000 K models onward	36 psi (2.5 Bar)	42 psi (2.9 Bar)

1000 H, J models:
  Up to 90 kg (198 lb) load - solo
  90 kg (198 lb) to max load* - pillion
	36 psi (2.5 Bar)
	42 psi (2.9 Bar)
		42 psi (2.9 Bar)
		42 psi (2.9 Bar)

*Refer to Dimensions and Weights in Reference section for details of maximum loading		

Notes

Chapter 1
Routine maintenance and Servicing

Contents

Degrees of difficulty

| **Easy,** suitable for novice with little experience | 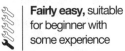 | **Fairly easy,** suitable for beginner with some experience | **Fairly difficult,** suitable for competent DIY mechanic | **Difficult,** suitable for experienced DIY mechanic | **Very difficult,** suitable for expert DIY or professional |

Specifications

Engine

Oil capacity at oil change:
  600 models .... 3.0 lit (3.2 US qt, 5.3 Imp pt)
  1000 models .... Not available
Oil capacity at oil and filter change:
  600 models .... 3.4 lit (3.6 US qt, 6.0 Imp pt)
  1000 models .... 3.8 lit (4.0 US qt, 6.7 Imp pt)
Oil capacity after disassembly:
  600 models .... 4.0 lit (4.2 US qt, 7.0 Imp pt)
  1000 models .... 4.5 lit (4.8 US qt, 8.0 Imp pt)
Coolant capacity:
  600 models .... 2.0 lit (2.1 US qt, 3.5 Imp pt)
  1000 models .... 3.0 lit (3.2 US qt, 5.3 Imp pt)
Spark plug type:
  All 600 models and 1000 T model onward .... NGK DPR8EA-9 or ND X24EPR-U9
  1000 H, J, K, L, M, N, P, R, S models .... NGK DPR9EA-9 or ND X27EPR-U9
Spark plug gap .... 0.8 - 0.9 mm (0.032 - 0.035 in)
Inlet valve clearance (cold):
  600 models .... 0.14 - 0.18 mm (0.006 - 0.007 in)
  1000 models .... 0.10 ± 0.02 mm (0.004 ± 0.001 in)
Exhaust valve clearance (cold):
  600 models .... 0.18 - 0.22 mm (0.007 - 0.009 in)
  1000 H, J, K, L, M, N models .... 0.16 ± 0.02 mm (0.006 ± 0.001 in)
  1000 P models onward .... 0.18 ± 0.02 mm (0.007 ± 0.001 in)
Idle speed:
  600 California models .... 1300 ± 100 rpm
  All other 600 models .... 1200 ± 100 rpm
  1000 L California models .... 1050 ± 100 rpm
  1000 P onward California models .... 1100 ± 100 rpm
  All other 1000 models .... 1000 ± 100 rpm

1

Miscellaneous

Freeplay adjustments:
Throttle cable freeplay - at twistgrip flange	2 - 6 mm (0.08 - 0.24 in)
Clutch cable freeplay (600 models) - at lever ball end	10 - 20 mm (0.4 - 0.8 in)
Final drive chain	15 - 25 mm (0.6 - 1.0 in)

Front forks:
Standard air pressure - all 600 models and 1000 H, J models	0 - 6 psi (0 - 0.4 Bar)

Tyre pressures - cold

	Front	**Rear**
1000 H and J models:		
Up to 90 kg (198 lb) - solo	36 psi (2.5 Bar)	42 psi (2.9 Bar)
90 kg (198 lb) to max load - pillion	42 psi (2.9 Bar)	42 psi (2.9 Bar)
All 600 models and 1000 K onwards	36 psi (2.5 Bar)	42 psi (2.9 Bar)
Refer to Dimensions and Weights in the Reference part of this Manual for details of maximum vehicle loading		
Tyre tread depth - minimum limit	1.5 mm (0.06 in)	2.0 mm (0.08 in)

At the time of writing, UK law requires that tread depth must be at least 1 mm over 3/4 of the tread breath all the way around the tyre.

Torque settings

	kgf m	lbf ft
Rear axle nut:		
600 models	9.0	65.0
1000 H, J, K, L, M, N models	9.5	69.0
1000 P models onward	9.3	67.0
Chain adjuster locknuts	2.2	16.0
Spark plugs	1.4	10.0
Front brake caliper bracket mounting bolts - 600 models and		
1000 H, J models (see text)	2.7	20.0
Front brake pad retaining pin	1.8	13.0
Front brake pad retaining pin plug (where fitted)	0.25	1.8
Rear brake caliper mounting bolt - 600 models and		
1000 H, J models	2.3	17.0
Rear brake pad pin retaining plate bolt	1.1	8.0
Engine oil drain plug:		
600 models	3.5	25.0
1000 H, J, K, L, M, N models	3.8	28.0
1000 P models onward	3.0	22.0
Oil filter	1.0	7.0
Cam follower adjuster screw locknut	2.3	17.0

Recommended fluids and lubricants

Engine:
Recommended oil	Honda 4-stroke oil or equivalent good quality SAE 10W40 SF or SG motor oil
Fuel grade	Unleaded, minimum octane rating 91 (RON/RM)
Coolant	50% distilled water/50% corrosion inhibited ethylene glycol antifreeze
Brake and clutch fluid	DOT 4 specification
Final drive chain	SAE 90 gear oil or aerosol lubricant suitable for O-ring chains
Wheel bearings and speedometer drive	High melting-point grease
Steering head bearings	General purpose grease
Swingarm and suspension linkage pivots	Molybdenum disulphide grease
All control pivots, stand pivots and throttle twistgrip	Chain and cable lubricant, motor oil or light grease
Control cables	Light machine oil or cable lube

Note: *The intervals listed below are recommended by the manufacturer. Your owner's manual may have different intervals for your model.*

Daily (pre-ride)
☐ See "Daily (pre-ride) checks" at the beginning of this manual.

Every 600 miles (1000 km)
☐ Adjust and lubricate the final drive chain (Section 1).

Six monthly, or every 4000 miles (6000 km)
Perform all of the daily (pre-ride) checks plus:

☐ Renew the spark plugs - US 600 and 1000 H and J models (Section 2).
☐ Check the spark plugs - US 1000 L-onwards and all UK models (Section 2).
☐ Clean the air cleaner element (Section 3).
☐ Clean the crankcase breather - 1000 models (Section 4).
☐ Check engine idle speed and adjust if necessary (Section 5).
☐ Check the battery (Section 6).
☐ Check the brake pads for wear (Section 7).
☐ Check the clutch operation - 600 models (Section 8).
☐ Lubricate all control cables and pivot points (Section 9).

Annually, or every 8000 miles (12,000 km)
All of the items above plus:

☐ Change the engine/transmission oil and filter (Section 10).
☐ Check and adjust the valve clearances (Section 11).
☐ Renew the spark plugs - US 1000 L and all UK models (Section 12).
☐ Check throttle and choke cable freeplay (Section 13).

☐ Synchronise the carburettors (Section 14).
☐ Check the clutch operation - 1000 models (Section 15).
☐ Check the fuel pipe for signs of leakage and clean or renew the fuel filters (as applicable) (Section 16).
☐ Check all coolant pipes and hoses for signs of leakage (Section 17).
☐ Check the secondary air supply system hoses for signs of damage and renew if necessary - US California models (Section 18).
☐ Check the operation of the steering and suspension (Section 19).
☐ Check the wheels for damage (Section 20).
☐ Check the brake system (Section 21).
☐ Check the drive chain slider for wear (Section 22).
☐ Check the side stand (Section 23).
☐ Check the headlight aim (Section 24).
☐ Check all nuts and bolts for tightness using the specified torque settings where given (Section 25).

Every 18 months, or every 12,000 miles (18,000 km)
All of the items above plus:

☐ Renew the air cleaner element (Section 26).
☐ Check evaporative emission control system hoses for signs of damage and renew if necessary - US California models (Section 27).

Two yearly, or every 12,000 miles (18,000 km)
All of the items above plus:

☐ Renew the brake fluid (Section 28).
☐ Renew the clutch fluid - 1000 models (Section 28).

Two yearly, or every 24,000 miles (36,000 km)
All of the items above plus:

☐ Renew the coolant (Section 29).

1

Component locations on CBR600 left side

1 Clutch cable upper adjuster	3 Carburettors	6 Drive chain	9 Oil filter
2 Valves, spark plugs	4 Fuel tap filter	7 Drive chain slider	10 Brake pads
	5 Fuel in-line filter	8 Engine oil drain bolt	

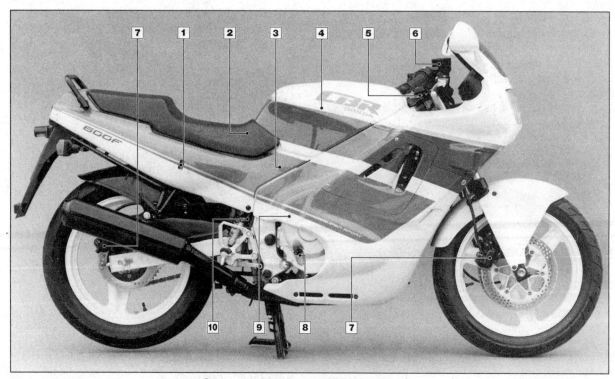

Component locations on CBR600 right side

1 Rear brake fluid reservoir	4 Air cleaner	7 Brake pads	9 Clutch cable lower adjuster
2 Battery	5 Steering head bearings	8 Engine oil filler	10 Rear brake light switch
3 Coolant tank	6 Front brake fluid reservoir		

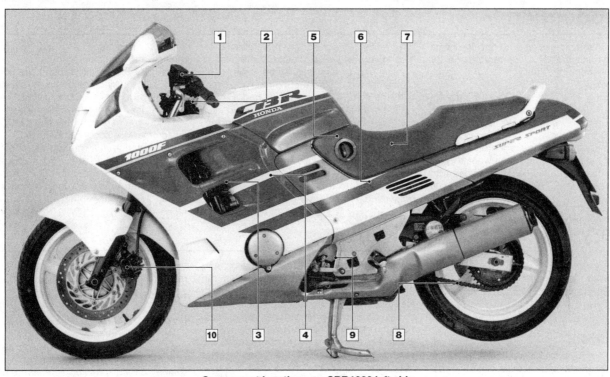

Component locations on CBR1000 left side

1 Clutch fluid reservoir	4 Carburettors	7 Battery	9 Drive chain slider
2 Steering head bearings	5 Fuel tap filter	8 Drive chain	10 Brake pads
3 Valves, spark plugs	6 In-line fuel filter (early models)		

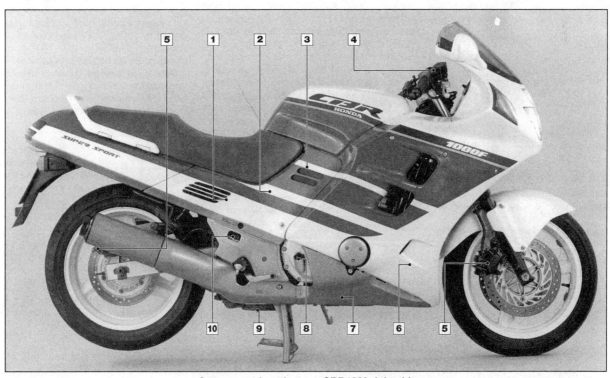

Component locations on CBR1000 right side

1 Rear brake fluid reservoir	4 Front brake fluid reservoir	7 Engine oil drain bolt	9 Crankcase breather hose plug
2 Coolant tank	5 Brake pads	8 Engine oil filler	10 Rear brake light switch
3 Air cleaner	6 Engine oil filter		

1

Introduction

1 This Chapter is designed to help the home mechanic maintain his/her motorcycle for safety, economy, long life and peak performance.

2 Deciding where to start or plug into the routine maintenance schedule depends on several factors. If you have a motorcycle whose warranty has recently expired, and if it has been maintained according to the warranty standards, you may want to pick up routine maintenance as it coincides with the next mileage or calendar interval. If you have owned the machine for some time but have never performed any maintenance on it, then you may want to start at the nearest interval and include some additional procedures to ensure that nothing important is overlooked. If you have just had a major engine overhaul, then you may want to start the maintenance routine from the beginning. If you have a used machine and have no knowledge of its history or maintenance record, you may desire to combine all the checks into one large service initially and then settle into the maintenance schedule prescribed.

3 Before beginning any maintenance or repair, the machine should be cleaned thoroughly, especially around the oil filter, spark plugs, cylinder head cover, sidepanels, carburettors, etc. Cleaning will help ensure that dirt does not contaminate the engine and will allow you to detect wear and damage that could otherwise easily go unnoticed.

4 Maintenance information is printed on decals attached to the motorcycle. If the information on the decals differs from that included here, use the information on the decal.

Every 600 miles (1000 km)

1 Drive chain -
adjustment and lubrication

Adjustment

1 To check the drive chain freeplay, place the machine on its centrestand with the rear wheel clear of the ground. Find the chain's tightest spot by rotating the rear wheel and feeling the amount of freeplay present on the bottom run of the chain, testing along the complete length of the chain. When the tightest spot has been found, push machine off its centre stand and support it on the side stand. Measure the total up and down movement available on the bottom run of the chain midway between the sprockets **(see illustration)**. This measurement should be within the limits given in the Specifications. If not the chain must be adjusted as follows.

2 Slacken the rear axle nut and loosen the chain adjuster locknuts. Tighten both adjuster nuts by an equal amount to draw the axle back until the drive chain freeplay is correct **(see illustration)**.

3 To preserve accurate wheel alignment, ensure that the same amount of lines (cast on the surface of each adjuster) are visible in the cutout of each swingarm fork end on both sides of the machine. A more accurate check of wheel alignment can be made by laying a plank of wood or drawing a length of string parallel to the machine so that it touches both walls of the rear tyre. Wheel alignment is correct when the plank or string is equidistant from both walls of the front tyre when tested on both sides of the machine **(see illustration)**.

4 Once wheel alignment is known to be correct, tighten the axle nut to the specified torque setting followed by the adjuster locknuts. Place the machine on its centre stand and check that the wheel spins freely.

5 Take note of the chain wear indicator labels on the swingarm ends and renew the chain if the arrowed alignment mark comes into the red 'replace chain' zone.

Lubrication

6 Although the chain fitted as standard equipment is of the O-ring type, grease being sealed into the internal bearing surfaces by O-rings at each end of the rollers, lubrication is still required to prevent the rollers from wearing on the sprocket teeth and to prevent the O-rings from drying up. A heavy (SAE 90) gear oil is best for this task; it will stay on the rollers longer than a lighter engine oil.

7 Whilst spinning the rear wheel, allow oil to dribble onto the rollers until all are oily, then apply a small amount to the O-rings on each side **(see illustration)**. An alternative is to use one of the proprietary aerosol-applied chain lubricants.

Caution: Some propellants used in aerosols cause the O-rings to deteriorate very rapidly, so make certain that the product is marked as being suitable for use with O-ring type chains (see illustration).

> **HAYNES HiNT** *Apply oil to the top of the lower chain run - centrifugal force will work it into the chain when the bike is moving.*

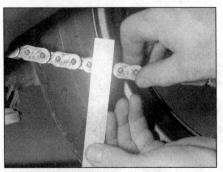

1.1 Measuring final drive chain freeplay

1.2 Rotate chain adjuster nuts by an equal amount

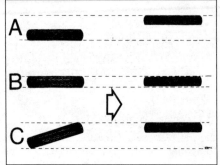

1.3 Method of checking wheel alignment
A and C incorrect, B correct

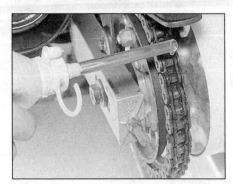

1.7 Lubricating the final drive chain

Six monthly, or every 4000 miles (6000 km)

2 Spark plugs - check

1 On 1000 H and J models remove both the upper fairing inner covers and left and right sidepanels. On 1000 K models onward remove the seat. On all 1000 models remove the fuel tank front mounting bolts then raise the tank up and support it on its prop stay. On 600 models remove both the left and right side covers from the fairing.

2 Carefully pull off the spark plug caps and remove any dirt or other foreign matter from the spark plug channels. Using a suitable plug spanner, unscrew and remove the spark plugs whilst keeping them clearly defined by their cylinder number.

3 Using feeler gauges, preferably of the wire type for greater accuracy, measure the gap between the electrodes and compare it with the figure given in the Specifications. If adjustment is required this can be carried out as described below, assuming that the plug is otherwise undamaged. In the event that any plug is heavily fouled or damaged in any way renewal is required; renew the plugs as a set. **Note:** *Ensure that the plugs are of the resistor type (indicated by the letter R) to ensure compliance with the ignition system. The same applies to the suppressor caps if these are ever renewed.*

4 If the spark plugs are still serviceable, carefully compare the appearance of their electrodes with the colour photographs at the end of this manual and note any information obtained from this. If any plug appears to show a fault, seek expert advice as soon as possible. The standard grade of spark plug should prove adequate in normal use and a change of specification (such as fitting a hotter or colder grade of plug) should not be made without expert advice from a Honda dealer.

5 Clean the plug electrodes by carefully scraping away the accumulated carbon deposits using a small knife blade or small files and abrasive paper; take care not to

bend the centre electrode or to chip or damage the ceramic insulator.
Caution: The cleaning of spark plugs on commercial sand-blasting equipment is not recommended due to the risk of abrasive particles being jammed in the gap between the insulator and plug metal body, only to fall clear later and drop into the engine; any plug that is too heavily fouled should be renewed.

6 Once clean, file the opposing faces of the electrodes flat using a small fine file. A magneto file or even a nail file is ideal for this purpose. Whichever method is chosen, make sure that every trace of abrasive and loose carbon is removed before the plug is installed. If this is not done, the debris will enter the engine and cause damage or rapid wear.

7 Whether a cleaned or new plug is fitted, always check the electrode gap before installing it. Use a spark plug adjusting tool or feeler gauges to measure the gap, and if adjustment is required, bend the outer (earth) electrode only. **Note:** *Never bend the centre electrode or the ceramic insulator nose will be damaged.*

8 Before the plugs are fitted, apply a fine coat of PBC or molybdenum disulphide grease to their threads. This will help prevent thread wear and damage on installation. and make their subsequent removal easier. Fit each plug finger-tight, then tighten it by a further 1/4 turn only, to ensure a gas-tight seal. Beware of

overtightening, and always use a plug spanner or socket of the correct size; tighten all spark plugs to the specified torque setting, where possible.

9 Never overtighten a spark plug otherwise there is a risk of stripping the thread from the cylinder head, especially as it is cast in light alloy. A stripped thread can be repaired without having to scrap the cylinder head by using a Helicoil wire thread insert. This is a low-cost service, operated by a number of dealers.

10 When refitting the suppressor caps, ensure that the HT leads are correctly routed; note that the leads are numbered as an aid to identification.

3 Air cleaner element - cleaning

1 On 600 models remove the fuel tank as described in Chapter 4. Slacken the screws which retain the top of the air cleaner housing, lift off the cover and remove the element **(see illustrations)**. On 1000 models remove the right sidepanel then slacken the three screws which retain the air cleaner housing side cover, removing it from the machine **(see illustration)**. Pull out the retaining clip from the bottom of the element and withdraw the element from the housing **(see illustrations)**.

3.1a On 600 models remove air cleaner housing top screws, remove cover . . .

3.1b . . . and air cleaner element

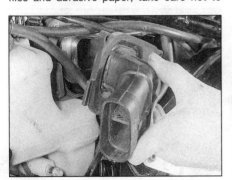

3.1c On 1000 models remove the air cleaner right side cover . . .

3.1d . . . withdraw the element retaining clip . . .

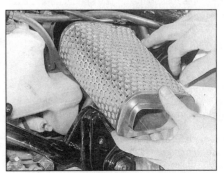

3.1e . . . and remove the element

1

3.3 On 600 models ensure arrow on element is facing forward

2 The element is of the dry paper type and can be cleaned by gently tapping the element on a solid surface to dislodge the dust and debris from the paper. If compressed air is available, use it to clean the element by blowing from the inside out. If the paper is extremely dirty or torn, the element must be renewed. **Note:** *On 1000 models drain the crankcase breather tube, as described in the following Section, before refitting the element.*
3 The element is installed by a reverse of the removal process. On 600 models note that the element must be installed so that the arrow on its frame is on the top surface, facing forwards **(see illustration)**. Ensure the element is correctly seated then refit the top of the air cleaner housing, tighten its retaining screws securely. Refit the fuel tank as described in Chapter 4. On 1000 models ensure the element is correctly positioned in the housing and secure it in place with its retaining clip. Refit the side cover to the air filter housing, ensuring it is correctly seated, and tighten its retaining screws securely. Refit the sidepanel.
4 It is essential that the element and housing sections or covers are correctly positioned and seat well to prevent unfiltered air entering and damaging the engine. The carburettors are also jetted to compensate for the presence of the element; if it is damaged, severely blocked or bypassed in any way or omitted, serious engine damage could result. Owners of US machines should also note that the air cleaner is subject to the anti-tampering legislation currently in force (see Chapter 4). For this reason the engine should never be run with the air cleaner element removed or disconnected.

4 Crankcase breather - draining (1000 models)

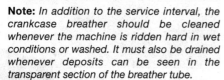

Note: *In addition to the service interval, the crankcase breather should be cleaned whenever the machine is ridden hard in wet conditions or washed. It must also be drained whenever deposits can be seen in the transparent section of the breather tube.*
1 The crankcase breather tube can be found

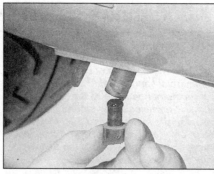

4.2 On 1000 models remove the crankcase breather drain plug and allow its contents to drain

on the underside of the machine, just behind the centre stand. The tube is connected to the air cleaner housing and is used to drain any water or oil present in the housing.
2 To drain the tube simply remove the plug from its end and allow the contents to drain out into a suitable container **(see illustration)**. When draining is complete refit the plug.

5 Engine idle speed - check

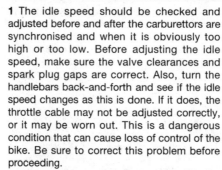

1 The idle speed should be checked and adjusted before and after the carburettors are synchronised and when it is obviously too high or too low. Before adjusting the idle speed, make sure the valve clearances and spark plug gaps are correct. Also, turn the handlebars back-and-forth and see if the idle speed changes as this is done. If it does, the throttle cable may not be adjusted correctly, or it may be worn out. This is a dangerous condition that can cause loss of control of the bike. Be sure to correct this problem before proceeding.
2 The engine should be at normal operating temperature, which is usually reached after 10 to 15 minutes of stop and go riding. Place the motorcycle on the centrestand and make sure the transmission is in Neutral.
3 Turn the throttle stop screw **(see illustration)**, until the idle speed listed in this Chapter's Specifications is obtained.

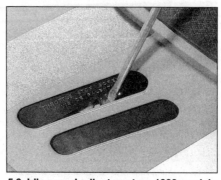

5.3 Idle speed adjustment on 1000 models

4 Snap the throttle open and shut a few times, then recheck the idle speed. If necessary, repeat the adjustment procedure.
5 If a smooth, steady idle can't be achieved, the fuel/air mixture may be incorrect. Refer to Chapter 4 for additional carburettor information.

6 Battery - checks

600 models

1 This model has a sealed battery, and thus requires no maintenance with regard to topping-up its electrolyte. All that should be done is to check that its terminals are clean and tight and that the casing is not damaged or electrolyte leaking. If the battery does need to be removed for any reason, refer to Chapter 8, Section 3 for details.

1000 models

2 Remove the seat then unhook the rubber strap and remove the battery cover and the tool kit. Remove the battery by disconnecting the leads and lifting it out of the machine. **Note:** *Always disconnect the negative (-) terminal first when disconnecting the battery terminals to prevent the risk of short circuits.*
3 The electrolyte level, visible through the translucent casing, should be between the two level marks on the battery casing. If not, remove the cell caps and top up to the upper level mark using only distilled water **(see illustration)**.
4 Check the battery for any signs of pale grey sediment at the bottom of the casing. This is caused by sulphation of the plates due to recharging at too high a rate or as a result of the battery being left discharged for long periods. A good battery should have little or no sediment visible and its plates should be straight and pale grey or brown in colour. If sediment deposits are deep enough to reach the bottom of the plates, or if the plates are buckled and have whitish deposits on them, the battery is faulty and must be renewed. Remember that a poor battery will give rise to a large number of minor electrical faults.

6.3 On 1000 models electrolyte level must be between marks on casing

7.7a On 1000 H, J and all 600 models position front brake pad spring in caliper . . .

7.7b . . . install brake pads . . .

7.7c . . . and refit pad retaining pins

5 On installation, check that the battery breather hose is not blocked and is correctly routed. Connect up the battery terminals, remembering to connect the negative (-) terminal last. Ensure that the terminals are tight and that the rubber cover is correctly fitted to the positive (+) terminal. Put the tool kit and cover back in place and secure the cover in position with the rubber strap.

All models

6 If the machine is not in regular use, disconnect the battery and give it a refresher charge every month to six weeks, as described in Chapter 8.

 HAYNES HINT *Battery terminal corrosion can be minimised by applying a layer of petroleum jelly to the terminals after the leads have been connected.*

7 Brake pads - wear check

> ⚠ **Warning: Brake pads contain asbestos. Take great care not to inhale any brake dust during the operation, and read the notes given in Safety first! concerning asbestos.**

1 The brake pads can be checked for wear without removing them from the caliper. On 600 models they can be checked through the gap between the caliper and bracket which is indicated by the cast arrow on the caliper surface. On 1000 models the front pads can be checked from the underside of the caliper, and the rear pads from the rear of the caliper.
2 On all models, the need for brake pad renewal can be determined by referring to the pad wear indicator on the friction material. Depending on the pad's manufacture, the wear limit indicator will be shown either as a series of grooves cut into the friction material, which will be visible until the pads have worn down to the bottom of the grooves, or as a wear groove or chamfer on the backing metal

side of the pad, the wear limit being when the friction material wears to the point where the groove or chamfer is exposed.
3 Due to the different types of pad fitted, it is recommended that the pad type be determined as soon as possible, before renewal becomes necessary. If there is any doubt about the pads' condition or if identification of pad type is difficult with the pads installed in the calipers, remove them as described below. If renewal is necessary, always renew both pads as a set, and in the case of the front brake, renew both sets at the same time.

Front brake - 1000 H, J and all 600 models

4 Remove both plugs from the caliper to reveal the pad pin retaining bolt heads; slacken both pad pins. Slacken and remove the caliper bracket mounting bolts and slide the caliper off the disc, taking care not to place any undue strain on the hydraulic hose. Remove both pad pins from the caliper and withdraw the brake pads, noting the correct position of the pad spring fitted to the caliper body.
5 Inspect the surface of each pad for contamination and check that the friction material has not worn beyond its service limit groove. If either pad is worn to or beyond the service limit at any point, fouled with oil or grease, or heavily scored or damaged by dirt and debris, both pads must be renewed as a

set. Note that it is not possible to degrease the friction material; if the pads are contaminated in any way they must be renewed.
6 If the pads are in good condition clean them carefully, using a fine wire brush which is completely free of oil or grease, to remove all traces of road dirt and corrosion. Using a pointed instrument, clean out the grooves in the friction material and dig out any embedded particles of foreign matter (as applicable). Any areas of glazing may be removed using emery cloth.
7 Ensure that the pad spring is correctly positioned in the caliper and remove all traces of corrosion from the pad retaining pins. Push the pistons as far back into the caliper as possible using hand pressure only; this is especially important if new pads are being fitted, due to the increased friction material thickness. Insert the pads into the caliper, and install the pad retaining pins, ensuring that they pass through both pads correctly **(see illustrations)**.
8 Slide the caliper assembly onto the disc and refit the caliper bracket mounting bolts, tightening them to the specified torque setting **(see illustration)**. Note: *The bottom left caliper bracket mounting bolt is also the anti-dive pin and should only be tightened to a torque setting of 1.2 kgf m (9 lbf ft).* Tighten the pad retaining pins to the specified torque setting and refit the pad pin plugs, tightening them securely **(see illustration)**.

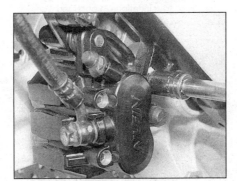

7.8a Install caliper and tighten caliper mounting bolts . . .

7.8b . . . and pad retaining pins to specified torque setting. Do not omit pad pin plugs

1

7.11a On 1000 H, J and all 600 models rear brake locate caliper pin with mounting bracket . . .

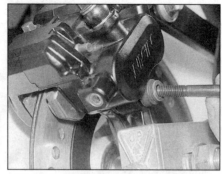

7.11b . . . then swing caliper down onto disc and insert its mounting bolt

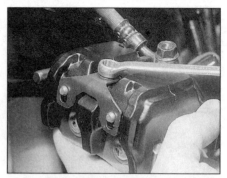

7.11c Ensure the pad pin retaining plate engages correctly with the pins and refit its retaining bolt

Rear brake - 1000 H, J and all 600 models

9 Slacken the pad pin retaining plate bolt and remove the plate from the caliper. Remove the caliper mounting bolt and rotate the caliper in a clockwise direction until it is clear of the disc. The caliper can then be removed from the machine by pulling it away from the wheel to free it from its mounting bracket, taking care not to place any undue strain on the brake hose. The pad pins can then be pulled out of the caliper using a pair of pointed-nose pliers, and the pads withdrawn, noting the correct position of the pad retaining spring in the caliper.

10 Inspect the pads as described above in paragraphs 5 and 6. Install the pads in the caliper as described in paragraph 7 before fitting the caliper as follows.

11 Remove all traces of corrosion from the caliper mounting pin then smear a small amount of silicone grease along its length. Refit the caliper to the mounting bracket, then swing the caliper down into position ensuring that the pads are positioned correctly on each side of the disc **(see illustration)**. Install the caliper mounting bolt, having first smeared silicone grease along its shank, and tighten it to the specified torque setting **(see illustration)**. Fit the pad pin retaining plate ensuring that it engages correctly with the slots in the pad pins and tighten its bolt to the specified torque setting **(see illustration)**.

Front and rear brake - 1000 K, L, M and N models

12 The brake pads on these models can be removed and installed whilst the caliper is fitted to the machine. Remove the pad pin plug from the caliper and slacken the pad retaining pin. Withdraw the pad retaining pin and slide the brake pads out of the caliper.

13 Inspect the pads as described above in paragraphs 5 and 6.

14 Check that the pad spring is in place in the caliper. Slide the pads into position ensuring that they locate correctly with the caliper mounting bracket, and refit the pad retaining pin **(see illustrations)**. **Note:** *If new pads are installed, it will first be necessary to push the pistons back into the caliper to gain the necessary clearance for the increased friction material thickness.* Tighten the pad retaining pin to the specified torque setting and refit the pad pin plug, tightening it securely **(see illustration)**.

Front and rear brake - 1000 P models onward

15 The brake pads can be removed and installed with the caliper fitted to the machine. Unscrew the pad retaining pin and press the spring plate on the other side of the caliper to allow the retaining pin to be withdrawn **(see illustrations)**. Slide the brake pads out of the caliper **(see illustration)**.

7.14a On 1000 K, L, M, N models slide pads into caliper

7.14b Refit pad retaining pin . . .

7.14c . . . followed by pad pin plug

7.15a Unscrew the pad retaining pin . . .

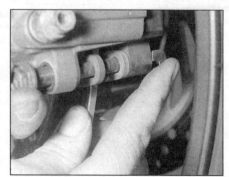

7.15b . . . and press the spring plate on the inside of the caliper to release the pad retaining pin

7.15c Withdraw the pads from the caliper

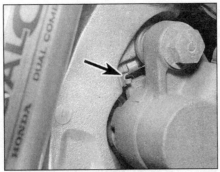

7.17 As the pads are inserted, ensure they engage the plate on the caliper mounting bracket (arrowed)

16 Inspect the pads as described above in paragraphs 5 and 6.

17 Check that the pad spring is in place in the caliper. Slide the pads into the caliper ensuring that they locate correctly with the plate on the caliper mounting bracket **(see illustration)**. **Note:** *If new pads are installed, it will first be necessary to push the pistons back into the caliper to gain the necessary clearance for the increased friction material thickness.* Slide the pad retaining pin into position so that it passes through the holes in each pad and check that the spring clip engages its end. Tighten the pad retaining pin the specified torque setting.

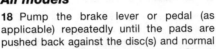

All models

18 Pump the brake lever or pedal (as applicable) repeatedly until the pads are pushed back against the disc(s) and normal operation of the brake has returned. Check the fluid level in the reservoir as described in "Daily (pre-ride) checks", noting that if new brake pads have been fitted it may be necessary to remove fluid from the reservoir.

19 Check the hydraulic system for leaks and ensure that the braking system is operating correctly. Remember that new pads, and to a lesser extent, cleaned pads will not function at peak efficiency until they have bedded in. Where new pads have been fitted, use the brake firmly but gently for the first 50 - 100 miles.

8 Clutch - check (600 models)

1 Check that the clutch cable operates smoothly and easily. If the clutch lever operation is heavy or stiff, lubricate the cable as described in the following Section. When the cable is operating smoothly it is necessary to check that the clutch lever is correctly adjusted. The clutch is correctly adjusted when there is 10 - 20 mm (0.4 - 0.8 in) freeplay, measured at the ball end of the l ever **(see illustration)**. If adjustment is required, use the handlebar end adjuster on the lever mounting bracket **(see illustration)**.

2 If there is insufficient range in the upper adjuster it will be necessary to remove the right side cover from the fairing and adjust the freeplay at the lower adjuster on the casing **(see illustration)**. Screw the upper adjuster fully inwards and slacken the locknut on the lower adjuster. Rotate the adjuster nut until the required freeplay is obtained at the handlebar lever, then securely tighten the lower adjuster locknut and refit the side cover to the fairing. If necessary, fine adjustments can then be made using the handlebar adjuster.

9 Control cables and pivot points - lubrication

Control cables

1 Check the outer cables for signs of damage, then inspect the exposed portions of the inner cables. Any signs of kinking or fraying will indicate that renewal is required. To obtain maximum life and reliability from the cables they should be thoroughly lubricated.

2 To lubricate the throttle, choke and clutch (600 models) cables, disconnect each cable at its lower end, then lubricate the cable with a pressure lube adapter **(see illustration)**. An alternative is to remove the cable from the

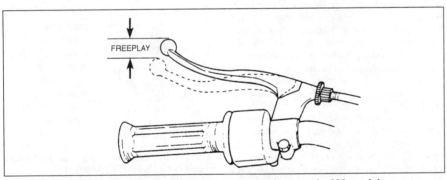

8.1a Clutch cable freeplay is measured at lever end - 600 models

8.1b Adjust clutch cable freeplay using upper . . .

8.2 . . . and lower adjusters

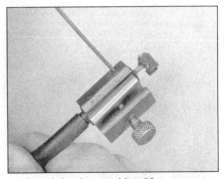

9.2a Lubricating a cable with a pressure lube adapter (make sure the tool seats around the inner cable)

machine, hang the cable upright, and make a small funnel arrangement using plasticine or by tapping a plastic bag around the upper end of the cable **(see illustration)**. Fill the funnel with oil and leave it overnight to drain through

3 The speedometer cable should be removed for examination and lubrication as described in Chapter 6.

Pivot points

4 The footpegs, clutch and brake levers, brake pedal, gearshift lever and side and centrestand pivots should be lubricated frequently. If the pivot is particularly dry, the component should be disassembled for thorough lubrication. However, if chain and cable lubricant is being used, it can be applied to the pivot joint gaps and will usually work its way into the areas where friction occurs. If motor oil or light grease is being used, apply it sparingly as it may attract dirt (which could cause the controls to bind or wear at an accelerated rate). **Note:** *One of the best lubricants for the control lever pivots is a dry-film lubricant (available from many sources by different names).*

5 Check that the stands are held securely in their raised positions by the return springs.

9.2b **Lubricating a control cable using a funnel type arrangement**

Annually, or every 8000 miles (12,000 km)

10 Engine/transmission oil and filter - change

Note: *The oil should be drained from the engine whilst it is at its normal operating temperature. This ensures that the oil is relatively thin and will therefore drain quicker and more completely, also any impurities will be held in suspension.*

1 Remove the fairing side sections, noting that on 1000 H and J models it is only necessary to remove the lower section (see Chapter 6).

2 On all models, start the engine and warm it up to normal operating temperature. Place the machine on its centrestand on level ground and position a suitably-sized container, of at least 4.5 litres (4.8 US qt, 8.0 Imp pt) capacity, beneath the engine unit and remove the drain plug from the sump **(see illustration)**. Remove the oil filler cap to assist draining.

> ⚠️ **Warning: Take great care to scalding your hands on the escaping oil or on the exhaust system.**

3 Oil filter removal is easy if access to the Honda service tool, Part Number 07HAA-PJ70100, can be obtained. This tool is a socket spanner which fits over the end of the filter allowing it to be removed using a ratchet. If this tool cannot be obtained the filter must be slackened using a strap spanner, although its use will be awkward and great care must be taken to avoid burning your hands on the exhaust system. Discard the filter.

4 Check the condition of the drain plug sealing washer, renewing it if necessary, and refit the drain plug to the sump. Apply a small amount of oil to O-ring of the new oil filter and screw the filter onto the crankcase **(see illustration)**. Tighten the drain plug, and if possible, the oil filter to their specified torque settings.

5 Fill the crankcase with the specified amount and grade of oil. Refit the filler cap and start the engine, allowing it to idle for a few minutes to distribute the new oil through the lubrication system. Switch off the engine and wait a few minutes to allow the oil level to settle. Check the oil level as described in "Daily (pre-ride) checks" and adjust as necessary.

6 The old oil drained from the engine cannot be reused in its present state and should be disposed of. Check with your local refuse disposal company, disposal facility or environmental agency to see whether they will accept the used oil for recycling. Don't pour used oil into drains or onto the ground.

Note: *It is antisocial and illegal to dump oil down the drain. To find the location of your local oil recycling bank, call this number free.*

OIL CARE FOLLOW THE CODE
OIL BANK LINE
0800 66 33 66

In the USA, note that any oil supplier must accept used oil for recycling.

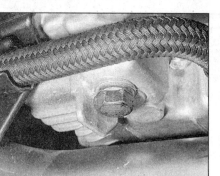

10.2 **Engine oil drain plug location - 600 models**

10.4 **Apply oil to filter O-ring prior to installation**

HAYNES HiNT *Check the old oil carefully. If the oil was drained into a clean pan, small pieces of metal or other material can be easily detected. If the oil is very metallic coloured, then the engine is experiencing wear from break-in (new engine) or from insufficient lubrication. If there are flakes or chips of metal in the oil, then something is drastically wrong internally and the engine will have to be disassembled for inspection and repair. If there are pieces of fibre-like material in the oil, the clutch is experiencing excessive wear and should be checked.*

11.1 On 1000 K models onward remove left engine protector

11.2 Remove crankshaft end cap and set crankshaft to TDC using index marks - 1000 model shown

11.5 Adjusting the valve clearances

11 Valve clearances - check
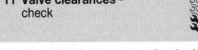

Note: *The valve clearances must be checked and adjusted with the engine cold, preferably after the machine has been left overnight.*

1 Remove the cylinder head cover as described in Chapter 2, Section 7. On 600 models remove the crankshaft and timing hole caps from the right crankcase cover. On 1000 models remove the cap from the left crankshaft end cover, noting that on 1000 K models onward it will first be necessary to remove the engine protector **(see illustration)**.

2 Using a suitable socket on the large hexagon nut on the end of the crank, turn the crankshaft in a clockwise direction on 600 models and an anticlockwise direction on 1000 models, until the T mark on the flywheel or crankcase aligns with the index mark visible on the crankcase cover or rotor (as applicable) and number 4 cylinder is at TDC on its compression stroke (ie inlet valve has just closed) **(see illustration)**.

3 With the engine in this position check the inlet valve clearances of number 2 and 4 cylinders and the exhaust valve clearances of cylinders 3 and 4. Using feeler gauges, measure the clearance between the follower and cam lobe. Turn the crankshaft through one complete turn (360°) so that number 1 cylinder is at TDC on its compression stroke, and check the inlet clearances of numbers 1 and 3 cylinders and the exhaust valve clearances on cylinders 1 and 2. All clearances must be within the specified limits given in the Specifications. If any are less than specified, action must be taken immediately to prevent damage to the valve and valve seat. If any are larger than specified the error must still be corrected but the problem is not quite as serious. If necessary, the clearances can be adjusted as described below using the screw and locknuts fitted to the cam followers.

4 On 1000 H, J and all 600 models the task of adjusting the valve clearances will be made considerably easier using the Honda locknut and adjusting screw wrenches, Part Numbers 07GMA-ML70120 and 07GMA-ML70110 respectively. On 1000 K models onward the clearances are adjusted using the aforementioned locknut spanner together with a modified 3 mm Allen key, cut to 65 - 68 mm (2.56 - 2.58 in) in length.

5 Slacken the locknut and turn the adjuster screw in or out until a feeler gauge of the appropriate size is a light sliding fit between the cam lobe and follower. Hold the screw and tighten the locknut to the specified torque setting. Recheck the clearance after the locknut has been tightened and re-adjust if necessary **(see illustration)**.

6 Once all clearances have been correctly set, turn the crankshaft through several revolutions then recheck all clearances before installing the cylinder head cover as described in Chapter 2. Always record the original and new clearance so that an accurate picture of the valve gear and its rate of wear can be built up.

12 Spark plugs - renewal (US 1000 L models onwards and all UK models)

1 Refer to Section 2 for details of this procedure.

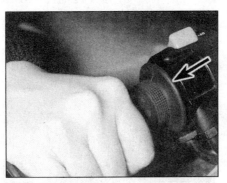

13.1a Throttle cable freeplay is measured in terms of twistgrip rotation at the grip flange (arrowed)

13 Throttle and choke cable - freeplay check

Throttle cable adjustment

1 There should be 2 - 6 mm (0.08 - 0.24 in) of freeplay in the throttle cables, measured in terms of twistgrip rotation **(see illustration)**. If this is not the case, slacken the locknut on the cable upper adjuster and rotate the adjuster until the required amount of freeplay is obtained then tighten the locknut. If it is not possible to obtain the correct freeplay with the upper adjuster, it will also be necessary to make adjustment at the lower adjuster, situated on the carburettors **(see illustration)**.

2 To gain access to the lower adjuster on 600 models it is necessary to remove the fuel tank as described in Chapter 4, and the air cleaner housing. On 1000 H and J models remove both the upper fairing inner covers and sidepanels, and on K models onward remove the seat. On all 1000 models, remove the fuel tank front mounting bolts, lift the tank up and support it on its prop stay. Screw the upper cable adjuster in to obtain the maximum possible freeplay, then slacken the lower adjuster locknut and set the cable freeplay using first the lower adjuster and then, if necessary, the upper adjuster. Once the

1

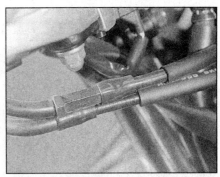

13.1b Adjust throttle cable freeplay using the upper . . .

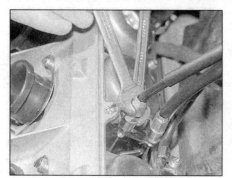

13.2 . . . and, if necessary, lower cable adjusters - 600 shown

13.5 Loosen cable retaining clamp to set choke cable freeplay

freeplay is correct tighten the locknuts securely **(see illustration)**.

3 Check that the throttle twistgrip operates smoothly and snaps shut quickly when released. Start the engine and allow it to idle, then move the handlebars from lock to lock. If the idle speed rises and falls as the handlebars are turned the throttle cables are incorrectly routed. To remedy, remove the retaining screws from the right handlebar switch and separate the two halves of the switch. Disconnect the cables from the twistgrip and re-route them along the smoothest possible route, ensuring that they are not kinked or foul any other component. Before connecting the cables lubricate them as described in Section 9, then reconnect the cables and check the freeplay, adjusting again if necessary.

Choke cable adjustment

4 Remove or raise the fuel tank as described in paragraph 3. Operate the handlebar mounted lever whilst observing the movement of the choke mechanism. The mechanism should extend smoothly when the lever is pulled, and return home fully when the lever is returned. If the choke mechanism does not operate smoothly this is probably due to a cable fault. Remove the retaining screws from the left handlebar switch and disconnect the cable at its upper end. Re-route the cable so it takes the smoothest route possible and lubricate it as described in Section 9. Reconnect the cable and tighten the handlebar switch screws securely. If this fails to improve the operation of the choke the cable must be renewed. Note that in very rare cases the fault could lie in the carburettors rather than the cable, necessitating the removal of the carburettors and examination of the choke plungers as described in Chapter 4.

5 Once the choke mechanism is operating smoothly it is necessary to ensure that there is a small amount of freeplay on the choke cable. It is recommended that there should be approximately 2 - 3 mm (0.08 - 0.12 in) of lever travel, measured at the base of the lever, before the mechanism starts to move. To adjust the cable, slacken the choke cable

clamping screw, situated on the carburettors, then move the lower end of the cable until the required amount of freeplay is obtained. Tighten the clamping screw securely **(see illustration)**.

14 Carburettors - synchronisation

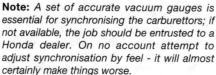

Note: *A set of accurate vacuum gauges is essential for synchronising the carburettors; if not available, the job should be entrusted to a Honda dealer. On no account attempt to adjust synchronisation by feel - it will almost certainly make things worse.*

Note: *The carburettors must be synchronised with the engine at its normal operating temperature and the machine on its centrestand.*

1 Before the carburettors can be synchronised, ensure that the throttle and choke mechanisms are operating correctly (see Section 13).

2 On 600 models, remove the fuel tank, as described in Chapter 4, and the left and right side fairings. Slacken and remove the four screws, one in each inlet tract, from the cylinder head and screw in the adapters. Connect the vacuum gauge hoses to the relevant adapters and arrange a temporary fuel supply, either by using a small temporary

tank or by using extra long fuel pipes to the now remote fuel tank on a nearby bench.

3 On all 1000 models raise the fuel tank up and support it on its prop stay. On 1000 H, J, K, L, M, N models, remove the rubber plug or vacuum tube (as applicable) from the vacuum take-off point on the top of each carburettor and connect the vacuum gauge hoses to the take-off points **(see illustration)**. On 1000 P models onward, release the fuel tap vacuum hose from No. 1 cylinder take-off point, the rubber plugs from Nos. 2 and 3 cylinder take-off points, and the screw and washer from No. 4 cylinder take-off point. Screw an adapter into No. 4 take-off point and connect the vacuum gauge hoses **(see illustration)**.

4 On all models, start the engine and allow it to warm up to normal operating temperature. If the gauges are fitted with damping adjustment, set this so that the needle flutter is just eliminated but so that they can still respond to small changes in pressure. Set the engine to the specified idle speed.

5 With the engine idling, check that all needles produce the same reading. A tolerance of 2 cm Hg on 1000 models and 4 cm Hg on 600 models is permissible but it is better to have all cylinders adjusted to the same reading; this is by no means as difficult as it would appear, requiring only a little care and patience. Note that it does not matter what the reading is, only that it is the same for all four cylinders. Stop the engine and allow it to cool down if it overheats.

6 The carburettors are adjusted by the three screws situated between each carburettor, in the throttle linkage **(see illustrations)**. Number two cylinder (all 600 models and 1000 H, J, K, L, M, N models) or number three cylinder (1000 P models onward) carburettor should be used as the base setting and the other three carburettors should be adjusted to the same. **Note:** *Do not press down on the screws whilst adjusting them, otherwise a false reading will be obtained.* When all the carburettors are synchronised, open and close the throttle quickly to settle the linkage, and recheck the gauge readings, readjusting if necessary.

7 When all the carburettors are correctly synchronised, stop the engine, disconnect the

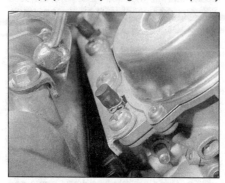

14.3a Vacuum take off point - 1000 H, J, K, L, M, N models

14.3b Vacuum take off point with gauge adapter in position - 1000 P models onward

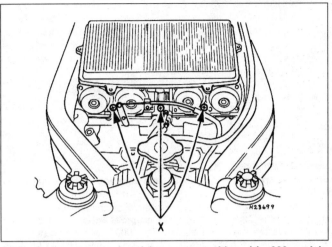

14.6a Carburettor synchronising screw positions (x) - 600 models

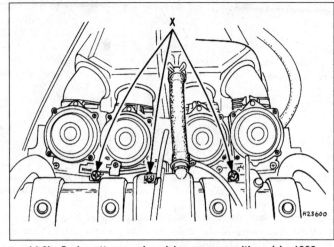

14.6b Carburettor synchronising screw positions (x) - 1000 models

gauges and remove the adapters (as applicable). Refit all the disturbed components. On 600 models (and No. 4 cylinder on 1000 P models onward) check the condition of the sealing washers fitted to the inlet tract screws, renewing them if necessary, and ensure the screws are tightened securely.

15 Clutch - check (1000 models)

1 Check the fluid level as described in Daily (pre-ride) checks.
2 Inspect the clutch hose for signs of leakage or deterioration, especially at the unions on the master cylinder and slave cylinder.
3 If there are traces of air in the system, the clutch should be bled as described in Chapter 7 using the procedure given for bleeding air from the hydraulic brake system.

16 Fuel pipe and filters - inspection

⚠ **Warning: Petrol (gasoline) is extremely flammable, especially when in the form of vapour. Take all precautions to prevent the risk of fire and read through Section 3 of Chapter 4 and the Safety first! Section of this Manual before carrying out the following operation.**
1 The fuel system hoses should be inspected for signs of damage and checked for security as described in Section 6 of Chapter 4.
2 The fuel tap should be removed from the machine and its fuel filter cleaned as described in Section 5 of Chapter 4 **(see illustration)**.
3 On 600 and 1000 H and J models remove the sidepanel and inspect the fuel pump filter for signs of clogging. If there are any traces of

debris visible through the translucent material of the filter, the filter must be renewed. **Note:** *The new filter must be installed with the arrow on the filter body pointing towards the outlet (fuel pump) side of the filter* **(see illustration).**

17 Cooling system - checks

1 With reference to Chapter 3, check the cooling system for leakage and damaged components. Pay particular attention to the hoses and check that all hose clips are correctly positioned and securely fastened.
2 Check the drainage hole on the underside of the water pump body for signs of leakage. Leakage from this hole indicates failure of the pump's mechanical seal.

18 Secondary air supply system - check (California models)

Note: *The air supply system is subject to anti-tampering legislation currently in force which means that the machine must never be used with any part of the system disconnected,*

missing, rendered inoperative or modified in any way.
1 Remove the necessary bodywork and check all the air supply system hoses for damage and deterioration, paying particular attention to the areas around the hose clips. Ensure that none of the hoses are kinked, pinched or split. If the renewal of any component is required use only genuine Honda replacement parts.
2 Refer to the vacuum hose routing label stuck to the air cleaner cover.

19 Steering and suspension - checks and adjustment

Checks

1 Place the machine on its centre stand and raise the front wheel clear of the ground using a suitable stand. Check the steering head bearings by grasping the bottom of both fork sliders, then pulling and pushing in a fore and aft direction; any freeplay should be felt between the fork bottom triple clamp (yoke) and the frame head lug. Check for overtightened bearings by placing the forks in a straightahead position and tapping lightly on

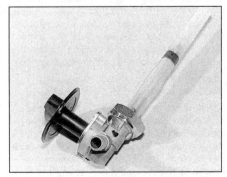

16.2 Remove the fuel tap and clean its filter

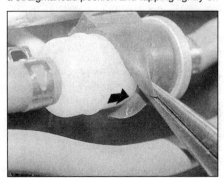

16.3 Ensure fuel pump filter is installed so that arrow faces pump

1

19.5 Remove cap to check front fork air pressure

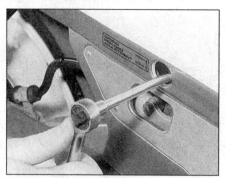

19.8 Adjusting rear suspension spring preload . . .

19.9 . . . and damping - 1000 K models onward

one handlebar end; the forks should fall away smoothly and easily to the opposite lock, taking into account the effect of cables and wiring, with no traces of notchiness. If necessary, adjust the steering head bearings using the information in Chapter 6.

HAYNES HiNT *Freeplay in the fork due to worn fork bushes can be misinterpreted for steering head bearing play - do not confuse the two.*

2 Ensure that the front forks work smoothly and progressively by pumping them up and down whilst the front brake is held on. Any faults revealed by this check should be investigated immediately; refer to Chapter 6, particularly if the oil seals are leaking.

3 Check that all the rear suspension pivot bolts are secure and that the pivots operate smoothly. With the machine placed on its centre stand and the rear wheel clear of the ground, check for freeplay in the swingarm by grasping its forked ends and pushing and pulling it horizontally. If freeplay is found, the swingarm or suspension linkage they must be removed and examined as described in Chapter 6.

Front fork adjustment

4 All 600 models and 1000 H, J models feature air-assisted front forks. **Note:** *When checking the air pressures do not use a tyre pressure gauge as they are not accurate enough and lose too much air when disconnected. A special suspension pressure gauge will be needed. When adding air to the front forks. Never use an air line, because these operate at far too high a pressure and could damage the seals. It is recommended that only a bicycle pump or one of the specialist aftermarket kits is used to add air; the latter usually comes equipped with its own built in gauge and is extremely accurate in use.*

5 When checking the air pressure raise the front wheel clear of the ground to prevent the pressure in the fork being artificially increased due to the weight of the machine. To achieve this it will be necessary to place the machine

on its centre stand and place a suitable sized block beneath the engine. Remove the cap from the top of each fork leg and check the pressure in both legs **(see illustration)**. The recommended pressure range is 0 - 6 psi (0 - 0.4 kg/cm²). Low air pressure settings provide a softer ride for light loads and smooth roads and high air pressure settings will provide a firmer ride for heavier loads and rougher road conditions. **Note:** *On no account must the pressure in the fork legs ever exceed 42 psi (3 kg/cm²) as this will almost certainly damage the fork seals.* Ensure that the pressure is equal in both legs and refit the caps to the top of the fork legs.

Rear shock absorber adjustment

600 models

6 On all 600 models the rear shock absorber has a 7-position spring preload adjuster fitted to the lower end of the unit. Position 1 is the softest setting through to position 7 which is the hardest. To adjust, remove the left sidepanel, and turn the preload adjuster to the required position using the C-spanner supplied in the machine's tool kit. Looking from the rear of the machine, turning the adjuster clockwise will decrease the preload and turning it anticlockwise will increase the preload.

7 On 600 L UK models and all US models the shock absorber also has a 3-position damping adjuster. The adjuster takes the form of a thumbwheel situated above the lower mounting bolt. Its position is indicated by the number on its bottom surface which aligns with the index mark on the top surface of the shock absorber. Position 1 is the softest setting and position 3 the hardest. Rotate the adjuster to the required setting ensuring that it clicks into position.

1000 models

8 The rear shock absorber has a 22-position spring preload adjuster. The adjuster is located behind the right sidepanel and can be turned using a suitable socket **(see illustration)**. Turning the adjuster clockwise increases the preload and hardens the ride, and turning it anticlockwise decreases the preload and softens the ride.

9 The shock absorber also features damping adjustment. The 1000 H and J models have a 3-position damping adjuster situated behind the left sidepanel. Its position is indicated by the arrow on the adjuster and the corresponding position on the shock absorber body. Position 1 is the softest setting and position 3 the hardest; position 2 is the standard setting. Set the adjuster to the required position using a suitable screwdriver, ensuring that it clicks into position. On 1000 K models onward the damping adjuster is situated on the lower end of the shock absorber and can be accessed just below the right footpeg **(see illustration)**. Turn the adjuster clockwise to increase the damping and harden the ride, and anticlockwise to reduce the damping and soften the ride.

20 Wheels - inspection

1 Check the complete wheel for cracks and chipping, particularly at the spoke roots and the edge of the rim. As a general rule a damaged wheel must be renewed as cracks will cause stress points which may lead to sudden failure under heavy load. Small nicks may be carefully radiused with a fine file and emery paper (No 600 - 1000) to relieve the stress. Note this will destroy the painted finish of the wheel and the wheel will thus require touching in with a suitable paint. If there is any doubt as to the condition of a wheel, advice should be sought from a Honda dealer or specialist wheel repairer.

2 Each wheel is painted to prevent corrosion. If damage occurs to the wheel and the paint is chipped the bared aluminium will soon start to corrode. A whitish grey oxide will form over the damaged area, which in itself is a protective coating. This deposit however, should be removed carefully as soon as possible and the damaged area repainted with a suitable paint.

3 To check the wheel bearings, position the bike on its centrestand with the wheel raised off the ground. Grasp the wheel at the top and bottom and attempt to rock it from side to side about its centre; if freeplay exists the bearings should be replaced (see Chapter 7).

4 Check the lateral runout of the rim by spinning the wheel and placing a fixed pointer close to the rim edge. If the maximum runout exceeds 2.0 mm (0.08 in) axially or radially, Honda recommend that the wheel be renewed. This is, however, a counsel of perfection; a runout somewhat greater than this can probably be accommodated without noticeable effect on the steering or stability of the machine. No means is available for straightening a warped wheel without resorting to the expense of having the wheel skimmed on all faces. If warpage was caused by impact during an accident, the safest measure is to renew the complete wheel. **Note:** *Worn wheel bearings may cause rim runout; these can be renewed as described in Chapter 7.*

5 Note: *Impact damage or serious corrosion has wider implications in that it could lead to a loss of pressure from the tubeless tyre. If in any doubt as to the wheel's condition, seek professional advice.*

21 Brake system - check

General check - all models

1 Make sure all brake fasteners are tight. Check that the fluid level in the reservoirs is correct (see "Daily (pre-ride) checks"). Look for leaks at the hose connections and check for cracks in the hoses. If the lever or pedal is spongy, bleed the brakes as described in Chapter 7.

Brake light switch check - all models

2 Check that both the front and rear stop lamps are functioning correctly. The front switch is located on the underside of the lever mounting bracket and is not adjustable in any way. If the switch is faulty it must be renewed.

3 The rear stop lamp switch is situated above the rear brake pedal. On 1000 models the switch is accessed through the hole in the sidepanel. To adjust the switch, hold the switch body to prevent it rotating and turn the adjuster nut. The switch should be set so that the stop lamp illuminates just as the rear brake starts to take effect **(see illustration).**

Dual Combined Brake System (DCBS) check - 1000 P models onward

4 This check must be performed with the motorcycle on its centrestand and the transmission in neutral.

5 Check that the rear tyre is off the ground. Using an 8 mm ring spanner on the left front caliper link bolt, apply a clockwise torque to the bolt and observe the secondary master cylinder pushrod and linkage **(see illustration).** With the torque applied, the linkage will operate the secondary master cylinder, which will transfer braking force to the outer two pistons of the rear brake caliper, preventing the rear wheel from being rotated. If the link bolt is inadvertently turned anticlockwise and loosens, make sure it is tightened securely. If the rear brake doesn't come on, there is a problem with the secondary master cylinder or proportional control valve (see Chapter 7 for details).

6 Chock the engine underneath the oil pan (sump) so that the front tyre is off the ground. Depress the rear brake pedal and check that the front wheel will not rotate.

22 Drive chain slider - wear check
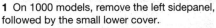

1 On 1000 models, remove the left sidepanel, followed by the small lower cover.

2 The chain slider is likely to be covered in dirt and excess lubricant from the chain, so clean it first. The nylon chain slider protects the swingarm and chain from direct contact,

but will wear down over a period of time. On 1000 P models onward, there is a line and arrow at the head of the slider which determines its wear limit; if the slider has worn down to or beyond the limit line it must be renewed. On all other models, make a visual check of the slider; if it looks like wearing through soon, renew it.

3 Renewal of the chain slider necessitates removal of the swingarm - refer to Chapter 6 for details.

23 Side stand - check

Side stand checks

1 Check the security of the side stand pivot bolt and check the rubber pad for wear. If the pad has worn down to the wear line, it must be renewed. On 1000 models, if the pad requires renewal, ensure that it is replaced with one marked 'over 260 lb only'.

2 Ensure that the side stand is securely held in the raised position by its return spring. Honda recommend that spring tension is checked using a spring balance hooked around the rubber pad of the stand. With the stand extended and the weight of the machine off the stand, pull on the spring balance and note the force required to retract the stand. This should be 2 - 3 kg (4.4 - 6.6 lbs) if the spring is functioning correctly.

Side stand switch check - K models onward

3 Sit on the machine, ensuring the side stand is the raised position. Start the engine, pull the clutch lever in, shift the transmission into first gear and then lower the side stand. As the stand is lowered the engine should cutout. If this is not the case the side stand switch operation is faulty and it should be checked as described in Chapter 5.

4 Lubricate the switch with a water dispersant fluid such as WD40.

1

21.3 Adjust rear stop lamp switch as described in text - 600 shown

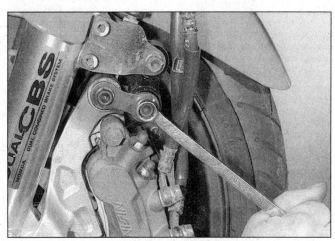

21.5 Checking the operation of the DCBS - 1000 P models onward

24 Headlight aim - check

1 An improperly adjusted headlight may cause problems for oncoming traffic or provide poor, unsafe illumination of the road ahead. Before adjusting the headlight, be sure to consult with local traffic laws and regulations.
2 The headlamp beam aim is set using the adjusters situated on the back of the headlamp unit. To gain access to these adjusters on 1000 H, J and all 600 models it is first necessary to remove the upper fairing inner sections, and on 1000 K models onward it is necessary to remove the maintenance cover from the underside of the upper fairing section (see illustration).
3 On 600 models the knob on the top right of the unit adjusts the horizontal aim of the beam, and the knob on the bottom left alters the vertical aim of the beam. On 1000 H and J models the knob on the top right of the unit alters the vertical aim and the horizontal aim is altered by rotating the bottom left adjuster with a suitable crosshead screwdriver. On 1000 K models onward, each bulb must be adjusted individually. The thumbwheels fitted on each side of the unit adjust the vertical setting of the relevant bulb whilst the horizontal adjusters are positioned in the centre of the unit and are adjusted using a crosshead screwdriver.

25 Fasteners - tightness check

1 Work around the machine checking all nuts and bolts for tightness. Pay particular attention to the engine mountings, exhaust mountings, rear suspension and swingarm

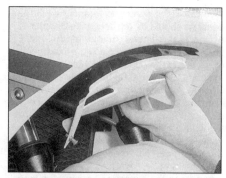

24.2 On 1000 K models onward, remove the maintenance cover to gain access to the headlamp adjusters

bolts, top and bottom triple clamp pinch bolts, wheel axles and all brake caliper bolts. Where possible use a torque wrench to check that all fasteners are tightened to their specified torque settings.

Every 18 months, or every 12,000 miles (18,000 km)

26 Air cleaner element - renewal

1 Refer to Section 3 for the air cleaner removal and installation procedure.

27 Evaporative emission control system hoses - check (California models)

Note: *The evaporative emission control system is subject to anti-tampering legislation currently in force which means the machine must never be used with any part of the system disconnected, missing, rendered inoperative or modified in any way.*

1 Remove the fuel tank as described in Chapter 4 and inspect all emission control system hoses for signs of damage or deterioration, paying particular attention to the areas around the hose clips. Ensure that none of the hoses are kinked, pinched or split. If the renewal of any component is required use only genuine Honda parts.

2 Refer to the vacuum hose routing label on the air cleaner cover.

Two yearly, or every 12,000 miles (18,000 km)

28 Brake and clutch fluid - renewal

Note: *Brake fluid is an excellent paint stripper and will attack painted and plastic components. Wash away any spilt fluid immediately with copious quantities of water.*
1 The hydraulic fluid must be renewed at the specified interval to preserve maximum brake/clutch efficiency by ensuring the fluid has not deteriorated to an unsafe level.
2 Before starting work obtain a new, sealed can of the recommended hydraulic fluid (you may need more for the DCBS of the 1000 P models onward) and carefully read the Section on brake bleeding in Chapter 7. Prepare the plastic tube and jar the same way as for bleeding, then open the bleed nipple and apply the lever or pedal (as appropriate) repeatedly.
Note: *Keep the master cylinder reservoir topped up at all times, otherwise air will enter the system and greatly lengthen the operation.*
3 Follow the procedure in Chapter 7 to bleed all air from the hydraulic components - this is particularly important in the case of the DCBS fitted to 1000 P models onward.

 HAYNES HiNT *The old hydraulic fluid is invariably darker in colour than the new, making it easier to see when it is pumped out and the new fluid has replaced it.*

4 Top up the master cylinder reservoir as described in "Daily (pre-ride) checks", and wash off any spilt fluid immediately. Finally check that the clutch/braking system is operating correctly before taking the machine on the road.

Two yearly, or every 24,000 miles (36,000 km)

29 Coolant - renewal

1 To minimise the build-up of deposits in the cooling system and ensure maximum protection against freezing the coolant must be renewed at the specified interval. The system should be drained, flushed out and filled with fresh coolant as described in Chapter 3.

Chapter 2
Engine, clutch and transmission

Contents

Degrees of difficulty

Easy, suitable for novice with little experience	**Fairly easy,** suitable for beginner with some experience	**Fairly difficult,** suitable for competent DIY mechanic	**Difficult,** suitable for experienced DIY mechanic	**Very difficult,** suitable for expert DIY or professional

Specifications

2

Engine

Type	DOHC, 16-valve, 4-cylinder, liquid-cooled
Capacity:	
600 models	598 cc (36.5 cu in)
1000 models	998 cc (60.9 cu in)
Bore:	
600 models	63.0 mm (2.48 in)
1000 models	77.0 mm (3.03 in)
Stroke:	
600 models	48.0 mm (1.89 in)
1000 models	53.6 mm (2.11 in)
Compression ratio:	
600 models	11.0:1
1000 models	10.5:1
Cylinder identification	Left to right, 1-2-3-4 (No 1 at alternator end)
Firing order	1-2-4-3
Compression pressure - at cranking speed with engine fully warmed up:	
600 models	185 ± 28 psi (13.0 ± 2.0 Bar)
1000 H, J, K, L, M, N models	177 ± 28 psi (12.5 ± 2.0 Bar)
1000 P models onward	149 - 206 psi (10.5 - 14.4 Bar)

Note: *compression pressure must not vary excessively between any two cylinders*

Camshafts

Cam lobe height:
  Inlet:
    600 California models .... 30.949 - 31.249 mm (1.2185 - 1.2303 in)
    Service limit .... 30.9 mm (1.217 in)
    All other 600 models .... 31.582 - 31.882 mm (1.2434 - 1.2552 in)
    Service limit .... 31.52 mm (1.241 in)
    1000 H, J, K, L, M models .... 35.608 - 35.808 mm (1.4019 - 1.4098 in)
    Service limit .... 35.55 mm (1.400 in)
    1000 N models .... 35.628 - 35.788 mm (1.4027 - 1.4090 in)
    Service limit .... 35.55 mm (1.400 in)
    UK 1000 P models onward .... 35.668 - 35.748 mm (1.4042 - 1.4074 in)
    Service limit .... 35.62 mm (1.402 in)
    US 1000 P models onward .... 34.907 - 34.987 mm (1.3743 - 1.3774 in)
    Service limit .... 34.85 mm (1.372 in)
  Exhaust:
    600 California models .... 30.980 - 31.280 mm (1.2197 - 1.2315 in)
    Service limit .... 30.93 mm (1.218 in)
    All other 600 models .... 31.550 - 31.580 mm (1.2421 - 1.2539 in)
    Service limit .... 31.50 mm (1.240 in)
    1000 H, J, K, L, M models .... 35.480 - 35.680 mm (1.3969 - 1.4047 in)
    Service limit .... 35.43 mm (1.395 in)
    1000 N models .... 35.500 - 35.660 mm (1.3976 - 1.4039 in)
    Service limit .... 35.43 mm (1.395 in)
    US 1000 P models onward .... 34.835 - 34.915 mm (1.3715 - 1.3746 in)
    Service limit .... 34.79 mm (1.370 in)
    UK 1000 P models onward .... 35.540 - 35.620 mm (1.3992 - 1.4024 in)
    Service limit .... 35.49 mm (1.397 in)
Camshaft journal OD:
  600 models .... 22.939 - 22.980 mm (0.9031 - 0.9047 in)
  Service limit .... 22.935 mm (0.9030 in)
  1000 H, J, K, L, M, N models .... Not available
  1000 P models onward:
    Number 1 and 4 journals .... 27.959 - 27.980 mm (1.1007 - 1.1016 in)
    Number 2 and 3 journals .... 27.929 - 27.950 mm (1.0996 - 1.1004 in)
Camshaft journal/cylinder head bearing oil clearance:
  Number 1 and 4 journals:
    600 models .... 0.020 - 0.062 mm (0.0008 - 0.0024 in)
    Service limit .... 0.10 mm (0.004 in)
    1000 H, J, K, L, M, N models .... 0.020 - 0.074 mm (0.0008 - 0.0029 in)
    1000 P models onward .... 0.020 - 0.062 mm (0.0008 - 0.0024 in)
    Service limit - all 1000 models .... 0.12 mm (0.005 in)
  Number 2 and 3 journals:
    600 models .... 0.020 - 0.082 mm (0.0008 - 0.0032 in)
    Service limit .... 0.12 mm (0.005 in)
    1000 H, J, K, L, M, N models .... 0.050 - 0.104 mm (0.0020 - 0.0041 in)
    1000 P models onward .... 0.050 - 0.092 mm (0.0020 - 0.0036 in)
    Service limit - all 1000 models .... 0.14 mm (0.006 in)
Camshaft runout:
  600 models .... Less than 0.05 mm (0.002 in)
  1000 models .... Less than 0.03 mm (0.001 in)

Pistons

Piston OD:
  600 models .... 62.960 - 62.990 mm (2.4787 - 2.4799 in)
  Service limit .... 62.90 mm (2.476 in)
  1000 models .... 76.960 - 76.990 mm (3.0299 - 3.0311 in)
  Service limit .... 76.86 mm (3.026 in)
Piston pin bore ID:
  600 models .... 16.002 - 16.008 mm (0.6300 - 0.6302 in)
  Service limit .... 16.05 mm (0.632 in)
  1000 models .... 20.002 - 20.008 mm (0.7875 - 0.7877 in)
  Service limit .... 20.06 mm (0.790 in)
Piston pin OD:
  600 models .... 15.994 - 16.000 mm (0.6297 - 0.6299 in)
  Service limit .... 15.98 mm (0.629 in)
  1000 models .... 19.994 - 20.000 mm (0.7872 - 0.7874 in)
  Service limit .... 19.98 mm (0.787 in)
Piston to piston pin clearance - all models .... 0.002 - 0.014 mm (0.0001 - 0.0006 in)
Service limit .... 0.04 mm (0.002 in)

Piston rings

Ring to groove clearance - 600 models:
Top ring . . . .   0.025 - 0.060 mm (0.0010 - 0.0023 in)
Second ring . . . .   0.015 - 0.050 mm (0.0006 - 0.0020 in)
Service limit . . . .   0.08 mm (0.003 in)
Ring to groove clearance - 1000 H, J, K, L, M, N models:
Top and second rings . . . .   0.015 - 0.045 mm (0.0006 - 0.0018 in)
Service limit . . . .   0.10 mm (0.004 in)
Ring to groove clearance - 1000 P models onward:
Top ring . . . .   0.025 - 0.055 mm (0.0010 - 0.0022 in)
Service limit . . . .   0.09 mm (0.004 in)
Second ring . . . .   0.015 - 0.045 mm (0.0006 - 0.0018 in)
Service limit . . . .   0.10 mm (0.004 in)
Ring end gap (installed) - 600 models:
Top ring . . . .   0.20 - 0.35 mm (0.008 - 0.014 in)
Service limit . . . .   0.50 mm (0.020 in)
Second ring . . . .   0.3 - 0.5 mm (0.01 - 0.02 in)
Service limit . . . .   0.6 mm (0.024 in)
Oil scraper ring side rails . . . .   0.2 - 0.8 mm (0.01 - 0.03 in)
Service limit . . . .   1.1 mm (0.04 in)
Ring end gap (installed) - 1000 models:
Top and second rings (H, J, K, L, M, N), second ring (P onward) . . .   0.32 - 0.47 mm (0.013 - 0.019 in)
Service limit . . . .   0.65 mm (0.026 in)
Top ring - P models onward . . . .   0.25 - 0.40 mm (0.010 - 0.016 in)
Service limit . . . .   0.58 mm (0.023 in)
Oil scraper ring side rail - all models . . . .   0.30 - 0.90 mm (0.012 - 0.035 in)
Service limit . . . .   1.1 mm (0.04 in)

Connecting rods and bearings

Small-end bearing ID:
600 models . . . .   16.016 - 16.034 mm (0.6305 - 0.6313 in)
Service limit . . . .   16.07 mm (0.6327 in)
1000 models . . . .   20.016 - 20.034 mm (0.7880 - 0.7887 in)
Service limit . . . .   20.08 mm (0.7905 in)
Big-end bearing standard ID:
600 models . . . .   36.000 - 36.016 mm (1.4173 - 1.4179 in)
1000 models . . . .   43.000 - 43.015 mm (1.5746 - 1.5749 in)
Big-end bearing size groups:
600 models:
Connecting rod marked 1 . . . .   36.000 - 36.008 mm (1.4173 - 1.4176 in)
Connecting rod marked 2 . . . .   36.008 - 36.016 mm (1.4176 - 1.4179 in)
1000 models:
Connecting rod marked 1 . . . .   43.000 - 43.007 mm (1.6929 - 1.6931 in)
Connecting rod marked 2 . . . .   43.008 - 43.015 mm (1.6932 - 1.6935 in)
Crankpin standard OD:
600 models . . . .   32.984 - 33.000 mm (1.2986 - 1.2992 in)
1000 models . . . .   39.987 - 40.003 mm (1.5742 - 1.5749 in)
Crankpin size groups:
600 models:
Crankshaft marked A . . . .   32.992 - 33.000 mm (1.2989 - 1.2992 in)
Crankshaft marked B . . . .   32.984 - 32.992 mm (1.2986 - 1.2989 in)
1000 models:
Crankshaft marked A . . . .   39.995 - 40.003 mm (1.5746 - 1.5749 in)
Crankshaft marked B . . . .   39.987 - 39.994 mm (1.5742 - 1.5745 in)
Big-end bearing insert thickness (colour code):
600 models:
Thin (yellow) . . . .   1.486 - 1.490 mm (0.0585 - 0.0587 in)
Medium (green) . . . .   1.490 - 1.494 mm (0.0587 - 0.0588 in)
Thick (brown) . . . .   1.494 - 1.498 mm (0.0588 - 0.0590 in)
1000 models:
Thin (yellow) . . . .   1.484 - 1.487 mm (0.05843 - 0.05854 in)
Medium (green) . . . .   1.488 - 1.491 mm (0.05858 - 0.05870 in)
Thick (brown) . . . .   1.492 - 1.496 mm (0.05874 - 0.05890 in)
Bearing insert/crankpin clearance - all models . . . .   0.028 - 0.052 mm (0.0011 - 0.0020 in)
Service limit:
600 models . . . .   0.06 mm (0.002 in)
1000 models . . . .   0.08 mm (0.003 in)

2

Connecting rods and bearings (continued)

Big-end bearing side clearance:
All 600 models and 1000 P models onward .... 0.05 - 0.20 mm (0.002 - 0.008 in)
1000 H, J, K, L, M, N models .... 0.05 - 0.25 mm (0.002 - 0.010 in)
Service limit - all models .... 0.3 mm (0.01 in)

Crankshaft and main bearings

Crankshaft runout:
600 models .... Less than 0.05 mm (0.002 in)
1000 models .... Less than 0.03 mm (0.001 in)
Crankcase main bearing ID:
600 models .... 36.000 - 36.024 mm (1.4173 - 1.4183 in)
1000 models .... 39.000 - 39.024 mm (1.5354 - 1.5363 in)
Main bearing size groups:
600 models:
Crankcase marked A .... 36.000 - 36.008 mm (1.4173 - 1.4176 in)
Crankcase marked B .... 36.008 - 36.016 mm (1.4176 - 1.4179 in)
Crankcase marked C .... 36.016 - 36.024 mm (1.4179 - 1.4183 in)
1000 models:
Crankcase marked A .... 39.000 - 39.007 mm (1.5354 - 1.5357 in)
Crankcase marked B .... 39.008 - 39.015 mm (1.5357 - 1.5360 in)
Crankcase marked C .... 39.016 - 39.024 mm (1.5360 - 1.5363 in)
Crankshaft journal OD:
600 models .... 32.984 - 33.000 mm (1.2986 - 1.2992 in)
1000 models .... 35.984 - 36.000 mm (1.5166 - 1.4173 in)
Crankshaft journal size groups:
600 models:
Crankshaft marked 1 .... 32.992 - 33.000 mm (1.2989 - 1.2992 in)
Crankshaft marked 2 .... 32.984 - 32.992 mm (1.2986 - 1.2989 in)
1000 models:
Crankshaft marked 1 .... 35.992 - 36.000 mm (1.4170 - 1.4173 in)
Crankshaft marked 2 .... 35.984 - 35.991 mm (1.4166 - 1.4169 in)
Main bearing insert thickness (colour code):
600 models:
Thin (pink) .... 1.480 - 1.484 mm (0.0583 - 0.0584 in)
Medium/thin (yellow) .... 1.484 - 1.488 mm (0.0584 - 0.0586 in)
Medium/thick (green) .... 1.488 - 1.492 mm (0.0586 - 0.0587 in)
Thick (brown) .... 1.492 - 1.496 mm (0.0587 - 0.0589 in)
1000 models:
Thin (pink) .... 1.496 - 1.499 mm (0.0589 - 0.0590 in)
Medium/thin (yellow) .... 1.500 - 1.503 mm (0.0590 - 0.0591 in)
Medium/thick (green) .... 1.504 - 1.507 mm (0.0592 - 0.0593 in)
Thick (brown) .... 1.508 - 1.512 mm (0.0593 - 0.0595 in)
Bearing insert/journal clearance:
600 models .... 0.023 - 0.047 mm (0.0009 - 0.0019 in)
Service limit .... 0.05 mm (0.002 in)
1000 models .... 0.021 - 0.045 mm (0.0008 - 0.0018 in)
Service limit .... 0.08 mm (0.003 in)

Cylinder block

Cylinder bore ID:
600 models .... 63.000 - 63.010 mm (2.4803 - 2.4087 in)
Service limit .... 63.10 mm (2.484 in)
1000 models .... 77.000 - 77.010 mm (3.0315 - 3.0319 in)
Service limit .... 77.10 mm (3.035 in)
Maximum taper:
600 models .... 0.10 mm (0.004 in)
1000 models .... 0.05 mm (0.002 in)
Maximum ovality:
600 models .... 0.10 mm (0.004 in)
1000 models .... 0.05 mm (0.002 in)
Piston/cylinder clearance:
1000 P models onward .... 0.010 - 0.040 mm (0.0004 - 0.0016 in)
All other models .... 0.010 - 0.050 mm (0.0004 - 0.0020 in)
Service limit - all models .... 0.10 mm (0.004 in)
Cylinder block maximum warpage:
600 models .... 0.10 mm (0.004 in)
1000 H, J, K, L, M, N models .... 0.07 mm (0.003 in)
1000 P models onward .... 0.05 mm (0.002 in)

Cylinder head

Maximum warpage:
- 600 models . . . .   0.10 mm (0.004 in)
- 1000 models . . . .   0.07 mm (0.003 in)

Starter clutch - 600 models

Driven gear boss OD . . . .   45.657 - 45.673 mm (1.7975 - 1.7981 in)
Service limit . . . .   45.57 mm (1.7941 in)

Valve guides and springs

Inlet valve clearance:
- 600 models . . . .   0.14 - 0.18 mm (0.006 - 0.007 in)
- 1000 models . . . .   0.10 ± 0.02 mm (0.004 ± 0.001 in)

Exhaust valve clearance:
- 600 models . . . .   0.18 - 0.22 mm (0.007 - 0.009 in)
- 1000 H, J, K, L, M, N models . . . .   0.16 ± 0.02 mm (0.004 ± 0.001 in)
- 1000 P models onward . . . .   0.18 ± 0.02 mm (0.007 ± 0.001 in)

Inlet valve stem OD:
- 600 models . . . .   4.975 - 4.990 mm (0.1959 - 0.1965 in)
- Service limit . . . .   4.97 mm (0.196 in)
- 1000 models . . . .   5.475 - 5.490 mm (0.2156 - 0.2161 in)
- Service limit . . . .   5.47 mm (0.215 in)

Exhaust valve stem OD:
- 600 models . . . .   4.955 - 4.970 mm (0.1951 - 0.1957 in)
- Service limit . . . .   4.94 mm (0.194 in)
- 1000 models . . . .   5.455 - 5.470 mm (0.2148 - 0.2154 in)
- Service limit . . . .   5.45 mm (0.215 in)

Valve guide ID - inlet and exhaust:
- 600 models . . . .   5.000 - 5.012 mm (0.1969 - 0.1973 in)
- Service limit . . . .   5.04 mm (0.198 in)
- 1000 models . . . .   5.500 - 5.512 mm (0.2165 - 0.2170 in)
- Service limit . . . .   5.55 mm (0.219 in)

Inlet valve/guide clearance:
- 600 models . . . .   Not available
- Service limit . . . .   0.07 mm (0.003 in)
- 1000 models . . . .   0.010 - 0.037 mm (0.0004 - 0.0015 in)
- Service limit . . . .   0.07 mm (0.003 in)

Exhaust valve/guide clearance:
- 600 models . . . .   Not available
- Service limit . . . .   0.09 mm (0.004 in)
- 1000 models . . . .   0.030 - 0.057 mm (0.0012 - 0.0022 in)
- Service limit . . . .   0.09 mm (0.004 in)

Valve seat width:
- All 600 models and 1000 P models onward . . . .   0.9 - 1.1 mm (0.035 - 0.043 in)
- Service limit . . . .   1.5 mm (0.06 in)
- 1000 H, J, K, L, M, N models . . . .   Not available

Inner valve spring free length:
- 600 models . . . .   33.4 mm (1.31 in)
- Service limit . . . .   32.1 mm (1.26 in)
- 1000 models . . . .   43.1 mm (1.70 in)
- Service limit . . . .   41.8 mm (1.65 in)

Outer valve spring free length:
- 600 models . . . .   34.2 mm (1.35 in)
- Service limit . . . .   32.7 mm (1.29 in)
- 1000 models . . . .   47.1 mm (1.85 in)
- Service limit . . . .   45.7 mm (1.80 in)

Clutch

Type . . . .   Wet, multi-plate
Friction plates:
- Number:
  - 600 models   6
  - 1000 models   9
- Thickness - 600 models:
  - Outer friction plate . . . .   3.22 - 3.38 mm (0.127 - 0.133 in)
  - Service limit . . . .   2.90 mm (0.114 in)
  - All other friction plates . . . .   3.42 - 3.58 mm (0.135 - 0.141 in)
  - Service limit . . . .   3.20 mm (0.126 in)

2

Clutch

Friction plates: (continued)
  Thickness - 1000 models:
    Inner friction plate .... 3.42 - 3.58 mm (0.135 - 0.141 in)
    All other friction plates .... 3.72 - 3.88 mm (0.146 - 0.153 in)
    Service limit - all plates .... 3.1 mm (0.12 in)
Plain plates:
  Number:
    600 models 5
    1000 models 8
  Plate warpage .... Less than 0.3 mm (0.12 in)
Clutch springs:
  Number:
    600 models 4
    1000 models 5
  Free length:
    600 models .... 42.5 mm (1.67 in)
    Service limit .... 41.0 mm (1.61 in)
    1000 models .... 46.7 mm (1.84 in)
    Service limit - H, J, K, L, M, N models .... 46.0 mm (1.81 in)
    Service limit - P models onward .... 44.7 mm (1.76 in)
Clutch drum centre collar:
  Inside diameter:
    600 models .... 21.993 - 22.007 mm (0.8659 - 0.8664 in)
    Service limit .... 22.05 mm (0.868 in)
    1000 models .... 27.995 - 28.012 mm (1.1022 - 1.1028 in)
    Service limit .... 28.08 mm (1.106 in)
  Height - 600 models .... 39.9 - 40.0 mm (1.571 - 1.575 in)
  Service limit .... 39.8 mm (1.57 in)
Mainshaft OD:
  600 models .... 21.980 - 21.991 mm (0.8654 - 0.8658 in)
  Service limit .... 21.94 mm (0.864 in)
  1000 models .... 27.980 - 27.993 mm (1.1016 - 1.1021 in)
  Service limit .... 27.97 mm (1.101 in)
Clutch drum ID - 1000 models .... 47.005 - 47.030 mm (1.8506 - 1.8516 in)
Service limit .... 47.10 mm (1.854 in)
Clutch master cylinder ID - 1000 models .... 14.000 - 14.043 mm (0.5512 - 0.5529 in)
Service limit .... 14.06 mm (0.554 in)
Clutch master cylinder piston OD - 1000 models .... 13.957 - 13.984 mm (0.5495 - 0.5506 in)
Service limit .... 13.94 mm (0.549 in)
Clutch slave cylinder ID - 1000 H, J, K, L, M, N models .... 35.700 - 35.762 mm (1.4055 - 1.4080 in)
Service limit .... 35.78 mm (1.409 in)
Clutch slave cylinder piston OD - 1000 H, J, K, L, M, N models ...... 35.650 - 35.672 mm (1.4035 - 1.4044 in)
Service limit .... 35.63 mm (1.403 in)
Clutch slave cylinder dimensions - 1000 P models onward .... Not available

Primary drive

Reduction ratio:
  600 models .... 1.775:1 (71/40 T)
  1000 models .... 1.786:1 (75/42 T)

Transmission

Type .... 6-speed, constant mesh

Ratios:	600 models	1000 models
1st	3.230:1 (42/13 T)	2.750:1 (33/12 T)
2nd	2.235:1 (38/17 T)	2.067:1 (31/15 T)
3rd	1.800:1 (36/20 T)	1.647:1 (28/17 T)
4th	1.500:1 (33/22 T)	1.368:1 (26/19 T)
5th	1.272:1 (28/22 T)	1.174:1 (27/23 T)
6th	1.130:1 (26/23 T)	1.045:1 (23/22 T)

Gear backlash service limits - 600 model:
  1st to 5th gear .... 0.30 mm (0.0118 in)
  6th gear .... 0.18 mm (0.0071 in)
Pinion ID:
  600 models:
    Mainshaft 5th and 6th gear pinions .... 28.000 - 28.021 mm (1.1024 - 1.1032 in)
    Service limit .... 28.04 mm (1.104 in)
    Countershaft 2nd, 3rd and 4th gear pinions .... 31.000 - 31.025 mm (1.2205 - 1.2215 in)
    Service limit .... 31.04 mm (1.222 in)

Transmission

Pinion ID: (continued)
  1000 models:
    Mainshaft 5th and 6th gear pinions .... 31.000 - 31.016 mm (1.2205 - 1.2211 in)
    Service limit .... 31.04 mm (1.222 in)
    Countershaft 3rd and 4th gear (H and J models), or 2nd
    and 4th gear (K models onward) pinions .... 33.000 - 33.016 mm (1.2992 - 1.2998 in)
    Service limit .... 33.04 mm (1.301 in)
Pinion bush OD:
  600 models:
    Mainshaft 5th and 6th gear bush .... 27.959 - 27.980 mm (1.1007 - 1.1016 in)
    Service limit .... 27.92 mm (1.099 in)
    Countershaft 2nd, 3rd and 4th gear bush .... 30.950 - 30.975 mm (1.2185 - 1.2195 in)
    Service limit .... 30.93 mm (1.218 in)
  1000 models:
    Mainshaft 5th and 6th gear bush .... 30.955 - 30.980 mm (1.2187 - 1.2197 in)
    Service limit .... 30.93 mm (1.218 in)
    Countershaft 2nd (K models onward), 3rd and 4th gear
    bush .... 32.955 - 32.980 mm (1.2974 - 1.2984 in)
    Service limit .... 32.93 mm (1.296 in)
Pinion to bush clearance:
  600 models:
    Mainshaft 5th and 6th gear .... 0.020 - 0.062 mm (0.0008 - 0.0024 in)
    Service limit .... 0.10 mm (0.0039 in)
    Countershaft 2nd, 3rd and 4th gear .... 0.025 - 0.070 mm (0.0010 - 0.0028 in)
    Service limit .... 0.11 mm (0.0043 in)
  1000 models - all gears .... 0.020 - 0.061 mm (0.0008 - 0.0024 in)
  Service limit .... 0.10 mm (0.0039 in)
Pinion bush ID - 1000 models only:
  Mainshaft 5th gear bushing .... 27.985 - 28.006 mm (1.1018 - 1.1026 in)
  Service limit .... 28.02 mm (1.103 in)
  Countershaft 3rd (H and J models), or 2nd (K models onward)
  bushing .... 29.985 - 30.006 mm (1.1805 - 1.1813 in)
  Service limit .... 30.02 mm (1.182 in)
Mainshaft OD at point of 5th gear bush - 1000 models .... 27.967 - 27.980 mm (1.1011 - 1.1016 in)
Service limit .... 27.94 mm (1.100 in)
Countershaft OD at point of 3rd (H and J models), or 2nd
(K models onward) bush - 1000 models .... 29.950 - 29.975 mm (1.791 - 1.1801 in)
Service limit .... 29.92 mm (1.178 in)
Bush to shaft clearance - 1000 models:
  Mainshaft 5th gear .... 0.005 - 0.039 mm (0.0002 - 0.0015 in)
  Service limit .... 0.06 mm (0.002 in)
  Countershaft 3rd (H and J models), or 2nd (K, L, M, N models) gear   0.005 - 0.056 mm (0.0002 - 0.0022 in)
  Countershaft 2nd gear (P models onward) .... 0.010 - 0.056 mm (0.0004 - 0.0022 in)
  Service limit - all models .... 0.06 mm (0.002 in)
Shift fork end width:
  600 models:
    Centre fork .... 5.93 - 6.00 mm (0.233 - 0.236 in)
    Service limit .... 5.60 mm (0.220 in)
    Left and right fork .... 5.43 - 5.50 mm (0.214 - 0.217 in)
    Service limit .... 5.10 mm (0.200 in)
  1000 H, J, K, L, M, N models - all forks .... 5.43 - 5.50 mm (0.214 - 0.217 in)
  Service limit .... 5.10 mm (0.200 in)
  1000 P models onward - centre fork .... 6.43 - 6.50 mm (0.253 - 0.256 in)
  Service limit .... 6.1 mm (0.24 in)
  1000 P models onward - right and left forks .... 5.43 - 5.50 mm (0.214 - 0.217 in)
  Service limit .... 5.10 mm (0.200 in)
Shift fork ID:
  600 models .... 12.000 - 12.021 mm (0.4724 - 0.4733 in)
  Service limit .... 12.04 mm (0.474 in)
  1000 models .... 14.000 - 14.018 mm (0.5512 - 0.5519 in)
  Service limit .... 14.04 mm (0.553 in)
Shift fork shaft OD:
  600 models .... 11.969 - 11.980 mm (0.4712 - 0.4717 in)
  Service limit .... 11.90 mm (0.469 in)
  1000 models .... 13.957 - 13.968 mm (0.5495 - 0.5499 in)
  Service limit .... 13.90 mm (0.547 in)

2

Final drive

Type	Chain and sprockets
Ratio:	
600 models	2.933:1 (44/15 T)
1000 H, J models	2.529:1 (43/17 T)
1000 K models onward	2.470:1 (42/17 T)
Chain size	50 (sealed type)
No. of links:	
600 models	110
1000 models	114

Torque settings

	kgf m	lbf ft
Cam follower holder bolts - 600 models	1.2	9.0
Camshaft cap bolts:		
600 models	1.2	9.0
1000 models	1.4	10.0
Camshaft sprocket bolts:		
600 models	2.1	15.0
1000 H, J, K, L, M, N models	1.7	12.0
1000 P models onward	2.0	14.0
Upper camchain guide bolts - 600 models	1.2	9.0
Cylinder head cover bolts	1.0	7.0
Camchain tensioner bolts - 1000 models	1.4	10.0
Cylinder head nuts:		
600 models	3.7	27.0
1000 models	4.6	33.0
Oil cooler pipe to oil cooler body bolts - 1000 models	0.9	6.5
Oil pump driven sprocket bolt	1.5	11.0
Clutch centre nut:		
600 models	8.5	61.0
1000 H, J models	9.0	65.0
1000 K models onward	12.8	93.0
Clutch slave cylinder banjo union bolt:		
1000 H, J models	3.0	22.0
1000 K models onward	3.5	25.0
Shift drum cam retaining pin bolt	2.3	17.0
Centre shift fork retaining bolt (early models)	1.8	13.0
Shift fork shaft retaining plate bolts - 1000 K models onward	1.2	9.0
Alternator rotor bolt - 600 models	8.5	61.0
Starter clutch bolt - 600 models	8.5	61.0
Crankcase fastening bolts - 600 models:		
6 mm	1.2	9.0
8 mm main bearing bolts	2.4	17.0
10 mm	4.0	29.0
Crankcase fastening bolts - 1000 H, J, K, L, M, N models:		
6 mm	1.2	9.0
8 mm	2.7	20.0
9 mm main bearing bolts	3.8	28.0
10 mm	4.0	29.0
Crankcase fastening bolts - 1000 P models onward:		
6 mm	Not available	
8 mm	2.4	17.0
9 mm main bearing bolts	3.7	27.0
10 mm bolt	3.9	28.0
Alternator driveshaft nut - 1000 models	5.0	36.0
Alternator base bolts - 1000 models:		
H, J, K, L, M, N models	2.9	21.0
P models onwards	2.5	18.0
Alternator drive chain tensioner and guide bolts - 1000 models	1.2	9.0
Oil pass plate bolts - 1000 models	1.2	9.0
Connecting rod bolts:		
600 models	2.4	17.0
1000 models	3.6	26.0

Torque settings (continued)

	kgf m	lbf ft
Engine mounting bolts:		
600 models	5.0	36.0
1000 models:		
Upper rear mounting bolt adjuster	0.8	6.0
Upper rear mounting bolt locknut	2.5	18.0
12 mm mounting bolt - H, J models	6.0	43.0
12 mm mounting bolt - K models onward	5.5	40.0
10 mm mounting bolt	4.5	33.0
Drive sprocket retaining bolt:		
600 models	5.5	40.0
1000 H, J models	9.0	65.0
1000 K models onward	5.2	38.0
Gearshift pedal pinch bolt	1.0	7.0
Exhaust system mountings:		
600 models:		
Header retaining nuts	1.2	9.0
All other mounting and clamp bolts	2.7	20.0
1000 models:		
Header retaining nuts	1.7	12.0
All other mounting and clamp bolts	2.2	16.0

1 General description

The engine/transmission unit is of water-cooled four-cylinder in-line design, fitted transversely across the frame. The sixteen valves are operated by double overhead camshafts, chain driven off the crankshaft. The engine/transmission unit is constructed in aluminium alloy with the crankcase being divided horizontally. The crankcase incorporates a wet sump, pressure fed lubrication system, and houses a chain driven dual rotor oil pump.

On 600 models the alternator is mounted directly on the right end of the crankshaft with the starter clutch being situated on the left end of the crankshaft. On 1000 models the alternator is mounted directly behind the cylinder block on the left side of the crankcase and is chain driven off the crankshaft. The starter clutch is also linked to the crankshaft by the same chain and forms part of the alternator driveshaft. On all models the water pump is mounted on the left side of the crankcase and is driven off the oil pump shaft.

The clutch is of the wet multi-plate type and is gear driven off the crankshaft. Final drive to the rear wheel is by chain and sprockets. The drive sprocket being mounted on the end of the countershaft (output shaft).

2 Major engine repair - general information

1 It is not always easy to determine when or if an engine should be completely overhauled, as a number of factors must be considered.
2 High mileage is not necessarily an indication that an overhaul is needed, while low mileage, on the other hand, does not preclude the need for an overhaul. Frequency of servicing is probably the single most important consideration. An engine that has regular and frequent oil and filter changes, as well as other required maintenance, will most likely give many miles of reliable service. Conversely, a neglected engine, or one which has not been broken (run) in properly, may require an overhaul very early in its life.
3 Exhaust smoke and excessive oil consumption are both indications that piston rings and/or valve guides are in need of attention, although make sure that the fault is not due to oil leakage. Refer to Section 31 and perform a cylinder compression check to determine for certain the nature and extent of the work required.
4 If the engine is making obvious knocking or rumbling noises, the connecting rod and/or main bearings are probably at fault.
5 Loss of power, rough running, excessive valve train noise and high fuel consumption rates may also point to the need for an overhaul, especially if they are all present at the same time. If a complete tune-up does not remedy the situation, major mechanical work is the only solution.
6 An engine overhaul generally involves restoring the internal parts to the specifications of a new engine. During an overhaul the piston rings are renewed and the cylinder walls are bored and/or honed. If a rebore is done, then new pistons will also be required. The main and big-end bearings are usually renewed during a major overhaul. Generally the valve seats are serviced as well, since they are usually in less than perfect condition at this point. While the engine is being overhauled, other components such as the carburettors and the starter motor can also be rebuilt. The end result should be a like new engine that will give as many trouble free miles as the original.
7 Before beginning the engine overhaul, read through the related procedures to familiarise yourself with the scope and requirements of the job. Overhauling an engine is not all that difficult, but it is time consuming. Plan on the motorcycle being tied up for a minimum of two weeks. Check on the availability of parts and make sure that any necessary special tools, equipment and supplies are obtained in advance.
8 Most work can be done with typical shop hand tools, although a number of precision measuring tools are required for inspecting parts to determine if they must be renewed. Often a dealer service department or motorcycle repair shop will handle the inspection of parts and offer advice concerning reconditioning and renewal. As a general rule, time is the primary cost of an overhaul so it does not pay to install worn or substandard parts.
9 As a final note, to ensure maximum life and minimum trouble from a rebuilt engine, everything must be assembled with care in a spotlessly clean environment.

3 Operations with the engine/transmission unit in the frame

The components and assemblies listed below can be removed without having to remove the engine unit from the frame. If however, a number of areas require attention at the same time, removal of the engine is recommended.
a) Clutch slave cylinder - 1000 models.
b) Engine sprocket.
c) Neutral switch.
d) Gearshift (selector) mechanism components.
e) Shift (selector) drum and forks - 1000 models.
f) Water pump.
g) Ignition system components.
h) Starter motor.

2

i) Alternator.
j) Clutch assembly.
k) Oil pan (sump), oil screen, oil pump and relief valve assembly.
l) Balancer shaft - 1000 models.
m) Cylinder head cover and camshafts.
n) Camchain tensioner.
o) Cylinder head.
p) Cylinder block and pistons.
q) Starter clutch - 600 models.

4 Operations with the engine/transmission unit removed from the frame

It is necessary to remove the engine/gearbox unit from the frame and separate the crankcase halves to gain access to the following components.
a) Crankshaft assembly.
b) Main and big-end bearings.
c) Connecting rods.
d) Camchain.
e) Oil pump drive chain - 1000 models.
f) Alternator drive chain and tensioner - 1000 models.
g) Starter clutch and alternator drive components - 1000 models.
h) Shift (selector) drum and forks - 600 models.
i) Gearbox shafts and pinions.

5 Engine - removal and installation

Note: Engine removal and installation should be carried out with the aid of an assistant; personal injury or damage could occur if the engine falls or is dropped. An hydraulic floor-type jack should be used to support and lower the engine to the floor if possible. These can be hired quite cheaply.

Removal

1 If the machine is dirty, wash it thoroughly before starting any major dismantling work. This will make work much easier and rule out the possibility of caked-on lumps of dirt falling into some vital component. Work can also be made easier by raising the machine to a suitable working height on an hydraulic ramp or a suitable platform.

2 Remove the fuel tank as described in Chapter 4, and the lower or side fairings (as applicable) as described in Chapter 6.

3 Place a suitably sized container beneath the engine unit and drain the engine oil as described in Chapter 1. Remove the oil filter and discard it. Disconnect the battery leads (negative lead first) and remove the battery from the machine. If the machine is to be left dismantled for some time, give the battery regular refresher charges as described in Chapter 8.

4 On 600 models slacken the eight nuts which secure the exhaust headers to the cylinder head and remove their mounting collars. Slacken and remove both the muffler and header mounting bolts and manoeuvre the complete exhaust system away from the machine. On 1000 models slacken the left muffler mounting clamp bolts and the muffler mounting bolt then remove the muffler. Remove the right muffler in a similar manner. Slacken the eight nuts which secure the headers to the cylinder head, followed by the header lower mounting bolt; the header assembly can then be lowered away from the machine.

5 Remove the carburettors as described in Chapter 4 then drain the coolant as described in Chapter 3. Remove the breather pipe from the rear of the cylinder head cover. Remove the bolts which secure the oil cooler hoses or pipes to the engine unit. Free the pipes or hoses from any retaining clamps or guides and tape them up out of the way of the engine. Remove the flexible coolant hoses from their unions on the water pump and cylinder head, and remove the radiator lower mounting bolts and nut (as applicable).

6 On California models, remove the secondary air system pipes and control valves (where located on the engine) from the front of the engine. On 1000 California models, remove the evaporative emission control system canister from the front of the engine. Take note of all hose connections and if necessary label them to ensure correct reassembly.

7 On 1000 models remove the three bolts which secure the clutch slave cylinder to the engine sprocket cover and withdraw the cylinder from the casing. Push the piston as far back as possible by hand and then slowly bring the clutch lever back to the handlebars and hold it there with a stout elastic band. This will prevent the slave cylinder piston from being expelled by the accidental operation of the clutch lever. On 1000 K models onward, slacken the speedometer cable retaining screw and withdraw the cable from the sprocket casing **(see illustration)**. Tie the slave cylinder and speedometer cable (as applicable) to the frame so that they do not hinder engine removal. Withdraw the clutch pushrod from the crankcase **(see illustration)**.

8 On all models slacken the gearshift pedal pinch bolt and remove the pedal from the shaft. Remove the engine sprocket cover noting the drive chain guide plate (600 models) and locating dowels fitted between the cover and crankcase. If the dowels are loose they should be removed and stored with the cover for safekeeping. On 1000 K models onward, note the speedometer drive joint fitted to the cover. The 1000 T models incorporate a noise damper in the sprocket cover which is retained by a plate and two screws.

9 Slacken the engine sprocket retaining bolt whilst locking the engine through the transmission (machine in gear - apply the rear brake hard to prevent rotation) and remove the bolt and washer. Pull the sprocket off the countershaft (output shaft) splines and disengage it from the chain, noting that it may be necessary to first slacken the drive chain to obtain the required amount of freeplay. Remove the sprocket and allow the chain to hang over the swingarm.

10 Disconnect the lead from the starter motor terminal and disconnect the electrical connections from the pulser coil(s), alternator, neutral and oil pressure switch (as applicable) and release all wiring from any cable ties or hooks which secure it to the frame **(see illustration)**. Pull the suppressor caps off the

5.7a On 1000 K models onward, slacken speedometer cable retaining screw and withdraw cable

5.7b Remove clutch slave cylinder as described in text and withdraw the pushrod - 1000 models

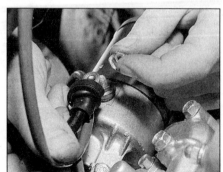
5.10a Disconnect the starter motor lead and all electrical connectors

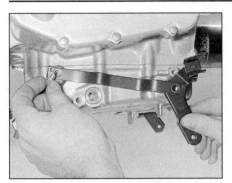

5.10b On 600 models remove the fairing mounting brackets . . .

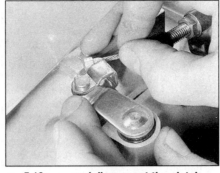

5.10c . . . and disconnect the clutch cable . . .

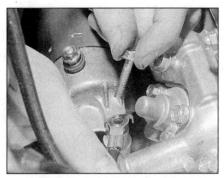

5.10d . . . and earth (ground) strap

spark plugs and position them clear of the engine. On 600 models remove the fairing mounting brackets from the right and left sides of the oil pan, disconnect the clutch cable from the engine, and remove the earth (ground) strap from the starter motor mounting bolt **(see illustrations)**. On 1000 models slacken the side stand bracket mounting bolts and remove it from the machine, noting that on K models onward it will also be necessary to disconnect the side stand switch wiring **(see illustrations)**.

11 On all models the engine unit should now only be retained by its mounting bolts. Check carefully that all components which may hinder the removal of the unit have been removed and that all cables and leads are wedged or tied out of the way. Position the jack beneath the engine unit to take the weight of the engine unit.

12 Slacken and remove both the right and left upper and lower engine front mounting bolts. Make a note of the correct position of any spacers fitted to the bolts to use as a guide on installation. Slacken both the upper and rear mounting bolts. **Note:** *On 1000 models there is an adjuster fitted to the upper rear mounting bolt on the right inner side of the frame. Loosen the adjuster locknut and screw the adjuster into the frame until there is a gap between the adjuster and engine.* On all models ensure the engine is securely supported then withdraw the rear mounting

bolts, again noting the position of any spacers. Turn the engine unit slightly so that the cylinder moves upwards and gently lower the engine out of the frame, taking great care not to damage the radiator. The engine unit can then be manoeuvred out of the side of the frame **(see illustration)**.

Installation

13 Remove all traces of corrosion from the engine mounting bolts and apply a smear of grease to their shanks to ease installation.

14 Position the engine unit beneath the frame then lift it up into position on the jack. Carefully manoeuvre the engine unit into position and insert the rear mounting bolts and spacers followed by the front mounting bolts and spacers. On 1000 models, once all the mounting bolts are in position tighten the upper rear mounting bolt adjuster to the specified torque setting; secure it in position by tightening the locknut to its specified torque setting. On all models tighten all the engine mounting bolts to the specified torque setting.

15 Connect the lead to the starter motor terminal, tighten its retaining nut securely, and refit its rubber insulating cap. Remake the electrical connections to the pulser coil(s), neutral and oil pressure switches and alternator (as applicable) ensuring that the wiring is correctly routed. Refit any cable ties that were removed and refit the wiring to any

relevant guide hooks or clamps. On 600 models install the fairing mounting brackets on the oil pan and reconnect the earth (ground) strap to one of the starter motor bolts. Connect the clutch cable to the operating arm and adjust it as described in Chapter 1 **(see illustration)**. On 1000 models refit the side stand bracket, tightening its mounting bolts securely, and on later models, connect the side stand switch wiring connector. On all models refit the suppressor caps to the spark plugs using the numbers on the HT leads to ensure they are correctly fitted.

16 Engage the engine sprocket with the drive chain, ensuring that the sprocket's marked face is outwards, then install it on the splines

5.10e On 1000 models disconnect the side stand switch wiring (K models onward) . . .

2

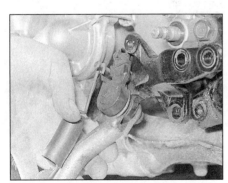

5.10f . . . and remove the side stand mounting bracket

5.12 Remove all mounting bolts and carefully lower engine out of frame

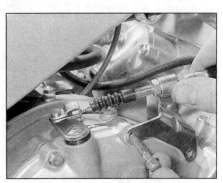

5.15 Connect clutch cable and adjust correctly - 600 models

5.16 Engage engine sprocket with drive chain and refit sprocket retaining bolt and washer

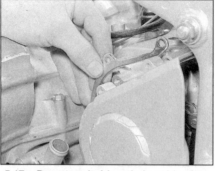

5.17a Do not omit drive chain guide plate when installing sprocket cover - 600 models

5.17b On 1000 K models onward, ensure speedometer drive joint aligns with sprocket bolt as cover is installed

on the countershaft (output shaft) **(see illustration)**. Fit the sprocket retaining bolt and washer and tighten it to the specified torque setting whilst locking the transmission as described in paragraph 8 to prevent the sprocket rotating. Check the drive chain tension as described in Chapter 1 and adjust if necessary.

17 Fit the two sprocket cover locating dowels (if removed) and install the cover, not omitting the drive chain guide plate (600 models) fitted between the cover and crankcase **(see illustration)**. **Note:** *On 1000 K models onward, when installing the cover ensure that the speedometer drive joint engages correctly with the sprocket retaining bolt (see*

illustration). Fit the gearshift pedal to the shaft, aligning the punch mark on the shaft with the punch mark on the pedal, and tighten the pedal pinch bolt to the specified torque **(see illustration).**

18 On 1000 models install the clutch pushrod ensuring that its rounded end is facing outwards. Ensure the clutch slave cylinder locating dowels are in position and fit a new gasket to the sprocket cover. Remove the elastic band from the clutch lever and push the slave cylinder piston in as far as possible using hand pressure only. Fit the slave cylinder to the sprocket cover and tighten its retaining bolts securely. Operate the clutch lever repeatedly to bring the piston in contact

with the pushrod; if there is evidence of air in the system it must be bled as described in Chapter 7. On 1000 K models onward, refit the speedometer cable to the sprocket cover and tighten its retaining screw securely.

19 On 1000 California models install the canister. On all California models, install the air control valves (where located on the engine) and the air pipes. Refer to the label on the air cleaner cover for correct connections.

20 On all models install the radiator lower mounting bolts and nut (as applicable) and tighten them securely. Refit the flexible coolant hoses to their unions on the water pump and cylinder head and securely clamp them in position. Renew the O-rings on the oil cooler pipes or hoses (as applicable) and refit them to the engine unit, tightening their retaining bolts securely. Ensure the hoses or pipes are correctly routed and pass through any relevant clamps or guides. Reconnect the breather pipe to the rear of the cylinder head. Refit the carburettors as described in Chapter 4.

21 Place new gaskets in the exhaust ports, using a dab of grease to stick them in place **(see illustration)**. On 600 models offer up the exhaust system, aligning the headers with the exhaust ports, and fit the muffler and header mounting bolts **(see illustrations)**. Refit the mounting collars to the header pipes and secure the headers in position by installing the eight mounting nuts, tightening them finger-

5.17c Align punch marks when installing gearshift pedal

5.21a Use grease to hold new gaskets in position

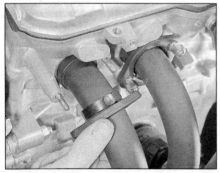

5.21b Align headers with the ports and refit the mounting collars . . .

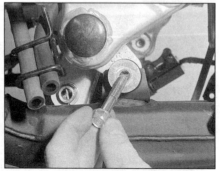

5.21c . . . and bolts

5.21d Refit muffler and tighten all mounting and clamping bolts to their specified torque settings

tight only at this stage. On 1000 models push the headers into the exhaust ports and secure them in position by fitting the lower mounting bolt and eight mounting nuts tightening all finger-tight only. Inspect the muffler gaskets for damage or deterioration, renewing if necessary, then install them on the header and refit their mounting bolts. On all models tighten all exhaust mounting and clamping bolts to their specified torque settings, starting from the front of the exhaust system and working backwards. **Note:** *Tighten the eight header retaining nuts evenly and progressively until the specified torque setting is reached.*

22 Reconnect the battery, remembering to connect the negative terminal last. Working as described in Chapter 1, install a new oil filter and add the required amount of oil to the engine. Fill the cooling system as described in Chapter 3. **Note:** *Be prepared for the oil and coolant levels to drop as soon as the engine is run. Therefore, temporarily install the fuel tank until the engine has been run and the coolant level is known to be correct. Do not install the lower fairing until the engine has been run and checked for oil or coolant leakage.*

6 Engine disassembly and reassembly - general note

Disassembly

1 Before any dismantling work is undertaken, the external surfaces of the unit should be thoroughly cleaned and degreased. This will prevent contamination of the engine internals, and will also make working a lot easier and cleaner. A high flash-point solvent, such as paraffin (kerosene) can be used, or better still, a proprietary engine degreaser such as Gunk or Jizer. Use old paintbrushes and toothbrushes to work the solvent into the various recesses of the engine casings. Take care to exclude solvent or water from the electrical components and inlet and exhaust ports.

> **Warning: The use of petrol (gasoline) as a cleaning agent should be avoided because of the risk of fire.**

2 When clean and dry, arrange the unit on the workbench, leaving a suitable clear area for working. Gather a selection of small containers and plastic bags so that parts can be grouped together in an easily identifiable manner. Some paper and a pen should be on hand to permit notes to be made and labels attached where necessary. A supply of clean rag is also required.

3 Before commencing work, read through the appropriate section so that some idea of the necessary procedure can be gained. When removing various engine components it should be noted that great force is seldom required, unless specified. In many cases, a

component's reluctance to be removed is indicative of an incorrect approach or removal method. If in any doubt, re-check with the text.

Reassembly

4 Before reassembly of the engine/transmission unit is commenced, the various components should be cleaned thoroughly and placed on a sheet of clean paper, close to the working area.

5 Make sure all traces of old gasket have been removed and that the mating surfaces are clean and undamaged. Great care should be taken when removing old gasket compound not to damage the mating surface. Most gasket compounds can be softened using a suitable solvent such as methylated spirits (stoddard solvent), acetone or cellulose thinner. The type of solvent required will depend on the type of compound used. Gasket compound of the non-hardening type can be removed using a soft brass-wire brush of the type used for cleaning suede shoes. A considerable amount of scrubbing can take place without fear of harming mating surfaces. Some difficulty may be encountered when attempting to remove gaskets of the self-vulcanising type, the use of which is becoming widespread, particularly as cylinder head and base gaskets. The gasket should be pared from the mating surface using a scalpel or small chisel with a finely honed edge. **Note:** *Do not resort to scraping with a sharp instrument unless necessary.*

6 Gather together all the necessary tools and have available an oil can filled with clean engine oil. Make sure that all new gaskets and seals are to hand, also all replacement parts required. Nothing is more frustrating than having to stop in the middle of a reassembly sequence because a vital gasket or replacement has been overlooked. As a general rule each moving engine component should be lubricated thoroughly as it is fitted into position.

7 Make sure that the reassembly area is clean and that there is adequate working space. Refer to the torque and clearance settings whenever they are given; many of the smaller bolts are easily sheared if overtightened. Always use the correct size screwdriver bit for crosshead screws and never use an ordinary screwdriver or punch. If any screws show evidence of maltreatment in the past, it is advisable to renew them as a complete set.

8 All mating surfaces must be carefully cleaned of all traces of old gaskets or jointing compound and must be absolutely flat and unmarked. Using a clean, lint-free cloth soaked in a high flash-point solvent, wipe over all the mating surfaces to remove all traces of oil and grease. Where necessary, apply a thin, continuous bead of sealant to the mating surfaces and assembly parts immediately.

9 Remember that if the mating surfaces are in good condition there should be no need for a thick film of sealant. The thinnest smear will

usually prove sufficient to seal the joint. **Note:** *If excess sealant is applied it will be pushed out to form a bead on each side of the joint. While the bead on the outside can be peeled off, the bead on the inside is free to break off and block oilways or cause similar problems!*

7 Camshafts and followers - removal, inspection and installation

Note: *The camshafts and followers can be removed with the engine in the frame.*

Removal

1 If the engine is in the frame, it will be necessary to first remove the lower or side fairing sections (as applicable). On 600 models remove the radiator lower mounting bolts and tie it out of the way of the cylinder head cover. On 1000 models remove the fuel tank as described in Chapter 4 and disconnect the throttle and choke cables from the carburettors. On all models pull the suppressor caps off the spark plugs **(see illustrations)**.

2 Disconnect the breather pipe from the rear of the cylinder head cover and slacken and remove the cylinder head cover retaining bolts. Carefully lift the cover, taking care not to damage the gasket, and manoeuvre it away from the engine unit.

3 Slacken the four bolts which secure the camchain upper guide to the cylinder head and lift it clear of the engine. On 600 models remove the camchain tensioner from the rear of the cylinder block and both inspection caps from the right crankcase cover. On 1000 models remove the cap from the crankshaft left end cover, noting that on K models onward it will first be necessary to remove the engine protector.

4 Slacken the four bolts which secure the sprockets to the camshafts and slide the sprockets off the camshaft shoulders. If necessary, the camshafts can be turned to gain access to the sprocket bolts by rotating the crankshaft.

Caution: Take great care not to drop the sprocket bolts down into the engine. If a bolt should drop into the engine do not turn the engine over until it has been retrieved. Failure to do so will result in extensive engine damage.

5 Slacken each of the camshaft bearing cap bolts by about one turn at a time. The camshafts are under pressure from the valve springs and will be pushed clear of the bearing surfaces in the cylinder head. Once valve spring pressure has been released, remove the bolts and place them with the bearing caps in a safe place. Also, if possible, remove all bearing cap dowels and store these with the caps. Disconnect the camchain from the sprockets and pass a screwdriver or loop of wire through the chain loop before removing the camshafts and sprockets from the cylinder head.

2

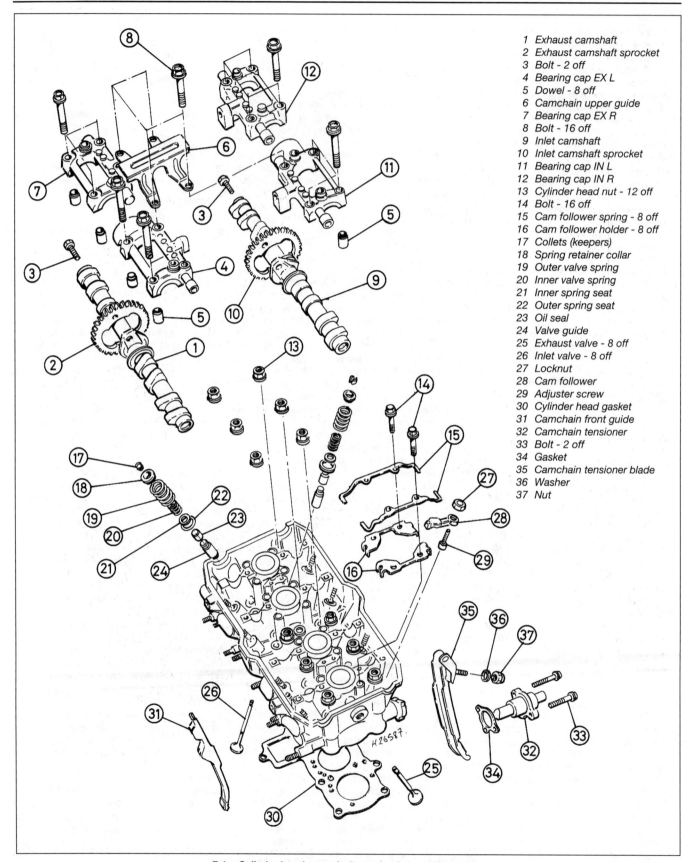

1 Exhaust camshaft
2 Exhaust camshaft sprocket
3 Bolt - 2 off
4 Bearing cap EX L
5 Dowel - 8 off
6 Camchain upper guide
7 Bearing cap EX R
8 Bolt - 16 off
9 Inlet camshaft
10 Inlet camshaft sprocket
11 Bearing cap IN L
12 Bearing cap IN R
13 Cylinder head nut - 12 off
14 Bolt - 16 off
15 Cam follower spring - 8 off
16 Cam follower holder - 8 off
17 Collets (keepers)
18 Spring retainer collar
19 Outer valve spring
20 Inner valve spring
21 Inner spring seat
22 Outer spring seat
23 Oil seal
24 Valve guide
25 Exhaust valve - 8 off
26 Inlet valve - 8 off
27 Locknut
28 Cam follower
29 Adjuster screw
30 Cylinder head gasket
31 Camchain front guide
32 Camchain tensioner
33 Bolt - 2 off
34 Gasket
35 Camchain tensioner blade
36 Washer
37 Nut

H 26587

7.1a Cylinder head, camshafts and valves - 600 models

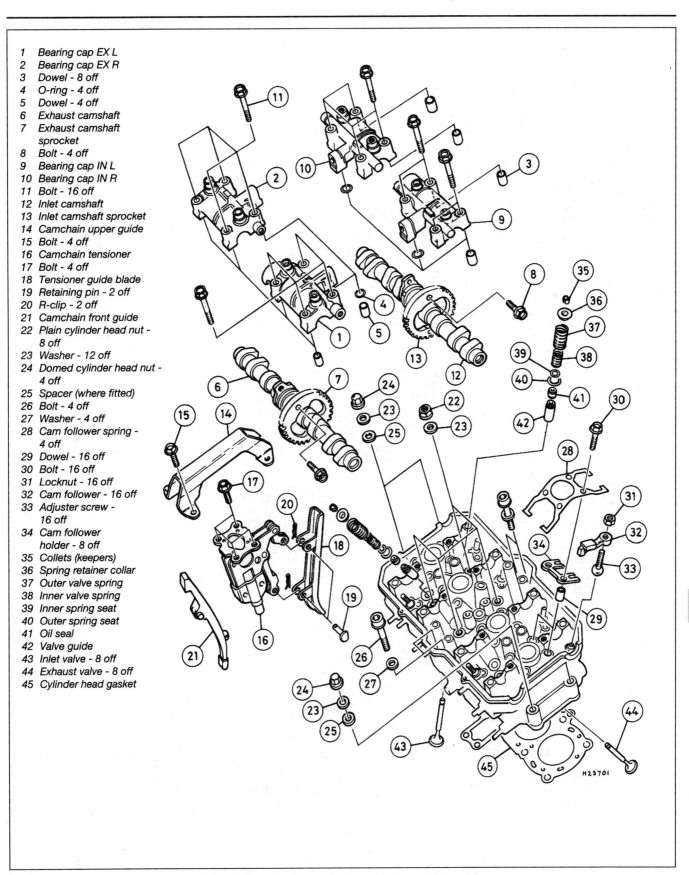

1   Bearing cap EX L
2   Bearing cap EX R
3   Dowel - 8 off
4   O-ring - 4 off
5   Dowel - 4 off
6   Exhaust camshaft
7   Exhaust camshaft
    sprocket
8   Bolt - 4 off
9   Bearing cap IN L
10 Bearing cap IN R
11 Bolt - 16 off
12 Inlet camshaft
13 Inlet camshaft sprocket
14 Camchain upper guide
15 Bolt - 4 off
16 Camchain tensioner
17 Bolt - 4 off
18 Tensioner guide blade
19 Retaining pin - 2 off
20 R-clip - 2 off
21 Camchain front guide
22 Plain cylinder head nut -
    8 off
23 Washer - 12 off
24 Domed cylinder head nut -
    4 off
25 Spacer (where fitted)
26 Bolt - 4 off
27 Washer - 4 off
28 Cam follower spring -
    4 off
29 Dowel - 16 off
30 Bolt - 16 off
31 Locknut - 16 off
32 Cam follower - 16 off
33 Adjuster screw -
    16 off
34 Cam follower
    holder - 8 off
35 Collets (keepers)
36 Spring retainer collar
37 Outer valve spring
38 Inner valve spring
39 Inner spring seat
40 Outer spring seat
41 Oil seal
42 Valve guide
43 Inlet valve - 8 off
44 Exhaust valve - 8 off
45 Cylinder head gasket

7.1b Cylinder head, camshafts and valves - 1000 models

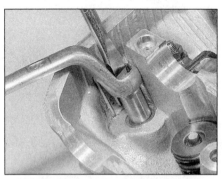

7.6 Remove cam follower adjuster screws as described in text

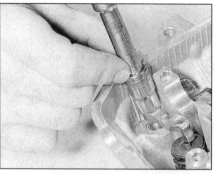

7.14 Installing a cam follower adjuster screw

6 The cam followers can be removed as follows. Remove the bolts which retain each cam follower holder and lift off the spring and holder. On 1000 models also remove the holder dowels from the cylinder head for safekeeping. Slacken and remove the adjuster locknut from the follower and remove the follower by rotating the adjuster screw in a clockwise direction. To remove the adjuster screws from the cylinder head, place one of the cam bearing cap dowels over the adjuster screw and refit the locknut. The adjuster screw can then be drawn out of the cylinder head by carefully tightening the locknut whilst retaining the adjuster screw **(see illustration)**.

Inspection

7 Inspect the camshaft lobes for signs of wear or scoring. Wear is normally evident in the form of visual flats worn on the peak of the lobes, and this may be checked by measuring each lobe at its widest point. If any lobe is worn to or beyond the service limit given in the Specifications the camshaft must be renewed. Scoring or similar damage can usually be attributed to partial failure of the lubrication system, possibly due to the oil and filter not having been renewed at the specified intervals. Before fitting a new camshaft, inspect the bearing surfaces of the cylinder head and cam followers.

8 If the cam lobes are scored it is likely that the surfaces of the cam followers are also damaged. If this is the case all the damaged followers must be renewed together with the camshaft.

9 If the camshaft bearing surfaces are scored or excessively worn, it is likely that the renewal of both the cylinder head and camshafts will be necessary. This is because the camshafts run directly in the cylinder head casting, using the alloy as a bearing surface. Note that it is not possible to purchase the camshaft bearing caps alone, as they are machined together with the cylinder head and are thus matched to it.

> **HAYNES HiNT**
>
> *Before renewing the camshafts or the cylinder head and bearing caps because of damage, check with local machine shops specialising in motorcycle engineering work. In the case of the camshafts, it may be possible for the cam lobes to be welded, reground and hardened at a cost far lower than that of a new camshaft. If the bearing surfaces in the cylinder head are damaged, it may be possible for them to be bored out to accept bearing inserts. Due to the cost of a new cylinder head and bearing caps, it is recommended that all options be explored.*

10 On 600 models measure the camshaft bearing journals, using a micrometer. If any journal has worn to or beyond the service limit, the camshaft(s) must be renewed. On all models the oil clearance between the camshaft journal and its bearing cap can be checked using Plastigage or by direct measurement.

The clearance must not exceed the service limit shown in the Specifications.

11 Camshaft runout can be checked by supporting each end of the camshaft on V-blocks, and measuring any runout using a dial gauge. If the runout exceeds the specified limit the camshaft must be renewed.

12 Inspect the upper camchain guide for wear or damage which will normally be fairly obvious, renewing it if necessary.

13 On 600 models inspect the camchain tensioner for wear or damage and check that the plunger moves in and out of the body smoothly. If this is not the case the tensioner must be renewed.

Installation

14 If the cam follower adjuster screws were removed, fit the screws to the relevant follower followed by the locknut **(see illustration)**. On 600 models set the adjuster screw so that the distance from the top of the locknut to the bottom of the screw is 20 mm (0.8 in), and on 1000 models set the screw so that the distance between the top surface of the screw and the bottom surface of the locknut is 7 mm (0.3 in). Secure the screw in position by tightening the locknut.

15 Install the follower assembly in the cylinder head by gently tapping the adjuster screw into position using a 10 mm socket, fitted to the locknut, as a drift. If the adjuster screws were not removed simply screw the follower onto the adjuster screw by rotating the screw itself. Fit the locknut and set up the adjuster screw as described above.

16 Refit the cam follower holder dowels to the cylinder head (1000 models only) and install the holders and springs, securing them in position with their retaining bolts **(see illustrations)**. Tighten the retaining bolts securely (1000 models) or to the specified torque setting (600 models).

17 Using a socket on the large hexagon nut on the end of the crankshaft, turn the crankshaft in a clockwise direction on 600 models and an anticlockwise direction on 1000 models, whilst keeping the camchain taut, until the T on the flywheel or crankcase aligns with the index mark visible on the crankcase cover or rotor (as applicable) **(see illustration)**.

7.16a Refit cam follower holders and springs . . .

7.16b . . . and secure them in position with their retaining bolts - 600 shown

7.17 Rotate crankshaft until T mark and index mark align - 600 shown

7.19a On 600 models install camshafts . . .

7.19b . . . so that the marks are facing upwards (inlet shown)

7.19c Refit bearing caps to the cylinder head noting the letters cast into each cap

18 Apply molybdenum disulphide grease to the camshaft journals and lobes and to the journals of the cylinder head and bearing caps. Install the camshafts and sprockets ensuring that the timing marks on the sprockets are facing to the right on 600 models and to the left on 1000 models. **Note:** *The inlet and exhaust camshafts are different, but can be easily identified by the cast IN or EX mark; ensure they are fitted correctly.*

19 Position the camshafts so that the cam lobes of number 4 cylinder are facing outwards (away from each other), and on 1000 models position the camshafts so that the cast IN and EX marks on the shafts are facing upwards **(see illustrations)**. Install the bearing caps dowels in the cylinder head and on 1000 models fit four new O-rings to the four inner dowel pins. Install the caps in their original positions using the mark cast into the top surface of each cap (IN R is the right inlet bearing cap for example) **(see illustration)**. Refit the camshaft bearing cap retaining bolts and tighten them evenly and progressively to the specified torque setting.

20 On 600 models, locate the cam sprockets with the drive chain so that the timing marks on each are level with the top surface of the cylinder head, and fit the sprockets to the camshafts **(see illustration)**. Apply a few drops of thread-locking compound to the

sprocket bolts and install the upper sprocket bolts, tightening them finger-tight only at this stage. Rotate the crankshaft through 1 complete turn (360°) until the T mark aligns with the index mark again, checking that the sprocket timing marks align again with the cylinder head, and fit the remaining sprocket bolts. Tighten all four cam sprocket bolts evenly and progressively to the specified torque setting.

21 On 1000 models rotate the cam sprockets so that the UP mark on each is facing upwards then locate the sprockets with the chain so that the IN mark on the inlet sprocket is level with the top surface of the cylinder head, and the EX mark on the exhaust sprocket is also level with the cylinder head surface. Fit the exhaust sprocket onto the camshaft then release the cam chain tensioner arm by pressing down on it with a screwdriver whilst fitting the inlet sprocket onto the camshaft. Apply thread-locking compound to the threads of the sprocket bolts and fit one bolt to each sprocket, noting that it may be necessary to rotate the crankshaft slightly to align the sprocket holes with the camshaft. Rotate the crankshaft through one complete turn (360°) and install the two remaining sprocket bolts. Turn the crankshaft through another complete turn and recheck that the IN and EX marks are

correctly aligned with the cylinder head surface. If this is the case, tighten all the sprocket retaining bolts to the specified torque setting and fill the camchain tensioner chamber with clean engine oil of the specified type.

22 On all models install the upper camchain guide to the cylinder head, ensuring that the arrow stamped on the guide is facing forward, and tighten its retaining bolts to the specified torque setting (600 models) or securely (1000 models) **(see illustration)**. On 600 models position a new gasket on the cylinder block and install the camchain tensioner, tightening its mounting bolts securely **(see illustration)**.

23 On all models rotate the crankshaft a few times, to settle all disturbed components, and check all valve clearances as described in Chapter 1, making adjustments as necessary. Lubricate all bearing surfaces with clean engine oil and wipe the cylinder head and cover gasket surfaces with a rag moistened with high flash-point solvent.

24 Examine the cylinder head cover gasket for signs of damage and renew it if necessary. Apply silicone sealant to the surfaces of the four semi-circular cutouts in the cylinder head. Clean the head cover gasket and fit it to the cover, ensuring that the arrow on the gasket is facing forwards; use a liquid gasket

2

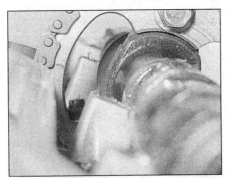

7.20 Align cam sprocket timing marks with cylinder head surface and tighten their retaining bolts to the specified torque setting

7.22a Refit the upper cam chain guide ensuring the arrow is facing forwards

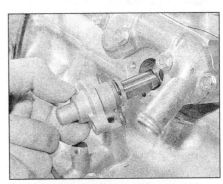

7.22b On 600 models refit camchain tensioner to the cylinder block

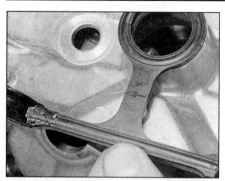

7.24a Fit gasket to the cylinder head cover ensuring the arrow on the gasket is facing forwards . . .

7.24b . . . and install cylinder head cover

not the case the tensioner body must be renewed. After inspection, drain the oil from the chamber and plunger.

Installation

7 Position the tensioner body inside the camchain's loop and fit the tensioner guide so that the chain runs up between the guide and body. Insert the guide retaining pins and secure them in position with their R-clips, taking great care not to drop the clips into the engine.

8 Refit the camchain tensioner mounting bolts and tighten them to the specified torque setting. Install the camshafts as described in the previous Section.

9 Cylinder head - removal, inspection and installation

Note: The cylinder head can be removed with the engine in the frame.

Removal

1 If the engine is in the frame, it will first be necessary to remove the fuel tank, carburettors, exhaust system, and camshafts and camchain tensioner using the information given in previous Sections of this Chapter. On California models it is also necessary to remove the secondary air system pipes and control valves.

2 Drain the cooling system as described in Chapter 3. Remove the retaining bolts that secure the metal coolant pipes to the rear of the cylinder head and carefully pull the pipes out, noting the O-rings around their unions.

600 models

3 Slacken the engine front upper mounting bolts on each side of the cylinder head, noting the spacer fitted between the frame and cylinder head on the right side. Remove the domed nut and washer from the rear of the cylinder head and lift out the rear camchain guide **(see illustrations)**.

compound to hold it in place **(see illustration)**. Install the cover on the engine unit so that the arrow cast on the top surface of the cover faces forward **(see illustration)**. Install the cylinder head cover retaining bolt seals ensuring that the UP mark on each seal faces upwards **(see illustration)**. Refit the cover retaining bolts and tighten them evenly and progressively to the specified torque setting, noting that the outer front cover bolts should be tightened first to ensure the cover gasket is correctly located. These bolts are marked with a triangle cast into the cylinder head cover surface **(see illustration)**.

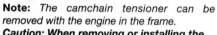

8 Camchain tensioner - removal, inspection and installation (1000 models)

Note: The camchain tensioner can be removed with the engine in the frame.
Caution: When removing or installing the tensioner, take care not to allow any item to drop down into the engine. If this should occur, do not turn the engine over until it has been retrieved. Failure to do so will result in extensive engine damage.

Removal

1 Remove the camshafts as described in previous Section.
2 Slacken the four bolts which secure the

camchain tensioner to the cylinder head and carefully lift the bolts away from the head. Withdraw the tensioner from the cylinder head and very carefully remove the R-clips from both tensioner guide retaining pins.

3 Remove the pins, separate the tensioner and guide, and manoeuvre the camchain out of position before removing the assembly. Pass a screwdriver through the chain to prevent it dropping down into the engine unit.

Inspection

4 Inspect the tensioner guide for signs of wear or damage and renew if necessary. Also inspect the camchain front guide which runs down the front of the cylinder block. If this is damaged it must also be renewed; refer to the cylinder head removal procedure in the following Section.

5 Turn the tensioner body upside down and drain all the oil from its chamber. Drain the oil from the plunger by moving the tensioner arm in and out slowly. The spring tension of the arm can only be tested in comparison with a new component. If there is any doubt as to the condition of the spring the tensioner must be renewed.

6 Fill the tensioner chamber up with clean engine oil and prime the plunger by slowly moving the tensioner arm in and out. If the tensioner is in good condition the tensioner arm should lock when moved quickly. If this is

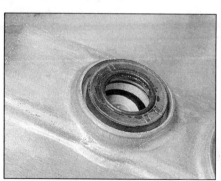

7.24c Ensure UP marks on head cover seals are facing upwards

7.24d Tighten the two bolts next to triangular marks first to ensure head cover is correctly positioned

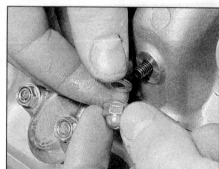

9.3a On 600 models remove domed nut and washer . . .

1000 models

4 On 1000 models drain the engine oil into a clean container as described in Chapter 1. Remove the two bolts which secure the oil cooler pipes to the front of the engine unit and separate them from the engine.

5 Remove the lower radiator mounting bracket from the cylinder head and disconnect the bottom radiator hose from its metal coolant pipe. Free the ignition coil/thermostat housing mounting bracket from the frame by removing its mounting bolts and remove the rubber heat protectors from each side of the cylinder head. Slacken the rear axle nut and the chain adjuster locknuts, then unscrew the adjuster nuts to obtain the maximum drive chain freeplay possible.

6 Slacken all the engine mounting bolts then place a jack or support beneath the machine to take the weight of the engine. Slacken, but do not yet remove, the locknut on the upper rear engine mounting adjuster, fitted on the right side of the frame, and screw in the adjuster until there is a gap between it and the engine. Remove all the engine mounting bolts except the upper rear bolt, noting the correct position of any spacers. Carefully jack the engine up into the frame pivoting it about the upper rear mounting bolt.

All models

7 On all models slacken the single bolt which secures the cylinder block to the crankcase and on 600 models remove the bolt which passes up through the front of the block, securing the head to the block **(see illustration)**. On 1000 models also remove the four bolts situated around the inside of the camchain tunnel.

8 Working in the reverse of the tightening sequence shown in illustration 9.12c, slacken the twelve cylinder head nuts by about one turn at a time until all pressure is released, then remove the nuts. Tap around the joint faces of the cylinder head with a soft-faced mallet to free the head. Once the seal has been broken, lift the head clear whilst feeding the camchain through the tunnel.

9 Remove the old head gasket and discard it.

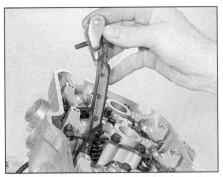

9.3b . . . and lift out rear camchain guide

If loose, remove the cylinder head locating dowels from the cylinder block and store them with the head for safekeeping. The front camchain guide can then be lifted out of the cylinder block **(see illustration)**.

Inspection

10 Remove all traces of carbon from the cylinder head using a blunt-ended scraper (the rounded end of an old steel rule will do). Finish off by polishing with metal polish to give a smooth shiny surface.

11 Check the condition of the spark plug threads. If the threads are worn or cross-threaded they can be reclaimed by the fitting of a Helicoil wire-thread insert. Most motorcycle repair shops operate this service which is simple, cheap and effective.

12 Lay the cylinder head on a sheet of 1/4 inch plate glass and check for distortion using feeler gauges. Aluminium alloy cylinder heads distort very easily, especially if the cylinder head nuts are tightened down unevenly. If the amount of distortion is only slight, it is permissible to rub the head down by wrapping a sheet of very fine emery cloth around the sheet of glass and rubbing in a rotary motion. Do not forget to check the corresponding surface of the cylinder block for warpage.

13 If the cylinder head is distorted beyond the service limit (as shown by frequent

9.7 On 600 models do not forget the bolt which secures head to the cylinder block

blowing of the cylinder head gasket), it will require skimming by a competent engineer experienced in this kind of work. This will of course raise the compression ratio of the engine and if too much is removed, the performance of the engine will be adversely affected. In extreme cases the valves might also strike the pistons, causing serious engine damage. If there is a risk of this happening, the only solution is to renew the cylinder head.

14 Refer to the following Section for information on overhauling the valves.

Installation

15 Ensure both cylinder head and block mating surfaces are clean and fit the locating dowels to the block (if removed). Install the camchain front guide, ensuring that its lugs are correctly located in the slots in the block, and fit a new head gasket over the dowels and studs **(see illustrations)**.

16 Carefully lower the cylinder head onto the block whilst feeding the camchain up through the head, noting that it may be necessary to lift the camchain guide slightly to allow the head to pass over it **(see illustration)**. Refit all the cylinder head nuts and bolts including their washers (where fitted). Using the correct tightening sequence, tighten the twelve cylinder head nuts evenly and progressively to the specified torque

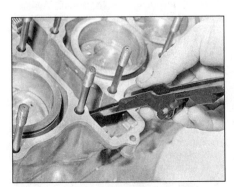

9.15a Install the front camchain guide . . .

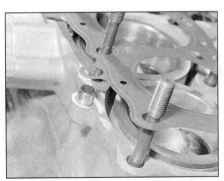

9.15b . . . and fit a new gasket over the dowels

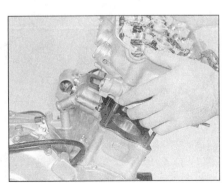

9.16a Lower the cylinder head onto the block . . .

2

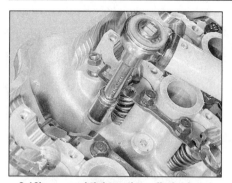

9.16b . . . and tighten the cylinder head nuts to specified torque setting as described in text

setting **(see illustrations)**. Once the cylinder head nuts are tight, tighten the cylinder head and block bolts securely.

600 models

17 On 600 models install the camchain rear guide in the camchain tunnel, fit a new sealing washer and secure the guide in position by tightening its domed retaining nut securely.

18 If the work is being carried out with the engine in the frame, refit the engine front upper mounting bolt on each side, not omitting the spacer fitted between the right side of the head and the frame. Tighten all disturbed engine mounting bolts to the specified torque setting.

1000 models

19 On 1000 models if the engine is in the frame, lower it back into its original position and install all the engine mounting bolts and spacers. Once all are in position tighten the engine upper rear mounting adjuster to the specified torque setting and secure it in position by tightening its locknut to its specified torque setting. Tighten all the engine mounting bolts to the specified torque settings then adjust the drive chain freeplay as described in Chapter 1.

20 Fit new O-rings to the oil cooler pipes and refit the pipes to the engine, tightening their retaining bolts to the specified torque setting. Install the rubber heat protectors on each side of the cylinder head and refit the radiator lower mounting bracket.

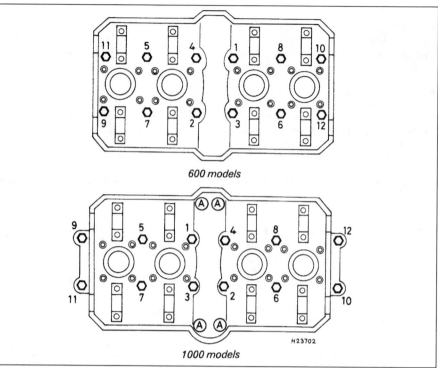

600 models

1000 models

9.16c Cylinder head nut tightening sequence

A - denotes four bolt positions

21 Connect the radiator bottom hose to its pipe and clamp it securely in position. Refit the ignition coil/thermostat housing mounting bracket bolts and tighten them securely. Replenish the engine oil and check the oil level as described in Chapter 1.

All models

22 On all models fit new O-rings to the cylinder head coolant pipes and refit the pipes to the head, tightening their retaining bolts securely **(see illustrations)**. Refill the cooling system as described in Chapter 3.

23 Install the camshafts, camchain tensioner, carburettors, fuel tank and exhaust system (as appropriate) using the information given in previous Sections of this Chapter. Reconnect the secondary air system components on California models; refer to the label on the air cleaner cover for hose connections.

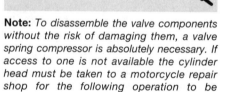

10 Valves - disassembly, inspection and reassembly

Note: *To disassemble the valve components without the risk of damaging them, a valve spring compressor is absolutely necessary. If access to one is not available the cylinder head must be taken to a motorcycle repair shop for the following operation to be performed.*

Disassembly

1 Before removing the valves from the cylinder head, obtain a container and partition it off into 16 separate sections. Clearly label each section with a cylinder number and valve position and place the valve components in their respective sections as they are removed. This will prevent mixing of valve components and ensure that they are installed in their original positions.

2 Remove the cam followers as described in Section 7. Compress the valve springs with a suitable valve spring compressor, and remove both valve collets (keepers). Carefully release the valve spring compressor and lift the spring retainer collar off the valve. Lift off both valve springs, noting that they should be fitted with their closer-pitched coils at the bottom, and then slide the valve out of the cylinder head. The oil seals can be carefully levered off the valve guide and both spring seats removed.

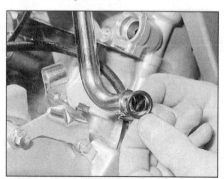

9.22a Do not omit the O-rings from the cylinder head coolant pipes . . .

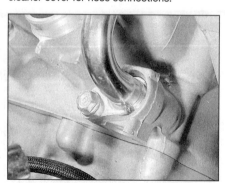

9.22b . . . and tighten their retaining bolts securely

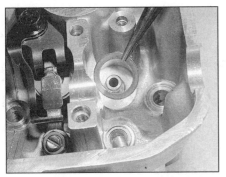

10.9a Install both the outer . . .

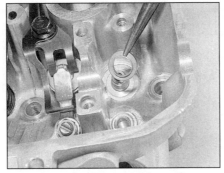

10.9b . . . and inner spring seats . . .

10.9c . . . and fit a new valve oil seal to the valve guide

Inspection

3 Inspect each valve for wear, overheating or burning and renew as a set if necessary. Normally the exhaust valves will need attention or renewal more frequently than the inlet valves, as the latter run at relatively low temperatures. If the valve face is pitted the valve must be renewed; do not attempt to cure this by grinding as this invariably causes the valve seat to become pocketed. Using a micrometer, measure the diameter of each valve stem at a number of points along its bearing surface. If at any point the diameter of the valve is less than the service limit given in the Specifications the valve must be renewed.
4 If possible, measure the internal bore of each valve guide at various points along its bearing surface both in the direction of the cam lobe and at right angles to it. If any measurement is beyond the specified service limit the guide must be renewed.
5 Inspect the cylinder head valve seats in each of the combustion chambers for signs of cracking, pitting or burning. Measure the width of the valve seat and check that it is within the specified limits. If the width of the valve seating area is not within the specified limits, varies significantly around its circumference, or is in any way damaged it must be re-cut. **Note:** *Valve guide renewal and re-cutting the valve seats are specialist jobs requiring a host of special tools. It is also*

remarkably easy to damage the cylinder head unless great care is taken during these operations.
6 Inspect the valve springs, retainers and collets (keepers) for signs of wear or damage, renewing as necessary. Measure the free length of both valve springs and renew the springs as a set if any have settled to less than the specified service limit.

Reassembly

7 The valves should be ground in using oil-bound grinding paste to remove any light pitting or to finish off a newly cut seat. Note that it is not normally necessary to resort to coarse grinding paste which is supplied in the dual-grade containers.
8 Commence by smearing a trace of fine grade grinding compound (carborundum paste) on the valve seat and apply a suction tool to the head of the valve. Oil the valve stem and insert the valve into its guide so that the valve and valve seat make contact with each other. With a semi-rotary motion, grind in the valve head to the seat, using a backwards and forwards motion. Lift the valve occasionally to ensure that the grinding paste is evenly distributed. Repeat the application until an unbroken ring of light grey matt finish is obtained on both the valve and seat - this denotes that the grinding operation is now complete.

Caution: Before moving onto the next valve, ensure all traces of grinding paste are removed from both the valve and seat and that none has entered the valve guide. If this precaution is not observed, rapid wear will take place due to the highly abrasive nature of the grinding paste.
9 Place both spring seats over the guides and press a new seal over each valve guide upper end **(see illustrations)**. Liberally oil the guide bore and the valve stem before inserting the valve into the guide **(see illustration)**. Refit the valve springs, ensuring that the closer-pitched coils are at the bottom (next to the cylinder head), and fit the spring retainer collar **(see illustrations)**. Check that both springs are correctly seated, compress them with the valve spring compressor, and install the collets (keepers). Remove the tool and give the end of each valve a sharp tap with a hammer to ensure that the collets (keepers) are correctly seated.
10 Install the cam followers as described in Section 7.

HAYNES HINT *You can check for proper sealing of the valves by pouring a small amount of solvent into each of the valve ports. If the solvent leaks past any valve into the combustion chamber area, the valve grinding operation on that valve should be repeated.*

2

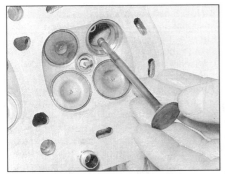

10.9d Liberally oil the valve stem and insert it into the guide

10.9e Refit the valve springs, ensuring that their closer-pitched coils are at the bottom . . .

10.9f . . . followed by the spring retainer. Compress the valve springs and install the collets (keepers)

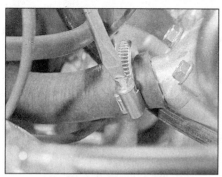

11.1a On 600 models disconnect the coolant hose from the rear of the block

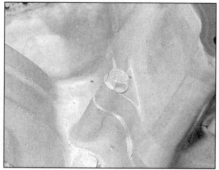

11.1b Remove the bolt which secures the block to the crankcase

11.7 On 600 models ensure oil jets are installed with their smaller holes uppermost

11 Cylinder block - removal, inspection and installation

Note: *The cylinder block can be removed with the engine in the frame.*

Removal

1 Remove the cylinder head as described in Section 9. On 600 models slacken the clamp which secures the flexible coolant hose to the rear of the block and prise the hose off its union **(see illustration)**. On 1000 models remove the two bolts which secure the metal coolant pipe to the front of the block and remove the pipe, noting the O-rings fitted to its unions. On all models remove the single bolt which secures the block to the crankcase **(see illustration)**.

2 Remove any residual road dirt from the base of the cylinder block then lift the block a couple of inches off the crankcase. Before the pistons emerge from the bottom of the bores, pack the crankcase mouth with clean rag to prevent any broken piston rings or other debris falling into the crankcase. Carefully lift the block off the studs and away from the engine. Note the cylinder block locating dowel pins and remove them for safekeeping if loose. Remove the cylinder base gasket and discard it. On 600 models also check that both oil jets are securely fitted to the crankcase, removing them for safekeeping if necessary.

Inspection

3 Remove all traces of gasket from the sealing faces of the block and check the upper sealing face of the block for warpage as described in Section 9 for the cylinder head.

4 Cylinder wear can be assessed by measuring the bore diameter at the top (just below the wear ridge), middle and bottom of the bore. Measure both along the piston pin axis and at right angles to it so that at least six measurements are taken. If any of the readings obtained exceed the service limit given in the Specifications, The cylinder block will have to be rebored and fitted with oversize pistons. Using the measurements obtained also check the taper and roundness (ovality) of the bore. If either of these exceed the specified service limit a rebore will be required.

5 Honda supply pistons in two oversizes, +0.25 mm (+0.01 in) and +0.50 mm (+0.02 in). If boring in excess of 0.5 mm becomes necessary it will be necessary to renew the cylinder block.

6 If new piston rings are to be run in a used bore, the bore surface must first be prepared by honing, or glaze-busting. This process, which can also be used to remove marks caused by very light piston seizure, involves the use of a cylinder bore honing tool usually in conjunction with an electric drill to break down the glazed surface which forms on any bore during normal service. The prepared bore will have a very lightly roughened surface

which will help the rings to bed in rapidly and fully. This is normally done as a matter of course after reboring. It also has the advantage of removing the lip from the top of the bore which could other wise damage the new top piston ring. Most motorcycle repair shops operate this service.

 Badly worn cylinder bores produce excessive smoking from the exhausts, initially in the form of a blue haze tending to develop into a white haze as the wear becomes more pronounced. The other indication is piston slap, a form of metallic rattle which occurs when there is little load on the engine. If the top of the bore is examined carefully, it will be found that there is a ridge on the thrust side; the depth of which will vary according to the rate of wear which has taken place.

Installation

7 On 600 models, if removed, install the oil jets in the crankcase top surface ensuring that their smaller holes are facing upwards **(see illustration)**.

8 On all models refit the dowels to the crankcase and install a new base gasket **(see illustration)**. Inspect the O-rings which are fitted over the lower end of each liner and renew any which are damaged.

9 Note that it is advisable to enlist the help of an assistant to refit the cylinder block. Lubricate the pistons and surface of the cylinder bores with clean engine oil. Pass the camchain through its tunnel in the block and slide the block into position.

10 The cylinder bores have a generous lead-in for the pistons at the bottom, although on a multi-cylinder engine such as this it would be an advantage to use the special Honda piston ring compressors. In the absence of these it is possible to lead the pistons into the bores gently, working across from one side to the other, guiding in one ring at a time whilst gently tapping on the cylinder block top surface **(see illustration)**.

11.8 Ensure dowels are in position and fit a new gasket

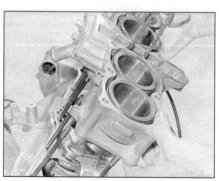

11.10 Carefully install the block as described in text

Caution: Great care must be taken not to put too much pressure on the piston rings as they are easily broken. The above process takes time and patience and must not be rushed. Once all the piston rings have entered the bore push the cylinder block down until it seats firmly on the base gasket.

11 Install the cylinder block retaining bolt, tightening it only finger-tight at this stage. Check that the crankshaft can be smoothly rotated whilst holding the block down and keeping the camchain taut.

12 On 600 models fit the coolant hose to the rear of the block, securing it in position by tightening its hose clamp securely. On 1000 models check the condition of the coolant pipe O-rings, renewing them if necessary, then refit the pipe to the block, tightening its retaining bolts securely.

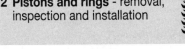

12 Pistons and rings - removal, inspection and installation

Note: *The pistons and rings can be removed with the engine in the frame.*

Removal

1 Remove the cylinder block as described in Section 11.

2 Remove the circlips from the pistons by inserting a small flat-bladed screwdriver into the groove in the piston boss and levering them out of position. Discard all circlips regardless of their apparent condition and use new ones on installation.

3 Press each piston pin out of position, noting that if the pins are a tight fit in the piston bosses it is advisable to warm the pistons before attempting to remove them. A rag which has been moistened in very hot water should be sufficient to expand the piston bosses when wrapped around the piston - take care to avoid scalding the hands! Do not use excessive force to remove the piston pins; if they are especially tight, make up a drawbolt arrangement to press them out of position. Using a spirit-based marker or scriber, mark each piston inside the skirt so that it can be refitted in its original bore on installation.

4 The piston rings can be removed by holding the piston in both hands and gently prising the ring ends apart until they can be lifted out of their grooves and onto the piston lands, one side at a time. The rings can then be slipped off the piston and put to one side for examination. Store the rings in the exact order that they were fitted as a guide to reassembly. If the rings are stuck in their grooves by excessive carbon deposits use three strips of thin metal to remove them **(see illustration)**. Be careful as the rings are brittle and will break easily if overstressed.

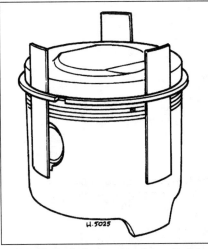

12.4 Method of removing rings stuck in their grooves by deposits

Inspection

5 If the cylinders are to rebored, the existing pistons and rings can de disregarded because they will be replaced with new items. If, however, the bores have been cleaned and checked as described in the preceding Section and are to be re-used, clean and check the pistons and rings as follows.

6 Remove all traces of carbon from the piston crowns using a blunt-ended scraper to avoid damaging the piston surface. Finish off by polishing the crowns of the pistons with metal polish to prevent carbon adhering so rapidly in future. **Note:** *Never use emery cloth on the soft aluminium alloy of the piston.*

7 Piston wear usually occurs at the skirt or lower end of the piston and takes the form of vertical streaks or score marks on the thrust side of the piston. Damage of this nature will necessitate renewal and is checked by measuring the outside diameter of the skirt at a point 10 mm (0.4 in) from the base of the piston and at right angles to the piston pin axis **(see illustration)**. If any piston has worn to or beyond its service limit, it must be renewed.

8 After the engine has covered a high mileage, it is possible that the ring grooves

12.7 Measuring piston diameter

may have become enlarged. Refit the rings to the piston and measure the clearance between the ring and groove using feeler gauges **(see illustration)**. If the gap exceeds the service limit the piston and/or piston rings must be renewed.

9 To measure the piston ring end gap, insert the ring into the lower end of its bore, using the crown of the bare piston to locate it. Ensure that it is square in the bore and measure the end gap of the ring using feeler gauges **(see illustration)**. If the ring gap exceeds the limits given, the rings should be renewed as a set.

10 It is also necessary to check the end gap when fitting new rings. If there is insufficient clearance, the rings will break up in the bore whilst the engine is running causing extensive engine damage. If necessary, the end gap can be increased by carefully filing the ends of the rings with a fine file. Support the ring on the end as much as possible to avoid breakage and ensure that the ring ends are kept square. Remove only a small amount at a time and keep rechecking the end gap in the bore.

11 Measure the outside diameter of the piston pin at several points along its bearing surface and renew it if it has worn beyond the service limit. If possible, also measure the internal diameter of the piston pin bore in the piston and the connecting rod small-end bore; compare these with the limits given in the Specifications, renewing components as necessary.

2

12.8 Checking piston ring groove clearance

12.9 Checking piston ring end gap

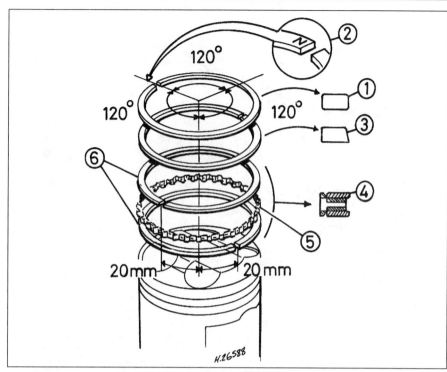

12.12 Piston ring end gap arrangement

1   Top ring
2   Top ring marking (N or R)
3   Second ring
4   Oil expander ring complete
5   Expander ring
6   Side rails

Installation

12 Refit the rings to the piston using the method employed on removal and position them as follows. The oil expander ring is fitted first followed by its side rails. Position the side rails so that thinner end gaps are at least 20 mm (0.8 in) each side of the oil expander ring end gap **(see illustration)**.

13 The second compression ring is easily identified by its tapered outer edge and must be fitted so that the widest point of the ring is at the bottom. The ring end gap should be positioned approximately 120° from that of the oil expander ring. The top ring is marked on one surface with either an N or R and must be installed with this mark on the upper surface of the ring and the ring end gap

positioned approximately 120° from the end gaps of both the second and oil expander ring **(see illustration)**. Ensure that all rings can move freely in their grooves.

14 Check that each piston has one new circlip fitted to it and insert the piston pin from the opposite side. If it is a tight fit, the piston should be warmed first. If the original pistons are being refitted, use the marks made on disassembly to ensure each piston is refitted to its correct bore.

15 Lubricate the piston pin and connecting rod bores with clean engine oil and lower each piston in turn over its respective connecting rod ensuring that the IN mark on the crown of the piston is on the inlet valve side. Push the piston pin through both piston bosses and the connecting rod small-end **(see illustration)**. If

12.15a Ensure piston is correctly positioned and insert the piston pin

12.15b Secure the piston pin in place using a new circlip

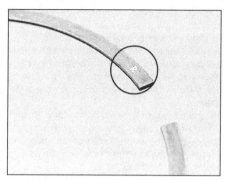

12.13 Top piston ring can be identified by mark on its upper surface

necessary the pins can be tapped carefully into position, using a hammer and suitable drift, whilst supporting the connecting rod and piston. Secure each piston pin in position with a second new circlip, ensuring that it is correctly seated in its groove **(see illustration)**.

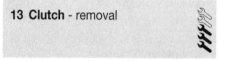

13 Clutch - removal

Note: *The clutch can be removed with the engine in the frame.*

1 If the engine is in the frame, drain the engine oil as described in Chapter 1, and remove the right lower or side fairing section (as appropriate) as described in Chapter 6. On 600 models it will also be necessary to remove the fuel tank as described in Chapter 4 and disconnect the three-pin block connector joining the three yellow alternator wires. Follow the procedure given under the relevant sub-heading **(see illustrations)**.

600 models

2 Slacken and remove all the right crankcase cover retaining bolts and, if the engine is in the frame, disconnect the cable from the clutch lifting arm, removing it along with its mounting bracket. Carefully lift the cover away from the engine whilst catching any residual oil which may be released as the cover is removed. Note the two locating dowels fitted to the crankcase and remove these for safekeeping if they are loose. Ensure that the clutch pushrod is securely in place in the crankcase cover.

3 Progressively slacken the clutch spring retaining bolts until spring pressure is released then remove the clutch lifting plate and springs.

4 The clutch centre is staked to the shaft for security. Prior to its removal, unstake the nut using a drill, taking great care not to damage the mainshaft (input shaft) threads.

5 In the absence of the Honda service tool, Part Number 07GMB-KT80100, it will be necessary to devise some method of preventing the clutch centre rotating as the

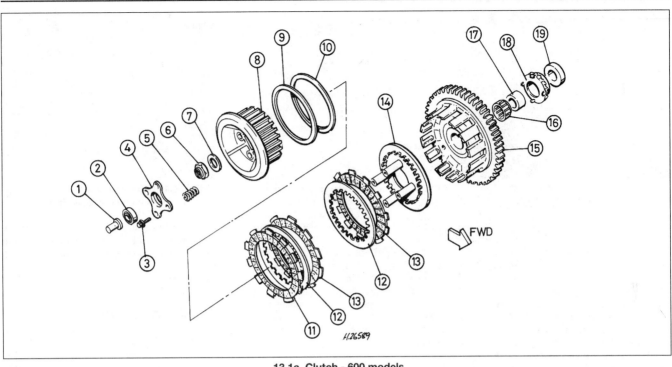

13.1a Clutch - 600 models

1 Pushrod	4 Lifting plate	8 Clutch centre	12 Plain plate - 5 off	16 Needle bearing
2 Bearing	5 Spring - 4 off	9 Spring seat	13 Friction plate - 5 off	17 Centre collar
3 Spring retaining bolt - 4 off	6 Nut	10 Anti-judder spring	14 Pressure plate	18 Oil pump drive gear
	7 Washer	11 Outer friction plate	15 Clutch drum	19 Spacer

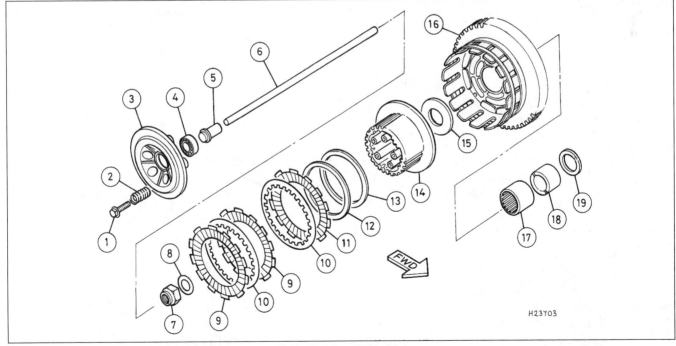

13.1b Clutch - 1000 models

1 Spring retaining bolt - 5 off	5 Pressure plate lifter	9 Friction plate - 8 off	13 Spring seat	16 Clutch drum
2 Spring - 5 off	6 Pushrod	10 Plain plate - 8 off	14 Clutch centre	17 Needle bearing
3 Pressure plate	7 Nut	11 Inner friction plate	15 Thrust washer (K models onward)	18 Centre collar
4 Bearing	8 Washer	12 Anti-judder spring		19 Thrust washer

13.5a On 600 models slacken clutch centre nut . . .

13.5b . . . whilst retaining the clutch centre as described in text

13.14 On 1000 models hold clutch centre as shown whilst slackening nut

centre nut is slackened. If the engine is in the frame, lock the clutch through the transmission, by selecting top gear and applying the rear brake hard whilst the nut is slackened. If the engine is out of the frame, pass a close-fitting ring spanner over the countershaft (output shaft) splines, select top gear and hold the spanner whilst the nut is slackened **(see illustrations)**.

6 Remove the nut and discard it; a new one must be used on installation. Remove the washer noting which way around it is fitted.

7 Withdraw the clutch centre followed by the outer friction plate. **Note:** *The outer friction plate is different to the others. Mark the plate in some way to ensure that it is refitted in its original position.* Remove the spring seat and anti-judder spring, noting which way around the spring is fitted, followed by the remaining plain and friction plates.

8 Remove the clutch pressure plate then withdraw the clutch drum and needle bearing.

9 To remove the oil pump drive assembly, slacken the bolt which secures the driven sprocket to the pump then remove both sprockets and the chain as an assembly. Slide the clutch drum centre collar off the mainshaft followed by the large spacer.

1000 models

10 Slacken and remove all the right crankcase cover retaining bolts, noting the correct positions of the two wiring clamps, and carefully lift the cover and heat protector bar away from the engine. Be prepared to catch any residual oil which will be released as the cover is removed.

11 Progressively slacken the clutch spring retaining bolts, until all spring pressure is released, and remove the clutch springs and their retaining bolts. Remove the pressure plate followed by the pressure plate lifter from the end of the pushrod and withdraw the pushrod itself.

12 Remove the friction and plain plates followed by the anti-judder spring, spring seat, inner plain plate and clutch centre. **Note:** *The inner friction plate is different to all the others. Mark this plate in some way to ensure it is fitted in its original position. Also make a note of which way around the anti-judder*

spring is fitted to use as a guide on reassembly.

13 The clutch nut is staked to the shaft for security. Prior to its removal, unstake the nut using a drill, taking great care not to damage the mainshaft (output shaft) threads. Note that the nut must be renewed on installation. A six-sided hexagonal nut is used on H and J models, and a bi-hexagonal nut on K models onward.

14 A holding tool will be required to prevent the clutch centre rotating whilst the nut is slackened **(see illustration)**. In the absence of the correct Honda service tool, Part Number 07724-0050001, a simple alternative can be made (see *Tool Tip*). Alternatively, if the engine is in the frame the centre can be retained as described in paragraph 4. Remove the nut and discard it; a new one must be used on reassembly. Remove the washer and clutch centre followed by the large thrust washer (K models onward).

15 Withdraw the clutch drum centre collar, using two pairs of pointed-nose pliers, and remove the needle roller bearing and clutch drum. Remove the thrust washer from the mainshaft.

14 Clutch - inspection

1 After an extended period of service the clutch friction plates will wear and promote clutch slip. Measure the thickness of each friction plate using a vernier caliper. If any plate has worn to or beyond the service limit given in the Specifications, the friction plates must be renewed as a set.

2 The plain plates should not show any signs of excess heating (blueing). Check for warpage using a flat surface and feeler gauges. If any plate exceeds the maximum

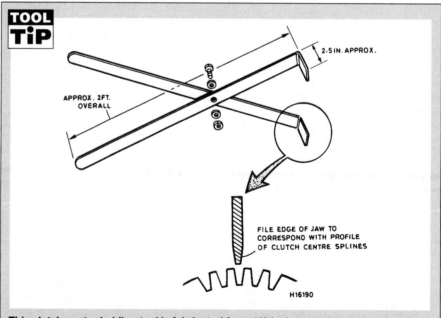

2.5 IN. APPROX.

APPROX. 2 FT. OVERALL

FILE EDGE OF JAW TO CORRESPOND WITH PROFILE OF CLUTCH CENTRE SPLINES

H16190

This clutch centre holding tool is fabricated from 1/8 inch steel strip and uses a nut and bolt as a pivot. The jaws should be filed or ground to suit the splines in the clutch centre and the handles should be about 2 - 3 feet in length to provide a secure grip.

14.9a Insert lifting arm into the cover, fit the return spring and roll pin . . .

14.9b . . . and hook the return spring over it

14.9c Insert the pushrod and check the operation of the lifting arm

permissible amount of warpage, or shows signs of blueing, all plain plates must be renewed as a set.

3 Inspect the clutch assembly for burrs and indentations on the edges of the protruding tangs of the friction plates and/or slots in the edge of the clutch outer drum with which they engage. Similarly wear can occur between the inner tongues of the plain plates and the slots in the clutch centre. Wear of this nature will cause clutch drag and slow disengagement during gear

changes, since the plates will snag when the pressure plate is lifted. With care a small amount of wear can be corrected by dressing with a fine file, but if this is excessive the worn components can be renewed. Also inspect the anti-judder spring and seat for signs of wear or distortion and renew if necessary.

4 Inspect the mainshaft (input shaft), clutch drum centre collar and clutch drum bearing surfaces for signs of wear and damage, along with the needle bearing. If access to the necessary measuring equipment can be gained, the condition of the above components can be judged by direct measurement. If any component shows signs of wear or damage, or has worn beyond its service limit given in the Specifications, it must be renewed.

5 Check the pressure plate lifting bearing for wear. On 600 models the bearing is fitted to the clutch lifting plate and on 1000 models it is fitted to the pressure plate. Ensure that the inner race of the bearing spins freely without any sign of notchiness and that there is no freeplay between the inner and outer races or the outer race and plate. If necessary, renew the bearing by driving the old bearing out of the plate and tapping the new bearing into position using a hammer and suitable tubular drift which bears only on the bearing's outer race.

6 Measure the free length of each clutch spring. If any one has settled to less than the service limit, the clutch springs must be renewed as a set.

600 models

7 Check that the clutch lifting arm and pushrod operate smoothly. Withdraw the

pushrod from the cover and check it for signs of wear or damage. Disengage the return spring from the lifting arm roll pin and then carefully tap the roll pin out of position. Withdraw the lifting arm from the cover and remove the return spring.

8 Inspect the needle bearings and seal fitted to the crankcase cover for signs of wear or damage, along with the lifting arm and return spring.

9 On reassembly apply grease to the oil seal lip, needle bearings and pushrod and carefully insert the lifter arm. Slide the return spring onto the arm then push the arm fully into position. Tap the roll pin back into position in the lifting arm and hook the return spring over it. Fit the pushrod to the crankcase cover and check the operation of the clutch lifting arm **(see illustrations).**

1000 models

10 Roll the clutch pushrod on a flat surface to check that it is not bent. If bent, it can be

straightened but if its hardened ends are worn it must be renewed.

11 The clutch master cylinder is similar to that used for the front brake and can be overhauled as described in Chapter 7.

12 Remove the fairing left section for access to the slave cylinder (see Chapter 6). Slacken the hydraulic hose union bolt on the slave cylinder - don't unscrew it or fluid will leak out. Remove the three mounting bolts and withdraw the slave cylinder from the sprocket cover.

13 Place the slave cylinder in a plastic bag (to contain brake fluid spills) and apply the clutch lever repeatedly to force the piston and spring out of the slave cylinder body. Unscrew the banjo union bolt to free the hydraulic hose from the slave cylinder.

14 Thoroughly clean the slave cylinder's internal components in clean brake fluid (don't use any type of petroleum-based solvent). Check the piston and cylinder bore for wear, scratches and rust, and renew either component if necessary **(see illustration).** If

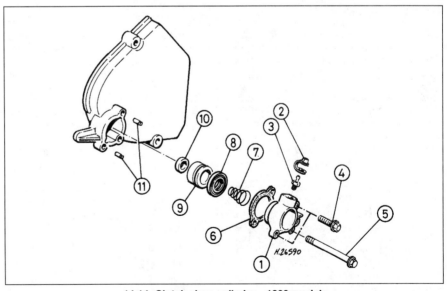

14.14 Clutch slave cylinder - 1000 models

1	Slave cylinder	5	Bolt	9	Piston
2	Cap	6	Gasket	10	Oil seal
3	Bleed nipple	7	Spring	11	Dowels
4	Bolts	8	Piston seal		

15.1a On 600 models slide the large spacer onto the mainshaft followed by the clutch drum centre collar

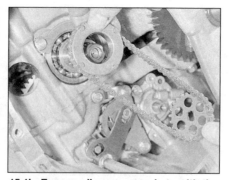

15.1b Engage oil pump sprockets with the drive chain and install them as an assembly

15.1c Apply thread-locking compound to driven sprocket bolt and tighten it to the specified torque setting

measuring equipment is available, the piston and slave cylinder bore diameters can be compared with the limits given in the Specifications.

15 The pushrod oil seal set in the end of the piston and the fluid seal set in the piston groove must be renewed as a matter of course. Make careful note of which way round both seals are fitted before prying them out of position. Install the new seals in the same fitted direction as the originals and lubricate their working surfaces with new hydraulic fluid.

16 Insert the smaller end of the spring into the piston. Lubricate the bore of the slave cylinder with new hydraulic fluid and insert the piston into the bore, fluid seal end first.

15.2a Lubricate the needle bearing and fit it onto the centre collar

17 Check that the two dowels are in place in the sprocket cover and place a new gasket over them. Install the slave cylinder, making sure that pushrod end locates in the piston oil seal. Secure the slave cylinder with the three bolts, noting that one of the bolts is longer than the other two.

18 Use new sealing washers on each side of the hydraulic hose union and tighten the banjo union bolt to the specified torque setting. Ensure that the union neck abuts the lug on the slave cylinder.

19 Fill the master cylinder reservoir with new hydraulic fluid and bleed the system as described in Chapter 7.

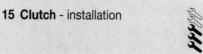

15 Clutch - installation

600 models

1 Slide the large spacer onto the mainshaft (input shaft) followed by the clutch drum centre collar **(see illustration)**. Assemble the oil pump drive and driven sprockets with the oil pump drive chain (ensure the dogs on the drive gear and the marks on the driven gear face outwards) and offer up the assembly to the engine unit, sliding the drive sprocket along the mainshaft, and engaging the driven sprocket

with the oil pump shaft **(see illustration)**. Apply thread-locking agent to the threads of the sprocket retaining bolt and tighten it to the specified torque setting **(see illustration)**.

2 Lubricate the needle bearing and fit it over the centre collar on the mainshaft **(see illustration)**. Apply molybdenum disulphide grease to the inner bearing surface of the clutch drum and install the clutch drum. **Note:** *Ensure that the dogs on the oil pump drive sprocket engage with the holes in the back of the clutch drum, and that the gear teeth of the primary driven gear on the back of the clutch drum mesh correctly with those of the primary drive gear (see illustration). Rotate the shafts concerned to ease alignment.*

3 Fit the spring seat to the clutch centre followed by the anti-judder spring, ensuring that the spring is fitted the correct way around **(see illustrations)**. Using the mark made on dismantling fit the outer friction plate to the clutch centre, followed by a plain plate then alternately install all the remaining friction and plain plates **(see illustrations)**. **Note:** *If new clutch plates are being fitted, apply a coating of oil to their surfaces to prevent seizure.*

4 Refit the pressure plate to the assembly, ensuring that it locates correctly with the slots in the clutch centre, and align all the friction plate tangs. Install the assembly into the clutch drum whilst aligning the friction plate tangs with the slots in the drum, and aligning

15.2b Ensure oil pump drive sprocket dogs engage with clutch drum holes when installing the drum

15.3a Fit the spring seat to the clutch centre . . .

15.3b . . . followed by the anti-judder spring . . .

15.3c . . . and the outer friction plate and plain plate

15.3d Alternately fit the remaining clutch plates then install the pressure plate

15.4 Align the friction plate tangs and install into the clutch drum

the clutch centre with the mainshaft splines **(see illustration)**.

5 Refit the washer, ensuring that the OUTSIDE mark is facing outwards, and fit a new clutch nut **(see illustration)**. Tighten the nut to the specified torque setting whilst holding the clutch centre using the method employed on removal. Once the nut has been tightened secure it in position by staking it into the groove in the mainshaft using a suitable hammer and punch **(see illustration)**.

6 Install the clutch springs, lifting plate and the clutch spring retaining bolts **(see illustration)**. Gradually tighten the four bolts evenly in a diagonal sequence, noting that when final tightening is reached the two bolts next to the punch marks on the lifting plate

must be secured first, followed by the two remaining bolts.

7 Refit the two crankcase cover locating dowels and fit a new gasket to the crankcase **(see illustration)**. Install the cover to the engine unit, ensuring that the pushrod is correctly fitted to the lifting arm **(see illustration)**. Install all the crankcase cover retaining bolts having first applied a few drops of thread-locking compound to the threads of the bolt directly above the crankshaft end cap. Ensure all crankcase cover bolts are securely tightened.

8 Replenish the engine oil as described in Chapter 1, reconnect the alternator wiring, refit the fuel tank as described in Chapter 4, and refit the fairing section.

1000 models

9 Fit the thrust washer to the mainshaft. Offer up the clutch drum, locating it with the primary drive gear, and slide the needle roller bearing and clutch centre collar along the mainshaft to locate the drum in position. Refit the large thrust washer (K models onward), followed by the clutch centre and washer.

10 Fit a new clutch nut - never re-use the old one. On K models onward, apply engine oil to the nut flange and threads. On all models, install the nut and tighten it to the specified torque setting whilst preventing the clutch centre from rotating using the method employed on dismantling **(see illustration)**. Secure the nut in position by staking it into the

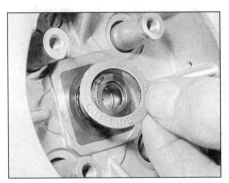

15.5a Ensure the thrust washer is fitted with OUTSIDE mark facing outwards

15.5b Fit a new clutch nut. Tighten it to the specified torque setting and stake it in position as described in text

15.6 Fit the clutch springs and lifting plate. Tighten the bolts as described in the text

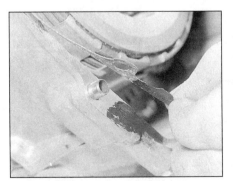

15.7a Ensure dowels are in position in the crankcase and fit a new gasket

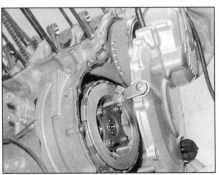

15.7b Install the right crankcase cover as described in text

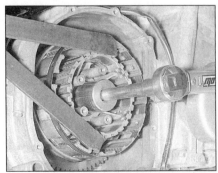

15.10a On 1000 models tighten the centre nut to the specified torque setting . . .

2

15.10b . . . and stake the nut into the mainshaft groove

15.11a Install the spring seat . . .

15.11b . . . followed by the anti-judder spring . . .

groove in the mainshaft using a suitable hammer and punch **(see illustration)**.

11 Install the spring seat and anti-judder spring to the clutch centre ensuring that the spring is fitted the correct way around **(see illustrations)**. Using the mark made on dismantling fit the inner friction plate to the clutch centre, followed by a plain plate, then alternately install the remaining friction and plain plates **(see illustrations)**. **Note:** *If new clutch plates are being fitted, apply oil to their surfaces to prevent possible seizure.*

12 Insert the pushrod into the centre of the mainshaft then grease the inside of the pressure plate lifter and fit it to the end of the pushrod **(see illustration)**. Install the clutch

pressure plate and refit the clutch springs and their retaining bolts **(see illustration)**. Tighten the clutch spring bolts evenly in a diagonal pattern and progressively in 2 - 3 steps until all are securely tightened.

13 Apply a smear of jointing compound to the crankcase surface to cover the area approximately 10 - 15 mm each side of the crankcase mating points. Fit a new gasket to the crankcase and install the cover and heat protector bar **(see illustration)**. Refit the crankcase cover retaining bolts, not omitting the two wiring clamps, and tighten them evenly and progressively working in a

diagonal sequence, until all are securely fastened **(see illustration)**.

14 Replenish the engine oil as described in Chapter 1 and refit the fairing section.

16 Gearshift (selector) mechanism - removal, inspection and installation

Note: *The gearshift (selector) mechanism can be removed with the engine in the frame.*

Removal

1 On 600 models if the engine is in the frame remove the clutch and oil pump drive chain

15.11c . . . and inner friction plate. Alternately install the remaining plain and friction plates

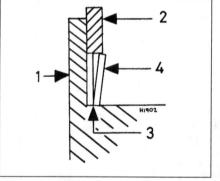

15.11d Correct fitting of clutch anti-judder spring

1 Clutch centre   3 Spring seat
2 Inner friction plate   4 Anti-judder spring

15.12a Insert pushrod and fit the pressure plate lifter

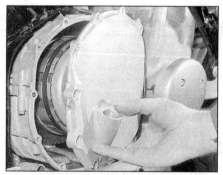

15.12b Refit the clutch pressure plate and clutch springs

15.13a Fit a new gasket as described in text and install the cover

15.13b Ensure the wiring clamps (arrowed) are correctly positioned when installing cover bolts

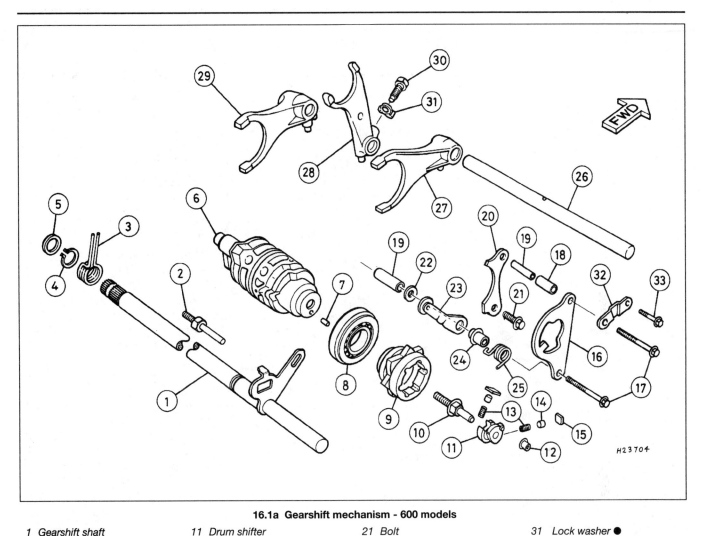

16.1a Gearshift mechanism - 600 models

1   Gearshift shaft
2   Spring anchor pin
3   Return spring
4   Circlip
5   Thrust washer
6   Shift drum
7   Locating pin
8   Bearing
9   Shift drum cam
10 Retaining pin bolt

11 Drum shifter
12 Collar
13 Spring - 2 off
14 Plunger - 2 off
15 Pawl - 2 off
16 Drum shifter retaining plate
17 Bolt - 2 off
18 Spacer
19 Dowel - 2 off
20 Shift drum retaining plate

21 Bolt
22 Thrust washer
23 Stopper (detent) arm
24 Collar
25 Return spring
26 Shift fork shaft
27 Right shift fork
28 Centre shift fork
29 Left shift fork
30 Retaining bolt ●

31 Lock washer ●
32 Shift fork shaft retaining
     plate ■
33 Bolt ■

● only fitted to H, J and
    US K models
■ only fitted to L and
    UK K models

2

assembly as described in Section 13 and disengage the gearshift pedal from its shaft **(see illustration)**. On 1000 models if the engine is in the frame drain the engine oil as described in Chapter 1, remove the water pump mounting bolts and the bolt which secures the metal coolant pipe to the front of the engine, then remove the pump from the crankcase and position it clear of the sprocket cover. **Note:** *It is not necessary to disconnect or drain any of the cooling system components.* Remove the final drive sprocket as described in Section 5. On 1000 K models onward, it will also be necessary to remove the sidestand mounting bracket **(see illustration)**.

2 On all 1000 models slacken and remove all the gearshift cover retaining bolts and carefully remove the cover and chain guide plate, taking care not to damage the seals on either the gearshift or countershaft splines. If loose, remove the gearshift cover locating dowels from the crankcase and store them with the cover for safekeeping.

3 On all models carefully withdraw the gearshift shaft from the crankcase, noting the thrust washer fitted between the shaft and crankcase, and remove the collar from the drum shifter mechanism pin. Slacken the two bolts which retain the drum shifter retaining plate and withdraw the plate and drum shifter as an assembly; note that this will involve

removal of the shift fork shaft retaining plate on later 600 models.
4 Disengage the stopper (detent) arm from the shift drum and remove the arm along with its return spring, collar and thrust washer. Note the two dowels which are fitted in the crankcase and remove these for safekeeping along with the spacer which is fitted over the upper dowel. If necessary, slacken the shift drum cam retaining pin bolt from the centre of the drum and remove the cam. Withdraw the shift drum cam locating pin from the drum.

Inspection

5 Carefully separate the drum shifter and retaining plate noting that the shifter pawls are

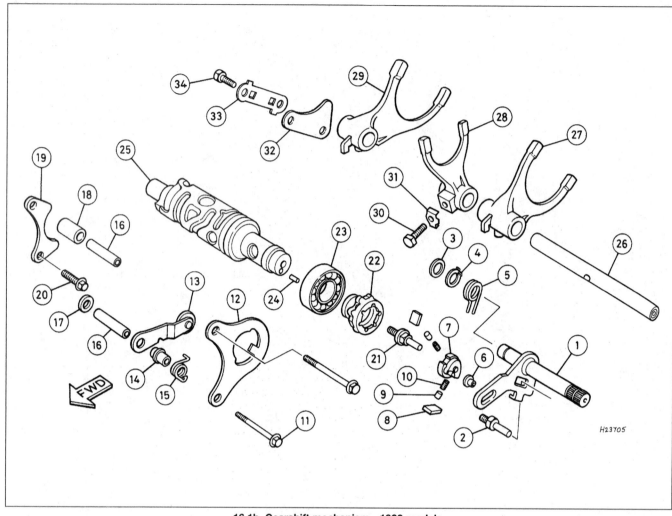

16.1b Gearshift mechanism - 1000 models

1 Gearshift shaft	11 Bolt - 2 off	21 Retaining pin bolt	30 Retaining bolt ●
2 Spring anchor pin	12 Drum shifter retaining plate	22 Shift drum cam	31 Lock washer ●
3 Thrust washer	13 Stopper (detent) arm	23 Bearing	32 Shift fork shaft retaining
4 Circlip	14 Collar	24 Locating pin	plate ■
5 Return spring	15 Return spring	25 Shift drum	33 Lock washer ■
6 Collar	16 Dowel - 2 off	26 Shift fork rod	34 Bolt ■
7 Drum shifter	17 Thrust washer	27 Left shift fork	
8 Pawl - 2 off	18 Spacer	28 Centre shift fork	● only fitted to H and J models
9 Plunger - 2 off	19 Shift drum retaining plate	29 Right shift fork	■ only fitted to K models onward
10 Spring - 2 off	20 Bolt		

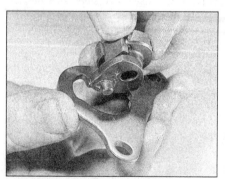

16.5a Carefully separate the drum shifter and retaining plate . . .

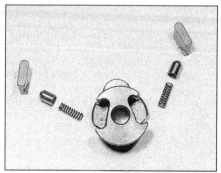

16.5b . . . and inspect drum shifter components for wear

spring-loaded; remove the pawls, plungers and springs from the shifter **(see illustrations). Note:** *The pawls are not interchangeable; mark them or make a note of their correct positions to ensure they are refitted correctly.* Inspect all components for signs of wear or damage, renewing components as necessary. Inspect the gearshift shaft, shift drum cam, stopper (detent) arm and collar for signs of wear or damage. If any component is damaged in any way the only satisfactory method of repair is renewal. The gearshift shaft and stopper arm return spring tension can only be checked by comparison with new items and should be renewed if there is any doubt about their condition.

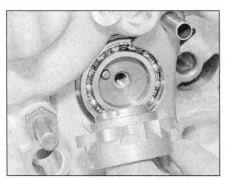

16.7a Locate shift drum cam with locating pin on installation

16.7b Apply thread-locking compound to the cam retaining pin bolt

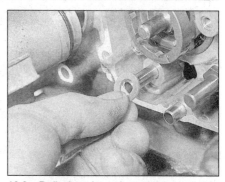

16.8a Refit dowels to the crankcase and fit thrust washer over lower dowel

6 On 1000 models check the condition of the three oil seals in the gearshift mechanism cover and renew any which show signs of deterioration or damage. Seals can be levered out of position using a flat-bladed screwdriver and the new items pressed into position. The seals can be tapped in using a hammer and a suitable tubular drift which bears only on the hard outer edge of the seal. Also inspect the gearshift shaft needle bearing for wear, renewing it if necessary.

Installation

7 If removed, refit the shift drum cam locating pin to the drum and install the cam **(see illustration)**. Apply a few drops of thread-locking compound to the threads of the cam retaining pin bolt and tighten it to the

specified torque setting **(see illustration)**.
8 Refit the dowels to the crankcase and fit the thrust washer over the lower dowel **(see illustration)**. Fit the collar and return spring to the stopper (detent) arm and install them as an assembly ensuring that the stopper arm engages correctly with the shift drum cam **(see illustration)**. Refit the spacer to the upper dowel.
9 Install the springs and plungers in the drum shifter and, using the marks made on dismantling, refit the pawls. Ensure the plungers are correctly located in the pawl grooves and refit the drum shifter assembly to its retaining plate **(see illustration)**. Install the drum shifter and retaining plate assembly to the engine and tighten the retaining plate

bolts securely **(see illustration)**. On later 600 models, do not forget to install the shift fork shaft retaining plate.
10 Fit the collar to the drum shifter pin and slide the thrust washer along the gearshift shaft **(see illustrations)**. Install the shaft ensuring that its return spring engages correctly with its locating pin and that the hole in the shaft plate locates with the drum shifter collar. Check that the gearshift shaft moves easily and centralises quickly with the pressure of the return spring. **Note:** *On 1000 K models onward, if the work is being carried out with the engine in the frame it may be necessary to fit the gearshift shaft into the cover and install as an assembly with the cover (see illustration)*. If this is the case

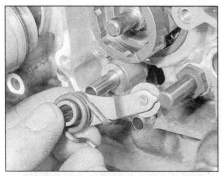

16.8b Fit the collar and spring to the stopper arm and install as an assembly

16.9a Fit spacer over upper dowel before refitting the drum shifter and retaining plate as an assembly . . .

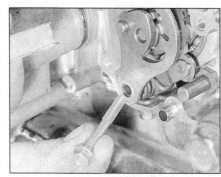

16.9b . . . and tighten its retaining bolts securely

16.10a Do not omit collar from drum shifter pin . . .

16.10b . . . or gearshift shaft thrust washer - 1000 shown

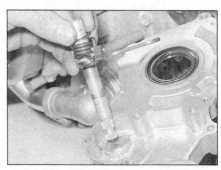

16.10c On 1000 K models onward, it may be necessary to fit gearshift lever to cover (see text)

2

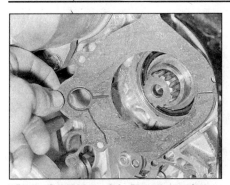

16.11a On 1000 models fit a new gasket as described in text . . .

16.11b . . . and refit the cover . . .

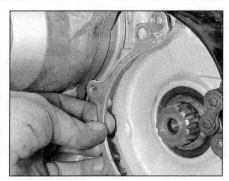

16.11c . . . and chain guide

great care must be taken to ensure the shaft plate and return spring engage correctly as the cover is installed. Check the operation of the gearshift shaft as soon as the cover is in position.

11 On 1000 models apply a smear of jointing compound to the crankcase surface to cover the area approximately 10 - 15 mm each side of the crankcase mating points. Ensure that the both dowels are in position in the crankcase and fit a new gasket **(see illustration)**. Apply grease to the lips of the cover oil seals then carefully refit the cover **(see illustration)**. Install all the cover retaining bolts and chain guide noting that the bolt fitted with a sealing washer must be fitted to the hole just below the drive sprocket **(see illustration)**. This hole is indicated by the triangular mark cast in the cover **(see illustration)**. Also apply a few drops of thread-locking compound to the threads of the lower chain guide bolt (indicated by an * mark on some models). Tighten the bolts evenly and progressively until all are securely fastened.

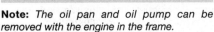

17 Oil pan (sump) and oil pump - removal, inspection and installation

Note: *The oil pan and oil pump can be removed with the engine in the frame.*
1 If the engine is in the frame, drain the

engine oil, and remove the complete lower fairing and exhaust system as described in Section 5. On 600 models it will also be necessary to disconnect the oil cooler hoses from each side of the oil pan (sump).

Removal

600 models

2 Slacken all twelve oil pan retaining bolts evenly and in a criss-cross sequence. Remove the oil pan and gasket from the crankcase. Note the two oil pan locating dowels and remove these for safekeeping along with their O-rings.
3 Slacken the two oil strainer retaining bolts and remove the strainer from the engine, noting the O-ring fitted to its union. Also remove the pressure relief valve - this is a push fit in the crankcase. If you wish to remove the oil pump, first remove the clutch and oil pump drive assembly as described in Section 13. Remove the two oil pump mounting bolts and manoeuvre the pump out of the engine unit, noting the two dowels fitted to the pump body **(see illustration)**.

1000 models

4 Slacken all sixteen oil pan retaining bolts evenly and in a criss-cross sequence. Three of the bolts are longer than the others on 1000 N models onward, and care must be taken to note which holes they come from; a paper or

cardboard template of the cover works well for this purpose and can also be used to mark the location of the wire clamps. Remove the oil pan from the engine.
5 Withdraw the oil strainer, pressure relief valve and the left and right side metal oil pipes, all of which are a push fit in the crankcase. Slacken the two bolts which secure the centre metal oil pipe in position and remove it from the machine. Note the O-rings which are fitted to all of the above components.
6 Remove the bolt which secures the driven sprocket to the oil pump, disengage the sprocket from the chain and remove it from the engine. Rotate the crankshaft until the slot on the water pump driveshaft is vertical then remove the three oil pump mounting bolts and slide the pump out of position. If loose, remove the three pump locating dowels from the crankcase noting the O-ring which is fitted over the large dowel.

Inspection

7 The oil pump and relief valve can be disassembled and checked as described in the relevant Sections of Chapter 4. Wash the oil strainer in a high flash-point solvent to remove all traces of foreign matter from the gauze. Inspect the gauze for signs of clogging or damage. If the gauze screen is split or clogged the strainer must be renewed. Renew all the O-rings as a matter of course.

16.11d Ensure bolt with the sealing washer is fitted next to the triangular mark on the cover

17.3 Remove oil pump mounting bolts and manoeuvre pump out of the crankcase - 600 shown

17.8a On 600 models fit the O-ring to the oil strainer . . .

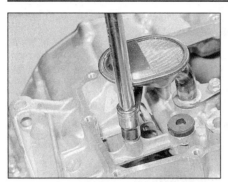

17.8b . . . and securely tighten its mounting bolts

17.9a Install the oil pan dowels and fit an O-ring over each one

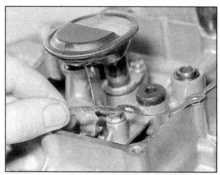

17.9b Use grease to stick a new oil pan gasket to the engine . . .

Installation

600 models

8 Ensure the dowels are fitted to the oil pump and install the pump in the engine unit so that its shaft locates correctly with the slot in the water pump driveshaft. Fit the two pump mounting bolts and tighten them securely. Refit the oil strainer to the underside of the pump, not omitting its O-ring, and tighten its retaining bolts securely **(see illustrations)**. Smear the relief valve O-ring with engine oil and carefully push the valve into position in the crankcase.

9 Refit both the oil pan dowels to the engine unit and fit an O-ring over each one **(see illustration)**. Install a new gasket, using a smear of grease to hold it in position, and refit the oil pan **(see illustrations)**. Install the oil pan retaining bolts and tighten evenly and progressively until all are securely fastened. Refit the clutch as described in Section 15.

1000 models

10 Fit the three oil pump dowels to the crankcase not omitting the O-ring which is fitted to the larger dowel. Manoeuvre the oil pump into position, aligning its shaft with the slot in the water pump driveshaft, and install the pump mounting bolts. Tighten the bolts securely and check that the pump shaft rotates freely.

11 Engage the oil pump driven sprocket with the drive chain, ensuring that the OUT mark on the sprocket face is facing the clutch, and locate it on the oil pump shaft. Apply a few drops of thread-locking compound to the sprocket retaining bolt and tighten it to the specified torque setting.

12 Apply a smear of oil to the oil pipe and relief valve O-rings and install them in the engine unit. Secure the centre oil pipe in position by tightening its retaining bolts securely. Fit the oil strainer to the pump, not omitting the O-ring, ensuring that the cutout in the strainer plate locates with the pin on the oil pump body. Fit a new gasket to the crankcase using a smear of grease to hold it in position, and install the oil pan. Refit the oil pan bolts, not forgetting the wiring clamps and the shorter bolt locations, and tighten them evenly and progressively until all are securely fastened.

---

18 Alternator rotor - removal and installation (600 models)

Note: *The alternator rotor can be removed with the engine in the frame.*
Note: *To remove the alternator rotor the special Honda rotor puller, Part Number 07733-0020001, or a pattern equivalent will be*

required. Do not attempt to remove the rotor using any other method.

Removal

1 Drain the engine oil, and remove the right crankcase cover as described in Section 13.
2 Slacken and remove the rotor retaining bolt and washer whilst holding the rotor to prevent it turning. In the absence of the special Honda service tool, Part Number 07725-0040000, the rotor can be retained using a strap wrench. Alternatively, the engine can be locked through the transmission by selecting top gear and applying the rear brake hard (engine in frame).
3 Screw the rotor puller tool into the centre of the rotor and pass a bar through the hole in the puller **(see illustration)**. Remove the rotor from the crankshaft end by tapping sharply on the end of the metal bar to release the rotor's grip on the tapered shaft.
4 Remove the Woodruff key from the crankshaft and store it safely inside the flywheel rotor.

Installation

5 Degrease the rotor and crankshaft tapers and remove any metal particles or swarf from the rotor magnet. Install the Woodruff key in the crankshaft taper **(see illustration)**.
6 Align the slot in the rotor taper with the Woodruff key and gently push the rotor onto

17.9c . . . and refit the oil pan

18.3 Puller must be used to remove alternator rotor

18.5 Ensure crankshaft taper is clean and install the Woodruff key

2

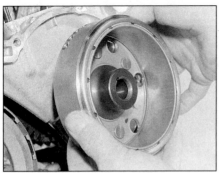

18.6a Align rotor slot with the Woodruff key whilst installing the rotor

the crankshaft **(see illustration)**. Gently tap the rotor centre with a soft-faced hammer to seat it on the crankshaft taper and refit the rotor retaining bolt and washer **(see illustration)**. Tighten the bolt to the specified torque setting whilst holding the rotor to prevent it from rotating.

7 Install the right crankcase cover as described in Section 15 and replenish the engine oil as described in Chapter 1.

19 Starter clutch - removal, inspection and installation (600 models)

Note: *The starter clutch can be removed with the engine in the frame.*

19.5a Remove the driven gear and needle bearing . . .

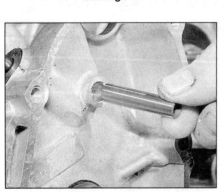

19.7a Refit the idler gear shaft to the crankcase . . .

18.6b Refit the rotor retaining bolt and washer and tighten to the specified torque setting

Removal

1 If the engine is in the frame, remove the left lower fairing and drain the engine oil as described in Chapter 1. Remove the fuel tank as described in Chapter 4. Trace the pulser coil wiring back from the left crankcase cover to its block connector and disconnect it from the main wiring loom.

2 Slacken all the bolts which retain the left crankcase cover and carefully remove cover. Be prepared to catch any surplus oil which may be released as the cover is removed. Unless the cover locating dowel is firmly fixed in the crankcase, remove it and store it with the cover.

3 Slacken and remove the starter clutch retaining bolt. **Note:** *If trouble is encountered*

19.5b . . . and inspect starter clutch rollers for signs of wear

19.7b . . . and install the idler gear

in slackening the bolt, the crankshaft can be held by locking it through the transmission as described in Section 13. Alternatively, if the pistons have been removed the crankshaft can be locked by passing a close-fitting bar through the connecting rod small-end bores. Once the bolt has been removed the pulser rotor, starter clutch and splined thrust washer can be slid off the crankshaft.

4 Remove the starter motor idler gear and pull the idler gear shaft out of the crankcase.

Inspection

5 Separate the starter clutch and driven gear and remove the needle bearing from the starter clutch shaft **(see illustrations)**. Inspect the needle bearing for wear together with the bearing surfaces of the driven gear and clutch. The starter clutch rollers should be unmarked with no signs of wear such as pitting or flat spots. The degree of wear on the driven gear can be assessed by measuring the outside diameter of its boss and comparing it with the service limit given in the Specifications. Renew any component which shows signs of wear or damage.

6 Inspect the starter idler gear and driven gear teeth and renew them as a pair if any teeth are chipped or missing. Check the idler shaft and gear bearing surfaces for signs of wear or damage, and renew if necessary.

Installation

7 Refit the idler gear shaft to the crankcase and slide on the idler gear **(see illustrations)**. Liberally oil the needle bearing and fit it to the starter clutch. Refit the driven gear and check that the gear will spin freely in one direction, but not the other.

8 Slide the splined thrust washer onto the crankshaft and install the starter clutch assembly, ensuring that the driven gear teeth engage correctly with those of the idler gear **(see illustration)**. Refit the pulser rotor over the crankshaft splines aligning the punch mark on the crankshaft end with the extra wide spline of the rotor **(see illustration)**. Install the starter clutch retaining bolt and washer and tighten it to the specified torque setting whilst retaining the crankshaft using

19.8a Fit the splined thrust washer over the crankshaft splines and install the starter clutch assembly

the method employed on dismantling (see illustration).

9 Ensure the mating surfaces of the cover and crankcase are clean and dry and refit the dowel pin. Fit a new gasket to the crankcase and carefully install the cover (see illustrations). Refit all the crankcase cover retaining bolts and tighten them securely.

10 If the operation is being carried out with the engine in the frame, reconnect the pulser coil wiring, refit the fuel tank, and replenish the engine oil.

20 Balancer shaft - removal, inspection and installation (1000 models)

Note: *The balancer shaft can be removed with the engine in the frame.*

Removal

1 Remove the oil pan (sump) as described in Section 17.

2 Remove the bolt which secures the balancer shaft clamp to the crankcase, followed by the shaft retaining bolt which passes up through the casting from the underside of the crankcase. Withdraw the shaft from the crankcase and rotate the balancer weight until it can be manoeuvred out of the crankcase, noting the shouldered thrust washers fitted to each end of the weight.

Inspection

3 Remove the gear from the end of the balancer weight and remove the cush drive rubbers. Withdraw the shaft from the centre of

19.8b Refit the pulser rotor as described in text and install starter clutch retaining bolt and washer . . .

19.8c . . . tighten it to the specified torque setting

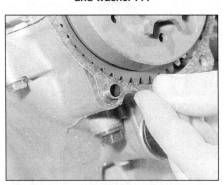
19.9a Ensure the dowel is in position in the crankcase and fit a new gasket

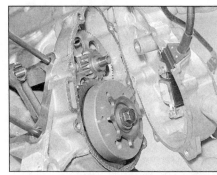
19.9b Install the left crankcase cover and tighten all its retaining bolts securely

the weight and withdraw the needle bearings and spacer (see illustration).

4 Inspect the needle bearings for wear or damage along with the bearing surfaces of weight and shaft. If any component shows signs of wear or scoring renew the shaft, bearings and weight as an assembly. Check the shouldered thrust washers for wear and renew if necessary.

5 Inspect the rubber segments of the cush drive for wear or deterioration such as compaction, perishing or breakage. Any damage will be self evident and the rubbers must be renewed as a set. Check the shaft O-ring for wear or damage and renew if necessary.

Installation

6 Apply oil to the cush drive rubbers and fit them onto the balancer weight. Refit the gear to the weight ensuring that the punch mark on the face of the gear aligns with index line on the opposite end of the balancer weight. Liberally oil the needle bearings and insert them into the balancer weight along with the spacer, positioned between them. Refit the shouldered thrust washers to each end of the weight ensuring that both are fitted with their shoulders facing inwards.

7 Using a spirit-based marker, mark the bottom surface of the weight so that the index mark will be visible when the weight is installed in the crankcase. Remove the cap from the left crankcase cover and rotate the crankshaft in a anticlockwise direction until the index mark on the rotor aligns with the T mark on the crankcase. Manoeuvre the balancer weight assembly into position in the crankcase and engage it with its drive gear so

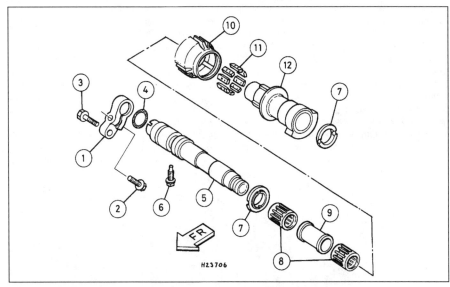
20.3 Balancer shaft - 1000 models

1 Clamp
2 Pinch bolt
3 Retaining bolt
4 O-ring
5 Balancer shaft
6 Shaft retaining bolt
7 Shouldered thrust washer - 2 off
8 Needle bearing - 2 off
9 Spacer
10 Gear
11 Cush drive rubbers
12 Weights

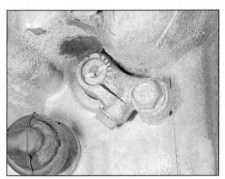

20.9 Adjust balancer shaft backlash using marks on the clamp

that the index mark on the weight aligns with the adjacent line on the crankcase surface.

8 Apply a smear of oil to the balancer shaft O-ring and insert the shaft. Secure the shaft in position by refitting the shaft retaining bolt to the underside of the crankcase and tightening it securely. Apply a small amount of gasket sealant to the threads of the balancer shaft retaining clamp bolt and refit it to the engine unit, tightening it securely. Install the oil pan (sump) as described in Section 17.

9 Once the oil pan has been installed it will be necessary to set the balancer shaft backlash as follows **(see illustration)**. Remove the balancer shaft clamp pinch bolt and rotate the shaft anticlockwise until it stops. Then rotate the shaft back in a clockwise direction until it has passed through the first of the graduations marked on the shaft clamp. Secure the shaft in position by tightening the clamp pinch bolt securely having first applied a few drops of thread-locking compound to its threads.

21 Shift (selector) drum and forks - removal, inspection and installation

Removal

600 models

1 To remove the shift drum and forks it is first necessary to split the crankcase halves as described in the following Section. The shift

drum and forks are located in the lower crankcase half.

2 On 600 H, J and US K models bend down the tabs of the lock washer fitted to the centre shift fork and remove its retaining bolt. On all models withdraw the shift fork shaft and remove the shift forks from the casing, noting the letter cast onto one surface of each fork. Slacken the bolt which secures the shift drum retaining plate to the casing and remove the bolt and plate. The shift drum can then be removed from the casing.

1000 models

Note: *The balancer shaft can be removed with the engine in the frame.*

3 If the engine is in the frame, remove the oil pump and clutch as described in Sections 17 and 13 of this Chapter, and the gearshift mechanism components as described in Section 16.

4 On H and J models bend down the tabs of the lock washer fitted to the centre shift fork and remove its retaining bolt. On K models onward, bend down the tabs of the shift fork shaft retaining plate lock washer then slacken its retaining bolts and remove the washer and plate. On all models withdraw the shift fork shaft.

5 Slacken the bolt which secures the shift drum retaining plate to the crankcase and remove it along with the retaining plate. Disengage the shift fork guide pins from their tracks in the drum and withdraw the shift drum. Remove the shift forks from the crankcase, noting the letter(s) cast onto one surface of each fork.

Inspection

6 The shift forks and shaft should be closely inspected to ensure that they are not badly damaged or worn. Measure the width of both fork ends and the internal diameter of the shaft bore. if either fork end or the shaft bore has worn beyond its service limit the shift fork(s) must be renewed.

7 The shift fork shaft can be checked for trueness by rolling it along a flat surface. A bent shaft will cause difficulty in selecting gears and make the gearshift action heavy. Measure the diameter of the shaft at the points where it is in contact with the shift

forks. If the shaft is bent or has worn beyond its service limit at any point it must be renewed.

8 Inspect the shift drum grooves and selector fork guide pins for signs of wear or damage. If either component shows signs of wear or damage the shift fork(s) and drum must be renewed. Check that the bearing fitted to the drum rotates freely and has no sign of freeplay between its inner and outer race. Renew the bearing if necessary.

Installation

600 models

9 Refit the shift drum in the lower crankcase half, fit the shift drum retaining plate and tighten its retaining bolt securely **(see illustration)**. The shift forks can be identified by the letter cast on each one; L denotes the left fork, C the centre, and R the right **(see illustration)**. **Note:** *All shift forks must be installed in the crankcase half so that the letter on each one faces towards the right side of the casing (clutch).* Locate the right fork with its groove in the shift drum and partially insert the shift fork shaft until it engages with the fork. Repeat the process for the centre and left fork and push the shaft fully home **(see illustration)**.

10 On H, J and US K models rotate the shift fork shaft until the hole in the shaft aligns with the centre fork bolt hole. Apply a few drops of thread-locking compound to the threads of the shift fork retaining bolt and refit it to the fork using a new lock washer. Tighten the bolt to the specified torque setting and secure it in position by bending up the tabs of the lock washer against the flats of the bolt.

1000 models

11 Apply molybdenum disulphide grease to the shift fork grooves of the gears prior to installing the forks. On H and J models the fork marked C is the centre fork and must be installed so that the C mark faces towards the right side of the crankcase (clutch side). The left fork is marked with an L and the right with an R. Both left and right forks must be installed so that their marks are facing towards the left side of the crankcase (drive sprocket side). On K models onward, the left fork is marked S2L, the centre fork S2C and

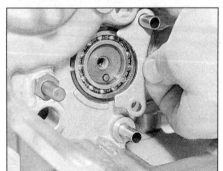

21.9a On 600 models insert the shift drum into the lower crankcase half and secure in position with the retaining plate

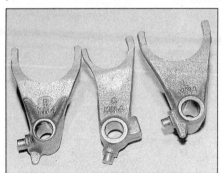

21.9b Shift forks can be identified using letters cast on each one

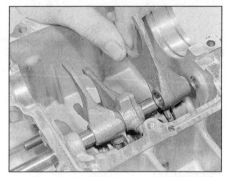

21.9c Install shift forks as described in text

22.7a On 600 models install oil jets as described in text

22.7b Do not omit crankcase locating dowels

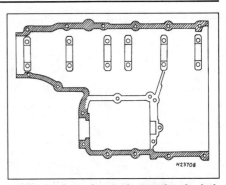

22.7c Apply gasket sealant to the shaded areas of lower crankcase - 600 models

the right fork S2R. All forks must be installed so that their marks face the left side of the crankcase (drive sprocket side).

12 Once the forks are correctly positioned refit the shift drum and its retaining plate. Apply a few drops of thread-locking compound to the threads of the retaining plate bolt and tighten it securely.

13 Engage the shift fork guide pins with their respective grooves in the drum and insert the shift fork shaft ensuring that it locates with all three shift forks. On H and J models rotate the shaft until the hole in the shaft aligns with the centre fork bolt hole. Refit the shift fork retaining bolt, using a new lock washer, and tighten it to the specified torque setting. On K models onward, refit the shift fork shaft retaining plate using a new lock washer and tighten both the retaining bolts to the specified torque setting. On all models secure the retaining bolt(s) in position by bending the lock washer tabs up against the flats of the bolt(s).

22 Crankcase -
separation and reassembly

1 The crankcase halves cannot be separated until the engine has been removed from the frame as described in Section 5 of this Chapter, and all preliminary dismantling has been carried out. If a full engine strip is being performed, then all operations described in Sections 7, 9, 11, 12, 13, 16, 17, 18, 19 and 21 on 600 models, and 7, 8, 9, 11, 12, 13, 16, 17, 20 and 21 on 1000 models must first be performed. If, however, it is wished only to examine the transmission shaft components then the operations described in Sections 9, 11, 12, 16 and 20 (as applicable) can be ignored. Note also that it is only necessary to remove the clutch assembly and gearshift mechanism components if the transmission shafts are to be disassembled, otherwise they can be left in position.

Separation

2 On 1000 models, if the starter clutch or alternator shaft is to be removed, slacken the bolt which secures the alternator shaft nut

cover to the upper side of the crankcase and lift off the cover. Lock up the crankshaft by passing a close-fitting bar through the connecting rod small-ends, then slacken and remove the nut.

3 On all models slacken and remove all the upper crankcase bolts (5 on 600 models and 3 on 1000 models). Invert the crankcase and progressively slacken the lower crankcase bolts in 2 - 3 steps, using a diagonal sequence, to prevent crankcase warpage. As each bolt is removed, store it in its relative position, along with any sealing washers or guides, in a cardboard template of the crankcase halves so that it can be refitted in its original position.

4 Separate the crankcase halves with the unit inverted on the bench. The crankshaft and main transmission shafts will remain in position in the upper half but take care not to dislodge or lose any main bearing inserts from the lower casing. If difficulty is encountered in breaking the seal between the crankcase halves, thoroughly check that all crankcase bolts and components have been removed before forcing the casings apart. Initial separation can be achieved by tapping gently with a soft-faced mallet.

Caution: Do not lever the cases apart with a screwdriver; this will only succeed in damaging the gasket face.

5 Lift off the lower crankcase half noting the three locating dowels. Remove the dowels and store them with the casing for safekeeping. On 600 models also note the oil jets fitted in the upper crankcase half; if these

22.8a Lower the lower crankcase half into position . . .

are loose they must also be removed for safekeeping.

Reassembly

6 Thoroughly clean the gasket faces of both casings and remove all old gasket compound - see Section 6. Check that all components are installed and that they can rotate smoothly and easily. Use a rag soaked in high flash-point solvent to wipe over the gasket surfaces of both halves to remove all traces of oil. Continue as described under the relevant following sub-heading.

600 models

7 Make sure the two oil jets are clear. Refit them in the upper crankcase half, noting that the jet nearest the crankshaft **(see illustration 22.7a)** is fitted with its smaller hole facing the lower crankcase half, and the jet next to the gearbox output shaft **(see illustration 24.9f)** is fitted with its larger hole facing the lower crankcase half. Refit the crankcase dowels to the lower casing **(see illustration)**. Apply a small amount of gasket compound to the outer gasket surface of the lower crankcase half **(see illustration)**. Take great care to leave a narrow margin around any oilways so that there is no risk of surplus compound blocking an oilway.

8 Ensure that the main bearing inserts are in position in the lower casing and carefully lower the lower crankcase half onto the upper half **(see illustration)**. Ensure that the shift forks engage with their respective slots in the transmission shafts as the halves are joined **(see illustration)**. Check that the lower

2

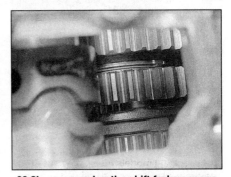

22.8b . . . ensuring the shift forks engage correctly with their relevant grooves

22.9a Install all main bearing bolts and washers and tighten them as described in text

crankcase half is correctly seated and that all shafts are free to rotate.

9 Install all the lower crankcase bolts and washers, using the cardboard template to ensure each bolt is fitted in its correct position. Do not omit the sealing washers from the twelve 8 mm main bearing bolts and the single 6 mm bolt (number 21 in the tightening sequence) **(see illustration)**. Tighten all the lower crankcase bolts in 2 or 3 stages, until all are tightened to their specified torque settings **(see illustration)**.

10 Turn the crankcase over and refit the upper crankcase bolts, ensuring that sealing washers are fitted to the two bolts next to the triangular marks cast on the crankcase surface **(see illustration)**. Tighten the upper 6 mm bolts to the specified torque setting.

1000 models

Note: *On 1000 P models onward, the twelve 9 mm main bearing bolts must be renewed on reassembly of the crankcases.*

11 Apply a small amount of gasket compound to the sealing faces of both the upper and lower crankcase halves. Take great care to leave a narrow margin around the main bearing inserts and oilways so that there is no risk of surplus compound blocking an oilway. Check the condition of the O-ring fitted onto the oil plate pipe in the upper crankcase half and renew it if necessary. Apply molybdenum disulphide grease to the crankshaft main bearings and the shift fork

22.10 Do not omit sealing washers from the bolts next to the triangular marks in crankcase upper surface

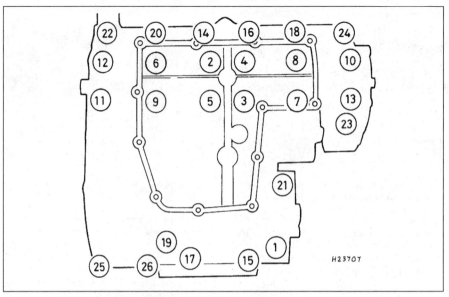

22.9b Crankcase lower half bolt tightening sequence - 600 models
Note: copper sealing washers fitted to bolts 2 to 13 and 21

grooves. **Note:** *If the balancer shaft is in position in the lower crankcase half the balancer shaft timing must be set, as described in Section 20.*

12 Ensure that the main bearing inserts are in position in the lower crankcase half and carefully lower the lower crankcase half onto the upper half. Ensure that the shift forks engage with their respective transmission slots and the balancer weight remains in position as the halves are joined. Check that the lower crankcase half is correctly seated and that all shafts are free to rotate.

13 Apply molybdenum disulphide grease to the threads and seats of the lower crankcase 8 mm bolts and install all the 8 mm and 6 mm lower crankcase bolts and sealing washers, using the cardboard template to ensure all are fitted in their original positions. Do not omit the sealing washers (H, J, K, L, M, N, P, R models only) from the twelve 9 mm main bearing bolts as they are installed (note that new 9 mm bolts must be used on P models onward). First tighten the 9 and 8 mm bolts in 2 to 3 stages, using a diagonal sequence, to their specified torque setting, then tighten all the 6 mm bolts to their specified torque setting.

14 Turn the crankcase over and install the three upper crankcase bolts ensuring that there is a sealing washer fitted to the two 8 mm bolts. Tighten the upper bolts to their specified torque settings.

15 If the starter clutch or alternator has been removed refit the nut and washer to the alternator shaft. Lock up the crankshaft by passing a close-fitting bar through the connecting rod small-end eyes and tighten the nut to the specified torque setting. Check the alternator shaft nut cover O-ring for damage, renewing it if necessary, and refit the cover to the crankcase. Install the cover

retaining bolt, along with its sealing washer, and tighten it securely.

All models

16 Check that the crankshaft and transmission shafts rotate smoothly and easily. If there are any signs of undue stiffness or of any other problem, the fault must be rectified before work can proceed.

23 Crankcase and covers - inspection and renovation

1 Small cracks or holes in aluminium castings may be repaired with an epoxy resin adhesive, such as Araldite, as a temporary measure. Permanent repairs can only be effected by argon-arc welding, and only a specialist in this process is in a position to advise on the economy or practicability of such a repair. Alternatively, you could consider the purchase of one of the low temperature aluminium fusion welding kits.

2 Damaged threads can be economically reclaimed by using a diamond section wire insert, of the Helicoil type, which is easily fitted after drilling and re-tapping the affected thread. Most motorcycle dealers and small engineering firms offer a service of this kind.

3 Sheared studs or screws can usually be removed with screw extractors, which consist of tapered, left-hand thread screws of very hard steel. These are inserted into a pre-drilled hole in the stud, and usually succeed in dislodging the most stubborn stud or screw. If a problem arises which seems beyond your scope, it is worth consulting a professional engineering firm before condemning an otherwise sound casing. Many of these firms advertise regularly in the motorcycle press.

24.9a On 600 models liberally oil the needle bearing and insert the mainshaft into the lower crankcase half

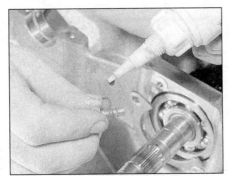

24.9b Apply thread-locking compound to the mainshaft retaining plate bolts . . .

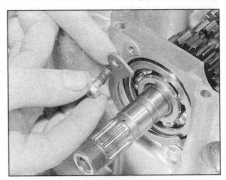

24.9c . . . and install the mainshaft retaining plate

24 Transmission shafts -
removal, inspection and installation

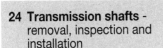

Removal

1 Separate the crankcase halves as described in Section 22.
2 On 600 models lift the countershaft (output shaft) out of the upper crankcase half and remove the countershaft bearing half ring retainer from the casing. Slacken the mainshaft (input shaft) retaining plate bolts, remove the retaining plate and withdraw the mainshaft assembly from the crankcase noting the needle bearing fitted to its left end.
3 On 1000 models simply lift the countershaft and mainshaft out of the upper crankcase half, and remove the half ring retainers, bearing locating pin and oil jet from the casing for safekeeping.

Inspection

4 Give the transmission shafts a close visual inspection for signs of wear or damage such as broken or chipped teeth, worn dogs or splines. Renew any parts found to be worn. The shaft assemblies can be disassembled and reassembled as described in the following Section. The transmission shafts are unlikely to sustain damage unless the engine has seized, placing an unusually high loading on the transmission, or the machine has

covered a very high mileage. Check the surface of the shaft, especially where a pinion turns on it, and renew the shaft if it has scored or picked up. Inspect the threads of the shafts and check them for trueness by setting them up in V-blocks and measuring any runout with a dial gauge. Damage of any kind can only be cured by renewal of the shaft concerned.
5 On 1000 models measure the diameter of the mainshaft at the point where the 5th gear bushing is fitted, and the countershaft at the point where the 3rd gear bushing (H and J models) or 2nd gear bushing (K models onward) is fitted, and the internal diameter of the relevant bushings. If either component has worn beyond its service limit it must be renewed. Calculate the bushing to shaft clearance and renew both components if the clearance exceeds the specified limit.
6 On all models measure the internal diameter of all gears which run on bushes and the external diameter of the bushings which they run on. If either component has worn to beyond its service limit it must be renewed. Using the above measurements calculate the gear to bushing clearance, if this exceeds the specified limit renew the relevant gear and bushing as a pair.
7 On 600 models if a dial gauge is available the backlash of each gear can be checked to measure tooth wear. This is done with both shafts installed in the crankcase half. If any gear is found to exceed the maximum

permissible backlash, both gears must be renewed as a matched pair.
8 Check that the outer race of the ball journal bearing fitted to each shaft rotates freely and has no sign of freeplay between its inner and outer races. Should either of the ball journal bearings require renewal, a bearing puller will be required to extract the bearing from its shaft. Note the position of the locating groove in the outer race of the bearing prior to removing it and ensure that the new bearing is fitted with the groove in the same position. Pull the bearing off of the shaft and fit the new bearing using a hammer and tubular drift which bears only on the inner race of the bearing.

Installation

9 On 600 models liberally oil the mainshaft needle bearing and insert the shaft into the upper crankcase half **(see illustration)**. Apply a few drops of thread-locking compound to the threads of the mainshaft retaining plate bolts and refit the plate to the casing, tightening its retaining bolts securely **(see illustrations)**. Refit the half ring retainer to its groove in the casing and install the countershaft, ensuring that the groove in its bearing locates with the half ring retainer and the oil seal lip locates with the groove in the casing **(see illustrations)**. Also ensure that the small pin in the ball journal bearing outer race is correctly positioned in the casing cutout **(see illustration)**.

2

24.9d Refit the half ring retainer to the casing . . .

24.9e . . . and install the countershaft . . .

24.9f . . . ensuring the oil seal and pin locate with the grooves in the casing

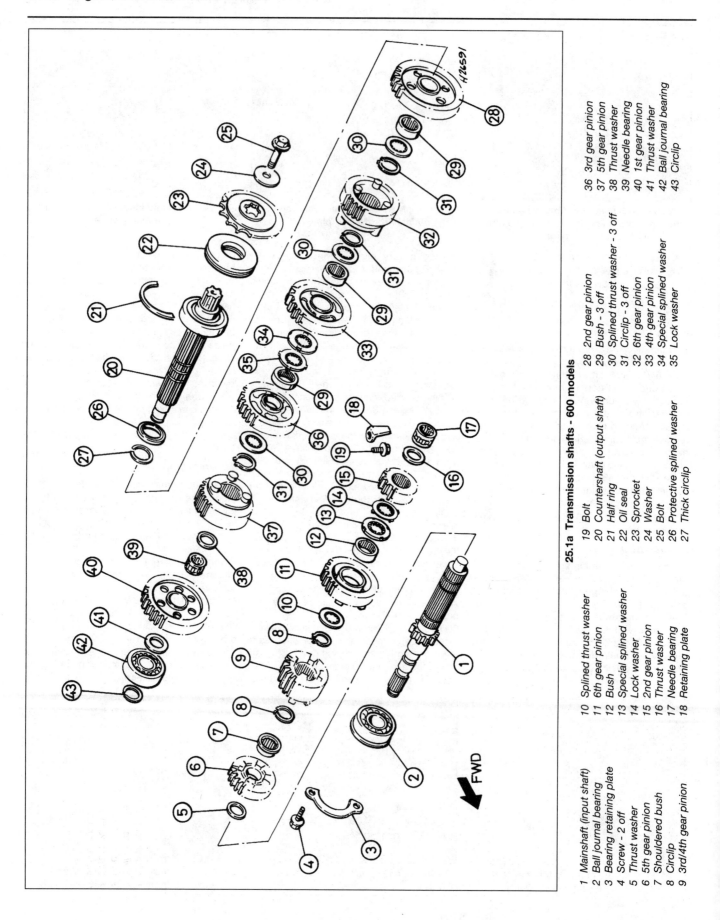

25.1a Transmission shafts - 600 models

1 Mainshaft (input shaft)
2 Ball journal bearing
3 Bearing retaining plate
4 Screw - 2 off
5 Thrust washer
6 5th gear pinion
7 Shouldered bush
8 Circlip
9 3rd/4th gear pinion

10 Splined thrust washer
11 6th gear pinion
12 Bush
13 Special splined washer
14 Lock washer
15 2nd gear pinion
16 Thrust washer
17 Needle bearing
18 Retaining plate

19 Bolt
20 Countershaft (output shaft)
21 Half ring
22 Oil seal
23 Sprocket
24 Washer
25 Bolt
26 Protective splined washer
27 Thick circlip

28 2nd gear pinion
29 Bush - 3 off
30 Splined thrust washer - 3 off
31 Circlip - 3 off
32 6th gear pinion
33 4th gear pinion
34 Special splined washer
35 Lock washer

36 3rd gear pinion
37 5th gear pinion
38 Thrust washer
39 Needle bearing
40 1st gear pinion
41 Thrust washer
42 Ball journal bearing
43 Circlip

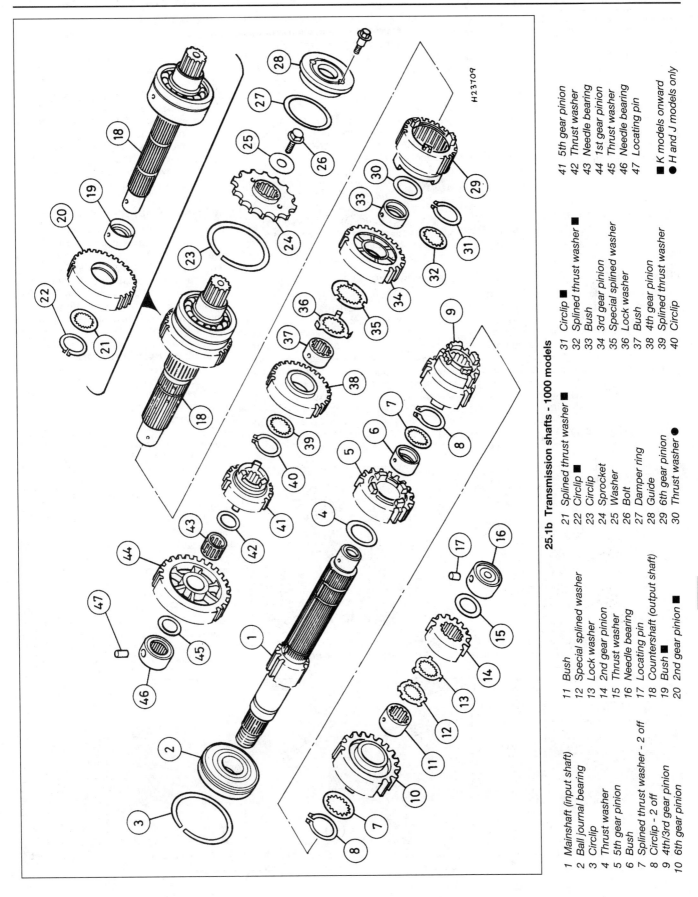

25.1b Transmission shafts - 1000 models

1 Mainshaft (input shaft)
2 Ball journal bearing
3 Circlip
4 Thrust washer
5 5th gear pinion
6 Bush
7 Splined thrust washer - 2 off
8 Circlip - 2 off
9 4th/3rd gear pinion
10 6th gear pinion
11 Bush
12 Special splined washer
13 Lock washer
14 2nd gear pinion
15 Thrust washer
16 Needle bearing
17 Locating pin
18 Countershaft (output shaft)
19 Bush ■
20 2nd gear pinion ■

21 Bush
22 Circlip ■
23 Circlip
24 Sprocket
25 Washer
26 Bolt
27 Damper ring
28 Guide
29 6th gear pinion
30 Thrust washer ●
31 Circlip ■
32 Splined thrust washer ■
33 Bush
34 3rd gear pinion
35 Special splined washer
36 Lock washer
37 Bush
38 4th gear pinion
39 Splined thrust washer
40 Circlip

41 5th gear pinion
42 Thrust washer
43 Needle bearing
44 1st gear pinion
45 Thrust washer
46 Needle bearing
47 Locating pin

■ K models onward
● H and J models only

10 On 1000 models install both the half ring retainers and the bearing locating pin and oil jet in the upper crankcase half noting that the oil jet is fitted to the countershaft cutout and the locating pin to the mainshaft cutout. Install both the mainshaft and countershaft ensuring the half ring retainers locate with the grooves in the bearings and the locating pin and oil jet engage with the holes in the needle bearing outer races.

11 On all models ensure that the transmission shafts rotate smoothly before proceeding further.

25 Transmission shafts - disassembly and reassembly

Disassembly

1 The transmission shafts should not be disturbed unless damage is obvious, such as chipped or worn teeth, unless or course careful examination of the whole assembly fails to pinpoint the source of the problem **(see illustrations)**.

2 Note: *The mainshaft and countershaft (input and output shaft) should be disassembled separately to avoid interchanging components.* Disassembling the shafts should pose no problem providing a good pair of circlip pliers is available. As each component is removed, place it in order

on a clean surface so that the reassembly sequence is self-evident and the risk of parts being fitted the wrong way around or in the wrong sequence is avoided. **Note:** *If inspected closely, it will be seen that all the thrust washers and circlips are chamfered on one side. Make a note of which side this chamfer faces on disassembly to use as a guide on reassembly.* Examine all thrust washers, renewing any which show signs of wear, and renew all circlips regardless of their apparent condition.

 HAYNES HiNT *When disassembling the transmission shafts, place the parts on a long rod or thread a wire through them to keep them in order and facing the proper direction.*

Reassembly

3 Having checked and renewed the transmission components as required, reassemble each shaft, referring to the accompanying line drawing and photographs, as applicable, for guidance. The correct assembly sequence is detailed below. Oil the shafts and pinion bushings liberally during assembly. When fitting the circlips to the shafts take care not to expand them any larger than is necessary to slide them over the shaft. When fitting a circlip to a splined shaft ensure that the ends of the circlip are positioned in the middle of the splines.

These two simple precautions ensure that the circlips are as secure as possible on the shaft.

4 If problems arise in identifying the various gear pinions which cannot be solved by reference to the accompanying illustrations; the number of teeth on each pinion can be used to identify them. Reference to the transmission specifications will show the number of teeth for each gear; the mainshaft pinions are listed first, followed by those of the countershaft. The problem should not arise, however, if the instructions given in paragraph 2 of this Section are followed carefully.

Mainshaft (input shaft) reassembly

5 The mainshaft is easily identified by its small integral 1st gear pinion. Holding the shaft by its right (threaded) end slide a plain thrust washer along the shaft followed by the 5th gear pinion, ensuring the dogs on the pinion are facing towards the left **(see illustration)**. Fit the splined 5th gear bush onto the shaft ensuring that the oil holes in the bush align with those in the shaft and fit the bush to the centre of the 5th gear pinion **(see illustration)**. **Note:** *On 600 models the bush has a shoulder; this must be on the left side of the bush.* Slide on a splined thrust washer (1000 models only) and secure all the above components in position with a circlip **(see illustration)**.

6 The 3rd/4th gear pinion is then fitted. On 600 models this must be fitted with its smaller diameter 3rd gear pinion towards the 5th gear pinion, and on 1000 models the larger diameter 4th gear pinion must face the 5th gear pinion **(see illustration)**. Fit a second circlip to the shaft and slide on another splined thrust washer **(see illustration)**.

7 Fit the 6th gear pinion bush onto the shaft, aligning its oil holes with the shaft oilways, and refit the 6th gear pinion with its dogs facing the right (threaded) end of the mainshaft **(see illustration)**. Slide the special splined washer up to the 6th gear pinion followed by the special lock washer ensuring that its tabs face the 6th gear pinion **(see illustration)**. Rotate the splined washer until its cutouts align with the lock washer tabs

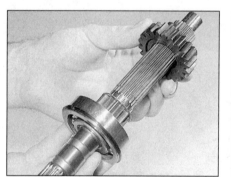
25.5a Take the mainshaft and slide on a plain thrust washer and the 5th gear pinion

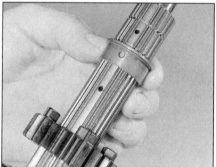
25.5b Install 5th gear bush as described in text - 600 shown

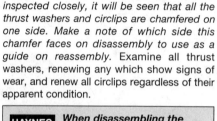

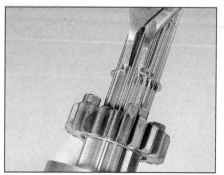
25.5c Secure components in position with first circlip

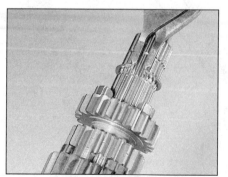
25.6a Install the 3rd/4th gear pinion as described in text and fit a second circlip . . .

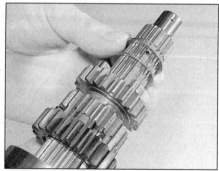
25.6b . . . followed by a splined thrust washer

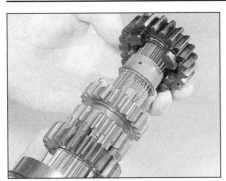

25.7a Install the 6th gear bush ensuring that its oil holes align with the shaft oilways and fit the 6th gear pinion

25.7b Slide on the special splined washer. Fit the special lock washer and engage its tabs with slots in the splined washer

25.7c Fit the 2nd gear pinion onto the shaft followed by a plain thrust washer . . .

then engage the lock washer with the splined washer to lock it in position. Fit the 2nd gear pinion to the mainshaft followed by a plain thrust washer **(see illustration)**. Liberally oil the needle bearing and install it on the end of the shaft **(see illustration)**.

Countershaft (output shaft) reassembly - 600 models

8 The countershaft is easily identified due to it having no integral pinions. Holding the shaft by its left (splined) end slide the special protective splined washer along the shaft so that its recessed surface is facing the left and secure it in position with the thickest circlip **(see illustrations)**.

9 Slide on the 2nd gear bushing ensuring that its holes align with the oilways in the shaft and fit the 2nd gear pinion with its recessed surface facing the right **(see illustration)**. Slide a splined washer along the shaft and secure all the above components in position with a circlip **(see illustrations)**. The 6th gear pinion is fitted with its shift fork groove facing the right end of the shaft and is retained by another circlip **(see illustration)**.

10 Fit a splined washer to the countershaft followed by the 4th gear bushing, again aligning the holes in the bushing with the shaft oilways **(see illustration)**. Slide the 4th gear pinion over the bushing, with its recessed surface facing the 6th gear pinion. Next fit the special splined washer, followed by the splined lock washer with its tabs facing the

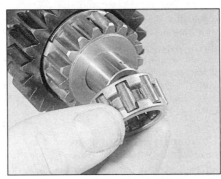

25.7d . . . and the needle bearing

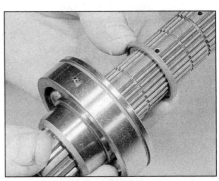

25.8a On 600 models fit the special protective splined washer as described in text . . .

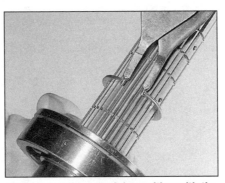

25.8b . . . and secure it in position with the thickest circlip

25.9a Slide the 2nd gear bush onto the shaft ensuring its holes align with shaft oilways and install the 2nd gear pinion

2

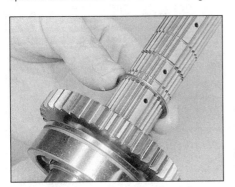

25.9b Slide on a splined thrust washer . . .

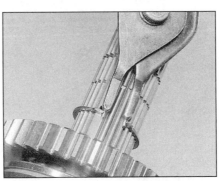

25.9c . . . and secure it in position with another circlip

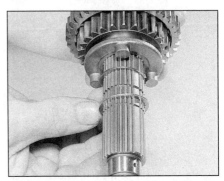

25.9d Install the 6th gear pinion followed by a circlip and splined thrust washer

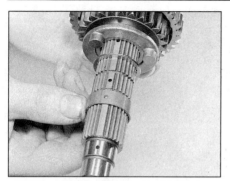

25.10a Align the 4th gear bush oil holes with the shaft oilways and slide it along the shaft

25.10b Fit the 4th gear pinion onto the bush and fit the special splined washer

25.10c Fit the special lock washer as described in text, followed by the 3rd gear bush aligning its holes with the shaft oilways . . .

left end of the shaft **(see illustrations)**. Rotate the splined washer until its cutouts align with the lock washer tabs then engage the lock washer with the splined washer to lock it in position.

11 Fit the 3rd gear bushing onto the shaft ensuring that its oil holes align with those in the shaft **(see illustration)**. Fit the 3rd gear pinion onto the bushing so that its recessed surface faces away from the 4th gear pinion. Slide on a splined thrust washer and secure it in position with another circlip **(see illustration)**.

12 The 5th gear pinion is fitted with its shift fork groove facing the left end of the shaft, followed by a plain thrust washer **(see illustration)**. Lubricate the needle bearing and fit it onto the shaft **(see illustration)**. Install the 1st gear pinion over the bearing and slide on another plain thrust washer **(see illustration)**. Fit the ball journal bearing to the end of the shaft so that its sealed surface is on the outside and secure all components in position with a circlip **(see illustration)**.

Countershaft (output shaft) reassembly - 1000 models

13 On 1000 H and J models the countershaft can be easily identified by its large integral 2nd gear pinion. Holding the shaft by its left (splined) end slide the 6th gear pinion along the shaft so that its shift fork groove is on the right side of the pinion, then fit a plain thrust washer.

14 On 1000 K models onward, the countershaft has no integral pinions. Holding the shaft by its left (splined) end slide on the 2nd gear bushing ensuring that its holes align with the shaft oilways. Fit the 2nd gear pinion over the bushing so that its recessed surface faces the right end of the shaft. Fit a splined thrust washer and secure it in position with a circlip. The 6th gear pinion is then fitted with its shift fork groove facing the right end of the shaft followed by another circlip. Slide a splined thrust washer up to the circlip.

15 On all 1000 models fit the 3rd gear

25.11a . . . and fit the 3rd gear pinion

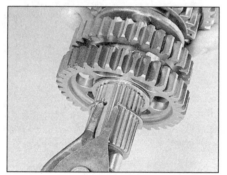

25.11b Slide on a splined thrust washer and secure it in position with a circlip

25.12a Fit the 5th gear pinion onto the shaft followed by a plain thrust washer

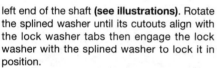

25.12b Liberally oil the needle bearing and install it on the shaft

25.12c Fit the 1st gear pinion onto the bearing and slide on another plain thrust washer

25.12d Install the ball journal bearing as described in text and secure it in position with a circlip

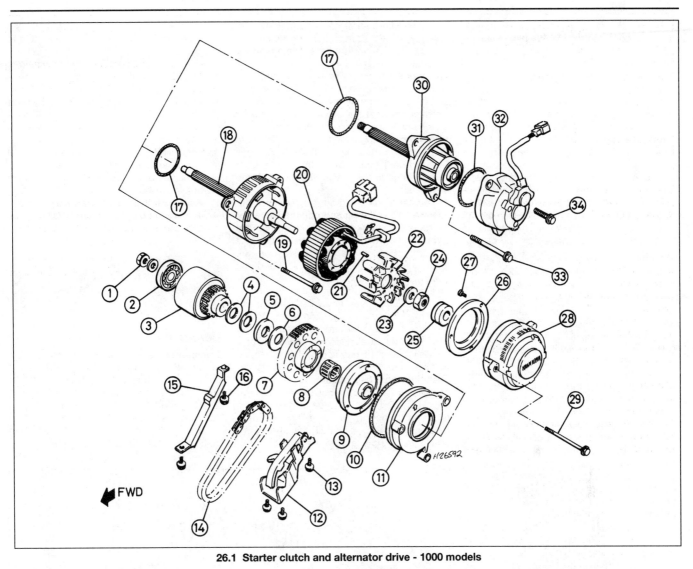

26.1 Starter clutch and alternator drive - 1000 models

1   Nut
2   Ball journal bearing
3   Damper
4   Belleville washer - 2 off
    (where fitted)
5   Collar
6   Washer
7   Starter clutch driven gear
8   Needle bearing
9   Starter clutch body

10 O-ring
11 Alternator base
12 Drive chain tensioner
13 Bolt - 3 off
14 Drive chain
15 Drive chain guide
16 Bolt - 2 off
17 O-ring
18 Alternator shaft and
    housing ●

19 Bolt - 3 off ●
20 Alternator windings ●
21 Locating pin ●
22 Rotor ●
23 Washer ●
24 Nut ●
25 Bearing ●
26 Inner cover ●
27 Screw and washer - 3 off ●
28 Alternator cover ●

29 Screw - 3 off ●
30 Alternator assembly ■
31 O-ring ■
32 Alternator cover and stator
    windings ■
33 Bolt - 3 off ■
34 Bolt - 3 off ■

● H and J models only
■ K models onward

2

bushing onto the shaft ensuring that its holes align with the shaft oilways. Fit the 3rd gear pinion over its bushing so that its recessed surface faces the 6th gear pinion. Slide the special splined thrust washer along the shaft followed by the splined lock washer ensuring the lock washer tabs are facing the left end of the shaft. Rotate the splined washer until its cutouts align with the lock washer tabs then engage the lock washer with the splined washer to lock it in position.

16 Slide the 4th gear pinion bushing along the shaft aligning its oil holes with those in the

shaft. Fit the 4th gear pinion over its bushing so that its recessed surface faces away from the 3rd gear pinion. Slide a splined thrust washer up to the 3rd gear pinion and secure it in place with a circlip.

17 The 5th gear pinion is then fitted with its shift fork groove facing the left end of the shaft, followed by a plain thrust washer. Liberally oil the needle bearing and fit it over the shaft. Install the 1st gear pinion over the bearing and slide on another plain thrust washer. Lubricate the second needle bearing and fit it to the end of the countershaft.

26 Starter clutch and alternator drive components - overhaul (1000 models)

Removal

1 Separate the crankcase halves as described in Section 22, and remove both the transmission shafts as described in Section 24 **(see illustration)**.

2 Bend down the locking tabs from the oil pass plate retaining bolts taking great care not

to break the tabs off. Slacken the three retaining bolts and remove the plate from the upper crankcase, noting the three O-rings fitted to the oil plate.

3 Slacken the three alternator drive chain tensioner mounting bolts and remove the tensioner from the casing. Remove the three bolts which secure the alternator base to the crankcase. Withdraw the alternator from the crankcase half whilst holding the starter clutch damper on the inside of the casing. The starter damper can then be lifted out of the casing and disengaged from the drive chain. Slide the collar and washer off the alternator shaft and remove the starter clutch.

4 If necessary, remove the bolt which retains the starter clutch idler gear shaft retaining plate and remove the plate from the casing. Withdraw the shaft and remove the idler gear.

Inspection

5 Check that the alternator shaft turns smoothly and quietly and shows no sign of freeplay between the shaft and base. If necessary the alternator can be dismantled as described in Chapter 8.

6 Remove the driven gear and needle bearing from the starter clutch. Inspect the needle bearing and the bearing surfaces of the driven gear and clutch for wear. Also check that the outer bearing surface of the driven gear is smooth and unmarked by contact with the clutch rollers. The rollers themselves must be undamaged with no signs of wear such as pitting or flat spots. If any component is found to be damaged or worn it must be renewed.

7 Check the teeth of both the starter idler and driven gear for signs of damage such as worn or chipped teeth, and renew them as a pair if damaged. Inspect the idler shaft and gear bearing surfaces for wear such as scoring.

8 Inspect the starter clutch damper for signs of wear or damage and renew if necessary.

9 Where fitted, separate the springs from the collar and measure the height of each spring. If the springs have been compressed to less than 1.8 mm (0.07 in) they must be renewed. On refitting glue the springs to the collar with a suitable adhesive.

10 Inspect the alternator drive chain tensioner blade for signs of wear or damage along with the tensioner guide which is fitted in the lower crankcase half. Damage or wear will be fairly obvious and require the renewal of the affected component. The strength of the tensioner and the drive chain can only be tested in comparison with new items. If any doubt exists about the condition of either the tensioner or chain they should be renewed.

11 Inspect the oil pass plate for signs of damage and clogging and renew if necessary. Note that the plate must be renewed if any of the locking tabs are broken. Renew the O-rings as a matter of course regardless of their apparent condition.

Installation

12 Position the starter idler gear in the crankcase and insert its shaft. Check the

condition of the shaft retaining plate O-ring, renewing it if necessary, and refit the plate to the casing tightening its retaining screw securely.

13 Liberally oil the needle bearing and fit it onto the starter clutch. Refit the driven gear and check that the gear will spin freely in one direction, but not the other. Slide the starter clutch assembly onto the alternator shaft followed by the plain washer and collar. Note that the collar must be fitted with the springs (where fitted) facing away from the starter clutch. Engage the starter damper with the drive chain.

14 Smear a small amount of oil over the alternator base O-ring and refit the alternator to the upper crankcase half noting that the arrow cast on the alternator base must face upwards. Ensure that the oilway on the alternator shaft aligns with the oil hole of the starter damper and locate the starter damper on the alternator shaft splines. Also ensure that starter clutch driven and idler gears mesh correctly. Apply a gasket compound to the threads of the alternator base bolts and tighten them to the specified torque setting.

15 Using a flat-bladed screwdriver, push the notch on the side of the tensioner body in and push the tensioner pushrod back into the tensioner body until the hole on the pushrod appears. Insert a small piece of wire through this hole to lock up the tensioner. With the tensioner locked up install it in the upper crankcase. Apply a few drops of thread-

locking compound to the threads of the tensioner mounting bolts and tighten them to the specified torque setting. Once all the tensioner bolts are tight remove the wire from the tensioner pushrod to tension the drive chain.

16 Fit the three O-rings onto the oil by pass plate and refit the plate to the casing. Apply a few drops of thread-locking compound to the oil plate retaining bolts and tighten them to their specified torque setting. Bend up the oil plate tabs against the flats of the bolts and stake the tips of the tabs to the bolt to secure the bolt in position.

17 Refit the transmission shafts as described in Section 24 and join the crankcase halves as described in Section 22.

27 Crankshaft and main bearings - removal, inspection and installation

Removal

1 Separate the crankcase halves as described in Section 22. On 600 models the crankshaft can then be lifted out of the casing and the camchain removed **(see illustration)**. On 1000 models remove the alternator drive components as described in the preceding Section to allow the crankshaft to be lifted out of the casing and the chains removed.

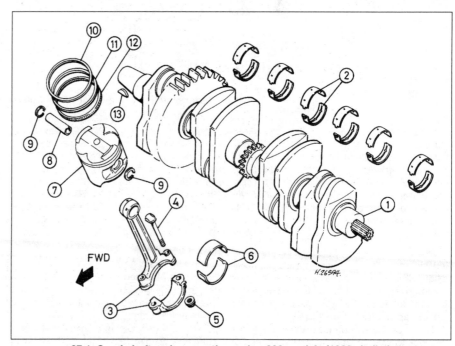

27.1 Crankshaft and connecting rods - 600 models (1000 similar)

1 Crankshaft	6 Big-end bearing shell -	10 Top compression ring
2 Main bearing shell - 12 off	8 off	11 Second compression ring
3 Connecting rods - 4 off	7 Piston - 4 off	12 Oil expander ring
4 Bolt - 8 off	8 Piston pin - 4 off	13 Woodruff key
5 Nut - 8 off	9 Circlip - 8 off	

Inspection

2 The crankshaft should be thoroughly cleaned using a high flash-point solvent. Be very careful to check that all oilways are completely free from dirt and other foreign matter.

3 Examine the crankshaft closely. Any obvious signs of damage such as marked bearings, damaged threads or sprockets will mean that it must be renewed. There are however many engineering firms, who advertise regularly in the motorcycle press, who can undertake major crankshaft repairs. In view of the expense of a new component it is worth trying such firms provided they are competent.

4 Crankshaft runout can be measured using a dial gauge with the crankshaft mounted on V-blocks. Rotate the crankshaft slowly through at least two complete turns noting the runout. If the crankshaft runout, measured at either centre main bearing journal, exceeds the service limit the crankshaft must be renewed.

5 Inspect closely the main bearing inserts (shells). The bearing surface should be smooth and of even texture, with no signs of scoring or streaking on its surface. If any insert is in less than perfect condition, all bearing inserts should be renewed as a set. In practice, it is advisable to renew the bearing inserts as a precautionary measure; they are relatively cheap and it is false economy to re-use worn parts.

6 The crankshaft journals should be given a close visual examination, paying particular attention where damaged bearing inserts have been discovered. If the journals are scored or pitted in any way a new crankshaft will be required. Note that undersizes are not available, precluding the option of re-grinding the crankshaft.

7 To select new inserts, use the manufacturer's size code system. The standard crankshaft main bearing journal is divided into two size groups to allow for manufacturing tolerances. The size group of each journal can be determined by the numbers stamped on the left crankshaft web **(see illustration)**. **Note:** *Ignore the letters - these refer to the big-end crankpins and are discussed in the following Section.* On the

27.7 Use crankshaft size code . . .

web will be an L followed by a series of six numbers, made up of the numbers 1 or 2, for example L 112121. The numbers indicate the diameter of each main bearing journal, starting with the left journal and finishing with the right journal.

8 The diameter of the crankcase main bearing journals is indicated in a similar manner using a series of six letters on the left end of the upper crankcase half **(see illustration)**. These will be made up of the letters A, B or C. The first letter indicates the diameter of the left journal and the last the diameter of the right journal. Both marks can be checked by direct measurement if the necessary equipment is available. The bearing inserts can then be selected using the table below. **Note:** *When ordering bearing inserts on 1000 models state whether the insert is for a centre or outer journal. This is necessary because the two centre journals are smaller than the outer journals.*

Crankshaft mark	Crankcase mark	Insert colour
1	A	Pink
1	B	Yellow
1	C	Green
2	A	Yellow
2	B	Green
2	C	Brown

9 Whether new inserts are to be fitted or the existing inserts are to be re-used, use Plastigage to check the clearance as follows. Remove all traces of oil from the bearing

27.8 . . . and crankcase markings to determine required bearing inserts - 600 shown

inserts and crankshaft journals and install the crankshaft in the upper crankcase half. Lay a strip of Plastigage over each of the main bearing journals, ensuring that it is not placed near the crankshaft oilways, then carefully lower the lower crankcase half into position, aligning the shift forks if necessary. **Note:** *Do not rotate the crankshaft.*

10 Install the twelve main bearing bolts and tighten them evenly and progressively to their specified torque setting using a diagonal sequence. Once all bolts are tight, slacken the bolts in a diagonal sequence to prevent the casings being warped, and lift off the lower crankcase half. Measure the thickness of the compressed Plastigage using the pre-marked indicator supplied with the kit, to determine the clearance. If the clearance is within the specified limits the inserts are satisfactory. If the clearance is excessive, even with new inserts (of the correct size), the main bearing journal is worn and expert advice should be obtained.

Installation

11 Ensure all the main bearing inserts are correctly seated in both the upper and lower crankcase halves and smear the insert surfaces with molybdenum disulphide grease **(see illustration)**. Refit the chain(s) to the crankshaft and install the crankshaft in the upper casing **(see illustrations)**. On 1000 models install the alternator drive components as described in Section 26.

2

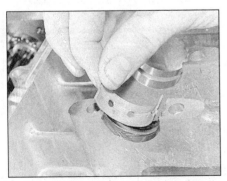

27.11a Ensure insert tab locates with crankcase groove on installation

27.11b Refit the chain(s) to the crankshaft . . .

27.11c . . . and install it in the upper crankcase half

28.3 Measuring big-end side clearance

28.5 Location of connecting rod size and weight group marks

28 Connecting rod and big-end bearings - removal, inspection and installation

Removal

1 Separate the crankcase halves as described in Section 22 of this Chapter. The connecting rods can be removed with the crankshaft either in place in the upper crankcase half or with the crankshaft removed. **Note:** *Before removing the connecting rods check the big-end side clearances as described in paragraph 3.*

2 Slacken and remove the big-end bearing cap nuts from each rod and remove it from the crankshaft. Mark each connecting rod with a spirit-based marker to ensure that they are refitted to their appropriate crankpin on installation.

Inspection

3 Inspect the connecting rods for signs of cracking or distortion, renewing any rod which is not in perfect condition. Check the connecting rod big-end side clearance, using feeler gauges **(see illustration)**. If the clearance exceeds the specified limit it will be necessary to renew the con-rod or crankshaft as necessary.

4 Inspect the piston pin and small-end bore of the con-rod for scoring or signs of wear. If access to the necessary measuring equipment is available, measure both these components and compare the readings obtained with the service limits given in the Specifications. If either component is damaged or worn renew both as a pair. Connecting rod distortion can only be properly assessed with a great deal of specialised equipment and should therefore only be checked by an expert. If any doubt remains about the condition of a rod it should be renewed.

5 If a connecting rod is to renewed, it is essential that it is of the correct weight group to minimise vibration. The weight is indicated by a letter stamped on the big-end cap of each rod **(see illustration)**. This letter together with the crankpin diameter mark (see paragraph 7) should be quoted when

purchasing new connecting rod(s).

6 Visually inspect the crankpin journals and inserts as described in paragraphs 5 and 6 of the preceding Section. New inserts can be selected as follows.

7 The standard crankpin journal diameter is divided into two size groups to allow for manufacturing tolerances. The size group of each crankpin can be determined by the letters which are stamped on the left end crank web. **Note:** *Ignore the numbers as these refer to the main bearing journals.* On the web will be an L followed by four letters, made up of the letters A and B, for example L ABAB. The letters indicate the diameter of each crankpin, starting with the left crankpin (number 1 cylinder) and finishing with the right crankpin (number 4 cylinder).

8 The connecting rods are also marked with the mark, in the form of either a number 1 or 2, being situated next to the weight mark. If the equipment is available, these marks can be checked by direct measurement. The bearing inserts can then be selected using the table below **(see illustration)**.

Connecting rod mark	Crankshaft mark	Insert colour
1	A	Yellow
1	B	Green
2	A	Green
2	B	Brown

9 Whether new inserts are to be fitted or the existing inserts are to be re-used, use Plastigage to check the clearance as follows. Remove all traces of oil from the bearing inserts and crankpin and lay strip of

Plastigage across the relevant crankpin. Carefully refit the connecting rod and tighten its bolts evenly and progressively to the specified torque setting. **Note:** *Do not rotate the connecting rod.*

10 Once both bolts are tightened to the specified torque setting carefully remove the con-rod from the crankshaft. Measure the thickness of the compressed Plastigage, using the indicator supplied with the kit, to determine the clearance. If the clearance is within the specified limits the inserts are satisfactory. If the clearance is excessive, even with new inserts (of the correct size), the crankpin is worn and expert advice should be obtained.

Installation

11 Ensure the insert locating tabs are correctly seated in the grooves in the connecting rod and bearing cap and smear the insert bearing surface with molybdenum disulphide grease **(see illustration)**.

12 Install the connecting rods to their original crankpin and refit the bearing cap **(see illustration)**. On 600 models the rods must be fitted so that their marked surfaces face the right end of the crankshaft (clutch), and on 1000 models install the rods so that their weight and crankpin diameter marks are at the rear. On all models ensure the bearing caps are installed in their original positions by aligning the weight and crankpin diameter marks.

13 Apply oil (600 models) or molybdenum disulphide grease (1000 models) to the connecting rod bolts and nuts and tighten them evenly, in 2 or 3 stages, to the specified torque setting. Check that the con-rod is free to rotate around its crankpin **(see illustration)**.

29 Starting and running the rebuilt engine

1 Attempt to start the engine using the normal procedure adopted for a cold engine. Do not be disillusioned if there is no sign of life initially. A certain amount of perseverance may prove necessary to coax the engine into

28.11 Install bearing inserts . . .

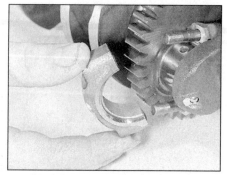

28.12 . . . and connecting rods as described in text . . .

28.13 . . . and tighten bearing cap bolts to the specified torque setting

activity even if new parts have not been fitted. Should the engine persist in not starting, check that the plugs have not become fouled by the oil used during reassembly. Failing this go through the troubleshooting section and work out what the fault is methodically.

2 When the engine does start, keep it running as slowly as possible to allow the oil to circulate. The oil pressure warning light should go out almost immediately the engine has started, although in certain instances a very short delay can occur whilst the oilways fill and the pressure builds. If the light does not go out the engine should be stopped before damage can occur, and the cause determined. Open the choke as soon as the engine will run without it. During the initial running, a certain amount of smoke may be in evidence due to the oil used in the reassembly sequence being burnt away. The resulting smoke should gradually subside.

3 Check the engine for blowing gaskets and leaks. Before using the machine on the road, check that all gears select properly, and that the controls function correctly.

4 Warm the engine up to normal operating temperature and thoroughly check for any oil or coolant leaks. If no leaks are present check both oil and coolant levels as described in Chapter 1 and top up as necessary. Do not forget to check these both before and after the machine has been run. Install the fairing as described in Chapter 6 and make a final check that all disturbed components have been securely tightened before taking the machine on the road.

30 Recommended break-in procedure

1 Any rebuilt machine will need time to settle down, even if parts have been installed in their original order. For this reason it is highly advisable to treat the machine gently for the first few miles to ensure oil has circulated throughout the lubrication system and that the new parts fitted have started to bed in.

2 Even greater care is necessary if the engine has been rebored or if a new crankshaft has been fitted. In the case of a rebore, the engine will have to be run in again, as if the machine were new. This means greater use of the transmission and a restraining hand on the throttle until at least 500 miles (800 km) have been covered. There is no point in keeping to any set speed limit; the main requirement is to keep a light loading on the engine and gradually work up performance until the 500 mile (800 km) mark is reached. These recommendations can be lessened to an extent when only a new crankshaft is fitted. Experience is the best guide since it is easy to tell when an engine is running freely.

3 If at any time a lubrication failure is suspected, stop the engine immediately and investigate the cause. If an engine is run without oil, even for a short period of time, irreparable damage is inevitable.

4 When the engine has cooled down completely after the initial run, recheck the various settings, especially the valve clearances. During the run most of the engine components will have settled into their normal working locations. Check the various levels, particularly that of the engine oil as it may have dropped slightly now that the various oil passages and recesses have filled.

2

Notes

Chapter 3
Cooling system

Contents

Degrees of difficulty

Easy, suitable for novice with little experience	Fairly easy, suitable for beginner with some experience	Fairly difficult, suitable for competent DIY mechanic	Difficult, suitable for experienced DIY mechanic	Very difficult, suitable for expert DIY or professional

3

Specifications

Coolant
Mixture type .... 50% distilled water, 50% corrosion inhibited ethylene glycol antifreeze
Total capacity:
600 models .... 2.0 lit (2.1 US qt, 3.5 Imp pt)
1000 models .... 3.0 lit (3.2 US qt, 5.3 Imp pt)

Radiator
Testing pressure:
600 models .... 18 psi (1.25 Bar)
1000 models .... 20 psi (1.40 Bar)
Cap valve opening pressure:
600 models .... 14 - 18 psi (0.95 - 1.25 Bar)
1000 models .... 16 - 20 psi (1.10 - 1.40 Bar)

Thermostat
Opening temperature .... 80 - 84°C (176 - 183°F)
Minimum valve lift .... 8 mm (0.32 in) @ 95°C (203°F)

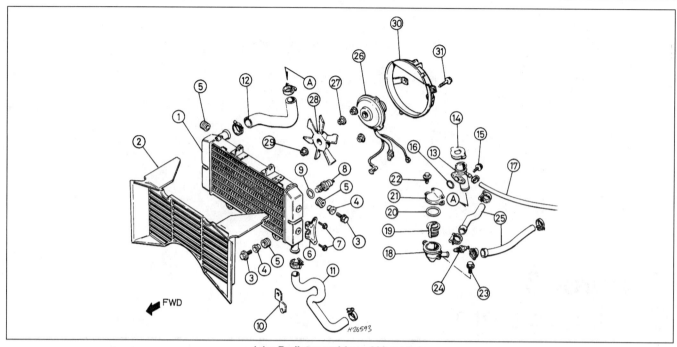

1.1a Radiator and fan - 600 models

1 Radiator	7 Screws	13 Filler neck	18 Thermostat
2 Grille	8 Fan switch	14 Pressure cap	housing
3 Bolts	9 O-ring	15 Bolts	19 Thermostat
4 Collars	10 Stays	16 O-ring	20 O-ring
5 Grommets	11 Bottom hose	17 Expansion tank	21 Cover
6 Oil hose clamps	12 Top hose	pipe	22 Bolts

23 Bolts	27 Nuts
24 Temperature	28 Fan
sender unit	29 Nut
25 Thermostat to	30 Fan shroud
engine hoses	31 Bolts
26 Fan motor	

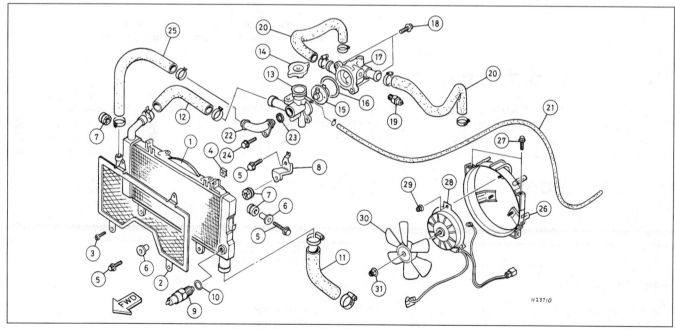

1.1b Radiator and fan - 1000 H and J models

1 Radiator	7 Grommets	13 Filler neck	18 Bolts
2 Grille	8 Stay	14 Pressure cap	19 Temperature
3 Screws	9 Fan switch	15 Thermostat	sender unit
4 Captive nuts	10 O-ring	16 O-ring	20 Thermostat to
5 Bolts	11 Bottom hose	17 Thermostat	engine hoses
6 Collars	12 Top hose	housing	21 Expansion tank

pipe	26 Fan shroud
22 Hose union	27 Bolts
23 O-ring	28 Fan motor
24 Bolt	29 Nuts
25 Filler neck to	30 Fan
radiator side hose	31 Nut

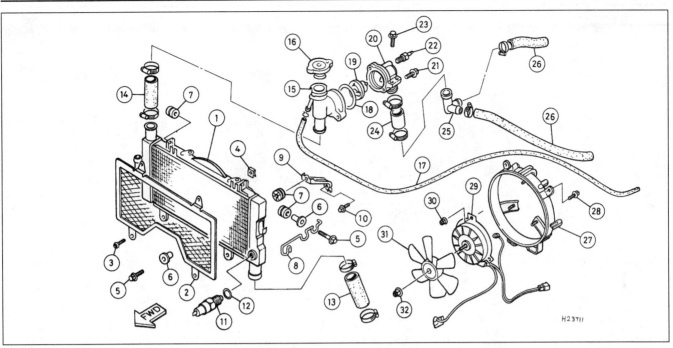

1.1c Radiator - 1000 K models onward

1 Radiator	7 Grommets	13 Bottom hose	18 O-ring	23 Bolts	27 Fan shroud
2 Grille	8 Clip	14 Top hose	19 Thermostat	24 Short connecting	28 Bolts
3 Screws	9 Stay	15 Filler neck	20 Thermostat housing	hose	29 Fan motor
4 Captive nuts	10 Bolt	16 Pressure cap	21 Bolts	25 Union	30 Nuts
5 Bolts	11 Fan switch	17 Expansion tank	22 Temperature	26 Thermostat to	31 Fan
6 Collars	12 O-ring	pipe	sender unit	engine hoses	32 Nut

1 General description

The cooling system uses a water/antifreeze coolant to carry away excess energy in the form of heat. The cylinders are surrounded by a water jacket from which the heated coolant is circulated by thermo-siphonic action in conjunction with a water pump, driven off the oil pump. The hot coolant passes upwards to the thermostat and through to the radiator mounted on the frame's front downtubes to take maximum advantage of the passing airflow. The coolant then flows across the radiator core, where it is cooled by the passing air, down to the water pump and back up to the engine where the cycle is repeated **(see illustrations)**.

A thermostat is fitted in the system to prevent the coolant flowing through the radiator when the engine is cold, therefore accelerating the speed at which the engine reaches normal operating temperature. A thermostatically controlled cooling fan is also fitted to aid cooling in extreme conditions.

The complete cooling system is partially sealed and pressurised, the pressure being controlled by a valve contained in the spring-loaded radiator cap. By pressurising the coolant the boiling point is raised, preventing premature boiling in adverse conditions. The overflow pipe from the system is connected to an expansion tank into which excess coolant is expelled under pressure. The discharged coolant automatically returns to the radiator when the engine cools.

 Warning: Do not remove the pressure cap from the radiator when the engine is hot. Scalding hot coolant and steam may be blown out under pressure, which could cause serious injury. When the engine has cooled, place a thick rag, like a towel over the pressure cap; slowly rotate the cap anti-clockwise to the first stop. This procedure allows any residual pressure to escape. When the steam has stopped escaping, press down on the cap while turning it anti-clockwise and remove it.

 Warning: Do not allow antifreeze to come in contact with your skin or painted surfaces of the motorcycle. Rinse off any spills immediately with plenty of water. Antifreeze is highly toxic if ingested. Never leave antifreeze lying around in an open container or in puddles on the floor; children and pets are attracted by its sweet smell and may drink it. Check with the local authorities about disposing of used antifreeze. Many communities will have collection centres which will see that antifreeze is disposed of safely.
Caution: At all times use the specified type of antifreeze, and always mix it with distilled water in the correct proportion. The antifreeze contains corrosion inhibitors which are essential to avoid damage to the cooling system. A lack of these inhibitors could lead to a build-up of corrosion which would block the coolant passages, resulting in overheating and severe engine damage. Distilled water must be used as opposed to tap water to avoid a build-up of scale which would also block the passages.

2 Radiator pressure cap - check

1 If problems such as overheating or loss of coolant occur, check the entire system as described in Chapter 1. The radiator cap opening pressure should be checked by a Honda dealer with the special tester required to do the job. If the cap is defective, replace it with a new one.

3

3.3 Carefully remove the radiator cap as described in text - 1000 K models onward shown

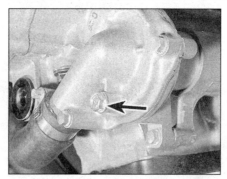

3.4a Coolant drain plug is situated on the water pump

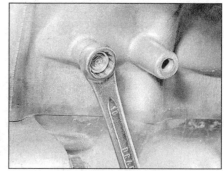

3.4b On 600 models there are also two drain plugs on the front of the cylinder block

3 Cooling system - draining

 Warning: To avoid the risk of personal injury, ensure the engine is cool before carrying out the following operation.

1 It will be necessary to drain the cooling system in order to change the coolant at the recommended interval or to permit engine overhaul or removal.

2 On 1000 H and J models slacken the two bolts which secure the front of the fuel tank to the frame and remove them along with the mounting plate. Remove the left sidepanel and then lift the front of the fuel tank up until the prop stay locks and the tank is securely supported. Remove the lower and left side sections of the fairing. On 1000 K models onward, remove the right upper fairing inner panel and the left lower fairing section. On all 600 models remove the fuel tank as described in Section 3 of Chapter 4, then remove the left lower fairing section. On all models refer to Chapter 6 for further information on fairing removal.

3 If the engine has been run recently, there will be some residual pressure in the system. If the engine is hot, steam and boiling water may be ejected which could cause scalding. As a precaution, place some rag over the radiator cap and remove it slowly to allow the pressure to escape **(see illustration)**.

4 Place a suitable container under the coolant drain plug, situated on the bottom of the water pump housing. Remove the drain plug and allow the coolant to drain into the container **(see illustration)**. Note: *On 600 models there are also two drain plugs on the front of the cylinder block; if it is wished to drain the system fully these must also be removed* **(see illustration)**.

5 If the coolant is reasonably new it can be re-used, provided it is kept clean and uncontaminated. If however, the system is to be refilled with new coolant it is advisable to give it a thorough flushing with tap water, if

possible using a hose which can be left running for a while. If the machine has done a fairly high mileage it may be advisable to carry out a more thorough flushing process as described in the following Section.

4 Cooling system - flushing

1 After an extended period of service the cooling system will slowly lose efficiency, due to the build-up of scale, deposits from the water and other foreign matter which will adhere to the internal surfaces of the radiator and water channels. This will be particularly so if distilled water has not been used in the mixture at all times. Removal of the deposits can be carried out easily, using a suitable flushing agent in the following manner.

2 After allowing the cooling system to drain, refit the drain plug and refill the system with clean water and a quantity of flushing agent. Any proprietary flushing agent in either liquid or dry form may be used, providing it is recommended for use with aluminium engines.

Caution: Never use a compound suitable for iron engines as it will react violently with the aluminium alloy. The manufacturer of the flushing agent will give instructions as to the quantity to be used.

3 Run the engine for ten minutes at operating temperature and drain the system. Repeat the procedure twice and then again using only cold water. Finally, refill the system as described in the following Section.

5 Cooling system - filling

Caution: Coolant will attack the painted surfaces of the machine. If any is spilt, it should be mopped up immediately and the affected area washed down with cold water.

1 Before filling the system, refit the drain plug using a new sealing washer, and tighten it securely. On 600 models, if the cylinder block drain plugs were removed refit them having first checked that their sealing O-rings are undamaged.

2 Fill the system slowly with the specified coolant to reduce the amount of air which will be trapped in the water jacket. Ideally, distilled water should be used for a basis for the coolant. If this is not readily available, rain water, caught in a non-metallic receptacle, is an adequate substitute. Similarly, it is permissible to use tap water which has been thoroughly boiled and allowed to cool down. In emergencies only, tap water can be used, especially if it is known to be of the soft type.

> **HAYNES HiNT** *Using non-distilled water will inevitably lead to early 'furring up' of the system and the need for more frequent flushing; the correct water/antifreeze mixture is 50/50. Do not allow the antifreeze level to fall below 40% as the anti-corrosion properties of the coolant will be reduced to an unacceptable level. Antifreeze of the ethylene-glycol-based type should be used - never use alcohol-based antifreeze in the engine.*

3 Once the system is filled, start the engine and allow it to idle. Flick the throttle twistgrip part open 3 or 4 times, so that the engine speed rises to approximately 4000 - 5000 rpm, then stop the engine. This process will bleed any trapped air bubbles from the system. Top up the coolant level to the base of the filler neck and refit the radiator cap.

4 Check the level of coolant in the expansion tank as described in Chapter 1, and top up to the upper level mark if necessary.

5 On 1000 H and J models, lower the fuel tank down, refit the mounting plate and tighten the mounting bolts to the specified torque setting. On 600 models install the fuel tank as described in Section 3 of Chapter 4. On all models, install all disturbed fairing components, referring to Section 19 of Chapter 6 for further information.

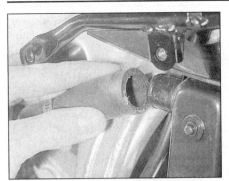

6.3a Disconnect both the top . . .

6.3b . . . and bottom coolant hoses from the radiator - 600 shown

6.3c On 1000 K models onward and all 600 models disconnect and remove the horn

6 Radiator - removal and installation

 Warning: To avoid the risk of personal injury, ensure the engine is cool before carrying out the following operation.

Removal

1 Remove the lower and side fairing sections (as applicable) as described in Chapter 6. On 1000 K models onward, remove the two front mounting bolts from the fuel tank and raise the tank up until its prop stay locks and the fuel tank is securely supported.

2 On all models drain the cooling system as described in Section 3 of this Chapter.

3 Slacken the hose clamps which secure the top and bottom coolant hoses to the radiator and carefully prise the hoses off their respective unions **(see illustrations)**. On 1000 K models onward and all 600 models, disconnect the horn wires and remove the horn from the machine **(see illustration)**. On all 600 models free the oil cooler hose clamps from each side of the radiator by removing their retaining bolts **(see illustration)**.

4 On all models, check that the cooling fan and fan switch wiring has been disconnected, then slacken and remove the three mounting

bolts and then manoeuvre the radiator away from the machine **(see illustrations)**.

5 If necessary, the cooling fan can be detached from the back of the radiator by slackening its retaining bolts. On 600 models the grille clips onto the radiator and on 1000 models it is retained by four screws.

6 The radiator is installed by a reversal of the removal sequence. If removed, refit the cooling fan to the back of the radiator and tighten its retaining bolts securely. Check that the fan wiring is correctly routed, and in no danger of being caught by the fan, and is retained by any relevant clips. Fit the grille, ensuring that it is securely clipped or screwed (as applicable) in position. Check the radiator rubber mountings for wear or deterioration and renew if necessary.

Installation

7 Install the radiator assembly to the frame and refit its mounting bolts, not omitting any collars; tighten them securely. Refit the hoses, tightening their retaining clamps securely, and reconnect the cooling fan and fan switch block connector. On 600 models do not forget to refit the oil hose clamps to the sides of the radiator. On 1000 K models onward and all 600 models install the horn.

8 Refill the cooling system, as described in Section 5 of this Chapter, and check for leaks before riding the machine.

7 Radiator - cleaning and inspection

1 The interior of the radiator can most easily be cleaned while the radiator is on the motorcycle, using the flushing procedure described in Section 4 of this Chapter. Additional flushing can be carried out by placing the hose in the uppermost union of the radiator and allowing the water to flow through for about ten minutes.

Caution: Under no circumstances should the hose be connected to the union mechanically as any sudden blockage in the radiator outlet would subject the radiator to the full pressure of the mains supply (about 50 psi). The radiator pressure should not exceed the testing pressure given in the Specifications.

2 Generally, if the radiator is found to be leaking, repair is impracticable and a new component must be fitted. Very small leaks may be stopped by the addition of a special sealing agent in the coolant, although if an agent of this type is used, follow the manufacturer's instructions carefully. Soldering, usually soft solder, may be used for caulking a large leak but this is a specialist repair best left to experts.

3 Remove any obstructions from the exterior

3

6.3d On 600 models remove oil cooler hose clamps from each side of the radiator

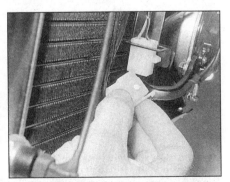

6.4a Do not forget to disconnect the cooling fan block connector . . .

6.4b . . . before removing radiator complete with cooling fan

core of the radiator using an air line. The conglomeration of moths, flies etc, usually collected in the radiator matrix severely reduces the cooling efficiency of the radiator.

4 If care is exercised, bent fins can be straightened by placing the flat of a screwdriver each side of the fin in question and carefully bending it into its original shape. Badly damaged fins cannot be repaired. If bent or damaged fins obstruct the airflow by more than 20%, a new radiator will have to be installed.

5 Inspect the radiator mounting rubbers for perishing or compaction. Renew the rubbers if there is any doubt about their condition, otherwise the radiator may suffer from excessive vibration.

8 Coolant hoses and pipes - removal, installation and checking for leaks

⚠️ **Warning: To avoid the risk of personal injury, ensure the engine is cool before carrying out the following operation.**

1 The cooling system can be regarded as semi-sealed, the only normal coolant loss being minute amounts through evaporation in the expansion tank. If significant quantities have vanished, it must be leaking at some point and the source of the leak should be promptly investigated.

2 The radiator hoses should be periodically inspected and renewed if any signs of cracking or perishing are discovered, the most likely areas being where they are clamped to their unions. Other areas which should be checked are the unions between the metal coolant pipes and the engine; all these unions are sealed with O-rings which in time could also perish and start to leak.

3 Before removing the hoses or coolant pipes drain the coolant as described in Section 3. Use a screwdriver to slacken the hose clamps, then slide them back along the hose and clear of the union spigot, noting that it may be necessary to remove the radiator mounting bolts, or alternatively the coolant

pipe retaining bolts, to allow the hose to be removed.

Caution: The radiator unions and the metal coolant pipes are fragile. Do not use excessive force when attempting to remove the hoses

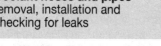

HAYNES HiNT *If a hose proves stubborn, release it by rotating it on its union before working it off. If all else fails, cut the hose with a sharp knife then slit it at each union so that it can be peeled off in two pieces. Whilst this is expensive it is preferable to buying a new radiator.*

4 Serious leakage will be self-evident, though slight leakage can be difficult to spot. It is likely that the leak will only be apparent when the machine is running and the system is under pressure, and even then the rate of escape may be such that the hot coolant evaporates as soon as it reaches the atmosphere, although traces of antifreeze should reveal the source of the leak. If not, it will be necessary to pressurise the system when cold to enable the leak to be traced. This operation requires specialist equipment and therefore must be entrusted to a Honda dealer.

5 Other possible sources of leakage are the O-rings on the water pump and thermostat housings, and the water pump's mechanical seal. The latter can easily be checked by examining the drainage hole in the base of the water pump body. If traces of coolant can be found around this hole, the seal is faulty and the pump must be renewed.

6 In very rare cases the leak may be due to a broken head gasket in which case the coolant will be drawn into the engine and expelled as vapour in the exhaust gases. If this proves to be the case it will be necessary to remove the cylinder head for further investigation.

7 On refitting hoses, first slide the clamps onto the hose and then work it on to its respective union. **Note:** *Do not use a lubricant of any kind. If necessary the hose can be softened by soaking it in very hot water before installing, although care is obviously*

necessary to prevent the risk of personal injury whilst doing this. When the hose is refitted rotate it on its unions to settle it in position before sliding the clamps into place and tightening them securely.

9 Thermostat - removal, testing and installation

⚠️ **Warning: To avoid the risk of personal injury, ensure the engine is cool before carrying out the following operation.**

1 The thermostat is automatic in operation and should give many years service without requiring attention. In the event of a failure, the valve will probably jam open, in which case the engine will take much longer than normal to warm up. Conversely, if the valve jams shut, the coolant will be unable to circulate and the engine will overheat. Neither condition is acceptable, and the fault must be investigated promptly.

Removal

2 Drain the cooling system as described in Section 3 of this Chapter.

3 On 600 models slacken the two bolts which secure the filler neck to the thermostat housing and separate the two components **(see illustration)**. Slacken the two bolts which retain the thermostat housing cover and lift off the cover **(see illustrations)**. On 1000 H and J models remove the two thermostat housing bolts and separate the housing. On 1000 K models onward, remove the two bolts securing the housing to the frame, followed by the bolts securing the housing to the filler neck; separate the two components. On all models, lift out the thermostat and O-ring **(see illustration)**.

Testing

4 Examine the thermostat visually before carrying out the test. If it remains in the open position at room temperature, it should be discarded.

5 Suspend the thermostat by a piece of wire in a container of cold water. Place a

9.3a On 600 models slacken the filler neck mounting bolts . . .

9.3b . . . remove the thermostat cover mounting bolts . . .

9.3c . . . and remove the cover . . .

9.3d . . . and thermostat

9.7a On installation ensure thermostat is correctly fitted . . .

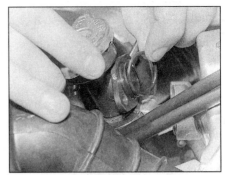

9.7b . . . and do not omit any O-rings - 600 shown

thermometer in the water so that the bulb is close to the thermostat. Heat the water, noting when the thermostat opens and how much valve lift it has when it is fully open, and compare the results with those given in the Specifications. If the readings obtained differ from those given, the thermostat is faulty and must be renewed.

6 In the event of thermostat failure, as an emergency measure only, it can be removed and the machine used without it. **Note:** *Take care when starting the engine from cold as it will take much longer than usual to warm up. Ensure that a new unit is fitted as soon as possible.*

Installation

7 Install the thermostat by reversing the removal sequence **(see illustrations)**. **Note:** *On all 1000 models ensure the thermostat is positioned so that its small by-pass hole is at the top.* Renew all O-rings regardless of their apparent condition, and tighten all bolts securely. Fill the system as described in Section 5 of this Chapter, then run the engine to check that the thermostat operates normally and there are no leaks.

10 Water pump - removal, inspection and installation

> **Warning: To avoid the risk of personal injury, ensure the engine is cool before carrying out the following operation.**

1 To prevent leakage of water or oil from the cooling system to the lubrication system and vice versa, two seals are fitted on the pump shaft. On the underside of the pump body there is also a drainage hole. If either seal fails this hole should allow the coolant or oil to escape and prevent the oil and coolant mixing.
2 The seal on the water pump side is of the mechanical type which bears on the rear face of the impeller. The second seal, which is mounted behind the mechanical seal is of the normal feathered lip type. However, neither seal is available as a separate item as the pump is a sealed unit. Therefore, if on inspection the drainage hole shows signs of

leakage, the pump must be removed as follows and renewed.

Removal

3 Drain the coolant as described in Section 3 of this Chapter. Drain the engine oil into a clean container as described in Chapter 1.
4 On 600 models, slacken the hose clamps which secure the flexible coolant hoses to the water pump cover and work both hoses off their unions. On 1000 models remove the bolt which retains the metal coolant pipe to the pump cover then slacken the bolt which secures the pipe clamp to the crankcase and pull the pipe clear of the pump. Slacken the clamps which secure the coolant hose and small-bore air bleed hose to the water pump; pull both hoses off their stubs on the pump.
5 On all models, slacken the two water pump mounting bolts and remove the pump from the machine. Then remove the remaining two bolts which retain the pump cover and separate the cover from the pump body.
6 As mentioned in paragraph 2, the pump assembly is a sealed unit and cannot be repaired. If either seal fails or the impeller is damaged or corroded it must be renewed. Renew all O-rings as a matter of course.

Installation

7 The water pump is installed by a reversal of the removal procedure. Fit new O-ring to the water pump body and cover then refit the cover to the pump body and tighten its retaining bolts securely **(see illustrations)**. Install the pump in the engine unit, ensuring

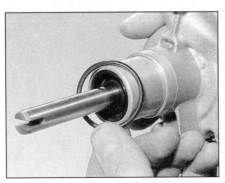

10.7b . . . and body

that the slot on the impeller shaft aligns with the projection on the oil pump shaft, and tighten the pump mounting bolts screws securely **(see illustration)**.
8 On 1000 models refit the air bleed hose to the top of the pump and the coolant outlet hose to the bottom of the pump; secure both hose with their clamps. Fit the metal coolant pipe, using a new O-ring, and tighten its retaining bolt securely. Install the pipe clamp.
9 On 600 models refit the coolant hoses and tighten both hose clamps securely.
10 On all models, replenish the engine oil as described in Chapter 1, and fill the cooling system as described in Section 5 of this Chapter. Finally, thoroughly check for leaks before taking the machine on the road.

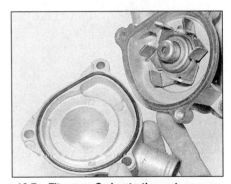

10.7a Fit a new O-ring to the water pump cover . . .

3

10.7c Align the slot in the pump shaft with the oil pump projection when installing the water pump

Notes

Chapter 4
Fuel and lubrication systems

Contents

Degrees of difficulty

Easy, suitable for novice with little experience	Fairly easy, suitable for beginner with some experience	Fairly difficult, suitable for competent DIY mechanic	Difficult, suitable for experienced DIY mechanic	Very difficult, suitable for expert DIY or professional

4

Specifications

Fuel tank capacity
Total including reserve:
    600 models .... 16.5 lit (4.36 US gal, 3.63 Imp gal)
    1000 H and J models .... 21.0 lit (5.60 US gal, 4.62 Imp gal)
    1000 K models onward .... 22.0 lit (5.81 US gal, 4.84 Imp gal)
Reserve:
    600 models .... 3.0 lit (0.79 US gal, 0.66 Imp gal)
    1000 models .... 3.5 lit (0.92 US gal, 0.77 Imp gal)

Fuel grade
Recommended grade .... Unleaded, minimum octane rating 91 (RON/RM)

Carburettors

	600 H, J and US 600 K	600 L and UK 600 K
Make	Keihin	Keihin
Throttle valve diameter	32.0 mm (1.26 in)	32.5 mm (1.28 in)
ID mark:		
UK models	VG22A	VG26A
California models	VG21A	VG27A
All other US models	VG20A	VG26F
Main jet:		
UK models	102	108
California models	105	108
All other US models	105	110
Pilot jet	35	38
Pilot screw - initial setting (turns out):		
California models:		
1 and 4 carburettors	2 1/2	2 5/8
2 and 3 carburettors	2 1/2	2 1/2
All other models	2 1/4	2 1/2
Float height:		
UK models	9.3 mm (0.37 in)	9.0 mm (0.35 in)
US models	8.0 mm (0.31 in)	9.0 mm (0.35 in)
Idle speed:		
California models	1300 ± 100 rpm	1300 ± 100 rpm
All other models	1200 ± 100 rpm	1200 ± 100 rpm

Carburettors

	1000 H, J	1000 K, L, M, N
Make	Keihin	Keihin
Throttle valve diameter	38.5 mm (1.52 in)	38.5 mm (1.52 in)
ID mark:		
UK models	VG80A	VG82A
California model	VG91A	VG91B
All other US models	VG90A	VG93A
Main jet:		
UK models	120	128
California models	120	120
All other US models	120	122
Pilot jet:		
UK models	38	40
US models	35	40
Pilot screw - initial setting (turns out):		
UK models	2	2 1/2
California models	2 3/4	2
All other US models	2	3
Pilot screw - final setting (turns out):		
California models	Not available	1 1/2
All other US models	Not available	2 1/2
Float height:		
UK models	9.0 mm (0.35 in)	9.0 mm (0.35 in)
US models	9.5 mm (0.37 in)	9.0 mm (0.35 in)
Idle speed:		
California models	1000 ± 100 rpm	1050 ± 100 rpm
All other models	1000 ± 100 rpm	1000 ± 100 rpm

Carburettors

	1000 P onwards
Make	Keihin
Throttle valve diameter	38 mm (1.5 mm)
ID mark:	
UK models	VP83B
California model	VP86A
All other US models	VP83D
Main jet	122
Pilot jet:	
UK models	42
US models	40
Pilot screw - initial setting (turns out):	
UK models	3
California models	2 1/2
All other US models	2
Float height	13.7 mm (0.54 in)
Idle speed	1000 ± 100 rpm

Engine lubrication

Recommended oil grade	Honda 4-stroke oil or equivalent good quality SAE 10W40 SF or SG motor oil

Capacity:

At oil change:

600 models	3.0 lit (3.2 US qt, 5.3 Imp pt)
1000 models	Not available

At oil and filter change:

600 models	3.4 lit (3.6 US qt, 6.0 Imp pt)
1000 models	3.8 lit (4.0 US qt, 6.7 Imp pt)

After disassembly:

600 models	4.0 lit (4.2 US qt, 7.0 Imp pt)
1000 models	4.5 lit (4.8 US qt, 8.0 Imp pt)

Oil pressure @ 5000 rpm:

600 models	71 psi @ 176°F (5.0 Bars @ 80°C)
1000 models	85 - 100 psi @ 176°F (6.0 - 7.0 Bars @ 80°C)

Oil pump

Inner rotor/outer rotor clearance	0.15 mm (0.006 in)
Service limit	0.20 mm (0.008 in)
Outer rotor/pump body clearance	0.15 - 0.22 mm (0.006 - 0.009 in)
Service limit	0.35 mm (0.014 in)
Rotor end play	0.02 - 0.07 mm (0.001 - 0.003 in)
Service limit	0.10 mm (0.004 in)

Torque settings

	kgf m	lbf ft
Oil pressure switch	1.2	9.0
Oil cooler mounting bolts - 1000 models	1.3	9.0
Oil pipe retaining bolts - 1000 models	0.9	7.0

1 General description

On 1000 H, J and all 600 models fuel is fed to the carburettors by means of an electric fuel pump. On 1000 K models onward, the fuel is gravity-fed to the carburettors, its flow being controlled by a vacuum-operated tap. All models uses a bank of four Keihin carburettors; those on P models onward are of the flat-slide type. Air is drawn into the intake system from a moulded plastic air cleaner casing containing a pleated paper type element.

Engine lubrication is of the wet sump type, the oil being contained in an oil pan at the bottom of the crankcase. The transmission is also lubricated from the same source, the whole engine unit being pressure fed by a troichoidal oil pump.

2 Fuel and lubrication systems - general information

1 For information on the following operations refer to the relevant Sections of Chapter 1.

a) Checking the fuel and emission system hoses.
b) Synchronising the carburettors.
c) Adjusting the throttle and choke cables.
d) Cleaning and renewing the fuel filters.
e) Changing the engine/transmission oil and filter.
f) Cleaning the air cleaner element.

2 For information on testing the fuel pump (1000 H, J and all 600 models only) and oil pressure switch refer to Chapter 8.

3 Precautions to be observed when servicing the fuel system

Warning: Petrol (gasoline) is extremely flammable, particularly when in the form of vapour. Precautions must be taken, as described below, to prevent the risk of fire of explosion when working on any part of the fuel system. Note that petrol (gasoline) vapour is heavier than air and will collect in poorly ventilated corners of buildings. Avoid getting it in the eyes or mouth and try to avoid skin contact. In case of accidents flush the affected area immediately with copious quantities of fresh water and seek prompt medical advice.

1 Always perform service procedures in a well-ventilated area to prevent a build-up of fumes.

2 Never work in a building containing a gas appliance with a pilot light, or any other form of naked flame. Ensure that there are no naked light bulbs or any sources of flame or sparks nearby.

3 Do not smoke (or allow anyone else to smoke) while in the vicinity of petrol (gasoline) or of components containing petrol (gasoline). Remember the possible presence of vapour from these sources and move well clear before smoking.

4 Check all electrical equipment belonging to the house, garage or workshop where work is being undertaken (see the Safety first! section of this manual). Remember that certain electrical appliances such as drills, cutters, etc, create sparks in the normal course of operation and must not be used near petrol (gasoline) or any component containing it. Again, remember the possible presence of petrol (gasoline) fumes before using electrical equipment.

5 Always mop up any spilt fuel and safely dispose of the shop towel or rag used.

6 Any stored petrol (gasoline), or any drained off during servicing work, must be kept in sealed containers that are suitable for holding petrol (gasoline), and clearly marked as such; the containers themselves should be kept in a safe place. Note that this last point applies equally to the fuel tank if removed from the machine; also remember to keep its filler cap closed at all times.

7 The fuel system consists of the fuel tank, with its filler cap and related vent pipes, the fuel pump (where applicable) and filters. Note that on California models, this includes the Evaporative Emission Control System components.

8 Read the Safety first! section of this manual carefully before starting work.

9 Owners of machines used in the US,

4

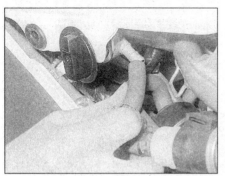

4.2a On 600 models disconnect the fuel pipe . . .

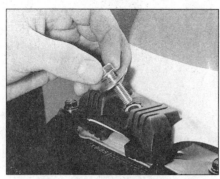

4.2b . . . and remove the fuel tank mounting bolts

particularly California, should note that their machines must comply at all times with Federal or State legislation governing the permissible levels of noise and of pollutants such as unburnt hydrocarbons, carbon monoxide, etc, that can be emitted by those machines. All vehicles offered for sale must comply with legislation in force at the date of manufacture and must not subsequently be altered in any way which will affect their emission of noise or of pollutants.

10 In practice, this means that adjustments

may not be made to any part of the fuel, ignition or exhaust systems by anyone who is not authorised or mechanically qualified to do so, or who does not have the tools, equipment and data necessary to properly carry out the task. Also if any part of these systems is to be renewed it must be replaced only by the genuine Honda components or by components which are approved under the relevant legislation, and the machine must never be used with any part of these systems removed, modified or damaged.

4 Fuel tank - removal, inspection and installation

Warning: Petrol (gasoline) is extremely flammable, especially when in the form of vapour. Take all precautions to prevent the risk of fire and read through Section 3 of this Chapter and the Safety first! Section of this Manual before carrying out the following operation.

Removal

1 Remove both right and left sidepanels and seat, and turn the fuel tap to the OFF position.
2 On 600 models disconnect the fuel pipe from the tap and remove the tank's front and rear mounting bolts **(see illustrations)**. Lift the fuel tank away from the machine, noting that on California models it will be necessary to disconnect the charcoal canister hose from the underside of the tank.
3 On 1000 H and J models remove the left and right inner covers from the upper fairing and disconnect the fuel level sender unit block connector. Remove both front mounting bolts

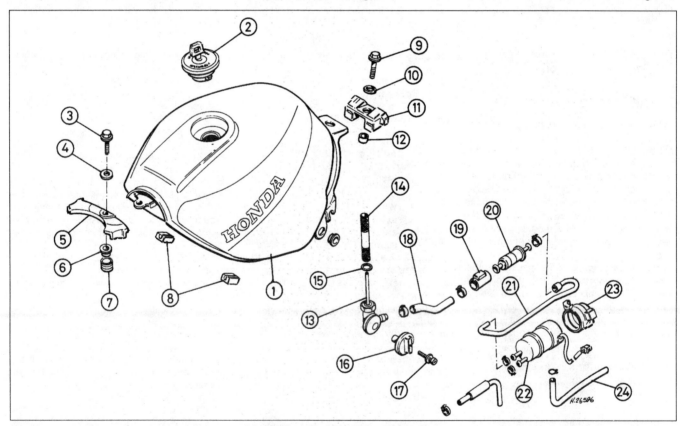

4.2c Fuel tank and fuel tap - 600 models

1 Fuel tank	6 Collar	11 Mounting rubber	16 Control knob	21 Filter to pump pipe
2 Filler cap	7 Grommet	12 Collar	17 Screw	22 Fuel pump
3 Front mounting bolt	8 Mounting rubbers	13 Fuel tap	18 Tap to filter pipe	23 Pump holder
4 Washer	9 Rear mounting bolt	14 Filter	19 Filter housing	24 Pump to carburettor
5 Mounting rubber	10 Washer	15 O-ring	20 Fuel filter	pipe

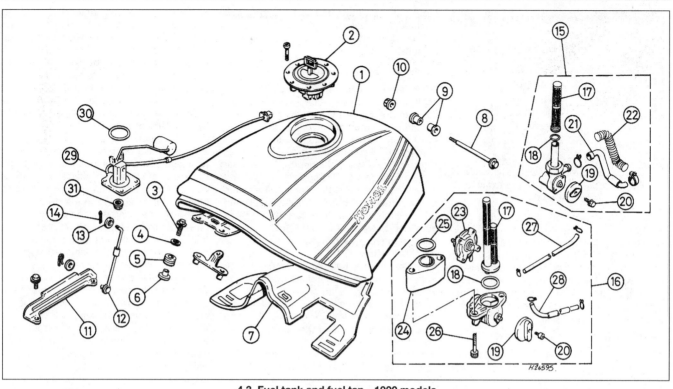

4.3 Fuel tank and fuel tap - 1000 models

1 Fuel tank	7 Tank insulator	14 R-clip	19 Control knob	26 Bolt - 2 off
2 Filler cap	8 Rear pivot bolt	15 Fuel tap -	20 Screw	27 Fuel pipe
3 Front mounting bolt -	9 Collars	H and J models	21 Fuel pipe	28 Vacuum pipe
2 off	10 Nut	16 Fuel tap -	22 Pipe guard	29 Fuel gauge sender
4 Washer - 2 off	11 Prop stay bracket	K models onward	23 Diaphragm	unit
5 Grommet - 2 off	12 Prop stay	17 Filter	24 Spacer	30 O-ring
6 Collar - 2 off	13 Washer	18 O-ring	25 O-ring	31 Nut - 4 off

and the rear pivot bolt from the fuel tank and disconnect the fuel pipe from the tap. Disconnect the prop stay and lift the tank away from the machine **(see illustration)**.

4 On 1000 K models onward, remove the tank's two front mounting bolts and disconnect the fuel level sender block connector **(see illustrations)**. Lift the tank up and remove the R-clip and washer which secures the prop stay to its bracket and disconnect the fuel and vacuum pipes (and vent pipe on US models) from the tap.

Remove the pivot bolt from the rear of the tank and lift the tank clear of the machine **(see illustrations)**.

Inspection

5 Inspect the tank mounting rubbers for signs of damage or deterioration and, if necessary, renew them before the tank is refitted.

6 Note that fuel tank repair, whether necessitated by accident or fuel leakage, is a task for the professional. Welding or brazing is not recommended unless the tank is first

purged of all fuel vapour; which is a difficult condition to achieve. Resin-based tank sealing compounds are a much more satisfactory method of curing leaks, and are usually available through suppliers who regularly advertise in the motorcycle press.

7 Accident damage will inevitably involve repainting the tank, but note that matching of modern paint finishes is a very difficult task, not to be lightly undertaken by the average owner. It is therefore recommended that the tank be removed by the owner and taken to a

4

4.4a On 1000 K models onward, remove the two front mounting bolts . . .

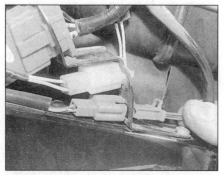

4.4b . . . disconnect the fuel level sender unit . . .

4.4c . . . and remove the rear pivot bolt

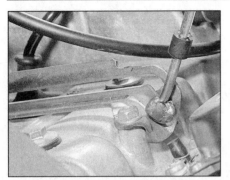

4.4d Disconnect fuel tank prop stay as described text

motorcycle dealer or similar expert for professional attention.

8 Repeated contamination of the tap filter, fuel pump filter (where applicable) and carburettor by water or rust and paint flakes indicates that the tank should be removed for flushing with clean fuel and internal inspection. Rust problems can be cured using a resin-based tank sealant.

Installation

9 To install the tank, reverse the procedure adopted for its removal. Ensure all the mounting rubbers are correctly positioned and refit all pipes to their original positions, securing them in place with their clips. Refit the tank to the frame and tighten its mounting bolts, not omitting any mounting collars, to the specified torque settings (where given).

10 Finally, turn the tap to the ON position and carry out a leak check on the fuel pipe connections before riding the machine.

 Warning: Any leaks found must be cured; as well as wasting fuel, any fuel dropping onto hot engine casings may well result in fire or explosion.

5 Fuel tap - removal, inspection and installation

 Warning: Petrol (gasoline) is extremely flammable, especially when in the form of vapour. Take all the precautions to prevent the risk of fire and read through Section 3 of this Chapter and the Safety first! Section of this Manual before carrying out the following operation.

1 Before the tap is removed it will be necessary to remove the fuel tank, and to drain all the fuel into a clean container suitable for holding petrol (gasoline) for temporary storage.

1000 H, J and all 600 models

2 Unscrew the tap from the fuel tank and lift it away, taking care not to damage the filter which projects inside the tank. On these

models the tap must be treated as a sealed unit, the only spare parts available being the fuel filter and body O-ring. If the unit is faulty it must be renewed.

1000 K models onward

3 The tap is vacuum-controlled and should allow fuel to flow only when there is a light vacuum present in the vacuum pipe, ie the engine running. In the event of failure, the most likely culprits are the vacuum pipe or diaphragm. If a leak develops in either of these the tap will not operate. Check the vacuum pipe for obvious splits or cracks, and renew if necessary. If the diaphragm itself is suspect, set the tap lever to ON or RES and connect the vacuum pipe to the tap. Suck gently on the vacuum pipe. If fuel does not flow, remove the tap for inspection as described below.

4 Slacken the two bolts which secure the tap to the tank and remove the tap along with its mounting spacer, taking care not to damage the filter. Slacken the four screws which retain the cover to the back of the unit and lift off the cover. Carefully remove the spring, spacer and diaphragm from the body.

5 Inspect the diaphragm very carefully for splits or tears holding it up to a good light source. If there is any sign of damage the complete diaphragm assembly must be renewed. Check the body for signs of cracks and remove all traces of dirt from inside it. Check the mounting spacer for signs of damage, renewing it if necessary, and renew both O-rings as a matter of course.

6 On reassembly ensure the diaphragm is correctly fitted and is not creased, then fit the spacer, spring and cover.

All models

7 Remove the fuel filter from the tap and clean it in fresh petrol (gasoline), taking precautions to prevent the risk of fire. Use a soft-bristled brush to remove any deposits from the filter. Inspect the filter for cracks or splits and renew it if any such damage is found. Before refitting, check that the main and reserve intakes of the tap are clean and unblocked.

8 Refit the tap to the fuel tank and install the tank as described in Section 4 of this Chapter. Thoroughly check for leaks before riding the machine.

6 Fuel system and associated pipes - general

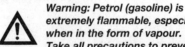 *Warning: Petrol (gasoline) is extremely flammable, especially when in the form of vapour. Take all precautions to prevent the risk of fire and read through Section 3 of this Chapter and the Safety first! Section of this Manual before carrying out the following operation.*

1 Thin-walled synthetic rubber tubing is used for many purposes, whether in the fuel system, emission control system or as drain or breather pipes. All hoses are of the push-on type, being secured by small wire clips. Normally it is necessary to renew pipes only if they become hard or split; it is unlikely that the clips will need frequent renewal as the main seal between pipe and union is effected by the interference fit.

2 Check carefully at periodic intervals (see Chapter 1) that the pipes are correctly fitted, undamaged, and secured to the frame by any clamps or ties provided. Check that they are correctly routed and that no drain or breather pipes are long enough to interfere with the final drive chain and engine sprocket or with the rear brake or suspension. If the pipes split, it is normally at the end, on or close to the union. In such cases the damaged length can be cut off and the hose refitted.

3 If any pipe has to be renewed, use only the genuine Honda replacement parts, particularly on emission control systems. Where pipes are moulded to a particular shape or where they are of an unusual size, this will be necessary anyway. The only exception to this is that it is permissible to use proprietary synthetic rubber or neoprene tubing for vacuum, breather and drain hoses and, in an emergency, for fuel hoses. Never use natural rubber tubing or clear plastic pipe; neither is suitable for such use.

7 Carburettors - removal and installation

 Warning: Petrol (gasoline) is extremely flammable, especially when in the form of vapour. Take all precautions to prevent the risk of fire and read through Section 3 of this Chapter and the Safety first! Section of this Manual before carrying out the following operation.

Removal

1 Remove the fuel tank as described in Section 4 of this Chapter

600 models

2 Remove the air cleaner element as described in Chapter 1. Remove the screws which secure the air cleaner casing to the carburettors then disconnect both breather pipes from the front of the casing and lift the casing away from the machine **(see illustrations)**. Disconnect the fuel pipe from its union between the centre two carburettors **(see illustration)**.

1000 H, J, K, L, M, N models

3 Remove the four mounting bolts which secure the air cleaner assembly to the frame

7.2a Remove air cleaner case screws . . .

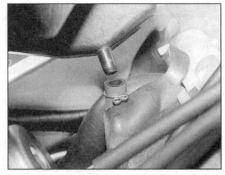

7.2b . . . and disconnect both breather hoses

7.2c Disconnect the fuel pipe from its union beneath the carburettors

and slacken all the clamps which secure the air cleaner pipes to the carburettors. Disconnect the breather pipe which joins the air cleaner to the valve (rocker) cover and on K, L, M, N models disconnect both breather pipes from their unions between Nos 1 and 2, and 3 and 4 carburettors.

4 On all models separate the air cleaner casing from the carburettors and move it as far rearwards as possible. Separate the fuel pipe at its joining union. On K, L, M, N California models disconnect all the relevant emission system pipes from the carburettors having taken note of their original positions. If necessary, mark the hoses with coloured tape to ensure that they are fitted correctly on installation.

1000 P onwards

5 Unbolt the air intake duct from both sides of the motorcycle **(see illustration)**.

6 Free the wiring and hoses from the air cleaner housing mounting bolt clips and remove the two mounting bolts **(see illustration)**. Disconnect the breather pipe from its stub on the valve cover and air cleaner assembly **(see illustration)**. On California models, label then disconnect the evaporative emission control hoses from the carburettors. On 1000 T models, disconnect the wiring to the throttle valve sensor on No. 1 carburettor.

7 Slacken the four clamps at the joint with the carburettors and move the air cleaner

assembly rearwards, away from the carburettors. Disconnect the air vent hose from its union on the top of the carburettors and the fuel hose from its union on the right underside of the carburettors **(see illustration)**.

All models

8 Place a suitable container below the carburettor float bowls then slacken the drain screws and drain any residual fuel from the carburettors. Tighten the drain screws securely on completion.

9 Slacken the clamps which secure the carburettors to their intake stubs and disengage the carburettors by pulling them rearwards. Slacken the choke cable clamp screw and disconnect the cable **(see illustrations)**.

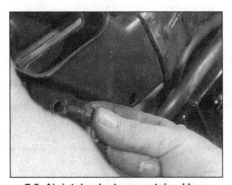

7.5 Air intake ducts are retained by a single bolt

7.6a Note how the hoses and wires are arranged before removing the air cleaner housing bolts

7.6b Breather hose connection to valve cover

4

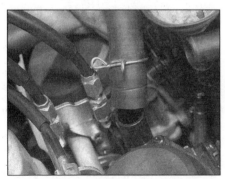

7.7 Air vent hose to carburettors

7.9a Release clamp screw to free choke cable outer . . .

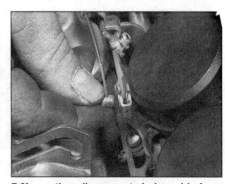

7.9b . . . then disconnect choke cable from its lever

7.9c Partially remove the carburettors . . .

7.9d . . . and disconnect the throttle cables from the pulley

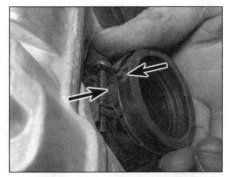

7.10 Hole in clamp must fit over peg on intake stub (arrowed) on 1000 P models onward

Slacken both throttle cable adjusters, to obtain maximum freeplay, then disconnect both cables from the carburettors and remove the carburettors from the machine **(see illustrations)**.

Installation

10 The carburettors are installed by reversing the removal sequence. Smear engine oil on the inside of the intake stubs to aid installation. On 1000 P models onwards, ensure that the intake stub clamps are positioned so that the hole in the clamp fits over the peg on the rubber stub **(see illustration)**.

11 Manoeuvre the bank of carburettors into position and loosely refit the throttle and choke cables. Ensure that the carburettors are pushed fully into the intake stubs, then tighten all the intake stub clamps securely. Adjust the throttle and choke cable freeplay as described in Chapter 1.

12 Reconnect all relevant pipes to their original positions and secure them in place with their clips. On 600 models install the air cleaner casing, not forgetting to connect the breather pipes, and fit the air cleaner element as described in Chapter 1. On 1000 models refit the air cleaner assembly to the carburettors, tightening all the air cleaner hose clamps securely, then refit its mounting bolts **(see illustrations)**. Refit the breather

pipe which links the air cleaner to the valve cover, and install all other vent and emission hoses (where applicable).

13 On all models, ensure that all pipes are correctly routed then install the fuel tank as described in Section 4 of this Chapter. **Note:** *Due to the nature of the fuel system (fuel only flows when the starter button is pressed), it will take some time for the carburettors to refill and for the engine to start. During this period do not operate the starter motor continuously. Operate the motor only for short periods of time (approximately 5 seconds), allowing time for it cool down in between.*

14 Finally, carry out a thorough check for leaks before riding the machine.

---

8 Carburettors - overhaul (all 600 models and 1000 H, J, K, L, M, N models)

> ⚠ **Warning: Petrol (gasoline) is extremely flammable, especially when in the form of vapour. Take all precautions to prevent the risk of fire and read through Section 3 of this Chapter and the Safety first! Section of this Manual before carrying out the following operation.**

Disassembly

1 Remove the carburettors from the machine as described in the previous Section. Do not separate the carburettors unless absolutely necessary; each carburettor can be dismantled sufficiently for all normal cleaning and adjustments while in place on the mounting brackets **(see illustration)**. If necessary, the carburettors can be separated as described in Section 10. Note that it is necessary to separate the carburettors to remove the choke plungers and on 1000 US models, the air cut-off valve components. **Note:** *Dismantle the carburettors separately to avoid interchanging parts.*   Working on one carburettor at a time, slacken and remove the four screws which retain the top covers. Lift off the cover and remove the spring from inside the piston. Carefully peel the diaphragm away from its sealing groove in the carburettor body and withdraw the combined diaphragm/piston assembly.

Caution: Do not use a sharp instrument to displace the diaphragm as it is easily damaged.

2 To remove the needle, push down on the retaining plate using an 8 mm socket, and turn it 90° anticlockwise (counterclockwise) **(see illustration)**. Then remove the plate and spring from the piston and withdraw the needle and washer **(see illustrations)**.

3 Remove the four screws which retain the float bowl to the bottom of the carburettor body and lift off the bowl to gain access to the various jets. Withdraw the float pivot pin, using a pair of pointed-nose pliers, and remove the float and needle valve assembly. Unscrew the valve seat from the carburettor and remove it along with its washer, noting the fuel filter situated behind it. Clean the fuel filter in fresh fuel and examine it for damage; renew it if necessary **(see illustration)**.

4 The main jet is a screw fit in the bottom of the needle jet and can be removed with a flat-bladed screwdriver **(see illustration)**. The needle jet is a screw fit in the carburettor body and can be unscrewed using a suitably-sized spanner or socket **(see illustration)**. The pilot

7.12a On 1000 P models onward, secure the hoses and wiring clamps on the right . . .

7.12b . . . and left sides

1 Top cover
2 Spring
3 Retaining plate
4 Spring
5 Needle
6 Washer
7 Diaphragm/piston assembly
8 Main jet
9 Needle jet
10 Pilot jet
11 Float valve seat and washer
12 Float valve
13 Float
14 Pivot pin
15 Pilot (mixture) screw - UK type
16 Pilot (mixture) screw - US type
17 Spring
18 Washer
19 O-ring
20 Air cut-off valve - 1000 only
21 Spring
22 Diaphragm
23 O-ring
24 Choke plunger
25 Spring
26 Retaining nut

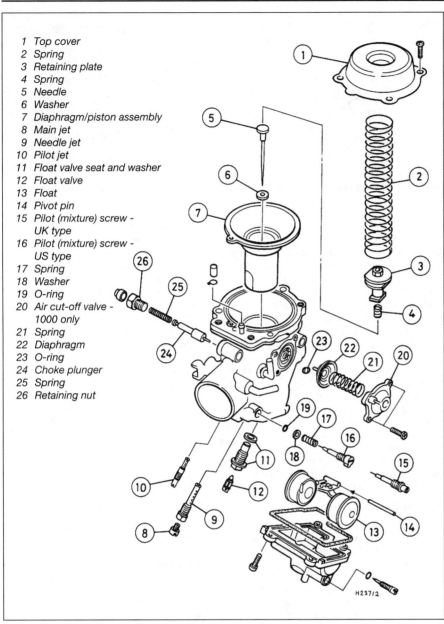

8.1 Carburettor - 1000 H, J, K, L, M, N models (600 similar)

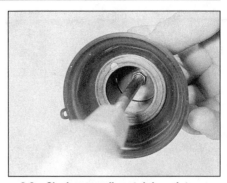

8.2a Slacken needle retaining plate as described in text . . .

8.2b . . . and remove the plate, spring . . .

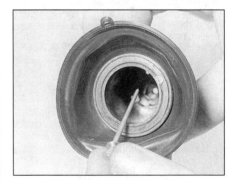

8.2c . . . needle and washer

8.3 Inspect needle valve seat filter for damage and renew if necessary

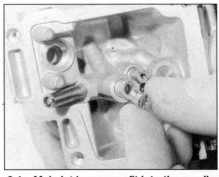

8.4a Main jet is a screw fit into the needle jet . . .

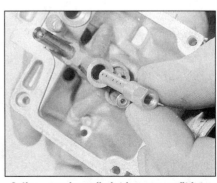

8.4b . . . and needle jet is a screw fit into the carburettor body

4

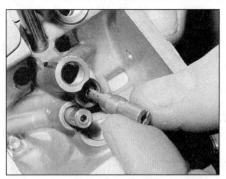

8.4c Pilot jet is situated beside main jet

8.6a Unscrew the choke plunger retaining nut . . .

8.6b . . . and withdraw the return spring . . .

jet is positioned adjacent to the main jet and can also be unscrewed using a small flat-bladed screwdriver (see illustration).

5 The pilot (mixture) screw is situated on the side of the carburettor body, just above the float bowl gasket face. It is recommended that its setting is not disturbed unless absolutely necessary because it will require setting up again on reassembly, as described in Section 11. If necessary, for cleaning or renewal, proceed as follows. On all US models the pilot screw will be concealed by a plastic limiter cap which must be removed to allow the pilot screw to be withdrawn. The cap will be cemented in place but can be removed using a pair of pliers. On all models screw the pilot screw in until it seats lightly, counting the number of turns necessary to achieve this, then remove the screw along with its spring, flat washer and O-ring. If the screw is bent or

8.6c . . . and plunger

damaged in anyway, all the pilot screws must be renewed as a set.

6 The choke assemblies can be removed, providing the carburettors have been separated (see Section 10), by unscrewing the nuts which retain them in the carburettor bodies (see illustrations). If any plunger does not operate smoothly and easily or is damaged in any way, it must be renewed. The return spring should also be renewed if at all suspect.

7 On 1000 US models remove the two screws which retain the air cut-off valve cover to the carburettor then lift off the cover and carefully remove the spring, diaphragm and O-ring. Check that the diaphragms are not split, perished or in any way damaged. Holding them up to a strong light will usual reveal even the smallest hole. The diaphragm must be renewed even if only slight damage is found as it is not repairable.

Inspection

8 Check that the needle is straight by rolling it on a flat surface such as a sheet of glass. If it is bent it must be renewed as a set together with the needle jet.

9 Check that the floats are in good order and are not punctured. If either float is punctured it will produce the wrong fuel level in the float chamber, leading to an over-rich mixture and flooding. If the floats are damaged in any way they must be renewed as a satisfactory repair will not be possible.

10 The needle valve and seat will wear after lengthy service and should be closely examined, with a magnifying glass if necessary. Wear usually takes the form of a groove or ridge, which will cause the needle to seat imperfectly. Test the spring-loaded tip on the bottom of the needle valve by pushing it into the body of the needle. The tip should return quickly and easily under spring pressure. If the needle valve or seat are damaged in any way both should be renewed as a set.

11 Before the carburettors are reassembled by a reversal of the disassembly procedure, they should be cleaned out thoroughly, preferably using compressed air. Avoid using a rag because there is always the risk of fine particles of lint obstructing the internal air passages or the jet orifices. Check carefully the condition of the carburettor body and float bowl, looking for distorted or damaged mating surfaces or any other signs of wear. If severe wear or damage is found, the carburettor assembly will have to be renewed. Check the condition of all O-rings and gaskets, renewing any that are worn or distorted.

Caution: Never use a piece of wire or sharp metal to clear a blocked jet. It is only too easy to enlarge a jet under these circumstances and increase the rate of fuel consumption.

12 On later models (K onward) a small air vent filter is also fitted (see illustration). On 600 models this is situated on the underside

8.12a Air vent filter location - 1000 K, L, M, N models

8.12b Separate filter housing . . .

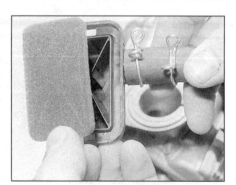

8.12c . . . and clean filter element as described in text

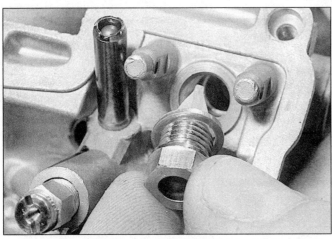

8.13a On reassembly do not omit needle valve seat washer

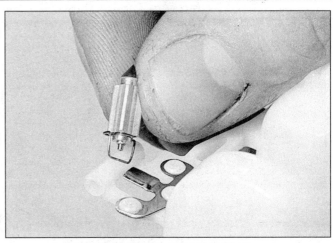

8.13b Fit the needle valve to the float . . .

of the air cleaner housing and on 1000 models it is located on the right side of the frame member which passes across the front of the cylinder head. Remove the vent filter assembly, separate the filter housing and remove the foam element **(see illustrations)**. Wash the element in soapy water and inspect it for signs of clogging or damage, renewing it if necessary. Ensure the element is dry and clean and reassemble the filter components.

13 Always use compressed air to clear a blockage; a tyre pump makes an admirable substitute when a compressed air line is not available. Do not use excessive force when assembling the carburettor because it is very easy to shear the small jets or some of the smaller screws **(see illustrations)**. **Note:** *If the carburettor is being set up from scratch it is important to check the float height before refitting the float bowl. To this end, refer to Section 11 before installing the carburettors.*

Reassembly

14 Insert the washer, needle and spring into the piston and refit the retaining plate. Push

down on the plate, using an 8 mm socket, and turn it 90° clockwise until it is locked in position. Insert the piston assembly into the carburettor body and lightly push it down, ensuring the needle is correctly aligned with the needle jet, then press the diaphragm outer edge into its groove ensuring the small tongue

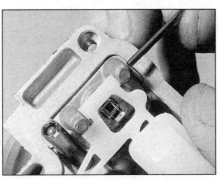

8.13c . . . and refit the float pivot pin

is correctly seated in the cutout **(see illustrations)**. Check that the diaphragm is not creased, and that the piston moves smoothly up and down the bore before refitting the spring and top cover **(see illustrations)**. On No 2 carburettor do not forget to refit the throttle cable bracket when installing the cover screws.

8.14a Insert the piston into the carburettor body ensuring the needle is correctly aligned with the needle jet

8.14b Ensure the diaphragm is correctly seated in the carburettor body . . .

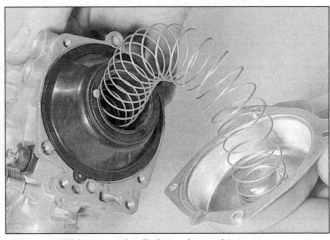

8.14c . . . and refit the spring and top cover

4

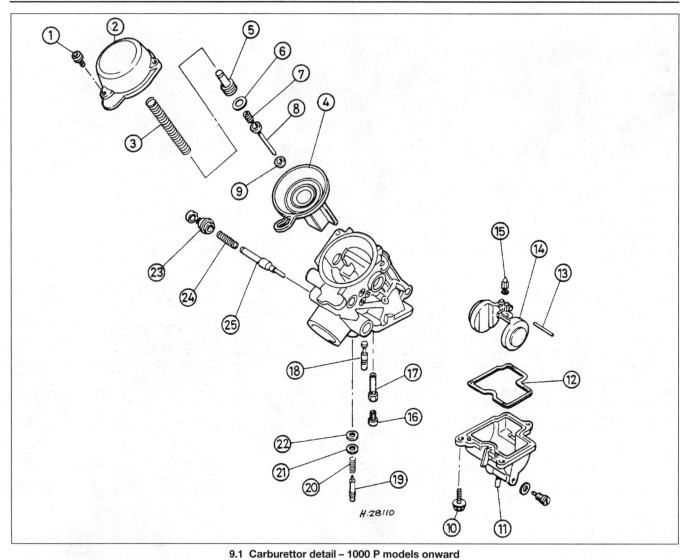

9.1 Carburettor detail – 1000 P models onward

1 Top cover screw	6 O-ring	11 Float chamber	16 Main jet	21 Washer
2 Top cover	7 Spring	12 Seal	17 Needle jet	22 O-ring
3 Spring	8 Needle	13 Float pivot pin	18 Pilot jet	23 Choke plunger nut
4 Piston and diaphragm	9 Sealing washer	14 Float	19 Pilot screw	24 Spring
5 Needle holder	10 Float chamber screw	15 Needle valve	20 Spring	25 Choke plunger

15 On 1000 US models refit the air cut-off valve diaphragm to the carburettor and fit a new O-ring, ensuring its flat surface faces the carburettor. Refit the spring and cover and tighten the retaining screws securely.

16 On all models, if removed, install the pilot (mixture) screws, screwing them in until they seat lightly, then unscrew each screw by the number of turns noted on dismantling. Note that if new screws are being fitted, set them to the initial position given in the Specifications at the start of this Chapter. Note that this is only an initial setting - once the carburettors are installed on the machine it will be necessary to adjust the pilot screws as described in Section 11.

17 Install the carburettors as described in the previous Section.

9 Carburettors - disassembly, inspection and reassembly (1000 P models onward)

⚠️ *Warning: Petrol (gasoline) is extremely flammable, especially when in the form of vapour. Take all precautions to prevent the risk of fire and read through Section 3 of this Chapter and the Safety first! Section of this Manual before carrying out the following operation.*

Disassembly

1 Remove the carburettors from the machine as described in Section 7. Do not separate the carburettors unless absolutely necessary; each carburettor can be dismantled sufficiently for all normal cleaning and adjustments while in place on the mounting brackets **(see illustration)**. If necessary, the carburettors can be separated as described in Section 10.

Caution: Keep the carburettors upright and do not allow them to rest on their air intake funnels.

2 Remove the three screws which retain the vacuum chamber cover and lift if off. Withdraw the large spring and carefully peel the edge of the diaphragm out of its groove, then withdraw the diaphragm/piston assembly **(see illustrations)**.

3 To remove the needle from the piston, thread one of the 4 mm vacuum chamber cover screws into the needle holder and using

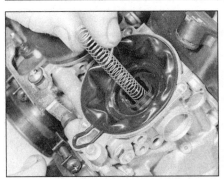

9.2a Remove the top cover and lift out the spring . . .

9.2b . . . followed by the piston/diaphragm assembly

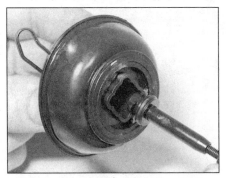

9.3 Screw a cover bolt into the needle holder and pull it free

pliers, pull the holder and needle out of the piston (see illustration). Once free of the piston, the washer, needle and coil spring can be removed from the holder. Don't push the needle from below to removed it because distortion of the needle is very likely.

4 Remove the three screws to free the float bowl from the base of the carburettor (see illustration). Access can now be gained to the jets and the float assembly.

5 Use a pair of pointed-nose pliers to withdraw the float pivot pin, then lift off the float assembly and needle valve (see illustration). The main jet is a screw fit in the bottom of the needle jet and can be removed with a flat-bladed screwdriver (see illustrations). The needle jet is a screw fit in the carburettor body and can be unscrewed using a suitably-sized spanner or socket (see illustrations). The pilot jet is positioned adjacent to the main jet and can also be unscrewed using a small flat-bladed screwdriver (see illustration).

6 The pilot (mixture) screw is situated at the front of the carburettor body, in the float bowl cutout (see illustration). It can be removed without disturbing the float bowl, although it is strongly advised that its setting is not altered unless absolutely necessary. If removed, the screw will require setting up as described in Section 11.

7 The pilot (mixture) screw can be removed by screwing it in until it seats lightly, counting

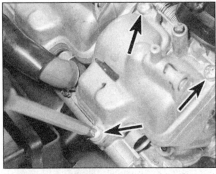

9.4 Float chamber is retained by three screws (arrowed)

9.5a Withdraw pivot pin to free float and needle

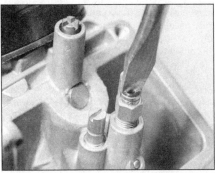

9.5b Unscrew the main jet . . .

9.5c . . . and remove it from the needle jet

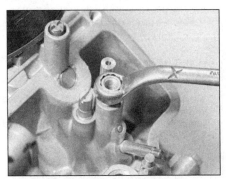

9.5d Unscrew the needle jet . . .

9.5e . . . and remove it from the carburettor body

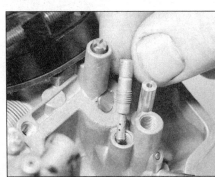

9.5f Pilot jet is a screw fit in carburettor

4

9.6 Pilot screws can be accessed without removing float chambers

9.8 Air funnels are retained by four screws

9.12 Check diaphragm carefully for signs of damage

the number of turns necessary to achieve this, then fully unscrewing the screw along with its spring, flat washer and O-ring. If the screw is bent or damaged in anyway, all the pilot screws must be renewed as a set. Done in this way, the number of turns recorded can be used to return the screw to its original position on reassembly.

8 The air intake funnel holders are secured by four screws **(see illustration)**. Once removed, the funnels can be separated from the holders.

9 A throttle valve sensor is fitted to the No. 1 carburettor on 1000 T models onward. The sensor is retained by three screws.

10 The choke assemblies can be removed, providing the carburettors have been separated (Sec 10), by unscrewing the nuts which retain them in the carburettor bodies. If any plunger does not operate smoothly and easily or is damaged in any way, it must be renewed. The return spring should also be renewed if at all suspect.

11 On US models remove the two screws which retain the air cut-off valve to the carburettor then lift off the valve components and recover the O-rings. Note that if the valve diaphragm is holed or perished the complete air cut-off valve assembly must be renewed - apart from the O-rings, individual parts cannot be purchased for the valve.

Inspection

12 Check that the needle is straight by rolling it on a flat surface such as a sheet of glass. If

it is bent it must be renewed as a set together with the needle jet. Check that the piston diaphragm is not holed or cracked **(see illustration)**.

13 Check that the floats are in good order and are not punctured. If either float is punctured it will produce the wrong fuel level in the float chamber, leading to an over-rich mixture and flooding. If the floats are damaged in any way they must be renewed as a satisfactory repair will not be possible.

14 The needle valve and seat will wear after lengthy service and should be closely examined, with a magnifying glass if necessary. Wear usually takes the form of a groove or ridge, which will cause the needle to seat imperfectly. Test the spring-loaded tip on the bottom of the needle valve by pushing it into the body of the needle. The tip should return quickly and easily under spring pressure. If the needle valve is worn or damaged in any way it should be renewed. The seat is part of the carburettor body; if it shows signs of severe wear, the carburettor must be renewed.

15 Check carefully the condition of the carburettor body and float bowl, looking for distorted or damaged mating surfaces or any other signs of wear. If severe wear or damage is found, the carburettor assembly will have to be renewed. Check the condition of all O-rings and gaskets, renewing any that are worn or distorted.

16 A small filter is located in the needle valve seat. Make a visual check that it is clear and use low pressure compressed air, applied

from inside the carburettor body, to clear any obstructions.

17 A small air vent filter is fitted to the ignition coil bracket **(see illustration)**. Unclip the cover from the base of the filter and remove the foam element. Wash the element in soapy water and inspect it for signs of clogging or damage, renewing it if necessary. Ensure the element is dry and clean and reassemble the filter components.

Reassembly

18 Before the carburettors are reassembled by a reversal of the disassembly procedure, they should be cleaned out thoroughly, preferably using compressed air. Avoid using a rag because there is always the risk of fine particles of lint obstructing the internal air passages or the jet orifices.

19 Always use compressed air to clear a blockage; a tyre pump makes an admirable substitute when a compressed air line is not available. Do not use excessive force when assembling the carburettor because it is very easy to shear the small jets or some of the smaller screws.

Caution: Never use a piece of wire or sharp metal to clear a blocked jet. It is only too easy to enlarge a jet under these circumstances and increase the rate of fuel consumption.

20 If the air funnel was disturbed, install the O-ring in the carburettor groove **(see illustration)**. Insert the air funnel into the holder and rotate it so that its tabs are locked in place **(see illustration)**. Align the cutout in

9.17 Air vent filter (arrowed) is mounted to ignition coil bracket

9.20a Install the O-ring in the carburettor groove

9.20b Insert air funnel in its holder and rotate it so that its tabs are locked in place

9.20c Align the cutout in the air funnel with the carburettor lug (arrowed)

9.22a Insert the jet needle and sealing washer into the piston . . .

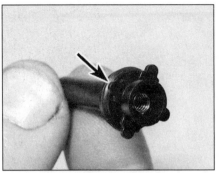

9.22b . . . and fit the needle holder and spring. Make sure the O-ring (arrowed) is correctly positioned

the air funnel with the carburettor lugs and install it; tighten the four screws securely **(see illustration)**.

21 If the pilot (mixture) screw was disturbed back it out to the previously recorded position, or if a new screw was fitted back it out to the initial positon given in the Specifications. Refer to Section 11 for pilot screw adjustment.

22 Fit the washer to the needle and insert the needle into the piston **(see illustration)**. Position a new O-ring in the groove of the holder and fit the spring inside the holder **(see illustration)**. Insert the holder into the piston and press it down until the O-ring is heard to click into the groove in the base of the piston. Insert the piston in the carburettor and seat the diaphragm edge and tab in the groove **(see illustration)**. Install the spring and vacuum cover top.

23 Engage the needle valve on the float and secure the float with the pivot pin **(see illustration)**. Before installing the float bowl, check the float height as described in Section 11. This is essential if a new float valve or float have been fitted or if fuel starvation or flooding have been experienced.

24 Install the carburettors as described in Section 7.

10 Carburettors -
separation and reassembly

⚠ *Warning: Petrol (gasoline) is extremely flammable, especially when in the form of vapour. Take all precautions to prevent the risk of fire and read through Section 3 of this Chapter and the Safety first! Section of this Manual before carrying out the following operation.*

1 Remove the carburettors from the machine as described in Section 7. Mark the body of each carburettor with its cylinder number to ensure that it is positioned correctly on reassembly. (The cylinders are numbered 1-2-3-4, left to right.)

600 models

2 Adjust the throttle stop screw until the bottom of the throttle valves align with the

9.22c Insert the piston and locate the diaphragm in the carburettor groove

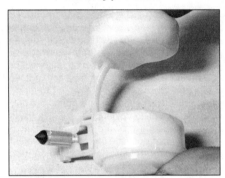

9.23 Make sure the needle valve is correctly located on the float

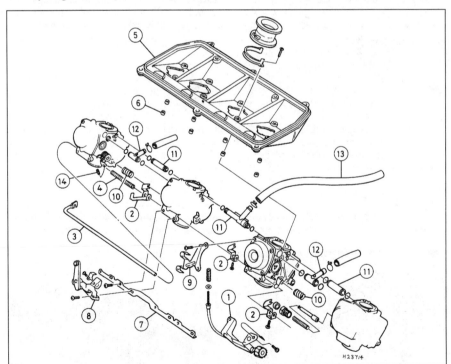

10.2 Carburettor linkage - 600 models

1 Idle speed adjuster	6 Dowels	11 Fuel unions
2 Choke arms	7 Front mounting bracket	12 Air unions
3 Choke linkage shaft	8 Choke cable bracket	13 Fuel pipe
4 Choke shaft spring	9 Throttle cable bracket	14 Synchronising screw
5 Rear mounting bracket	10 Throttle linkage spring	springs

4

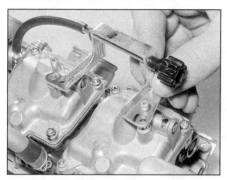

10.4 Remove throttle stop screw bracket before separating Nos. 1 and 2 carburettors

10.6a Renew all fuel and air union O-rings as a matter of course

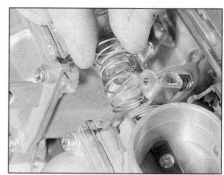

10.6b Do not omit the large throttle linkage spring when joining the carburettors

bypass holes in the carburettor venturis. Slacken the three screws (one on each choke operating arm) and withdraw the choke linkage shaft and spring (see illustration). The choke arms can then also be removed.

3 Bend up their lock washer tabs and remove the eight screws from the rear mounting bracket. Lift off the rear mounting bracket noting the locating dowel pins. Remove these for safekeeping if they are not firmly stuck in the carburettor bodies. Then remove the eight screws which retain the front mounting bracket to the top of the carburettors.

4 Before separating the carburettors make a note of how the throttle linkage springs are arranged to ensure that they are fitted correctly on reassembly. Then carefully separate the carburettors whilst taking care

not to damage the fuel and air unions between each unit or to lose the springs from the throttle linkages. Note that before No 1 and No 2 carburettors can be separated it will be necessary to remove the throttle stop screw mounting bracket from the float bowls (see illustration).

5 The carburettors are reassembled by a reverse of the separation procedure. Inspect the fuel and air unions for signs of deterioration, renewing them if necessary, and renew all the O-rings regardless of their apparent condition. Also renew the lock washers on the mounting bracket screws.

6 Carefully fit the air and fuel unions to No 1 carburettor, taking care not to damage the O-rings, then refit No 2 carburettor, not omitting the large throttle linkage spring fitted between

the two carburettors (see illustrations). Note that a smear of engine oil on the O-rings will aid installation. Once the carburettors are correctly joined, refit the small spring to the synchronising screw linkage, ensuring that it is correctly positioned. Rejoin numbers 3 and 4 carburettors using the same procedure.

7 Once the two pairs of carburettors are correctly assembled refit the throttle stop screw mounting bracket to the float bowls of No 1 and No 2 carburettors, tightening its retaining screws finger-tight only. Fit the fuel T-piece to No 2 carburettor then rejoin both pairs of carburettors and install the large spring in the throttle linkage. Do not forget to fit the small synchronising spring one the two pairs are joined.

8 Fit the front mounting bracket to the carburettors and install all the screws, tightening them finger-tight only. Place the carburettors on a flat surface, such as a sheet of glass, to ensure they are correctly aligned then tighten the front mounting bracket screws evenly and progressively in the specified order (see illustrations). Ensure all the dowels are fitted to the rear of the carburettors and install the rear mounting bracket (see illustration). Refit the mounting screws using new lock washers and tighten the screws evenly and progressively in the specified order (see illustrations). Secure the screws in place by bending down the tabs of the lock washers.

9 Refit the choke arms to the front mounting

10.8a Install front mounting bracket and tighten screws as described in text

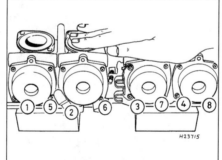

10.8b Tightening sequence for carburettor front mounting screws

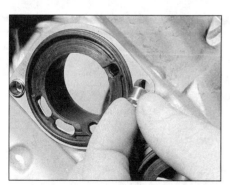

10.8c Ensure all air cleaner case dowels are in position

10.8d Tighten air cleaner case screws as described in text

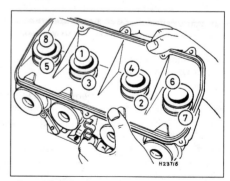

10.8e Tightening sequence for carburettor rear mounting screws - 600 model

10.9a Engage the choke arms with the plungers . . .

10.9b . . . then install the choke shaft and tighten choke arm screws securely

bracket ensuring that they engage correctly with each choke plunger (see illustration). Insert the choke linkage shaft and spring, then tighten the choke arm screws securely (see illustrations).

1000 H, J, K, L, M, N models

10 Disconnect the fuel pipe from the carburettors then slacken all the rear mounting bracket screws and remove the bracket (see illustration). Straighten and remove the split pin and washer from the throttle linkage between Nos 2 and 3 carburettors and separate the linkage.
11 Slacken all the front mounting bracket screws and remove the bracket from the assembly. Make a note of how the throttle linkage springs are arranged then slacken all the choke operating arm screws. The carburettors can then be separated, and the choke linkage shaft dismantled, whilst taking care not to damage the fuel or air unions or lose the small synchronising springs.
12 Before reassembling the carburettors inspect the fuel and air unions for deterioration, renewing them if necessary. Renew all O-rings as a matter of course.
13 Join Nos 1 and 2, then Nos 3 and 4 carburettors as described above in paragraph 6.
14 Refit Nos 1 and 2 carburettors to the rear mounting bracket, not forgetting to refit the throttle stop screw mounting bracket, and tighten the mounting screws finger-tight only. Refit the choke arms to Nos 1 and 2

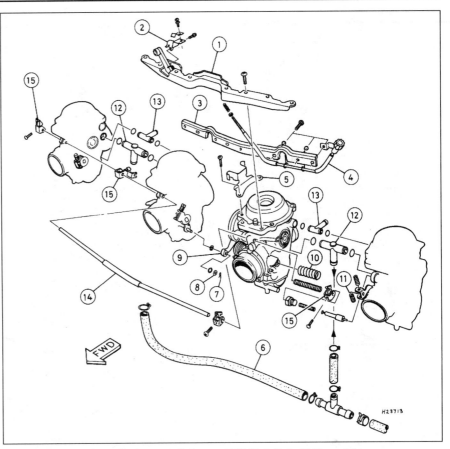

10.10 Carburettor linkage - 1000 H, J, K, L, M, N models

1 Front mounting bracket	6 Fuel pipe	11 Synchronising screw spring
2 Choke cable clamp	7 R-clip	12 Fuel union
3 Rear mounting bracket	8 Washer	13 Air union
4 Idle speed adjuster	9 Throttle link arm	14 Choke linkage shaft
5 Throttle cable bracket	10 Throttle linkage spring	15 Choke arms

carburettors and install the linkage shaft and spring. Ensure all choke components are correctly positioned and tighten the choke arm screws loosely.
15 Refit the choke arms to Nos 3 and 4 carburettors then slide the assembly onto the choke shaft, ensuring it passes through both carburettors and arms, and refit the rear mounting bracket screws. Tighten all the rear

mounting bracket screws evenly and progressively in the specified order (see illustration).
16 Install the front mounting bracket, ensuring that the choke lever engages correctly with the shaft, and tighten its mounting screws evenly and progressively in the specified order (see illustration 10.8b). Check that the choke arms are correctly

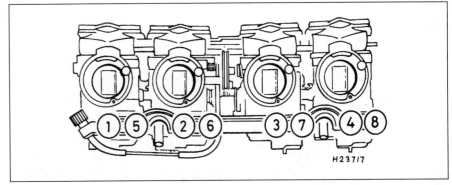

10.15 Tightening sequence for carburettor rear mounting screws - 1000 H, J, K, L, M, N models

4

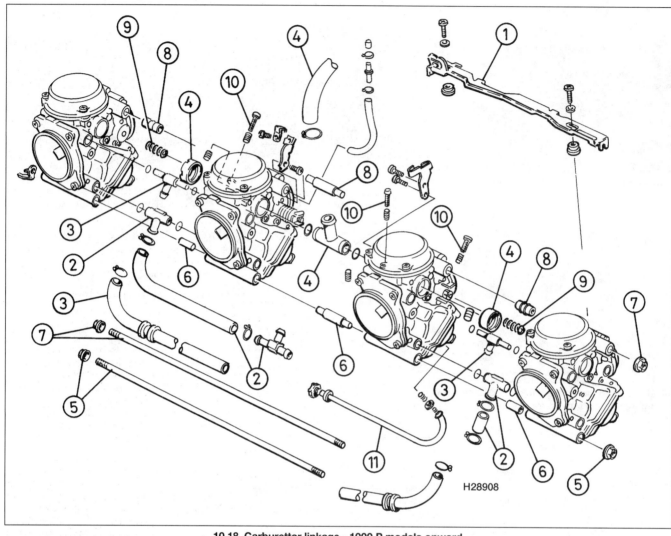

10.18 Carburettor linkage - 1000 P models onward

1 Choke linkage shaft	4 Air vent hose and unions	7 6 mm joining bolt and nuts	10 Synchronising screws
2 Fuel hose and unions	5 5 mm joining bolt and nuts	8 6 mm dowels	11 Idle speed adjuster
3 Breather hose and unions	6 5 mm dowels	9 Throttle linkage springs	

engaged with the plungers then tighten all the choke arm screws securely. Rejoin the throttle linkage between Nos 2 and 3 carburettors and refit the washer, securing it in position with a new split pin. Refit the fuel pipe.

1000 P models onward

17 To prevent damage to the air funnels, it is advised that they are removed. Remove the four screws and lift the holders and air funnels off the carburettors **(see illustration 9.8)**. Recover the O-rings.

18 Carburettor Nos 1 and 2 are separated from Nos 3 and 4. Release the fuel pipe spring clips and pull the fuel pipes off the unions between each pair of carburettors **(see illustration)**. Similarly, on all models except California, free the air vent pipes from their unions between each pair of carburettors.

19 Remove the two screws with their plastic washers which retain the choke shaft (see

illustration). Unhook the choke shaft return spring from between Nos 1 and 2 carburettors and remove the shaft complete with spring and plastic washers **(see illustrations)**.

Remove the choke cable clamp from the bracket on No 2 carburettor.

20 Make a note of how the throttle valve synchronisation screw springs are fitted to ensure

10.19a Choke shaft is retained by two screws with plastic washers

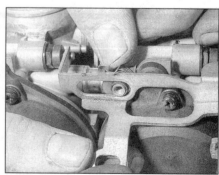

10.19b Unhook the return spring . . .

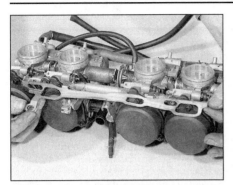

10.19c . . . and withdraw the choke shaft

10.19d Note the shouldered washer and return spring positions

10.20a Take note of the throttle linkage springs and synchronising spring positions before separating the carburettors

that they are installed correctly on reassembly **(see illustration)**. Unscrew the nuts from one end of the two joining bolts and withdraw the joining bolts fully from the other side **(see illustration)**. Note that the bolts are of different diameter.

21 Carefully separate carburettors No 2 and 3, leaving Nos 1 and 2, and Nos 3 and 4 still joined. Retrieve the synchronisation springs, the two dowels and the vent hose T-piece union as they are separated.

22 Separate carburettor Nos 1 and 2 by gently pulling them apart. Retrieve the throttle linkage spring, synchronisation springs, both dowels, air vent T-piece, fuel T-piece and breather joint. Carry out the same procedure to separate carburettor Nos 3 and 4.

23 Before reassembling the carburettors inspect the fuel and air unions for deterioration, renewing them if necessary. Renew all O-rings as a matter of course.

24 Carefully fit the air, breather and fuel unions to No 1 carburettor, taking care not to damage the O-rings. Install the dowels, noting that their diameter differ, then refit No 2 carburettor, not omitting the large throttle linkage spring fitted between the two carburettors. Note that a smear of engine oil on the O-rings will aid installation. Once the carburettors are correctly joined, refit the small springs to the synchronising screw linkage, ensuring that they are correctly positioned. Rejoin Nos 3 and 4 carburettors using the same procedure.

25 Fit the vent hose T-piece union and the two dowels to No 2 carburettor and join the two pairs of carburettors. Insert the synchronising spring in the throttle linkage. Thread the two joining bolts into place and secure with the nuts. Tighten the nuts evenly to the specified torque setting, noting that no more than 3.0 mm of thread should extend from the outer face of the top nuts and no more than 2.4 mm from the outer face of the lower nuts **(see illustration)**.

26 Mount the choke cable clamp to its bracket on No 2 carburettor and reconnect the choke shaft with the choke valve plungers. Note that the plastic washer should be located underneath the shaft and the return spring should be located between Nos 1 and 2 carburettors. Secure the choke shaft with the retaining screws and their plastic washers.

27 Push the air vent pipes and fuel pipes onto their unions and secure them with the spring clips.

28 Install the air intake funnels as described in Section 9.

All models

29 Check the operation of both the choke and throttle linkages ensuring that both operate smoothly and return quickly under spring pressure. Install the carburettors as described in Section 7. Check the idle speed, adjusting it if necessary, and then go on to check the carburettor synchronisation. Both operations are described in Chapter 1.

11 Carburettors - adjustment

 Warning: Petrol (gasoline) is extremely flammable, especially when in the form of vapour. Take all precautions to prevent the risk of fire and read through Section 3 of this Chapter and the Safety first! Section of this Manual before carrying out the following operation.

1 The first step in carburettor adjustment is to ensure that the jet sizes and float height are correct, which will require the removal and disassembly of the carburettors as described in Sections 7 and 8 or 9 (as applicable).

2 Before any dismantling is undertaken eliminate all other possible causes of running problems, checking in particular the spark plugs, air cleaner element and the operation of the choke mechanism. Checking and cleaning these items will often resolve a mysterious flat spot or misfire.

10.20b Remove the two nuts (arrowed) to separate the carburettors

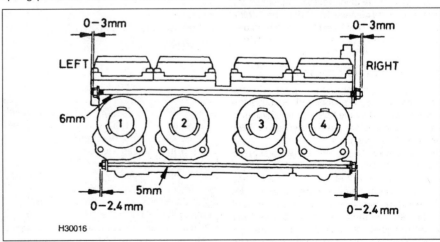

10.25 Carburettor joining bolt nut positions

4

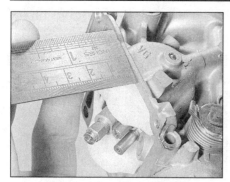

11.3 Checking the float height

Float height

3 If the carburettors have been removed for the purpose of checking jet sizes, the float height should be measured at the same time. It is unlikely that once this is set up correctly, there will be a significant amount of variation, unless the float needle or seat have worn. These should be checked and renewed as required. With the float bowl removed slowly rotate the carburettors until the floats move under gravity until the valve is just closed, but not so far that the needle's spring-loaded tip is compressed. Measure the distance between the gasket face and the bottom of the float with an accurate ruler **(see illustration)**. The correct setting should be as given in the Specifications Section. If adjustment is required it can be made by bending, by a very small amount, the small tang to which the float needle is attached. Repeat the procedure on the other carburettors.

4 Once the float heights are known to be correct refit the float bowls and install the carburettors on the machine as described in Section 7.

Pilot (mixture) screw

Note: *The pilot screws on 1000 P models onward are located in the base of the carburettor bodies, making access impossible with a conventional flat-bladed screwdriver. Honda produce a special tool (Pt. No. 07908-4220201 in the UK, 07MMA-MT3010A and 07PMA-MZ2011A in the US) which has a flexible drive.*

5 If the pilot screws have been renewed or disturbed they must be adjusted as follows. **Note:** *Do not adjust the pilot screws unnecessarily; there is little to be gained from unwarranted adjustment. The pilot screws are preset at the factory and certain US models are fitted with a limiter cap to prevent unnecessary adjustment. The limiter cap is cemented in place, but can be removed with pliers.*

6 Turn each pilot screw in until it seats lightly, then unscrew it by the number of turns shown in the Specifications at the start of this Chapter. This is only an initial setting and the pilot screws must then be adjusted as

described below. **Note:** *On 1000 K, L, M, N US models there is also a specified final setting, although it is recommended that the following procedure is used.*

7 Start the engine, warming it up to normal operating temperature, then set the machine to its specified idle speed by rotating the throttle stop screw. Turn all the pilot screws out a further half a turn whilst noting the effect on the engine speed. If the engine speed increases by 50 rpm or more, turn all the screws out a further half a turn. Repeat this procedure until the engine speed fails to rise, then reset the engine to the specified idle speed using the throttle stop screw. Using No 2 carburettor on all 600 models, No 1 carburettor on 1000 H, J, K, L, M, N models, and No 3 carburettor on 1000 P models onward, slowly turn the pilot screw in whilst noting the effect this has on the idle speed. Once the idle speed has dropped 50 rpm, stop and back the screw off by one complete turn, then reset the engine to the specified idle speed. Repeat this procedure on the remaining three pilot screws.

8 On all 600 and 1000 H, J, K, L, M, N US models, once the pilot screws are correctly set it is necessary to fit a new limiter cap to each screw. The cap must be cemented onto the pilot screw (using Loctite 601), whilst taking care not to move the screw's position, and positioned so that its lug is tight against the stop on the carburettor body. The cap will prevent the screw being turned anticlockwise (counterclockwise), which would richen the mixture, and allows only a small amount of movement clockwise.

9 On all models, ensure that the engine idles smoothly and does not falter and stop after the throttle twistgrip has been opened and closed a few times. Finally adjust the throttle cables and check that the throttle operates smoothly and returns quickly before taking the machine on the road.

Engine idle speed

10 Refer to the procedure in Chapter 1.

12 Emission control systems - general (California models)

1 To comply with legislation in the state of California, machines are fitted with two emission control systems; a system which reduces the amount of toxic emissions in the exhaust gases and another system which prevents the vapours from any part of the fuel system escaping into the atmosphere.

2 The exhaust emission control system consists of a secondary air supply system which introduces filtered air into the exhaust gases in the exhaust port. Fresh air is drawn into the exhaust port through a reed valve arrangement whenever there is a negative pulse in the exhaust system. This charge of

fresh air promotes the burning of the unburnt exhaust gases and changes a considerable amount of hydrocarbons and carbon monoxide into relatively harmless carbon dioxide and water.

3 The evaporative emission control system works as follows. Fuel vapour from the fuel tank and carburettor is directed into a charcoal canister where it is absorbed and stored whilst the engine is stopped. When the engine is run and the purge control valve diaphragm is open, fuel vapour in the charcoal canister is drawn into the engine through the carburettor and replaced with fresh air.

4 Both systems are automatic in operation and should not normally require attention. The only maintenance needed is to carry out a regular check of the system hoses as described in Chapter 1. However, if at any time either system is suspected of being faulty the machine must be taken to a Honda dealer who will have the necessary equipment to check the condition of the emission system components. Faults in the exhaust emission control system will lead to the tickover becoming unstable and a reduction in engine power, often accompanied by backfiring. Faults in the evaporative emission system will lead to the engine being difficult to start.

5 Note that both systems are subject to anti-tampering legislation currently in force which means the machine must never be used with any part of its emission control systems disconnected, missing, rendered inoperative or modified in any way. Use only genuine Honda replacement parts if renewal of any component is required.

13 Air cleaner - general

Caution: Never run the engine with the air cleaner disconnected or the element removed. Apart from the risk of increased engine wear due to unfiltered air being allowed to enter, the carburettors are jetted to compensate for the presence of the air cleaner and a dangerously weak mixture, which could lead to overheating and possible engine damage, will result if it is omitted.

1 The care and maintenance of the air cleaner element is described in Chapter 1.

2 US owners should note that the air cleaner is subject to the anti-tampering legislation currently in force, which means the machine must never be run with the element removed or rendered inoperative, or with the assembly modified in any way. Furthermore, only genuine Honda replacement parts may be used if the renewal of any component is necessary.

3 Refer to Section 7 of this Chapter for air cleaner attachment details.

14 Lubrication system - checking the oil pressure

1 The efficiency of the lubrication system is dependent on the oil pump delivering oil at the correct pressure. This can be checked using an oil pressure gauge and adapter; Honda supply a gauge and adapter (Pt. Nos. 07506-3000000 and 07510-4220100).

2 The oil pressure is checked by removing the oil pressure switch and screwing the adapter and gauge into the crankcase as follows. On 600 models the switch is located on the top right side of the crankcase, just behind the engine number, and on 1000 models it is situated on the right side of the crankcase, just below the right crankshaft end cover.

3 Remove the necessary fairing sections to gain access to the oil pressure switch (see Chapter 6). Prior to carrying out the pressure test, check the engine oil level and top up if necessary. Start the engine and warm it up to normal operating temperature. Stop the engine, disconnect the wire from the oil pressure switch, and unscrew the switch from the crankcase whilst taking great care not to burn your hands on the hot engine unit.

⚠ **Warning: On 1000 models hot oil may be expelled as the switch is removed. Position a clean container below the switch to catch any oil. On all models screw the pressure gauge and adapter into the crankcase and on 1000 models pour any oil which may have been released as the switch was removed back into the crankcase, topping up if necessary with fresh oil.**

4 Start the engine and increase the engine speed to 5000 rpm, noting the reading obtained on the pressure gauge. If the system is working normally, the pressure should be within the range given in the Specifications at the start of this Chapter. If it exceeds the higher figure by a considerable amount it is likely that the relief valve is stuck closed. If this is the case the relief valve must be removed and inspected as described in Section 16. If the oil pressure is significantly below the lower figure the oil pump should be removed for inspection as described in the following Section.

Caution: On no account should the machine be used with low oil pressure, as plain bearing engines in particular rely on oil pressure as much as oil quantity for effective lubrication.

5 On installation remove all traces of oil from the threads of the pressure switch and apply a small amount of sealant to the threads. Refit the switch to the crankcase and tighten it to the specified torque setting. Reconnect the wire to the switch and refit the fairing components.

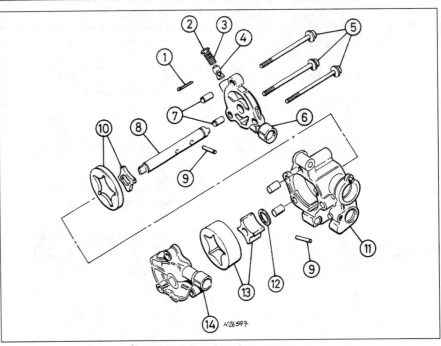

15.2 Oil pump

1 Split pin	5 Bolts	8 Driveshaft	11 Pump body
2 Spring seat	6 Cover (cooler side)	9 Drive pins	12 Thrust washer
3 Spring	7 Dowel pins	10 Rotors (cooler side)	13 Rotors (pump side)
4 Relief valve			14 Cover (pump side)

15 Oil pump - removal, inspection and installation

Removal

1 Remove the oil pump as described in Section 17 of Chapter 2.

Inspection

2 Straighten and remove the split pin which retains the pump relief valve components and withdraw the spring seat, spring and relief valve from the pump **(see illustration)**. Slacken the bolts or screws which secure the covers to the pump and lift off the covers noting the dowel pins. Remove both the pump (thick) and cooler (thin) rotors from the body, then remove the drive pins from the shaft and withdraw the shaft. Note the thrust washer fitted behind the drive pin on the pump rotor side of the body.

3 Wash all the pump components in a high flash-point solvent and allow them to dry. Inspect the rotors, pump body and relief valve for signs of scoring, chipping or other surface damage which will be evident if metallic particles have found their way into the oil pump assembly. If any component shows signs of wear or damage the pump must be renewed as a complete assembly; no individual replacement parts being available.

4 Temporarily install both sets of rotors in the pump body and refit the pump shaft. Using feeler gauges, measure the clearance between the inner rotor tip and the outer rotor, and between the outer rotor and pump body **(see illustrations)**. Then lay a straightedge

4

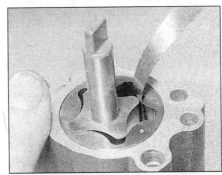

15.4a Check inner rotor tip to outer rotor clearance . . .

15.4b . . . and outer rotor to pump body clearance

15.4c Measuring pump rotor end play

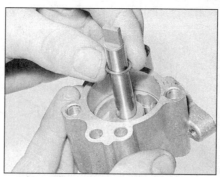

15.6a Install thrust washer on the pump rotor side of the body . . .

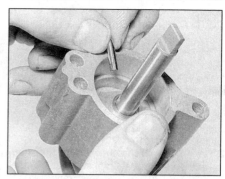

15.6b . . . and refit pump rotor drive pin

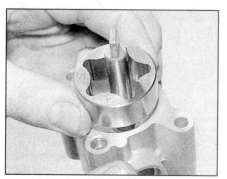

15.6c Install outer rotors as described in text . . .

15.6d . . . and ensure inner rotor slot engages correctly with the drive pin

across each end of the pump and measure the end play of each set of rotors **(see illustration)**. If any measurement exceeds the service limits shown in the Specifications, the pump assembly must be renewed.

5 Apply clean engine oil to all the pump components and assemble them as follows. **Note:** *The pump components must be absolutely clean and free of dirt and foreign matter or damage to the pump will occur.*

6 Install the thrust washer on the pump rotor side of the body then fit the pump rotor drive pin to the pump shaft and install the shaft **(see illustrations)**. Fit the pump outer rotor noting the punch mark on one of its surfaces **(see illustration)**. On 600 models the rotor must be fitted with this mark facing the pump body, and on 1000 models the rotor must be fitted so that the mark faces away from the pump body. Install the inner rotor ensuring that its slot engages correctly with the drive pin **(see illustration)**. Check that the two locating dowels are fitted to the pump cover and fit it to the body.

7 Invert the pump and fit the cooler rotor drive pin to the shaft. Install the outer cooler rotor, ensuring that the punch mark is facing away from the pump body, and refit the inner rotor ensuring it locates with its drive pin. Check that the dowel pin(s) is in position then refit the cover and tighten the cover retaining screws or bolts securely **(see illustrations)**.

8 Fit the relief valve piston, spring and spring

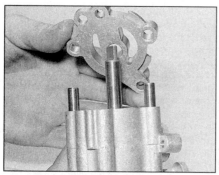

15.7a Do not omit dowel pins when refitting end covers

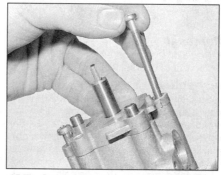

15.7b Secure covers in position with their retaining screws

15.8a Refit the relief valve piston to the pump . . .

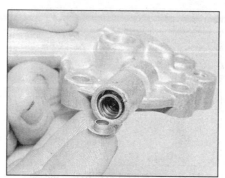

15.8b . . . followed by the spring and spring seat . . .

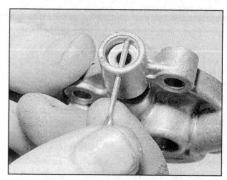

15.8c . . . and secure relief valve components in position with a new split pin

16.1 Oil pressure relief valve is a push fit into the crankcase

16.2a Remove the relief valve circlip . . .

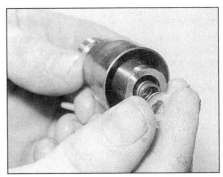

16.2b . . . and withdraw the washer . . .

seat and secure them in position with a new split pin (see illustrations).

Installation

9 Check that the pump shaft rotates freely and easily and install the pump as described in Section 17 of Chapter 2.

16 Oil pressure relief valve - removal, inspection and installation

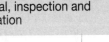

1 Remove the oil pan (sump) as described in Section 17 of Chapter 2 and pull the relief valve from its location in the crankcase (see illustration).

2 Remove the circlip from the relief valve body and withdraw the washer, spring and piston (see illustrations). Wash all components in a high flash-point solvent and inspect the piston and valve bore for signs of scoring or other damage. Also check the spring for any sign of fatigue. If any component is worn or damaged in any way the relief valve must be renewed.

3 Lubricate all components with clean engine oil then refit the piston, spring and washer to the body and secure them in position with the circlip. Ensure the circlip is correctly located in its groove and check that the piston moves smoothly up and down the valve body. Inspect the relief valve O-ring, renewing if necessary, and lubricate it with engine oil

before refitting the valve to the crankcase (see illustration). Install the oil pan (sump) as described in Section 17 of Chapter 2.

17 Oil cooler, hoses and pipes - removal, inspection and installation

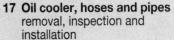

1 Remove the fairing as described in Chapter 6, then drain the engine oil into a clean container as described in Chapter 1.

2 To remove the oil cooler, slacken the two union bolts which retain each hose and disconnect them from the cooler (see illustration). Remove the oil cooler mounting bolts and lower the cooler matrix away from

16.2c . . . spring . . .

16.2d . . . and piston from the valve body

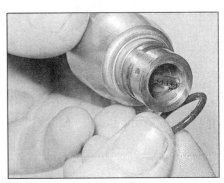

16.3 Inspect the relief valve O-ring and renew if necessary

4

17.2a To remove the oil cooler, slacken the bolts which retain each hose to the oil cooler matrix . . .

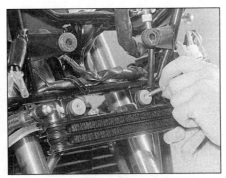

17.2b . . . and remove the oil cooler mounting bolts

17.2c Hose bottom connection - 600 shown

the machine **(see illustration)**. If it is necessary to remove the hoses completely, slacken the bolt which secures each hose to the oil pan on 600 models, or the bolts which mount the pipes onto the crankcase on 1000 models, then free the hoses or pipes from their retaining clips and remove them from the machine **(see illustration).**

3 Remove any obstructions from the cooler matrix using an air line; the conglomeration of moths and flies, etc, usually collected in the cooler matrix severely reduces its cooling efficiency. If care is exercised, bent fins can be straightened by placing the flat of a screwdriver either side of the fin in question and carefully bending it into its original shape.

4 Inspect the oil cooler, hoses and pipes for signs of leakage or damage. If any component shows signs of leakage or damage it must be renewed as repair is not possible.

5 On installation fit new O-rings to the unions. On 600 models refit the oil hoses to the sump and refit the oil cooler. Ensure the hoses are correctly routed and retained by any of the necessary clips then tighten both the cooler and hose retaining bolts securely. On 1000 models refit the pipes to the crankcase and install the oil cooler. Tighten both the oil cooler and pipe retaining bolts to their specified torque settings.

6 Replenish the engine oil as described in Chapter 1 and refit the fairing as described in Chapter 6.

Chapter 5
Ignition system

Contents

Degrees of difficulty

Easy, suitable for novice with little experience	Fairly easy, suitable for beginner with some experience	Fairly difficult, suitable for competent DIY mechanic	Difficult, suitable for experienced DIY mechanic	Very difficult, suitable for expert DIY or professional

Specifications

General
Firing order	1-2-4-3
Cylinder identification	1-2-3-4 left to right (No 1 at alternator end)

Ignition timing
Initial:
600 K and L models	14.5° BTDC @ specified idle speed
All other models	10° BTDC @ specified idle speed

Full advance:
600 models	Not available
1000 H, J, K, L, M, N models	38° BTDC @ 5000 rpm
1000 P models onward	40° BTDC @ 5000 rpm

Pulser coil
Resistance:
600 models	450 - 550 ohm @ 20°C (68°F)
1000 models	460 - 580 ohm @ 20°C (68°F)

Ignition HT coil
Primary winding resistance:
600 models	2.5 - 3.1 ohm @ 20°C (68°F)
1000 H, J, K, L, M, N models	2.6 - 3.2 ohm @ 20°C (68°F)
1000 P models onward	2.5 - 3.2 ohm @ 20°C (68°F)

Secondary winding resistance - with HT lead and suppressor cap:
600 models	21 - 25 K ohm @ 20°C (68°F)
1000 H, J, K, L, M, N models	17 - 23 K ohm @ 20°C (68°F)
1000 P models onward	21 - 27 K ohm @ 20°C (68°F)

Secondary winding resistance - without HT lead and suppressor cap:
600 models	11 - 15 K ohm @ 20°C (68°F)
1000 H, J, K, L, M, N models	13 - 17 K ohm @ 20°C (68°F)
1000 P models onward	11 - 17 K ohm @ 20°C (68°F)

Spark plug
Type:
All 600 models and 1000 T model onward	NGK DPR8EA-9 or ND X24EPR-U9
1000 H, J, K, L, M, N, P, R, S models	NGK DPR9EA-9 or ND X27EPR-U9
Plug gap	0.8 - 0.9 mm (0.032 - 0.035 in)

Torque settings
	kgf m	lbf ft
Pulser coil rotor bolt - 1000 models	4.9	35.0
Pulser coil mounting bolts - 600 models	0.5	3.8

5

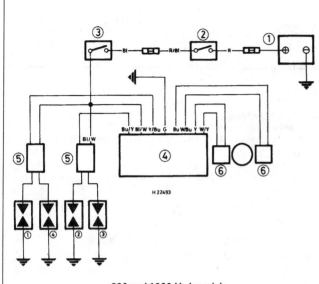

600 and 1000 H, J models

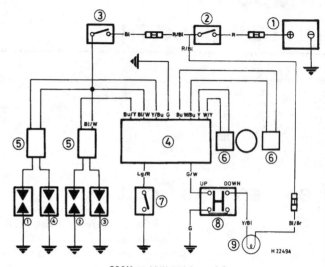

600K and UK 600 L models

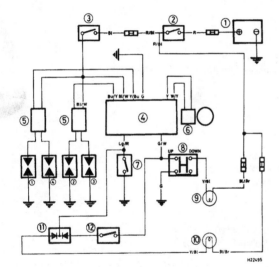

US 600 L model

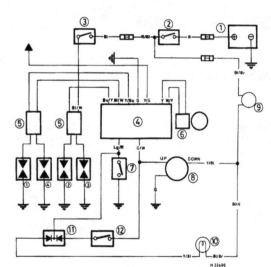

1000 K, L, M, N models

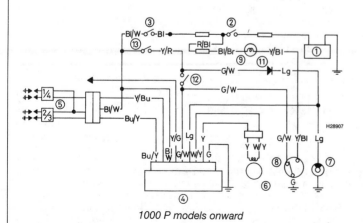

1000 P models onward

1.1 Ignition system circuit diagrams

1 Battery
2 Ignition switch
3 Engine kill switch
4 Spark unit
5 Ignition coils
6 Pulser coil(s)
7 Neutral switch
8 Side stand switch
9 Side stand warning light
10 Neutral warning light

11 Diode
12 Clutch switch
13 Starter switch
Bl Black
Bu Blue
G Green
Lg Light green
R Red
W White
Y Yellow

1 General description

These models are fitted with a magnetically-triggered electronic ignition system, which due to its lack of mechanical parts is totally maintenance-free. The system comprises a rotor, pulser coil(s), spark unit and two ignition HT coils. The raised trigger on the rotor, which is fitted to the left end of the crankshaft, magnetically operates the pulser coil(s) as the crankshaft rotates. The pulser coil(s) send a signal to the spark unit which then supplies the ignition coils with the power necessary to produce a spark at the plugs **(see illustration)**.

Each coil supplies two spark plugs. Cylinders 1 and 4 operate off one coil and cylinders 2 and 3 off the other. For any given cylinder, the plug is fired twice for every engine cycle, but one of the sparks occurs during the exhaust stroke and therefore performs no useful function. This arrangement is usually known as a 'spare spark' or 'wasted spark' system.

2 Spark plugs - general

1 For information on spark plug removal, renewal and maintenance, and installation refer to Chapter 1.

3 Ignition system - fault diagnosis

1 As no means of adjustment is available, any fault in the system can only be attributed to failure of a system component or a simple wiring fault. Of the two possibilities, the latter is by far the most likely. In the event of failure, check the system in a logical fashion, as described below.
2 Remove the spark plugs from No 3 and No 4 cylinders, giving them a quick visual check, noting any obvious signs of flooding or oiling. Fit the plugs into their plug caps and rest them on the cylinder head so that the metal body of each plug is in good contact with the cylinder head metal. The electrode ends of the plugs should be positioned so that sparking can be checked as the engine is spun over using the starter motor.

> ⚠ **Warning: The energy levels in electronic systems can be very high. On no account should the ignition be switched on whilst the plugs or plug caps are being held. Shocks from the HT circuit can be most unpleasant. Secondly, it is vital that the**

plugs are soundly earthed when the system is checked for sparking. The ignition system components can be seriously damaged if the HT circuit becomes isolated.

3 Having observed the above Warning, check that the kill switch is in the RUN position, turn the ignition switch to ON and turn the engine over on the starter motor. If the system is in good condition a regular, fat blue spark should be evident at the plug electrodes. If the spark appears thin or yellowish, or is non-existent, further investigation will be necessary. Before proceeding further, turn the ignition off and remove the key as a safety measure.
4 Ignition faults can be divided into two categories, namely those where the ignition system has failed completely, and those which are due to a partial failure. The likely faults are listed below, starting with the most probable source of failure. Work through the list systematically, referring to the subsequent sections of this Chapter for full details of the necessary checks and tests. **Note:** *Before checking the following items ensure that the battery is fully charged and that all fuses are sound.*
  a) *Loose, corroded or damaged wiring connections, broken or shorted wiring between any of the component parts of the ignition system.*
  b) *Faulty ignition or engine kill switch.*
  c) *Faulty neutral or side stand switch (K models onward).*
  d) *Faulty pulser coil(s).*
  e) *Faulty ignition HT coil(s).*
  f) *Faulty spark unit.*

4 Ignition system - checking the wiring

1 The wiring should be checked visually, noting any signs of corrosion around the various terminals and connectors. If the fault has developed in wet conditions it follows that water may have entered any of the connectors or switches, causing a short circuit. A temporary cure can be effected by spraying the relevant area with one of the proprietary de-watering aerosols such as WD40 or similar. A more permanent solution is to dismantle the switch or connector and coat the exposed parts with silicone grease to prevent the ingress of water. The exposed backs of connectors can be sealed off using a silicone rubber sealant.
2 Light corrosion can normally be cured by scraping or sanding the affected area, although in serious cases it may prove necessary to renew the switch or connector affected. Check the wiring for chafing or breakage, particularly where it passes close to part of the frame or its fittings. As a temporary measure damaged insulation can be repaired

with PVC tape, but the wire concerned should be renewed at the earliest opportunity.
3 Using the appropriate wiring diagram at the end of this manual, check each wire for breakage or short circuits using a multimeter set on the resistance scale or a dry battery and bulb, wired as shown in illustration 2.1 in Chapter 8. In each case, there should be continuity between the ends of each wire.

5 Ignition and engine kill switches - testing

1 The ignition system is controlled by the ignition or main switch, mounted on the top yoke. The switch has several terminals, of which two are involved in controlling the ignition system. These are the ignition terminal (red/black lead) and the power supply from the battery (red lead). The two terminals are connected when the switch is in the ON position and the connection should be broken when the switch is in the OFF position.
2 If the operation of the switch is suspect, trace the wiring back from the switch, disconnect its block connector from the main wiring loom. Check the operation of the switch using a multimeter set to the resistance (ohms) scale.
3 The engine kill switch situated in the right-hand handlebar switch cluster can be tested in a similar manner. Trace the wiring back from the switch and disconnect it from the main wiring loom. Using the multimeter, continuity should be present between the black and black/white terminals when the switch is in the RUN position and high resistance (open-circuit) should be shown when the switch is in the OFF position.
4 If either switch is found to be faulty it must be renewed. Although the switches are effectively sealed units (no replacement parts being available), there is nothing to be lost by attempting a repair. Depending on the owner's skill, worn contacts may be reclaimed by building them up with solder or in some cases, simply by cleaning them with a water dispersant spray.

6 Side stand and neutral switches - testing (K models onward)

General information

1 The side stand and neutral switches are linked to the ignition system to provide a safety feature which prevents the machine being ridden with the side stand down **(see illustration)**. If at any time the transmission is put into gear whilst the side stand is down, the power from the spark unit will be

5

6.1 Side stand switch location - 600 K and L models

automatically transmitted to earth (ground). This effectively breaks the ignition system and kills the engine.

2 A clutch switch and diode are also incorporated in the ignition system from L models onward. The clutch switch overrides the neutral and side stand switches when the lever is pulled in. If necessary, the clutch switch and diode can be tested as described in Chapter 8.

Side stand switch

3 To test the side stand switch it is first necessary to remove the left side panel on 1000 models, and the fuel tank on 600 models. Trace the wiring back from the switch and disconnect its 3-pin block connector (containing green/white, yellow/black and green wires) from the main wiring loom.

4 Using a multimeter set to the resistance (ohms) scale, check for continuity between the green/white and green wires and the yellow and black and green wires on the switch side of the connector. If the switch is in good condition there should be continuity between the green/white and green wires only when the sidestand is up, and continuity between the yellow/black and green wires only when the side stand is down. If this is not the case the switch must be renewed.

5 To gain access to the switch it will be necessary to remove the lower or left lower (as applicable) fairing section. Slacken the bolt(s) which secure the switch to the frame and remove it from the machine. On installation tighten the switch retaining bolt(s) securely and ensure the wiring is correctly routed. **Note:** *On 1000 models ensure that the switch contact aligns with the side stand hole and the cutout in the switch body locates with the return spring pin.*

Neutral switch

6 To test the neutral switch it is necessary to remove the right side panel on 1000 models, and the fuel tank on 600 models. Disconnect the single light green/red wire from the main loom and check for continuity between the wire and earth (ground). If the switch is in good condition, there should be continuity when the transmission is in neutral and high resistance (open-circuit) when it is in gear. If not, the switch is faulty and must be renewed.

The neutral switch is situated on the rear underside of the crankcase on 1000 models and on the left side of the crankcase, just above the water pump, on 600 models.

7 Pulser coil(s) - testing, removal and installation

1 On 600 models remove the fuel tank and on 1000 models remove the left side panel.
2 On 1000 K models onward, and US 600 L models disconnect the 2-pin block connector containing the white/yellow and yellow wires. Using a multimeter set to the ohms x 100 scale, measure the resistance between the two wires on the coil side of the connector.
3 On all other models disconnect the red (600 models) or black (1000 models) 4-pin block connector. Using a multimeter set to the ohms x 100 scale, measure the resistance between the white/yellow and yellow wires, and the white/blue and blue wires.
4 On all models compare the readings obtained with those shown in the Specifications at the start of this Chapter. The pulser coil(s) must be renewed if the reading obtained differs greatly from that given, particularly if the meter indicates a short-circuit (no measurable resistance) or an open-circuit (infinite, or very high resistance).
5 If the coil(s) are thought to be faulty, first check that this is not due to a damaged or broken wire from the coil to the connector; pinched or broken wires can usually be easily repaired by the average owner. Pulser coil(s) can be removed and renewed as follows.

600 models

6 To renew the pulser coil(s) first remove the left side fairing section as described in Chapter 6 and drain the engine oil into a clean container as described in Chapter 1.
7 Slacken all the bolts which retain the left crankshaft cover and remove the cover from the machine noting the dowel which is fitted to the crankcase. This should be removed for safekeeping if loose. Slacken the bolts which secure the pulser coil(s) and remove them from the cover **(see illustration).**

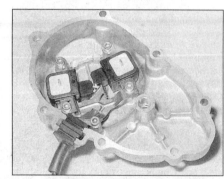

7.7 On 600 models the pulser coil(s) are mounted on the inside of the left crankshaft cover

8 Installation is by a reversal of the removal procedure. Refit the pulser coil(s) to the cover then tighten their retaining bolts to the specified torque setting, having first applied a few drops of thread-locking compound to their threads. Ensure that the dowel is in position in the crankcase. Check that the crankcase and cover sealing faces are clean and refit the cover to the machine using a new gasket. Tighten all cover bolts evenly and securely and install the fairing section.
9 Top up the engine oil as described in Chapter 1.

1000 models

10 Remove the left side fairing section as described in Chapter 6. On K models onward, slacken the three bolts which secure the left engine protector, removing it from the machine, then slacken the protector mounting bracket bolts and remove the bracket.
11 On all models position a clean container beneath the left crankshaft cover, to catch any oil which may be released, then remove all the bolts which retain the left crankshaft end cover and lift off the cover along with the heat protector bar (H and J models only). Discard the cover gasket and obtain a new one for installation.
12 Remove the rotor retaining bolt from the end of the crankshaft and remove the rotor. Slacken the pulser coil retaining bolts, displace the grommet, and remove the coil(s) from the crankcase.
13 On installation, refit the pulser coil(s), tightening their retaining bolts securely, and refit the rotor ensuring that the projections on its back locate correctly with the cutout and hole in the crankshaft end. Apply thread-locking compound to the threads of the rotor bolt and tighten it to the specified torque setting.
14 Ensure that both the crankcase and cover sealing surfaces are clean and that the grommet is correctly positioned. Install the end cover, and heat protector bar (where fitted), using a **new** gasket and tighten its retaining bolts securely. On K models onward, refit the engine protector and bracket. On all models install the fairing components as described in Chapter 6.
15 Top up the engine oil as described in Chapter 1.

8 Ignition HT coils - testing, removal and installation

1 If either ignition coil is suspected of failure it can be tested by measuring the resistance of its primary and secondary windings. On 1000 models this test can be carried out with the coils in place on the frame but on 600 models the coils must be removed. On 600 models the coils are mounted on the frame, just behind the carburettors, and on 1000 models

8.1 Ignition HT coil location - 1000 models

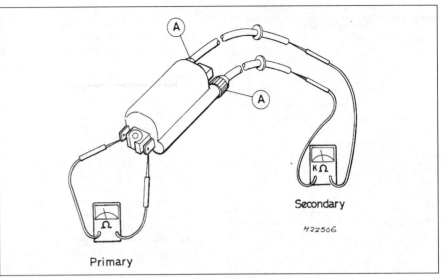

8.4 Ignition HT coil test connections

Release connectors (A) to make secondary winding test without HT leads and suppressor caps

they are mounted on the frame below the front of the fuel tank **(see illustration)**.

2 On 600 models remove the fuel tank as described in Chapter 4. Make a note of how the low tension wires are arranged then disconnect them from the coils. Pull the suppressor caps off the spark plugs then slacken the coil mounting bolts and remove the coils.

3 On 1000 H and J models remove the lower inner covers from the upper fairing then on all 1000 models remove the fuel tank front mounting bolts then lift up the tank and support it with the prop stay. Ensure the tank is securely supported and pull the suppressor caps off the spark plugs.

4 On all models, set the meter to the ohms x 1 scale and measure the resistance between the low tension terminals **(see illustration)**. This will give a resistance reading of the primary windings and should be within the limits given in the Specifications.

5 To check the condition of the secondary windings, set the meter to the K ohm scale and connect the meter probes to the two spark plug caps, noting the reading obtained **(see illustration 8.4)**. If this reading is not within the range shown in the Specifications, unscrew the HT leads from the coil then measure the resistance between the HT terminals. If both values obtained differ greatly from those specified it is likely that the coil is defective.

> **HAYNES HiNT** *If only the first reading obtained is suspect then it can be assumed that the fault lies in the HT leads and suppressor caps rather than the coil itself - leads and caps are available separately from the coils.*

6 Should any of the above checks not produce the expected result, the coil should be taken to a Honda dealer or auto-electrician for a more thorough check. If the coil is confirmed to be faulty, it must be renewed; the coil is a sealed unit and cannot therefore be repaired.

9 Spark unit - location and testing

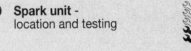

1 If the test shown in the preceding Sections have failed to isolate the cause of an ignition fault it is likely that the spark unit itself is faulty. **Note:** *Test details are available for the spark unit, but they relate to a special test unit only available to a Honda dealer. It is therefore totally impracticable for the owner to check* the unit with home workshop equipment.

2 The spark unit is located behind the right sidepanel on 600 models **(see illustration)** and behind the right side of the seat cowling on 1000 models. On 1000 models, to gain access to the unit first remove the seat and side panels, followed by the grab rail and seat cowling mounting bolts, then lift the grab rail clear of the machine. Disengage the bulbholders from the back of the stop/tail lamp and carefully remove the seat cowling **(see illustrations)**.

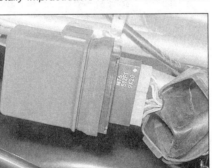

9.2a On 600 models spark unit is located behind the right sidepanel

9.2b On 1000 models it will first be necessary to remove the grab rail ...

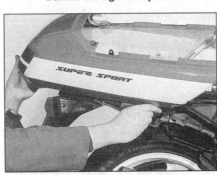

9.2c ... and seat cowling ...

9.2d ...to gain access to the spark unit - K models onward shown

5

10 HT leads and suppressor caps - inspection

1 Erratic running faults and problems with the engine suddenly cutting out in wet weather can often be attributed to leakage from the high tension leads and suppressor caps. If this fault is present, it will often be possible to see tiny sparks around the leads and caps at night. One cause of this is the accumulation of mud and road grime around the leads, and the first thing to check is that the leads and caps are clean. It is possible to cure the problem by cleaning the components and sealing them with an aerosol ignition sealer, which will leave an insulating coating on both components.

2 Water dispersant sprays are also highly recommended where the system has become swamped with water.

3 The suppressor leads and caps may break down internally. If this is suspected both components can be tested as described in Section 8 of this Chapter and renewed as necessary.

11 Ignition timing - check

1 Since no provision exists for adjusting the ignition timing and since no component is subject to mechanical wear, there is no need for regular checks; only if investigating a fault such as a loss of power or a misfire should the ignition timing be checked.

2 The ignition timing can be checked only whilst the engine is running using a stroboscopic lamp; therefore a suitable timing lamp will be required. The inexpensive neon lamps should be adequate in theory, but in practice may produce a pulse of such low intensity that the timing mark remains indistinct. If possible, one of the more precise xenon tube lamps should be employed powered by an external source of the appropriate voltage. **Note:** *Do not use the machine's own battery as an incorrect reading may result from stray impulses within the machine's electrical system.*

3 On 600 models remove the right lower fairing section and on 1000 H and J models remove the left side fairing section and the lower inner cover from the upper fairing, and on 1000 K models onward, remove the left engine protector. On all 1000 models, remove the fuel tank front mounting bolts then lift up the tank and support it with the prop stay.

4 On all models warm the engine up to normal operating temperature and remove the inspection cap from the crankshaft cover. Stop the engine and connect the timing light to No. 1 or 4 spark plug lead. Start the engine and aim the light in the inspection hole.

600 models

5 With the machine idling at the specified speed the F mark on the rotor should align with the index mark on the casing. Slowly increase the engine speed noting that the F mark should move anticlockwise (counter-clockwise) in relation to the engine speed. Stop the engine and repeat the test on all the remaining spark plug leads.

1000 H, J, K, L, M, N models

6 With the machine idling at the specified speed, the index mark on the rotor should align with the F mark on the crankcase. Slowly increase the engine speed noting that the index mark on the rotor should move clockwise in relation to the engine speed. **Note:** *On K, L, M, N models the index mark should align with the advance index mark on the crankcase at 5000 rpm.*

1000 P models onward

7 With the machine idling at the specified speed, the index mark on the rotor should align with the three dots next to the F mark on the crankcase. Slowly increase the engine speed to check the ignition advance. From approximately 1600 rpm the index mark on the rotor should begin to move clockwise, away from the three dots next to the F mark.

All models

8 As already stated, there is no means of adjustment of the ignition timing on these machines. If the ignition timing is incorrect one of the ignition system components is at fault and the system must be tested as described in the preceding Sections of this Chapter and the faulty component renewed.

Chapter 6
Frame and suspension

Contents

Degrees of difficulty

Easy, suitable for novice with little experience		**Fairly easy,** suitable for beginner with some experience		**Fairly difficult,** suitable for competent DIY mechanic		**Difficult,** suitable for experienced DIY mechanic		**Very difficult,** suitable for expert DIY or professional	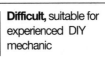

Specifications

Forks

Spring free length:	
600 models	397.3 mm (15.64 in)
1000 H, J models	468.8 - 478.2 mm (18.46 - 18.83 in)
1000 K, L, M, N models	419.9 mm (16.53 in)
1000 P models onward	446.3 mm (17.57 in)
Service limit:	
600 models	389.3 mm (15.33 in)
1000 H, J models	464.0 mm (18.30 in)
1000 K, L, M, N models	411.5 mm (16.20 in)
1000 P models onward	437.4 mm (17.22 in)
Fork tube (stanchion) max runout	0.2 mm (0.008 in)
Oil capacity - per leg:	
600 models:	
Right leg	361 cc (12.2 US fl oz, 12.7 Imp fl oz)
Left leg	371 cc (12.5 US fl oz, 13.0 Imp fl oz)
1000 H, J models:	
Right leg	485 cc (16.4 US fl oz, 17.0 Imp fl oz)
Left leg	495 cc (16.7 US fl oz, 17.4 Imp fl oz)
1000 K, L, M, N models - both legs	409 cc (13.8 US fl oz, 14.3 Imp fl oz)
1000 P models onward - both legs	418 cc (14.1 US fl oz, 14.7 Imp fl oz)
Oil level:*	
600 models	120 mm (4.7 in)
1000 H, J models	148 mm (5.8 in)
1000 K models onward	172 mm (6.8 in)
Fork oil grade	ATF (Automatic Transmission Fluid) or Fork oil

* Oil level is measured from the top of the tube with the fork spring removed and the leg fully compressed

Rear shock absorber

Spring free length:	
600 models	148.9 mm (5.86 in)
1000 H, J models	137.4 mm (5.41 in)
1000 K, L, M, N models	177.1 mm (6.97 in)
Service limit:	
600 models	146.0 mm (5.75 in)
1000 H, J models	134.5 mm (5.30 in)
1000 K, L, M, N models	173.6 mm (6.83 in)

6

Torque settings

	kgf m	lbf ft
Fork top bolt:		
600 models	2.2	16.0
1000 models	2.3	17.0
Damper rod socket (Allen) bolt	2.0	14.5
Damper rod locknut - 1000 K models onward	2.0	14.5
Triple clamp (yoke) bolts:		
Top		
All 600 models and 1000 H, J models	1.1	8.0
1000 K models onward	2.3	17.0
Bottom:		
600 models	3.5	25.0
1000 models	5.0	36.0
Steering stem adjuster nut (see text):		
600 models	2.2	16.0
1000 models	2.5	18.0
Steering stem top nut	10.3	76.0
Handlebar pinch bolts	2.7	20.0
Anti-dive cover bolts	0.4	2.8
Swingarm pivot nut:		
600 models	6.5	47.0
1000 H, J, K, L, M, N models	11.0	80.0
1000 P models onward	10.8	78.0
Rear shock absorber mounting bolts:		
600 models	5.5	40.0
1000 H, J, K, L, M, N models	4.5	33.0
1000 P models onward	4.2	30.0
Rear shock absorber damper rod locknut - 600 models	6.5	47.0
Rear shock absorber linkage pivot bolts:		
600 models	5.5	40.0
1000 H and J models	4.5	33.0
1000 K models onward:		
Connecting link to frame bolt	6.0	43.0
All other bolts - K, L, M, N models	4.5	33.0
All other bolts - P models onward	4.2	30.0
Torque arm mounting bolt	2.2	16.0
Left footpeg bracket bolts - 600 models	2.7	20.0
Muffler (exhaust) mounting bolt and clamp bolts	2.2	16.0

1 General description

All models covered in this manual employ a diamond-shaped frame which uses the engine unit as a stressed member. The frame is constructed in box-section steel.

Front suspension is by a pair of oil-damped, coil spring, telescopic fork legs. The 1000 H, J and all 600 models incorporate an anti-dive system on the left fork leg which increases the damping rate of the forks under braking.

Rear suspension is by Honda's Pro-Link system in which the swingarm acts on a gas-charged, hydraulically-damped suspension unit via a two-piece linkage.

2 Frame and suspension -
maintenance and adjustments

1 For information on the following operations refer to the relevant Section of Chapter 1.

a) *Checking the suspension and steering (front and rear).*
b) *Adjusting the suspension settings.*

3 Forks - removal and installation

Removal

1 Remove the front wheel as described in Chapter 7. On 1000 P models onward, remove the two secondary master cylinder mounting bolts (these also secure reflectors on US models) and free the cylinder from the left fork leg. Also on 1000 P models onward, remove the brake pipe union retaining block from the right fork leg. Remove the front mudguard (fender).

2 Carefully prise off the circlip from the top of each fork tube **(see illustration)**. Slacken each handlebar casting pinch bolt and lift the castings off the fork tubes **(see illustration)**. Support each handlebar assembly to prevent straining the hydraulic hose(s) and control

cables and keep the master cylinder(s) upright to prevent the possible leakage of fluid.

3 If the fork legs are to be dismantled, it is preferable to slacken the top bolts whilst they are still held in the triple clamps (yokes). To do this, first remove the cap from the top of the fork, then on all models with air-assisted forks depress the air valve to release the air pressure from each fork leg. Slacken the fork top bolts with a suitable spanner.

3.2a Prise the circlip off of the top of the fork tube . . .

3.2b . . . slacken the handlebar pinch bolt and lift the handlebar off of the tube

3.4 Slacken the triple clamp pinch bolts and remove the fork legs with a twisting motion

3.5a Position the fork legs as described in text . . .

4 Slacken the top and bottom triple clamp (yoke) pinch bolts and remove the forks by twisting them and pulling them downwards (see illustration).

HAYNES HiNT *If the forks are seized in the triple clamps (yokes), spray the area with penetrating oil and allow time for it to soak in.*

Installation

5 Installation is by the reverse of the removal procedure. Remove all traces off corrosion from the triple clamps (yokes) and slide the fork legs back into place. Position each leg so that the groove on the fork tube aligns with the top surface of the top triple clamp then tighten the top and bottom triple clamp pinch bolts to the specified torque setting (see illustrations).

6 If the fork legs have been dismantled, the fork top bolts should now be tightened to the specified torque setting (see illustration).

7 Refit the handlebar castings to the top of the fork tubes, ensuring that the lug on the bottom of each casting is correctly located with the cutout on the top triple clamp (yoke), and tighten the pinch bolts to the specified torque setting. Install the circlip in the groove at the top of each fork leg.

8 Install the front wheel and fender as

3.5b . . . and tighten the triple clamp pinch bolts to the specified torque setting

described in Chapter 7. Check the fork air pressure (where applicable) as described in Chapter 1 and refit the caps to the top of each fork tube. Finally, check the operation of the front forks and brake before riding the machine.

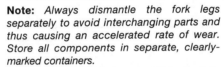

4 Forks - disassembly and reassembly

Note: *Always dismantle the fork legs separately to avoid interchanging parts and thus causing an accelerated rate of wear. Store all components in separate, clearly-marked containers.*

1 Remove the fork legs as described in Section 3. Clamp the fork slider (lower leg) securely in a vice equipped with soft jaws, being careful not to overtighten it. Then slacken the damper assembly retaining socket (Allen) bolt which passes up through the bottom of the slider. Release the fork leg from the vice.

1000 K models onwards

2 Unscrew the top bolt until it is free from the top of the fork tube (see illustration overleaf). If the top bolt was not slackened whilst the tube was installed in the triple clamps, it will be necessary to temporarily hold the tube carefully in the vice whilst it is

3.6 If the fork leg has been dismantled, tighten the top bolt to the specified torque setting

slackened; take care not to damage the tube's surface. Invert the leg over a suitable container and pump the tube in and out to remove as much oil as possible.

3 Carefully clamp the fork slider (lower leg) in the vice and unscrew the top bolt from the damper rod whilst retaining the locknut with a suitable open-ended spanner. With the aid of an assistant, push the spring spacer downwards, to compress the fork spring, and remove the stepped spring collar from the damper rod. Slowly release the spacer until all the spring pressure has been relieved, then withdraw the spring seats (one each side of the spacer), spacer and fork spring from the tube. Invert the fork leg over the container again and pump the damper rod in and out to remove any more fork oil.

4 Carefully prise out the dust seal from the top of the slider to reveal the fork seal retaining circlip. Carefully remove the circlip whilst taking care not to damage the surface of the tube. Remove the previously-slackened damper socket (Allen) bolt from the bottom of the slider and withdraw the damper assembly from the tube.

5 To separate the tube from the slider it will be necessary to displace the top bush and oil seal. The lower bush should not pass through the top bush, and this can be used to good effect. Push the tube gently inwards until it stops against the damper seat (take care not to do this forcibly or the seat may be damaged), then pull the tube sharply outwards until the lower bush strikes the top bush. Repeat this operation until the top bush and seal are tapped out of the slider.

6 With the tube removed, the oil seal, washer (noting which way up it is fitted) and top bush can be slid off its upper end. Slip the oil seal protector off the top of the slider on 1000 P models onward. Tip the damper seat out of the slider.

Caution: Do not remove the lower bush from the tube unless it is to be renewed..

7 To dismantle the damper assembly first remove the damper rod locknut from its upper end. Clamp the damper assembly upside down in a vice equipped with soft jaws, taking care not to overtighten and damage its

6

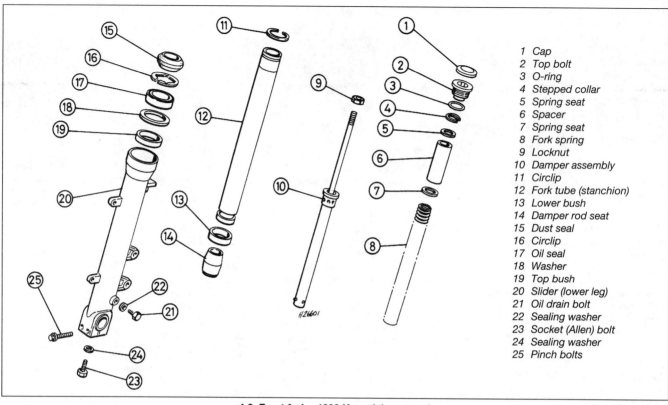

1 Cap
2 Top bolt
3 O-ring
4 Stepped collar
5 Spring seat
6 Spacer
7 Spring seat
8 Fork spring
9 Locknut
10 Damper assembly
11 Circlip
12 Fork tube (stanchion)
13 Lower bush
14 Damper rod seat
15 Dust seal
16 Circlip
17 Oil seal
18 Washer
19 Top bush
20 Slider (lower leg)
21 Oil drain bolt
22 Sealing washer
23 Socket (Allen) bolt
24 Sealing washer
25 Pinch bolts

4.2 Front fork - 1000 K models onward

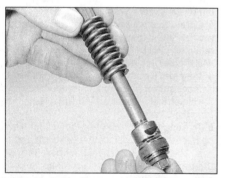

4.9a Refit the damper rod rebound spring and insert the damper rod into the damper body

surface. Note the circlip at the bottom of the damper. Depress the bottom piece with a suitably sized bar and prise out the circlip using a small flat-bladed screwdriver. The bottom piece can then be pushed out of position using the damper rod itself, and the damper rod and spring withdrawn from the damper body.

8 After checking the fork components for wear and damage as described in the next Section, reassembly can commence. Ensure that all components are clean. Always fit a new oil seal. The bushes can be re-used, but only if they are in perfect condition. It is recommended, however, that they are renewed as a precautionary measure. The lower bush is split to permit its removal over the end of the tube. Do not open the split any more than is essential to ease it into place. Renew all O-rings as a matter of course.

9 Refit the rebound spring to the damper rod (see illustration). Apply clean fork oil to the piston ring and bottom piece O-ring and insert the rod and bottom piece into the damper body (see illustration). Secure the bottom piece in position with the circlip, ensuring that it is correctly located in its groove (see illustration). Refit the damper rod locknut so that its chamfered edge faces downwards (towards the piston), screwing it fully onto the damper rod (see illustration).

10 On 1000 P models onward, install the protector on the fork slider. On all models, insert the damper assembly into the upper

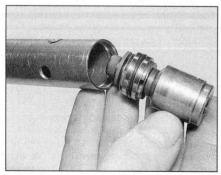

4.9b Fit the bottom piece into the damper body...

4.9c ...and secure it in position with the circlip

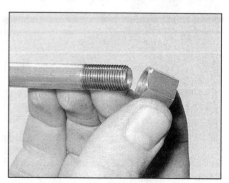

4.9d Fit the damper rod locknut so that its chamfered edge is facing downwards

end of the tube **(see illustration)**. Pass a length of wooden dowel, or the fork spring and spacer, up through the tube to hold the damper assembly in position and fit the damper seat to the end of the damper body **(see illustration)**. Oil the tube and bush, and support it vertically with the damper piston uppermost. Lower the slider over the tube assembly and refit the damper socket (Allen) bolt using a new sealing washer **(see illustration)**. Apply thread-locking compound to the threads of the bolt and tighten it to the specified torque setting. **Note:** *If necessary, temporarily install the fork spring, spacer and top bolt to stop the damper assembly from rotating as the bolt is tightened.*

11 Oil the top bush and slide it down over the tube, followed by the washer, ensuring that the washer is fitted with its chamfered surface downwards. Smear the **new** oil seal lips with grease and slide it over the tube so that its marked surface is facing upwards (away from the slider). Drive the oil seal into place in the slider **(see illustration)**. Once the oil seal is correctly seated remove the drift and plain washer and refit the circlip, ensuring that it is correctly located in its groove **(see illustration)**. Lubricate the lips of the dust seal then slide it down the fork tube and press it into position **(see illustration)**.

 HAYNES HiNT *A length of tubing with an inside diameter slightly larger than the fork tube and an outside diameter slightly smaller than the slider recess can be used to drive the oil seal into place. Place a large plain washer against the oil seal and then tap it home using the tubular drift as a form of slide-hammer. Take care not to scratch the tube during this operation; it is best to make sure that the tube is pushed fully inwards so that any accidental scoring is confined to the area above the seal.*

12 Slowly pour in the specified amount and grade of fork oil whilst pushing the damper rod up and down. Once the oil has been added, slowly pump the fork tube in and out at least five times, and pump the damper rod

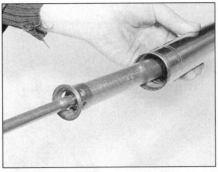

4.10a Insert the damper assembly into the upper end of the tube

at least another 10 times. This will ensure that the fork oil is evenly distributed.

13 Fully insert both the tube and damper rod then check the fork oil level. Add or subtract fork oil until the oil is at the specified level listed in the Specifications Section of this Chapter.

14 Clamp the slider securely in a vice and fully extend the damper rod. Secure a piece of wire around the rod; the wire can then be used to hold the rod in the extended position whilst the stepped spring collar is installed. Ensure that the locknut is screwed fully onto the damper rod and that there is at least 10.5 mm (0.41 in) between the top surface of the nut and the damper rod end.

15 Insert the fork spring, ensuring that its tapered end is at the bottom, followed by a spring seat, the spacer, and a second spring seat **(see illustrations)**. With the aid of an

4.11a Tap the oil seal into place with a suitable tubular drift . . .

4.11c . . . and refit the dust seal

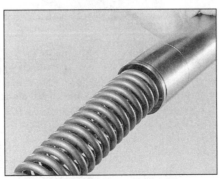

4.15a Install the fork spring as described in text . . .

4.10b Refit the damper seat to the end of the damper body and lower the slider down over the fork tube assembly

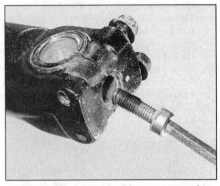

4.10c Apply thread-locking compound to the damper assembly bolt and tighten it to the specified torque setting

4.11b . . . then secure it in position with its circlip . . .

4.15b . . . and refit the spacer and spring seats

6

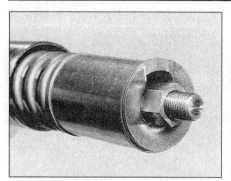

4.15c Compress the spring and install the stepped spring collar

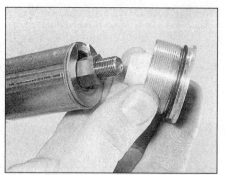

4.16a Screw the top bolt fully onto the damper rod . . .

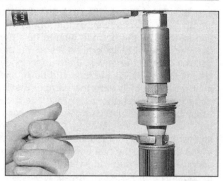

4.16b . . . and tighten it to the specified torque setting

assistant push down on the spacer, compressing the fork spring, whilst retaining the damper rod and install the stepped spring collar **(see illustration)**.

16 Fit a new O-ring to the top bolt and screw it fully onto the damper rod by hand, until it touches the locknut, then tighten the locknut to the specified torque setting (if possible) **(see illustrations)**. Screw the top bolt into the fork tube. **Note:** *The top bolt can be tightened*

to the specified torque setting at this stage if it can be held firmly enough but do not risk over-tightening and damaging the tube in the vice. A better method is to tighten the top bolt when the fork leg has been installed and are securely clamped in the triple clamps **(see illustration 3.6)**.

1000 H, J and all 600 models

17 Extend the fork leg and unscrew the top

bolt from the top of the tube, whilst taking care not to allow it to be expelled forcibly by spring pressure, as the last threads of the bolt are unscrewed. Once the top bolt has been removed withdraw the spacer, spring seat and fork spring, noting which way up the spring is fitted **(see illustration)**. Invert the fork leg over a suitable container and pump the tube vigorously to expel as much oil as possible.

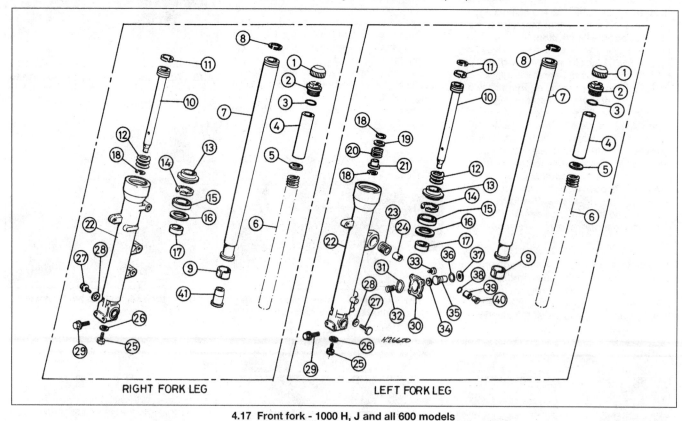

RIGHT FORK LEG

LEFT FORK LEG

4.17 Front fork - 1000 H, J and all 600 models

1 Cap	7 Fork tube	14 Circlip	22 Slider (lower leg)	29 Pinch bolts	35 Piston
2 Top bolt and air	(stanchion)	15 Oil seal	23 Needle roller	30 Anti-dive valve	36 O-ring
valve	8 Circlip	16 Washer	bearing	cover	37 Piston seal
3 O-ring	9 Lower bush	17 Top bush	24 Collar	31 Cover O-ring	38 Circlip
4 Spacer	10 Damper rod	18 Circlip	25 Socket (Allen) bolt	32 Spring	39 Bush
5 Spring seat	11 Piston ring	19 Spring seat	26 Sealing washer	33 Socket (Allen)	40 Collar
6 Fork spring	12 Rebound spring	20 Spring	27 Oil drain bolt	bolts	41 Damper rod seat
	13 Dust seal	21 Oil lock valve	28 Sealing washer	34 Rubber stopper	

4.21a On 1000 H, J and all 600 models lubricate the piston O-ring and refit the piston to the cover

4.21b Insert the piston collar . . .

4.21c . . . and secure it in position with the circlip

18 Prise out the dust seal from the top of the slider to gain access to the oil seal retaining circlip. Carefully remove the circlip whilst taking care not to scratch the surface of the tube. Remove the damper rod retaining socket (Allen) bolt from the bottom of the slider. If the damper rod slackens but rotates in the tube rather than unscrewing, refit the spring, spring seat and spacer, and top bolt. Compress the leg to hold the damper rod in place whilst the bolt is unscrewed. The tube can then be separated from the slider as described above in paragraph 5. Note that there is only a damper rod seat fitted to the right fork assembly.

19 To remove the damper rod from the left tube, prise the first circlip off the damper rod and withdraw the oil lock valve, spring and spring seat. Prise off the second circlip then

tip the damper rod and rebound spring out of the tube. On the right fork leg simply remove the circlip from the damper rod to permit its removal.

20 To disassemble the anti-dive assembly on the left slider, remove the four socket bolts which retain the assembly and remove it from the slider. Prise off the circlip from the piston collar, remove the collar, and withdraw the piston. Check all components for signs of wear and damage, renewing as necessary. Renew the piston and cover O-rings as a matter of course.

21 Anti-dive components are installed by a reverse of the removal procedure. Lubricate the piston and O-ring and insert it into the cover **(see illustration)**. Refit the collar to the piston and secure in position with the circlip **(see illustrations)**. Refit the spring to the

piston, ensuring that its tapered end is facing the piston and refit the assembly to the slider using a new O-ring **(see illustration)**. Apply thread-locking agent to the retaining bolts and tighten them to the specified torque setting **(see illustration)**. Once the cover is in position check that the piston moves smoothly and returns quickly under spring pressure.

22 Reassembly can commence once all components have been cleaned and checked as described in paragraph 8 and the next section.

23 Refit the rebound spring to the damper rod and slide it into place in the tube **(see illustration)**. On the left fork leg refit the first circlip to its groove on the damper rod followed by the spring seat, spring and oil lock valve **(see illustrations)**. Secure all

4.21d Ensure the spring is fitted as described in text

4.21e Apply thread-locking compound to the anti-dive cover bolts and tighten them to the specified torque setting

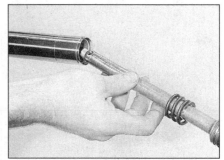

4.23a Refit the rebound spring to the damper rod and insert the rod into the fork tube

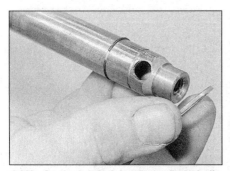

4.23b On the left fork leg fit the first circlip to the damper rod, followed by the spring seat . . .

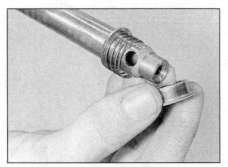

4.23c . . . spring and oil lock valve . . .

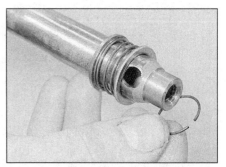

4.23d . . . and then secure all components in position with a second circlip

6

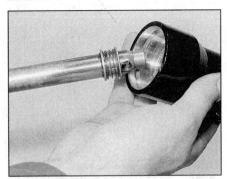

4.24a Insert the tube assembly into the slider - left leg shown

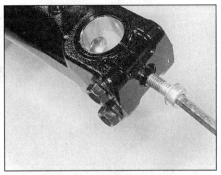

4.24b Apply thread-locking compound to the damper rod bolt and tighten it to the specified torque setting

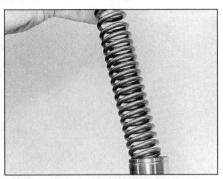

4.27a Install the fork spring as described in text . . .

components in position with the second circlip, ensuring it is correctly fitted in its groove **(see illustration)**. On the right fork leg refit the circlip to the groove on the damper rod and fit the damper rod seat to the end of the rod.

24 Pass a length of dowel, or the fork spring and spacer, up through the tube to hold the damper rod in place. Oil the tube and support it vertically with the damper rod uppermost. Lower the slider over the tube and refit the damper rod socket (Allen) bolt using a new sealing washer **(see illustrations)**. Apply thread-locking compound to the threads of the bolt and tighten it to the specified torque setting. **Note:** *If necessary, temporarily refit the fork spring, spacer and top bolt to prevent the damper rod from rotating.*

4.27b . . . and refit the spring seat . . .

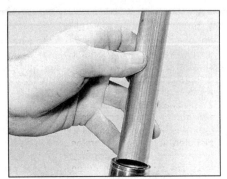

4.27c . . . and spacer

25 Refit the top bush, washer, oil seal, circlip and dust seal as described above in paragraphs 14 through 16.

26 Fill the fork leg with the specified amount and type of oil and pump the fork leg slowly to distribute the oil evenly. Compress the leg fully and check the oil level. Add or subtract oil, as necessary, until it is at the level given in the Specifications at the start of this Chapter.

27 Clamp the tube securely in a vice and insert the fork spring, ensuring that its tighter-pitched coils or tapered end (as appropriate) are/is at the bottom **(see illustration)**. Refit the spring seat and spacer and fit a new O-ring to the top bolt **(see illustrations)**. Refit the top bolt to the tube **(see illustration)**. **Note:** *The top bolt can be tightened to the specified torque setting at this stage if it can be held firmly enough, but do not risk over tightening the tube in the vice. A better method is to tighten the top bolt when the fork leg is securely clamped in the triple clamps.*

All models

28 When reassembly is complete install the fork legs in the triple clamps as described in Section 3.

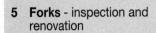

5 Forks - inspection and renovation

1 If the forks have been damaged in an accident, it is essential to inspect both triple

4.27d Fit a new O-ring to the top bolt and fit it to the fork tube

clamps (yokes), the fork tubes (stanchions) and the sliders (lower legs) for distortion and hairline cracks. Distorted components must be renewed, do not attempt to straighten them.

2 The parts most likely to wear are the sliding surfaces of the bushes. These control the play in the forks and are designed to wear before damage occurs to the tube or slider. If there are signs of scoring or obvious wear, the bushes must be renewed. Only in extreme cases will the tube or slider be worn; in these cases the affected item must be renewed **(see illustration)**.

3 Check the tube for signs of scoring. Damage of this type can be caused by dirt trapped below a damaged or worn dust seal and can be avoided by ensuring that it is renewed whenever the oil seal is renewed. If there has been impact damage, check that the tube is straight by rolling them on a flat surface. If the equipment is available the runout can be measured by setting the tube up in vee-blocks and measuring the runout with a dial gauge. If runout exceeds the maximum limit the tube must be renewed. Do not attempt to straighten a bent fork tube.

4 The oil seals should be renewed whenever they are disturbed, as should all sealing O-rings and sealing washers. Check carefully the condition of the damper rod piston ring(s) and renew if there is any doubt about their condition. Note that on 1000 K models onward, none of the damper assembly parts

5.2 Lower fork bush is split for easy removal

5.4a Inspect damper rod piston rings for damage and renew if necessary

5.4b Renew all O-rings regardless of condition

5.7 Slip out inner sleeve for access to needle roller bearings in left fork slider - 1000 P models onward

are available separately; if any part of the assembly is faulty, it must be renewed as a complete unit **(see illustrations)**.

5 Measure the free length of the fork springs; if either has settled to less than the specified length both springs must be renewed as a pair.

6 On all 600 and 1000 H and J models check the needle roller bearing and collar fitted to the left slider. If either component shows signs of wear or damage they must be renewed as a set. The bearing can be removed and installed using a drawbolt tool as described in Section 12 of this Chapter.

7 On 1000 P models onward, check the brake caliper pivot needle roller bearings set in the left slider. If they need replacing, slip out the inner sleeve and pry the dust seals from each side of the pivot using a flat-bladed screwdriver **(see illustration)**. The bearings can be removed and installed using a drawbolt tool.

8 Thoroughly clean all components and dry them ready for reassembly.

6 Steering stem - removal and installation

Caution: Although not strictly necessary, before removing the steering head it is recommended that the fuel tank be removed. This will prevent the paintwork being accidentally damaged.

1 Remove the forks as described in Section 3 of this Chapter. Trace the wiring back from the ignition switch to its block connector and disconnect it from the main wiring loom. On all 600 models remove the two bolts which secure the brake hose union to the bottom triple clamp (yoke), and on all 1000 models remove the bolt(s) which retains the brake hose guide to the bottom triple clamp.

2 Prise off the cap from the steering stem top nut and slacken and remove the nut. The top triple clamp can then be lifted off the steering stem along with the ignition switch.

3 Straighten the tabs of the adjuster nut lock

washer then, using a suitable C-spanner slacken and remove the adjuster nut locknut. Remove the lock washer and discard it; a new one must be fitted on reassembly. Support the bottom triple clamp and slacken the adjuster nut. Lift off the nut and dust seal from the top of the steering head and gently lower the bottom triple clamp and steering stem out of the frame. Lift out the upper bearing inner race, followed by the bearing itself.

4 Remove all traces of old grease from the bearings and races and check them for wear or damage as described in the following Section.

5 The steering stem is installed by a reverse of the removal procedure. Smear a liberal quantity of general purpose grease on the bearing inner and outer races.

6 Carefully lift the steering stem into position and refit the upper bearing and inner race. Apply grease to the underside of the dust seal and fit it to the steering stem. Refit the adjuster nut and tighten it using hand pressure only.

7 To preload the bearings to the torque specified by the manufacturer (see Specifications) it will be necessary to use the service tool, Pt No 07916-3710100, which consists of a socket designed to fit over the steering stem and into the cutouts of the adjuster nut. Using the service tool, tighten the adjuster nut to the specified torque setting then turn the steering stem from lock to lock approximately 5 times to settle the bearings and races in position. After preloading the bearings, slacken the adjuster nut one full turn then tighten it again to the specified torque setting. **Note:** *It is important to check the feel of the steering afterwards as described below; if it is too tight re-adjust the bearings as described below.*

8 If the service tool is not available, tighten the adjuster nut hard using a conventional C-spanner to preload the bearings then adjust as follows.

9 Slacken the adjuster nut slightly until pressure is just released, then turn it slowly clockwise until resistance is just evident. *Caution: Take great care not to apply excessive pressure because this will apply too high a loading on the bearings and*

cause premature failure. The object is to set the adjuster nut so that the bearings are under a very light loading, just enough to remove any free play.

10 Fit a **new** lock washer to the adjuster nut and bend down two opposite tabs into the grooves of the adjuster nut. Refit the locknut and tighten it finger-tight only. Hold the adjuster nut, to prevent it from moving, and tighten the locknut approximately 90° more until its slots align with the remaining lock washer tabs. Secure the locknut in position by bending up both the tabs into its slots.

11 Refit the top triple clamp to the steering stem and refit the stem top nut. Temporarily fit the fork legs, to align the triple clamps, tighten the steering stem top nut to the specified torque setting and refit the cap. Reconnect the ignition switch block connector to the main wiring loom. Refit the brake hose union or guide (as applicable), tightening its retaining bolt(s) securely.

12 Install the fork legs as described in Section 3 of this Chapter. As soon as the forks and front wheel are installed, check that the steering head bearings are correctly adjusted; referring to Chapter 1 for details.

13 Thoroughly check the operation of the front forks and brake before riding the machine.

7 Steering head bearings - inspection and renewal

1 For straight line steering to be consistently good, the steering head bearings must be in absolutely perfect condition. Even the smallest amount of wear may cause steering wobble at high speeds and judder during front wheel braking.

2 The bearing tracks of the races should be polished and free from indentations. Inspect the ball bearings for signs of wear, damage or discoloration, and examine the bearing retainer ring for signs of cracks or splits. If there are signs of wear on any of the above components both upper and lower bearing assemblies must be renewed as a set.

6

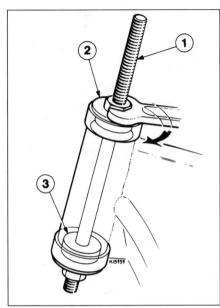

7.3 Drawbolt tool for installing bearing outer races

1 Long bolt or threaded rod
2 Thick washer
3 Guide for lower outer race

3 The outer races are an interference fit in the steering head and can be tapped from position with a suitable drift. Tap firmly and evenly around each race to ensure that it is driven out squarely. It may prove advantageous to curve the end of the drift slightly to improve access. Alternatively, the races can be removed using a slide-hammer type bearing extractor; these can often be hired from tool shops. The new outer races can be pressed into the head using a drawbolt tool **(see illustration)**, or by using a large diameter drift, such as a socket, which bears only on the outer edge of the race.

4 The lower inner race is a press fit on the steering stem and will require levering off the stem. Use two screwdrivers placed on opposite sides of the race to work it free. Once it has been removed inspect the dust seal which is fitted below it for signs of wear or damage and renew it if necessary. On

installation, first fit the dust seal, then smear grease on the stem and bearing-to-stem surface. Slide the bearing down over the stem as far as possible using hand pressure, then use a length of tubing with an internal diameter slightly larger than the steering stem to tap the new race into position. Ensure that the tubing does not come in contact with the bearing surface at any time.

8 Frame - inspection and renovation

1 The frame is unlikely to require attention unless accident damage has occurred. In some cases, renewal of the frame is the only satisfactory course of action if it is badly out of alignment. Only a few frame repair specialists have the jigs and mandrels necessary for resetting the frame to the required standards of accuracy and even then there is no easy means of assessing to what extent the frame may have been overstressed.

2 After the machine has covered a considerable mileage, it is advisable to examine the frame closely for signs of cracking or splitting at the welded joints. Rust can also cause weakness at these joints. Minor damage can be repaired by welding or brazing, depending on the extent and nature of the damage.

3 Remember that a frame which is out of alignment will cause handling problems. If misalignment is suspected as the result of an accident, it will be necessary to strip the machine completely so that the frame can be thoroughly checked, and if necessary renewed.

9 Rear shock absorber - removal and installation

1 Place the machine on its centre stand and remove both the right and left side panels. Place a block of wood under the rear wheel to prevent it from dropping when the shock

absorber mounting bolts are removed, then follow the procedure given under the relevant sub-heading.

600 models

2 Slacken and remove the shock absorber's upper and lower mounting bolts and manoeuvre the shock absorber out of the frame.

3 Installation is the reverse of the removal procedure. Check that the mounting bolts are unworn, renewing them if necessary, and apply molybdenum disulphide grease to their shanks. Fit the shock absorber so that the lug on its lower spring seat is facing upwards and install both the upper and lower mounting bolts, tightening them to the specified torque setting **(see illustrations)**.

1000 H and J models

4 Remove the three bolts which retain the left muffler (silencer) cowling and remove the cowling, noting the insulating washers positioned behind it. Follow the same procedure to remove the right muffler (silencer) cowling. Loosen both bolts on the clamp which secures the left muffler to the header (exhaust) pipe, then slacken its mounting bolt and remove the muffler from the machine. Remove both pivot bolts which secure the rear suspension connecting link to the frame and relay arm and manoeuvre the connecting link out of position. Remove the shock absorber's upper and lower mounting bolts and lower it out of the frame.

5 The shock absorber is installed by a reverse of the removal process. Check all mounting and pivot bolts for signs of wear or damage, renewing them if necessary, and smear their shanks with molybdenum disulphide grease. Manoeuvre the shock absorber into place, ensuring that the spring preload adjuster faces the right side, and refit its upper and lower mounting bolts. Tighten the shock absorber mounting bolts to the specified torque setting. Install the connecting link and refit both its pivot bolts, tightening them to the specified torque setting.

6 Check the muffler gasket for wear or damage and renew it if necessary. Install the muffler and refit its mounting bolt. Tighten

9.3a On 600 models install the rear shock absorber . . .

9.3b . . . and tighten both its upper . . .

9.3c . . . and lower mounting bolts to the specified torque setting

9.8 On 1000 K models onward, the shock absorber can be manoeuvred out the right side of the machine

both the clamp bolts and mounting bolt to their specified torque setting. Refit the muffler cowlings, not omitting the insulating washers that are fitted between each cowling and muffler, and tighten its retaining screws securely.

1000 K models onward

7 Remove the shock absorber linkage as described in Section 11.

8 Slacken and remove the shock absorber upper mounting bolt and lower the shock absorber out of the frame (see illustration).

9 The shock absorber is installed by a reverse of the removal procedure. Inspect all mounting and pivot bolts for signs of wear, renewing them if necessary, and smear their shanks with molybdenum disulphide grease. Offer up the shock absorber, ensuring that the spring preload adjuster is facing the right side, refit its upper mounting bolt and tighten it to the specified torque setting.

10 Install the shock absorber linkage as described in Section 11.

All models

11 Remove the block of wood from beneath the rear wheel and refit the sidepanels. Thoroughly check the operation of the rear suspension before riding the machine.

---

10 Rear shock absorber - disassembly, inspection and reassembly

Note: To dismantle the shock absorber it is necessary to have access to a suitable spring compressor (600 models) or a hydraulic press and special Honda service tool (1000 H, J, K, L, M, N models). If these are not available, take the unit to a Honda dealer who will have the necessary service tools to dismantle the unit.

600 models

1 Fit the spring compressor to the shock absorber and compress the spring until all spring pressure is removed from the circlip at the top of the unit. Remove the circlip and slowly release the spring compressor. Slide the upper seat, spring, dust seal, lower seat,

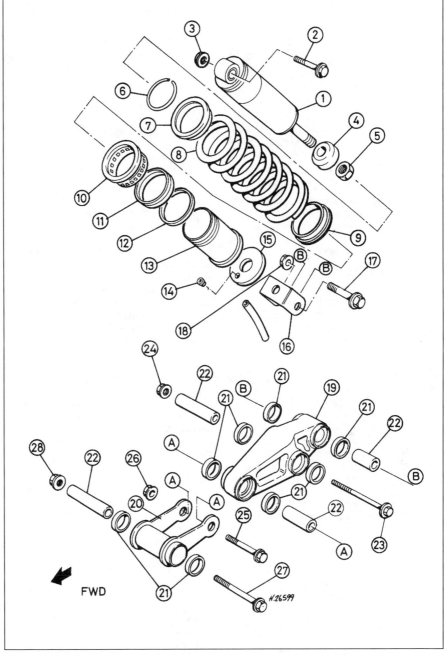

10.1 Rear shock absorber and linkage - 600 models

1 Shock absorber damper	12 Ring	22 Inner sleeves
2 Top mounting bolt	13 Spring guide	23 Relay arm-to-swingarm
3 Nut	14 Pipe union	pivot bolt
4 Damper rubber	15 Lower seat stopper	24 Nut
5 Locknut	16 Lower mounting joint	25 Connecting link-to-relay
6 Circlip	17 Shock absorber-to-relay	arm pivot bolt
7 Upper seat	arm bolt	26 Nut
8 Spring	18 Nut	27 Connecting link-to-frame
9 Lower seat	19 Relay arm	pivot bolt
10 Adjuster	20 Connecting link	28 Nut
11 Dust seal	21 Dust seals	

adjuster and spring guide off the damper assembly whilst noting exactly how they are fitted (see illustration).

2 Where fitted, remove the damper adjuster detent assembly then slacken the adjuster knob grub screw and remove the adjuster

6

10.2a If necessary, remove the damper adjuster detent assembly . . .

10.2b . . . and the adjuster knob

from the shock **(see illustrations)**. Slide the damper rubber and lower seat stopper away from the lower mounting joint and slacken the locknut. Remove the mounting joint and locknut and slide the seat stopper and damper rubber off the damper rod.

3 Inspect the damper unit for signs of oil leakage or damage.

4 Centre punch the damper unit body at a point approximately 25 mm (1.0 in) from the top surface of the body. Place the unit inside a large clear plastic bag and clamp it in a vice so that the unit is upright. Inflate the bag and insert an electric drill with a sharp 2 - 3 mm (5/64 - 1/8 in) drill bit through the open end of the bag and carefully drill through the body of the damper unit at the point which has been centre-punched **(see illustration)**.

 Warning: The damper unit is filled with nitrogen gas and is therefore pressurised. DO NOT attempt to disassemble the unit; if faulty the damper unit must be renewed. Should it become necessary to dispose of the damper unit do not just throw it away. It is first necessary to release the gas pressure as follows.

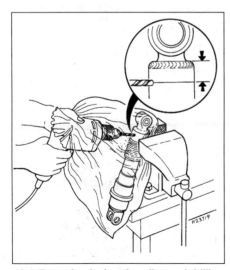

10.4 Rear shock absorber disposal drilling point - 600 models

Refer to text for details

 Warning: This operation involves drilling a hole in the damper unit body and it is essential that proper eye protection is worn.
As shown in the accompanying figures, the manufacturer specifies that the drill and damper be placed inside a plastic bag during the operation as protection against the escaping gas. Do not drill the hole any farther down the body than is specified, otherwise you may drill into the oil chamber, causing oil to be expelled under pressure. Also ensure that the drill bit is sharp; a blunt bit could cause an excessive build-up of heat which could lead to an explosion and severe personal injury.
Unless the owner feels that he/she has the necessary skill and experience to carry out this operation, it is recommended that the unit be taken to a Honda Service Agent for disposal.

5 If the damper unit is in a serviceable condition, go on to check the rest of its components. Remove the inner sleeve from the upper mounting lug and check both the sleeve, bush and dust seals and caps for wear or damage and renew as necessary. If damaged, both the collar and bush must be renewed as a pair. Carefully prise the dust seals and caps out of position using a small flat-bladed screwdriver; the rubber bush can be removed and installed using a drawbolt arrangement as described in Section 12. Apply molybdenum disulphide grease to the outer surface of the inner sleeve before inserting it into the rubber bush.

10.9 On 1000 models check the operation of the preload adjuster as described in text

6 Measure the free length of the shock absorber spring. If it has been set to less than the service limit, given in the Specifications at the start of this Chapter, it must be renewed. Check all other shock absorber components for signs of wear or damage, renewing them as necessary.

7 Reassemble the unit as follows. Slide the damper rubber onto the damper rod, ensuring that its tapered surface faces the damper unit, and refit the lower seat stopper. Apply thread-locking compound to the threads of the damper rod and screw the locknut fully onto it. Screw the mounting joint onto the damper rod until it is tight against the locknut then tighten the locknut to the specified torque setting. Slide the damper rubber and seat stopper down on to the mounting joint, ensuring that the joint is correctly positioned between tabs on the seat stopper.

8 Refit the spring guide to the damper, locating the slot in the guide with the tab on the seat stopper. Slide on the preload adjuster, ensuring that it is the correct way around, followed by the lower seat, dust seal, spring and upper seat. Compress the spring, using the specified spring compressor, and refit the circlip to the top of the damper. Check that the circlip is correctly located in its groove and slowly release the spring compressor.

1000 H and J models

9 Before disassembling the shock absorber, check the operation of the preload adjuster **(see illustration)**. Inspect the adjuster for signs of leakage or damage, and check that its adjuster knob turns freely from the HIGH to LOW settings. Check the operation of the adjuster by measuring the stroke of the adjuster whilst turning the knob from the LOW to the HIGH setting. It should have a stroke of approximately 9 mm (0.35 in). If this is not the case, the shock absorber must be disassembled and the adjuster renewed.

10 As mentioned at the very beginning of this section, a service tool (Pt No 07964-ME90000) and hydraulic press are required to disassemble the shock absorber safely. To disassemble the unit, first remove the screw from the lower spring seat and set the preload adjuster to the LOW position. Fit the service tool to the top of the damper unit and position the shock absorber upright in the press so that its lower spring seat is securely supported. Carefully use the hydraulic press to compress the unit until all spring pressure is released from the circlip fitted below the lower spring seat. Then remove the circlip and slowly release the hydraulic pressure on the spring.

11 Remove the shock absorber from the press and slide the lower seat, dust seal and spring off the damper **(see illustration)**. Slide off both the upper spring seats, noting how they are fitted, followed by the stopper ring and preload adjuster.

12 Inspect the shock absorber components as described above in paragraphs 3, 5 and 6.

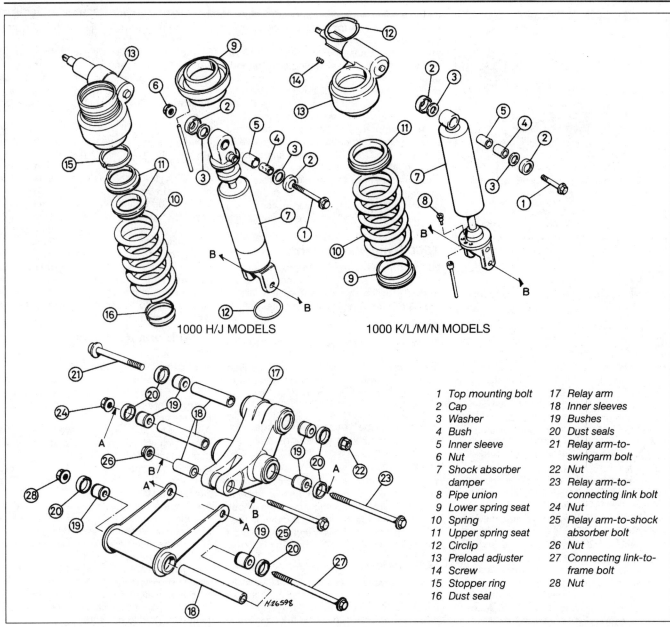

10.11 Rear shock absorber and linkage - 1000 models

1 Top mounting bolt
2 Cap
3 Washer
4 Bush
5 Inner sleeve
6 Nut
7 Shock absorber
   damper
8 Pipe union
9 Lower spring seat
10 Spring
11 Upper spring seat
12 Circlip
13 Preload adjuster
14 Screw
15 Stopper ring
16 Dust seal

17 Relay arm
18 Inner sleeves
19 Bushes
20 Dust seals
21 Relay arm-to-
   swingarm bolt
22 Nut
23 Relay arm-to-
   connecting link bolt
24 Nut
25 Relay arm-to-shock
   absorber bolt
26 Nut
27 Connecting link-to-
   frame bolt
28 Nut

Note: *If necessary, the damper unit can be disposed using the information in paragraph 4 whilst noting that the unit should be centre punched at a point approximately 13 mm (0.5 in) UP from the LOWER surface of the damper, and that the unit should be gripped UPSIDE DOWN in the vice while the hole is drilled (**see illustration**).*

13 The shock absorber is reassembled as follows. First slide the preload adjuster onto the damper ensuring that its screw is located in the slot in the upper mounting joint. Next refit the stopper ring, both the upper spring seats, ensuring they are fitted in their original positions, and the dust seal. Slide the spring onto the assembly ensuring that its tighter-pitched coils are at the bottom. Fit the lower

seat and align its screw hole with the small circular recess on the damper body.

14 Refit the service tool to the top of the damper unit and fit the assembly to the press ensuring that the lower seat is securely supported. Use the press to compress the spring and refit the circlip to the damper body. Check that the circlip is correctly located in its groove and then slowly release the pressure and remove the assembly from the press. Check that the hole in the lower seat is still aligned with the recess in the damper and install the screw, tightening it securely.

1000 K, L, M and N models

15 Before disassembling the shock absorber test the preload adjuster as described above

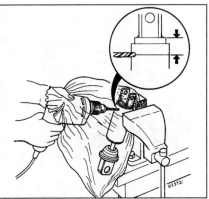

10.12 Rear shock absorber disposal drilling point - 1000 H and J models

Refer to text for details

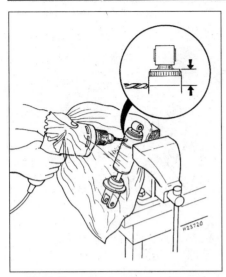

10.18 Rear shock absorber disposal drilling point - 1000 K, L, M, N models

Refer to text for details

in paragraph 9.

16 To disassemble the shock absorber service tool (Pt No 07KMF-MS20100) and an hydraulic press will be needed. To disassemble the unit, first remove the screw from the preload adjuster and set the preload adjuster to the LOW position. Fit the service tool to the upper end of the shock absorber and fit the assembly in the press ensuring that the lower mounting point is securely supported. Carefully use the press to compress the spring until the spring pressure is removed from the circlip fitted above the preload adjuster. Prise the circlip out of its groove and then slowly release the pressure on the spring and remove the assembly from the press.

17 Remove the service tool and slide the circlip, preload adjuster, upper spring seat, spring and lower spring seat off the damper **(see illustration 10.11)**.

18 Inspect all components as described above in paragraphs 3, 5 and 6. **Note:** *If necessary, the damper unit can be disposed of using the information in paragraph 4 noting that the body should be centre-punched, and*

the hole drilled, at a point approximately 13 mm (0.5 in) from the top surface of the damper body **(see illustration)**.

19 The shock absorber is reassembled as follows. Slide the lower spring seat, spring, upper spring seat, preload adjuster and the circlip onto the damper unit and fit the service tool to the upper end of the assembly. Fit the assembly into the press, ensuring it is securely supported, and compress the spring until the snap can be fitted to the groove in the damper. Once the circlip is correctly located, slowly release the pressure on the spring and remove the shock absorber from the press. Align the screw hole of the preload adjuster with the small circular recess on the damper body and refit the screw, tightening it securely.

1000 P models onward

20 With the exception of the top mounting eye bush and seals, no replacement parts are available for the shock absorber. If it fails, it must therefore be replaced with a new unit.

All models

21 Install the shock absorber in the frame as described in the previous Section and reset the preload adjustment to the required position. Thoroughly check the operation of the rear suspension before riding the machine.

11 Rear shock absorber linkage - removal and installation

1 Place the machine on its centre stand and place a block of wood under the rear wheel to prevent it from dropping when the shock absorber linkage bolts are removed, then follow the procedure given under the relevant sub-heading.

600 models

2 Remove both the left and right sidepanels. Slacken and remove the shock absorber lower mounting bolt and the relay arm to swingarm pivot bolt. Remove the connecting link to frame pivot bolt and lower the relay arm and connecting link assembly away from the

machine. Remove the pivot bolt which secures the connecting link to the relay arm and separate the two components.

3 Withdraw the inner sleeves from the relay arm and connecting link and inspect all components for wear or damage, as described in the following Section **(see illustration 10.1)**. Install the linkage as follows.

4 Lubricate all the seals, needle roller bearings, inner sleeves and the pivot bolt shanks with molybdenum disulphide grease. Insert all the inner sleeves and refit the connecting link to the relay arm, tightening the pivot bolt to the specified torque setting.

5 Install the connecting link and relay arm assembly in the machine and refit the connecting link to frame bolt, tightening it to the specified torque setting **(see illustration)**. **Note:** *The linkage must be fitted so that the UP mark on the side of the relay arm is facing upwards.* Fit the relay arm to swingarm pivot bolt and the shock absorber lower bolt and tighten both to the specified torque setting **(see illustrations)**. Refit the left and right.

1000 H and J models

6 Remove the left muffler and connecting link as described in paragraph 4 of Section 9.

7 Slacken and remove the shock absorber lower mounting bolt and the relay arm to swingarm pivot bolt and remove the relay arm from the machine.

8 Withdraw the inner sleeves from the connecting link and relay arm and inspect all components for wear or damage, as described in the following Section, before installing the linkage as follows **(see illustration 10.11)**.

9 Lubricate all the seals, needle roller bearings, bushes, inner sleeves and pivot bolts with molybdenum disulphide grease and slide all the inner sleeves into position. Install the relay arm and fit the relay arm-to-swingarm pivot bolt, followed by the shock absorber lower mounting bolt, tightening both to the specified torque setting. Refit the connecting link and tighten both its pivot bolts to the specified torque setting.

10 Install the muffler as described in Section 9, paragraph 6.

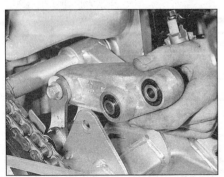

11.5a On 600 models the relay arm must be installed with the UP mark facing upwards

11.5b Fit the relay arm to swingarm pivot bolt . . .

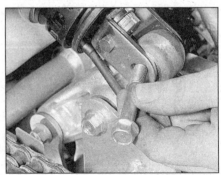

11.5c . . . and the shock absorber lower mounting bolt

11.11a On 1000 K models onward remove the pivot side covers . . .

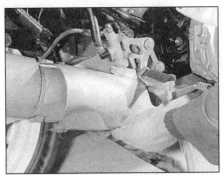

11.11b . . . and muffler cowlings as described in text

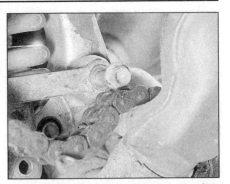

11.14 Install the relay arm and connecting link individually and insert the relay arm to connecting arm pivot bolt

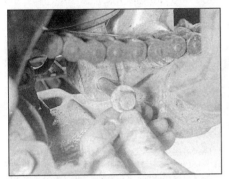

11.15a Install the shock absorber lower mounting bolt . . .

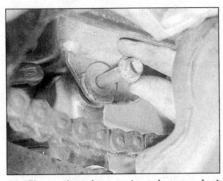

11.15b . . . the relay arm to swingarm pivot bolt . . .

11.15c . . . and the connecting link to frame pivot

1000 K models onward

11 Remove the left sidepanel, then slacken the two bolts which retain the left pivot side cover and remove the cover **(see illustration)**. Remove the five retaining bolts from the left muffler cowling, noting the correct position of its mounting collars, and lower the cowling away from the muffler. Remove the right pivot side cover and muffler cowling in a similar way **(see illustration)**.

12 Slacken and remove the shock absorber lower mounting bolt, the connecting link to frame pivot bolt and the relay arm to swingarm pivot bolt, then remove the nut from the connecting link to relay arm pivot bolt. Lift up the rear wheel, to gain the clearance necessary to remove the connecting link to relay arm bolt, and place another block under the wheel to hold it in that position. Withdraw the bolt and remove the linkage components from the machine.

13 Withdraw the inner sleeves from the connecting link and relay arm and inspect the components for wear or damage, as described in the following Section **(see illustration 10.11)**. Install them as follows.

14 Lubricate all the seals, needle roller bearings, bushes, inner sleeves and pivot bolts with molybdenum disulphide grease and slide all the inner sleeves into position. Offer up the linkage components, ensuring that the hole in the connecting link is on the right side,

and fit the relay arm to connecting link pivot bolt **(see illustration)**.

15 Lower the rear wheel back down to its original height and refit the shock absorber lower mounting bolt, the relay arm to swingarm pivot bolt and the connecting link to frame pivot bolt **(see illustrations)**. Tighten all bolts to their specified torque settings.

16 Install the muffler cowlings, not omitting the mounting collars, and tighten the retaining bolts securely. Refit both pivot side covers, tightening their retaining screws securely. Install the sidepanels.

All models

17 Remove the block of wood from beneath the rear wheel and push the machine off the centre stand. Thoroughly check the operation of the rear suspension before riding the machine.

12 Rear shock absorber linkage
- inspection and renovation

1 Thoroughly clean all components, removing all traces of dirt, corrosion and old grease.
2 Inspect all components closely, looking for obvious signs of wear such as heavy scoring, or for damage such as cracks or distortion.
3 Carefully lever out the dust seals, using a flat-bladed screwdriver, and check them for signs of wear or damage; renew them if necessary. Worn bushes or bearings can be drifted out of their bores, but note that removal will destroy them; new bushes or bearings should be obtained before work commences. The new bushes or bearings should be pressed or drawn into their bores

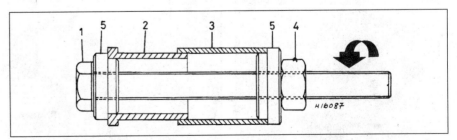

12.3 Drawbolt tool for installing bearings or bushes in rear suspension components

1 Long bolt or threaded rod
2 Bearing or bush
3 Component's housing
4 Nut
5 Large washers

6

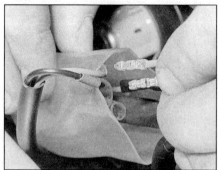

13.2a Disconnect the turn signal wiring . . .

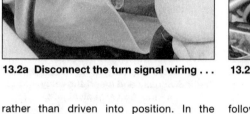

13.2b . . . and remove the left rear footpeg bracket

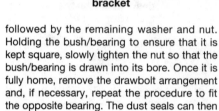

13.2c Slacken the fender mounting bolts and manoeuvre it away from the machine

rather than driven into position. In the absence of a press, a suitable drawbolt arrangement can be made up as described below **(see illustration)**.

4 It will be necessary to obtain a long bolt or a length of threaded rod from a local engineering works. The bolt or rod should be about one inch longer than the combined length of either the relay arm or connecting link, and one bearing or bush (as applicable). Also required are suitable nuts and two large robust washers. In the case of the threaded rod, fit one nut to one end of the rod and stake it in place for convenience.

5 Fit one of the washers over the bolt or rod so that it rests against the head, then pass the assembly through the relevant bore. Over the projecting end place the bush or bearing which should be greased to ease installation,

13.6a Withdraw the inner sleeve . . .

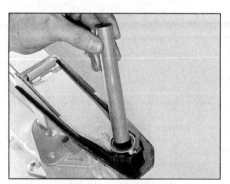

13.6b . . . and spacer and check for wear or damage

followed by the remaining washer and nut. Holding the bush/bearing to ensure that it is kept square, slowly tighten the nut so that the bush/bearing is drawn into its bore. Once it is fully home, remove the drawbolt arrangement and, if necessary, repeat the procedure to fit the opposite bearing. The dust seals can then be pressed into place.

13 Swingarm -
removal and installation

Removal

1 Remove the rear wheel as described in Chapter 7.

600 models

2 Remove both sidepanels then slacken and remove all the left rear footpeg bracket mounting bolts, then disconnect the turn signal lamp wiring and lift the footpeg bracket away from the machine **(see illustrations)**. Slacken the four bolts which secure the rear fender to the swingarm and manoeuvre the fender out of position **(see illustration)**. Straighten and remove the split pin from the torque arm to swingarm mounting bolt and remove the bolt to disconnect the two components. Note the collar which is fitted to the torque arm mounting lug on the swingarm and remove it for safekeeping. Slacken and remove the relay arm to swingarm pivot bolt and the shock absorber lower mounting bolt.

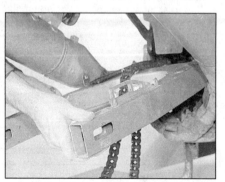

13.7a Offer up the swingarm . . .

1000 H and J models

3 Slacken the six bolts which secure the rear fender to the swingarm and manoeuvre the fender out of position. Straighten and remove the split pin from the torque arm to swingarm mounting bolt and remove the bolt to disconnect the two components. Remove the torque arm mounting collar from the swingarm for safekeeping. Remove the rear shock absorber as described in Section 9.

1000 K models onward

4 Remove the shock absorber as described in Section 9. Remove the three bolts which secure the chainguard to the swingarm and lift the guard away from the machine.

All models

5 Remove the nut from the swingarm pivot shaft and withdraw the shaft whilst supporting the swingarm. If the shaft is stuck firmly in place with corrosion apply a penetrating fluid, such as WD40, and allow time for this to work. Rotate the pivot shaft head in an attempt to free it, or in stubborn cases use a long drift to drive the shaft out. Manoeuvre the swingarm out of the frame.

6 Remove the collar from the right side of the swingarm and withdraw the inner sleeve and collar from the left side of the swingarm **(see illustrations)**. Inspect all components for wear or damage as described in the following Section before installing the swingarm as follows.

7 Lubricate the seals, bearings, collars and inner sleeve, and the pivot shaft with general

13.7b . . . and insert the pivot shaft

13.7c Refit the pivot shaft nut and tighten it to the specified torque setting

purpose grease and refit the collars and inner sleeve to the swingarm. Offer up the swingarm and insert the pivot shaft **(see illustrations)**. Refit the pivot shaft nut and tighten it to the specified torque setting **(see illustration)**.

Installation

600 models

8 Install the shock absorber lower mounting bolt and the relay arm to swingarm pivot bolt

and tighten both to the specified torque setting. Refit the torque arm mounting collar to the swingarm and install the mounting bolt. Tighten the bolt to the specified torque setting, and secure it in position with a **new** split pin. Install the rear fender and tighten its retaining bolts securely. Refit the left rear footpeg bracket, not forgetting to reconnect the turn signal wiring; tighten its mounting bolts to the specified torque setting. Refit both side panels.

1000 H and J models

9 Install the shock absorber as described in Section 9. Refit the torque arm to swingarm mounting collar and bolt and tighten the bolt to the specified torque setting. Secure the torque arm bolt in position using a **new** split pin and install the rear fender, tightening its retaining bolts securely.

1000 K models onward

10 Install the chainguard on the swingarm and tighten its retaining bolts securely. Install the shock absorber as described in Section 9.

All models

11 Install the rear wheel as described in

Chapter 7. Thoroughly check the operation of the rear suspension and brake before riding the machine.

14 Swingarm - inspection and renovation

1 Thoroughly clean all components, removing all traces of dirt, corrosion and old grease.
2 Inspect all components closely, looking for obvious signs of wear such as heavy scoring, or for damage such as cracks or distortion due to accident damage **(see illustration)**. Any damaged or worn component must be renewed.
3 Check the pivot shaft for wear. If the shank is seen to be stepped or badly scored, it must be renewed. Remove all traces of corrosion and hardened grease from the shaft before checking it for straightness by rolling it on a flat surface such as a sheet of plate glass; if it is not perfectly straight it must be renewed. Check also that its threads and those of the retaining nut are in good condition.

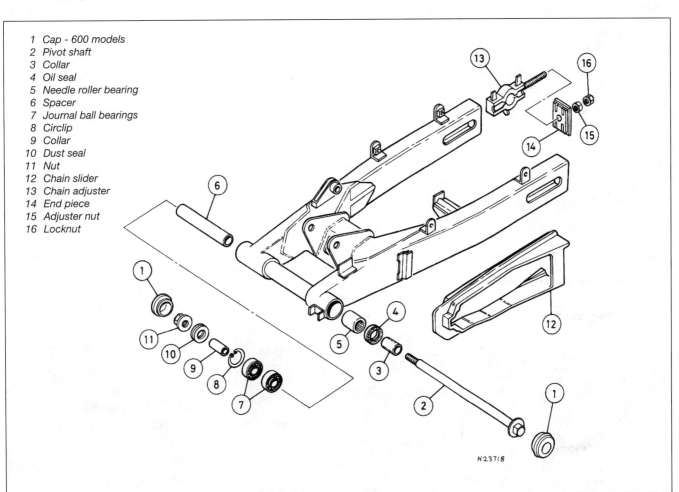

1 Cap - 600 models
2 Pivot shaft
3 Collar
4 Oil seal
5 Needle roller bearing
6 Spacer
7 Journal ball bearings
8 Circlip
9 Collar
10 Dust seal
11 Nut
12 Chain slider
13 Chain adjuster
14 End piece
15 Adjuster nut
16 Locknut

14.2 Swingarm - 600 models (1000 similar)

14.4 Carefully remove dust seals and inspect them for wear

14.5 Right side bearings are retained by a circlip

16.2a Remove instrument panel mounting bolts . . .

4 Lever out the dust seals, using a flat-bladed screwdriver, and inspect them for signs of wear or damage, renewing them if necessary (see illustration).

5 The two right side bearings (radial ball type) can be driven out of position simultaneously, using a hammer and suitable drift, once the circlip has been removed from the right side of the swingarm (see illustration). Move the drift around the edge of the inner bearing whilst drifting it out of position, so that the bearing leaves the swingarm squarely.

6 Wash the bearings thoroughly in a high flash-point solvent to remove all traces of the old grease. Check the bearing tracks and balls for wear, pitting or damage to the hardened surfaces. A small amount of side-to-side movement in the bearing is normal but no radial movement should be detectable. Check the bearings for play and roughness when they are spun by hand. All bearings will emit a small amount of noise when spun but they should not chatter or sound rough. If there is any doubt about the condition of the bearings they should be renewed. Pack the bearings with grease and drift them separately into position using a suitable tubular drift which bears only on the bearing's outer race. Secure the bearings in position with the circlip, ensuring that it is correctly seated in its groove.

7 The single needle roller bearing fitted to the left side of the swingarm can, if necessary, be

removed and renewed as described in Section 12 of this Chapter.

8 Inspect the drive chain slider fitted to the left lug of the swingarm arm. If this shows any sign of wear it should be renewed. Refer to Chapter 1 for details.

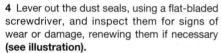

15 Footpegs, stands and controls - inspection and repair

1 At regular intervals all footpegs, the centre and side stands, the brake pedal and the gearshift lever pivots should be checked and lubricated. Check that all mounting nuts and bolts are securely fastened, using the recommended torque settings where these are given. Check that any securing split pins are correctly fitted.

2 Check that the bearing surfaces of all pivots are well greased and unworn, renewing any component that is excessively worn. If lubrication is required dismantle the assembly to ensure that the grease can be packed fully into the bearing surface. Return springs, where fitted, must be in good condition with no traces of fatigue and securely mounted.

3 If accident damage necessitates a repair, check first that the damaged component is not cracked or broken. Such damage may be repaired by welding, if the pieces are taken to an expert, but since this will destroy the finish, renewal is usually the most satisfactory course of action.

16 Instrument panel - removal and installation

1 Slacken all the screws which retain the upper fairing inner covers and remove the covers from the machine. On 1000 K, L, M and N models also remove the instrument panel cover, and on 1000 P models onward, also remove the windshield and instrument panel cover. If necessary, refer to Section 19 for further information.

2 Remove the instrument panel mounting bolts and partially withdraw the instrument panel (see illustration). Disconnect the speedometer cable by slackening its knurled retaining ring and disconnect the instrument panel block connector(s) (see illustrations). On 1000 P models onward, note how the wiring block connectors locate in their clamps on the underside of the instrument panel. Carefully lift the panel away from the machine (see illustration).

3 If necessary, the panel can be disassembled by removing all the screws from the back of the panel assembly and removing the top cover and lens. The speedometer head can then be removed once its two retaining screws have been slackened. Before removing the tachometer and temperature or fuel gauge (as applicable) it will be necessary to disconnect their electrical connections from the back of the panel. Note the original

16.2b . . . and disconnect the instrument panel wiring

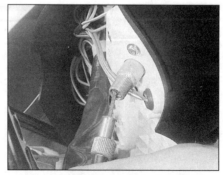

16.2c Unscrew the speedometer cable retaining ring . . .

16.2d . . . and remove the instrument panel

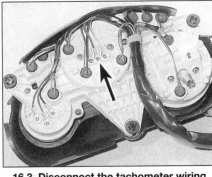

16.3 Disconnect the tachometer wiring connectors (arrowed) before attempting to remove it

position of each wire to ensure that it is fitted correctly on reassembly **(see illustration)**.

4 The instrument head itself is generally reliable, and is the least likely culprit in the event of failure, this normally being attributed to the cable (speedometer) or wiring (tachometer) rather than the instrument mechanism. If however, it is noted that the speedometer has ceased to function whilst the odometer (mileage recorder) still functions, the instrument can be assumed to have failed. The instrument heads can be considered as sealed units with no form of repair being practicable at home; if faulty the instrument head must be renewed. The only alternative is to seek the assistance of one of the companies who specialise in this type of repair.

5 The instrument panel is reassembled and installed by a straightforward reverse of the removal procedure. Fit the instruments to the panel and reconnect the wiring (where necessary) to the relevant terminals. Refit the top cover and lens to the assembly and secure it in place with its retaining screws. *Caution: Do not overtighten any of the instrument panel screws as they are easily overstressed.*

6 Check that the panel mounting rubbers are in good condition, renewing them if necessary, and install the panel. Refit the speedometer cable and tighten its retaining ring securely. Reconnect the instrument block connector(s). Refit the instrument panel mounting bolts, not omitting the mounting collars, and tighten them securely.

7 Refit the instrument panel cover (and windshield on 1000 P models onward) and inner covers (as applicable) and tighten all retaining screws securely. Check that the panel warning lights function correctly before riding the machine.

17 Speedometer drive cable - inspection and maintenance

1 If the speedometer suddenly fails, or if its movement is jerky or sluggish, check whether the cable has broken. Remove the inner cable

to check that it is adequately lubricated and not worn due to a trapped or kinked outer cable.

2 The cable should be removed at regular intervals so that it can be checked for wear and damage and so that the inner cable can be lubricated.

3 The cable is secured at its upper end by a knurled sleeve nut, and is retained by a screw at its lower end which secures it to the speedometer drive gearbox. On 1000 K models onward the speedometer drive is taken off the countershaft (output shaft), the cable location being on the engine sprocket cover, whereas on all other models it is on the left side of the front wheel. Most cables have a tight spot, but if the resistance is severe and a wavering instrument needle has been noted, the cable should be renewed. Withdraw the inner cable and clean it with solvent to remove all traces of old grease. Examine the cable for broken strands or other damage.

> **Warning: Do not check the cable for broken strands by passing it through the fingers or palm of the hand, this may well cause a painful injury if a broken strand snags the skin. It is best to wrap a piece of rag around the cable and pull the cable through it, any broken strands will snag on the rag.**

4 Regrease the cable with high melting-point grease, taking care not grease the upper six inches of the cable, nearest the instrument. If this precaution is not observed, grease will work its way into the instrument head and immobilise its sensitive movement.

5 When refitting the cable, always ensure that it has a smooth, easy run to minimise wear, and that the O-ring fitted to the lower end of the cable is in good condition. Check that the cable is secured where necessary by any clamps or ties provided to keep it away from any hot or moving parts.

18 Speedometer drive - inspection and maintenance

1000 H, J and all 600 models

1 The speedometer drive gearbox is mounted on the left side of the wheel hub, and can be removed once the wheel has been removed as described in Chapter 7. The gearbox components should be greased whenever the wheel is removed.

2 The drive plate fitted in the wheel hub can be removed once the grease seal has been levered out of position. If the tangs of the drive plate are bent or damaged it must be renewed. On installation ensure that the drive plate tabs locate with the slots in the hub and refit the grease seal. Smear a small amount of grease over the drive plate and seal lips.

3 Remove the plastic drive gear, along with the two washers, from the gearbox housing.

Remove all traces of old grease from the gearbox components and inspect them for wear and damage. If the driven gear in the housing is worn or seized in position, the gearbox must be renewed as a complete assembly (it is not possible to remove the gear from the housing). However, if only the plastic drive gear is worn this can be renewed individually. Pack the gearbox with high melting-point grease and fit the washers and drive gear.

4 Refit the speedometer gearbox to the hub ensuring that the slots in the drive gear engage correctly with the drive plate tangs. Note that the most common fault with this type of speedometer drive is that the drive plate tangs are flattened by careless refitting of the gearbox.

5 Install the front wheel as described in Chapter 7.

1000 K models onward

6 The speedometer gearbox is located in the engine sprocket cover and is driven off the end of the countershaft (output shaft). The gearbox must be regarded as a sealed unit and requires no maintenance.

7 To inspect the gearbox it is necessary to remove the engine sprocket cover as described in Chapter 2. If the driven gear is seized or fails to turn when the drive gear is rotated, the complete sprocket cover assembly must be renewed (it is not possible to remove the components from the casing). The only part available individually is the joint which links the drive gear to the countershaft.

8 Install the sprocket cover as described in Chapter 2, ensuring that the speedometer joint is fitted correctly to the speedometer drive gear and engages correctly with the drive sprocket retaining bolt.

19 Fairing - removal and installation

Caution: Do not overtighten any fairing or windshield mounting bolt or screw; both components are easily damaged if overstressed.

600 models

1 Remove both sidepanels then slacken the two screws which retain each lower fairing side cover and remove both the left and right side covers.

2 Remove the four bolts and two screws which secure the left lower fairing section in position and lower the section away from the machine **(see illustration overleaf)**. The left lower fairing section can then be removed once all its retaining bolts and screws have been released. Use the same procedure to remove the right lower fairing section.

3 Slacken the two screws which retain each upper fairing lower inner cover and remove

6

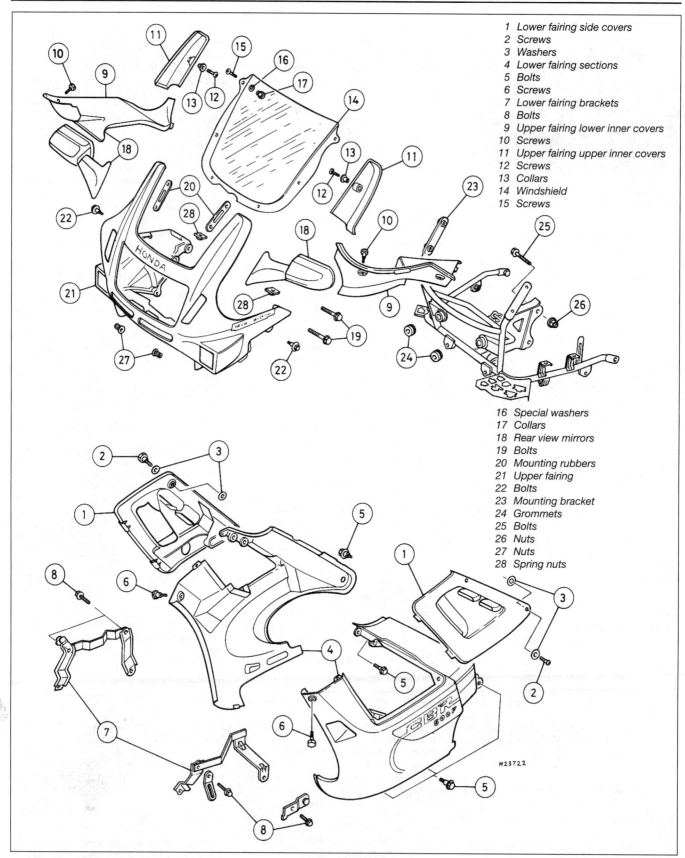

1 Lower fairing side covers
2 Screws
3 Washers
4 Lower fairing sections
5 Bolts
6 Screws
7 Lower fairing brackets
8 Bolts
9 Upper fairing lower inner covers
10 Screws
11 Upper fairing upper inner covers
12 Screws
13 Collars
14 Windshield
15 Screws

16 Special washers
17 Collars
18 Rear view mirrors
19 Bolts
20 Mounting rubbers
21 Upper fairing
22 Bolts
23 Mounting bracket
24 Grommets
25 Bolts
26 Nuts
27 Nuts
28 Spring nuts

H23722

19.2 Fairing - 600 models

19.6a On 600 models ensure the upper fairing mounting rubbers are correctly fitted . . .

19.6b . . . connect the headlamp connector . . .

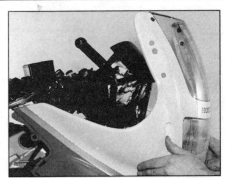

19.6c . . . and install the upper fairing

both the left and right lower inner covers from the machine.

4 Remove the single screw which retains each upper fairing upper inner cover and remove both covers from inside the fairing. Note that it is not necessary to remove the windshield in order to remove the upper fairing, but if required proceed as follows. Slacken the windshield mounting screws and remove them along with the collars and special washers. Carefully lift the windshield away from the upper fairing.

5 To remove the upper fairing, first disconnect the right and left turn signal block connectors. Displace the rubber cover of each rear view mirror to reveal the mirror mounting

bolts. Slacken the bolts and remove both left and right mirrors. Remove the two bolts which secure the lower edge of the upper fairing to the bracket and pull the fairing away from the machine, noting the two mounting rubbers fitted between the upper fairing and bracket at each rear view mirror mounting point. Disconnect the headlamp (and position lamp - UK only) wiring from the rear of the headlamp unit and remove the upper fairing.

6 The fairing is installed by a reverse of the removal procedure. Offer up the upper fairing section to the mounting bracket, ensuring that the mounting rubbers are correctly positioned between the fairing and bracket, and reconnect the headlamp (and position lamp -

UK only) wiring connectors **(see illustrations)**. Install the rear view mirrors and the upper fairing mounting bolts and tighten both the fairing and mirror mounting bolts securely **(see illustrations)**. Refit the rubber covers to conceal the mirror mounting bolts. Connect the turn signal block connectors **(see illustration)**.

7 Carefully install the windshield to the upper fairing (if removed) and refit the mounting collars and screws, ensuring that the washers are fitted between the collars and windshield **(see illustrations)**. Refit the upper inner covers to the inside of the upper fairing and tighten their retaining screws.

8 Install the upper fairing lower inner covers,

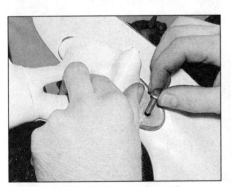

19.6d Install both the rear view mirrors . . .

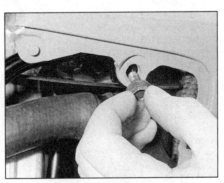

19.6e . . . and the upper fairing mounting bolts - tighten all bolts securely

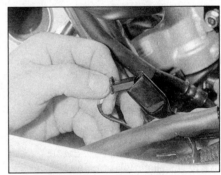

19.6f Reconnect both the left and right turn signal block connectors

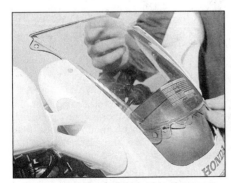

19.7a Install the windshield to the upper fairing . . .

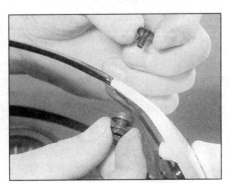

19.7b . . . and secure it in position with its mounting collars

19.7c Install the upper inner covers and tighten their retaining screws securely

6

19.8 Ensure lower inner covers locate correctly with the upper fairing on installation

19.9 Refit both lower fairing sections and tighten all mounting bolts securely

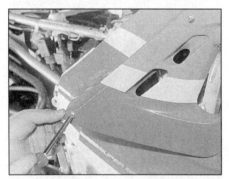

19.10 Install the lower fairing side covers and secure them in position with their retaining screws

ensuring the tabs on the covers locate correctly with the slots in the upper fairing, and secure them in position with their retaining screws **(see illustration)**.

9 Install the left lower fairing section carefully aligning its locating tabs with the upper fairing and inner cover. Refit all its mounting bolts and screws, not omitting any collars which are fitted, and tighten them all securely **(see illustration)**. Refit the right lower fairing section in a similar way tightening all its fasteners securely.

10 Refit both lower fairing side covers, ensuring their tabs locate with the grooves of the lower fairing, and secure them in position with the retaining screws **(see illustration)**. Install the sidepanels.

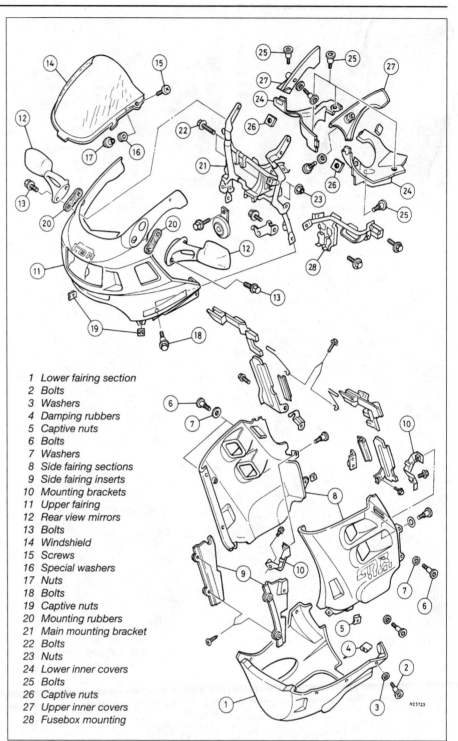

1 Lower fairing section
2 Bolts
3 Washers
4 Damping rubbers
5 Captive nuts
6 Bolts
7 Washers
8 Side fairing sections
9 Side fairing inserts
10 Mounting brackets
11 Upper fairing
12 Rear view mirrors
13 Bolts
14 Windshield
15 Screws
16 Special washers
17 Nuts
18 Bolts
19 Captive nuts
20 Mounting rubbers
21 Main mounting bracket
22 Bolts
23 Nuts
24 Lower inner covers
25 Bolts
26 Captive nuts
27 Upper inner covers
28 Fusebox mounting

19.12 Fairing - 1000 H and J models

1000 H and J models

11 Remove the two screws which secure each muffler cowling and remove the cowlings from the machine, noting the insulating washers fitted between the cowling and muffler. Remove both side panels.

12 Slacken and remove the six bolts which secure the lower fairing section (belly pan) to the side fairings and lower it away from the machine. Both the left and right side fairing sections can then be removed once their mounting bolts have been slackened; each is retained by four bolts **(see illustration)**.

13 Release the three bolts which retain the lower inner covers then lift the covers out of the upper fairing.

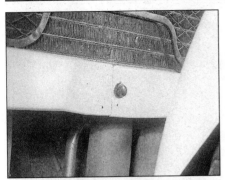

19.17a On 1000 K, L, M, N models release the three clips which secure the lower fairing sections together as described in text

19.17b Remove all the lower fairing section mounting bolts . . .

19.17c . . . and remove them from the machine

14 The windshield and upper fairing can be removed and installed as described above in paragraphs 4 to 7.

15 Installation is a reversal of the removal procedure, noting that when fitting the side fairing sections, ensure they locate correctly with the upper fairing and inner covers.

16 When installing the left and right muffler cowlings, do not omit the insulating washers behind each cowling.

1000 K, L, M and N models

17 First remove the left and right side panels. Pull out the three trim clips, situated behind the front wheel, which secure the right and left lower fairing sections together **(see illustration)**. Remove the six bolts which

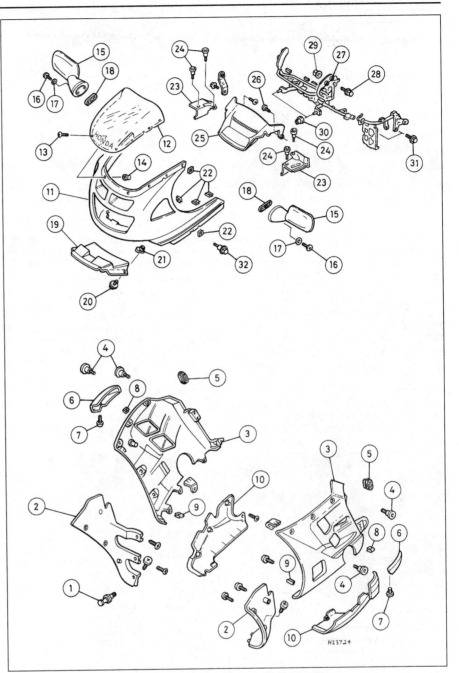

19.17d Fairing - 1000 K, L, M, N models

1 Clips	11 Upper fairing	22 Captive nuts
2 Lower fairing front inserts	12 Windshield	23 Upper fairing inner covers
3 Lower fairing sections	13 Screws	24 Bolts
4 Bolts	14 Collars	25 Instrument panel cover
5 Grommets	15 Rear view mirrors	26 Screws
6 Protectors	16 Bolts	27 Mounting bracket
7 Screws	17 Special washers	28 Bolts
8 Captive nuts	18 Mounting rubbers	29 Nuts
9 Captive nuts	19 Upper fairing air guide	30 Grommets
10 Lower fairing lower section	20 Clips	31 Bolts
	21 Fasteners	32 Bolts

retain each lower fairing section and lower both right and left sections away from the machine **(see illustrations)**.

Caution: Support the area of fairing around each clip as it is withdrawn to avoid damaging the fairing.

6

19.18a Each inner fairing cover is retained by three bolts

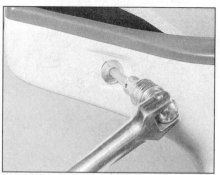

19.18b Slacken the instrument panel cover retaining bolts . . .

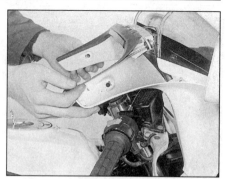

19.18c . . . and carefully remove it from the machine

18 Slacken the three bolts which secure each upper fairing inner cover in position and lift them clear **(see illustration)**. Slacken and remove the four instrument panel cover screws and partially remove the panel. Disconnect the warning lamp block connector and lift the panel away from the upper fairing **(see illustrations)**.

19 To remove the upper fairing first disconnect the headlamp and turn signal block connectors, situated on the left side of the upper fairing **(see illustration)**. Displace the rubber covers from the rear view mirror stems and slacken the mirror mounting bolts. Remove the mirrors, along with their rubber mountings, and remove the upper fairing

mounting bolts (one on each side) from the lower edge of the fairing **(see illustration)**. The fairing can then be lifted away from the machine **(see illustration)**.

20 The fairing is installed by a reverse of the removal procedure. Offer up the upper fairing section and refit its mounting bolts. Refit the rear view mirrors, noting that their rubber mountings must be fitted so that the FR mark faces forwards. Tighten the mirror and fairing mounting bolts securely then refit the protective rubber covers to the mirrors. Reconnect the headlamp and turn signal block connectors ensuring that all connectors pass through their retaining bracket.

21 Reconnect the warning lamp block

connector and install the instrument panel cover in the upper fairing, securing it in position with its mounting bolts. Refit the left and right inner covers and tighten their retaining bolts securely.

22 Install the left lower fairing section, ensuring that it is correctly located with the upper fairing, and tighten its retaining bolts securely. Then refit the right lower fairing section taking care to ensure that it locates correctly with both the upper and left lower fairing sections. Fit the three clips which secure the two halves of the lower fairing together then refit the right lower section retaining bolts, tightening them securely. Refit the side panels.

1000 P models onward

23 First remove the left and right side panels.

24 Withdraw the two trim clips to free the maintenance cover from the underside of the upper fairing **(see illustration)**. Simply pull the head of the clips out to allow the body of the clip to be withdrawn. Withdraw the two screws revealed by removal of the maintenance cover **(see illustration)**. Remove the three trim clips which secure the lower halves together at the front of the fairing **(see illustrations)**.

25 Remove the three screws which retain the side protector cover **(see illustration)**. Remove the single screw which retains the side protector piece **(see illustration)**.

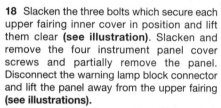

19.19a Disconnect the block connectors situated on the left side of the upper fairing . . .

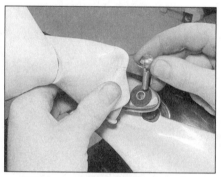

19.19b . . . and remove the rear view mirrors

19.19c Remove the upper fairing mounting bolts and manoeuvre it away from the machine

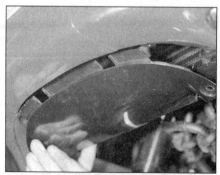

19.24a Maintenance cover is retained by two trim clips

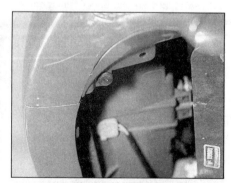

19.24b Remove the two screws underneath the maintenance cover

19.24c Fairing lower halves are secured by trim clips . . .

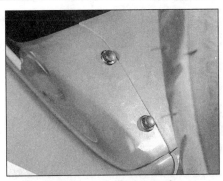

19.24d . . . on the front edge

19.25a Remove the side protector cover

Withdraw the spring clip linking the two lower panel halves on the underside **(see illustration)**. Remove the three bolts from the top edge of the lower panel, the two bolts from the rear edge, the single bolt from the rear lower corner and the single screw located under the side protector **(see illustration)**. Carefully remove the lower fairing panels.

26 To remove the upper fairing, both lower sections must first be removed (see paragraphs 23 to 25). Remove the five screws to free the windshield from the upper fairing; retrieve the washers and nuts if they are loose **(see illustration)**.

27 Remove the upper fairing inner panels; each is secured by a single screw and tabs which engage with the upper fairing and

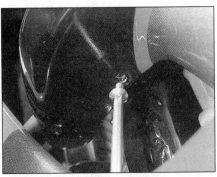

19.25b Side protector piece is retained by a single screw

19.25c Fairing lower panel halves are secured by a spring clip (arrowed) at the bottom

19.25d Fairing lower panel fastener locations (arrowed)

19.26 Removing the windshield from the upper fairing

19.27a Inner covers are retained by a single screw

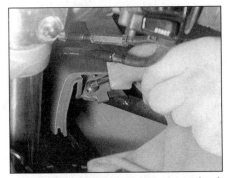

19.27b Instrument panel cover is retained by a screw on each side at the bottom corner . . .

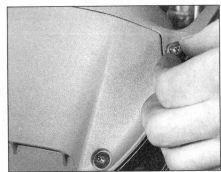

19.27c . . . front face . . .

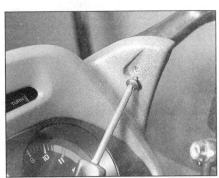

19.27d . . . and top corner

6

19.27e The instrument panel can then be lifted free

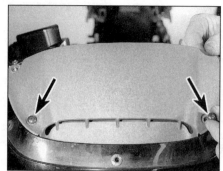

19.27f Air duct is retained by two screws (arrowed)

19.28 Rear view mirrors are retained by two bolts

instrument panel cover **(see illustration)**. Remove the six screws which secure the instrument panel cover to the upper fairing and lift the cover off the instruments **(see illustrations)**. Remove the two remaining screws and slide the air duct out of the upper fairing **(see illustration)**.

28 Peel back the rubber cover from the mirror stalk and unscrew the two mirror mounting bolts **(see illustration)**. Note the exact position of the mounting bracket rubber dampers and plate as each mirror is withdrawn from the fairing.

29 Remove the two bolts on each side of the upper fairing and gently pull the upper fairing forwards off its mounting pegs **(see** illustrations**)**. When access is available, reach in and unplug the wiring connectors to the headlamps, position lamps and turn signals. If the upper fairing halves require separation, remove the four screws retaining the headlight unit and remove the headlight **(see illustration)**. The two halves are secured by six screws **(see illustration)**.

30 The upper fairing is installed in a reverse of the removal procedure, noting the following:

a) *Engage the fairing pegs in the two holes in the headlamp unit* **(see illustration)**.

b) *When installing the mirrors, the damping rubber marking must face outwards and the arrows on the mounting plate must*

point up and forwards **(see illustration)**.

31 The lower fairing sections are installed in a reverse of the removal procedure, noting that care must be taken to correctly engage the hinge arrangement which joins the bottom edges and secure it with the spring clip. To secure the trim clips at the front joint and on the maintenance cover, install the clip and push its head in to lock it in position.

All models

32 Check that the fairing is securely mounted, and that all the electrics function correctly, before riding the machine. Also check the headlamp aim if the upper fairing has been removed.

19.29a Remove the two bolts (arrowed) on each side of the upper fairing . . .

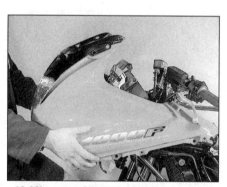

19.29b . . . and remove the upper fairing

19.29c Headlamp unit is retained by four screws (arrowed)

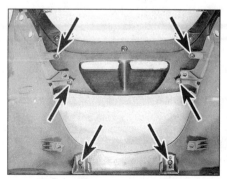

19.29d Upper fairing sections are retained by six screws (arrowed)

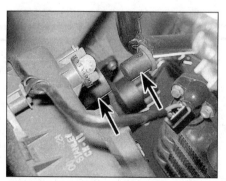

19.30a Fairing peg must engage headlamp unit hole (arrowed)

19.30b Take note of damping rubber and mounting plate markings when fitting the mirrors

Chapter 7
Wheels, brakes and tyres

Contents

Degrees of difficulty

Easy, suitable for novice with little experience	Fairly easy, suitable for beginner with some experience	Fairly difficult, suitable for competent DIY mechanic 	Difficult, suitable for experienced DIY mechanic	Very difficult, suitable for expert DIY or professional

Specifications

Wheels

Runout (radial and axial) . . . . 2.0 mm (0.08 in)
Axle runout . . . . 0.2 mm (0.01 in)

Brakes

Disc thickness (service limit):
  Front:
    1000 K models onward . . . . 4.0 mm (0.16 in)
    All 600 models and 1000 H, J models . . . . 3.5 mm (0.14 in)
  Rear:
    1000 K, L, M, N models . . . . 5.0 mm (0.20 in)
    1000 P models onward . . . . 4.0 mm (0.16 in)
    All 600 models and 1000 H, J models . . . . 4.0 mm (0.16 in)
Disc maximum runout - all models . . . . 0.3 mm (0.01 in)
Caliper bore ID - all 600 models and 1000 H, J, K, L, M, N models:
  Front:
    1000 H, J models . . . . 30.230 - 30.280 mm (1.1900 - 1.1920 in)
    Service limit . . . . 30.290 mm (1.1930 in)
    All 600 models, US 1000 L, M models . . . . 27.000 - 27.050 mm (1.0630 - 1.0650 in)
    Service limit . . . . 27.060 mm (1.0651 in)
    UK 1000 K, L, M, N models . . . . 25.400 - 25.450 mm (1.0000 - 1.0020 in)
    Service limit . . . . 25.460 mm (1.0020)
  Rear - all models . . . . 27.000 - 27.050 mm (1.0630 - 1.0650 in)
  Service limit . . . . 27.060 mm (1.0651 in)

7

Brakes (continued)

Caliper bore ID - 1000 P models onward (front and rear):
  Standard
    22.6 mm bore .... 22.650 - 22.700 mm (0.8917 - 0.8937 in)
    25.4 mm bore .... 25.400 - 25.450 mm (1.0000 - 1.0020 in)
    27.0 mm bore .... 27.000 - 27.050 mm (1.0630 - 1.0650 in)
  Service limit
    22.6 mm bore .... 22.710 mm (0.8940 in)
    25.4 mm bore .... 25.460 mm (1.0024 in)
    27.0 mm bore .... 27.060 mm (1.0654 in)
Caliper piston OD - all 600 models and 1000 H, J, K, L, M, N models:
  Front:
    1000 H, J models .... 30.165 - 30.198 mm (1.1879 - 1.1889 in)
    Service limit .... 30.160 mm (1.1970 in)
    All 600 models, US 1000 L, M models .... 26.918 - 26.968 mm (1.0598 - 1.0617 in)
    Service limit .... 26.910 mm (1.0590 in)
    UK 1000 K, L, M, N models .... 25.335 - 25.368 mm (0.9974 - 0.9987 in)
    Service limit .... 25.330 mm (0.9970 in)
  Rear - all models .... 26.918 - 26.968 mm (1.0598 - 1.0617 in)
  Service limit .... 26.910 mm (1.0590 in)
Caliper piston OD - 1000 P models onward (front and rear):
  Standard
    22.6 mm bore .... 22.585 - 22.618 mm (0.8892 - 0.8905 in)
    25.4 mm bore .... 25.318 - 25.368 mm (0.9968 - 0.9987 in)
    27.0 mm bore .... 26.916 - 26.968 mm (1.0597 - 1.0617 in)
  Service limit
    22.6 mm bore .... 22.560 mm (0.8820 in)
    25.4 mm bore .... 25.310 mm (0.9965 in)
    27.0 mm bore .... 26.910 mm (1.0594 in)
Master cylinder bore ID:
  Front:
    1000 H and J models .... 15.870 - 15.913 mm (0.6248 - 0.6265 in)
    Service limit .... 15.930 mm (0.6270 in)
    US 1000 L, M and all 600 models .... 14.000 - 14.043 mm (0.5512 - 0.5529 in)
    Service limit .... 14.055 mm (0.5533 in)
    US 1000 P models onward, UK 1000 K models onward .... 12.700 - 12.743 mm (0.5000 - 0.5017 in)
    Service limit .... 12.760 mm (0.5020 in)
  Rear:
    All 600 models, 1000 H, J, K, L, M, N .... 12.700 - 12.743 mm (0.5000 - 0.5017 in)
    Service limit .... 12.760 mm (0.5020 in)
    1000 P models onward .... 17.460 - 17.503 mm (0.6874 - 0.6891 in)
    Service limit .... 17.515 mm (0.6896 in)
Master cylinder piston OD:
  Front:
    1000 H and J models .... 15.827 - 15.854 mm (0.6231 - 0.6242 in)
    Service limit .... 15.820 mm (0.6230 in)
    US 1000 L, M and all 600 models .... 13.957 - 13.984 mm (0.5495 - 0.5506 in)
    Service limit .... 13.950 mm (0.5490 in)
    US P models onward, UK 1000 K models onward .... 12.657 - 12.684 mm (0.4983 - 0.4994 in)
    Service limit .... 12.650 mm (0.4980 in)
  Rear:
    All 600 models, 1000 H, J, K, L, M, N models .... 12.657 - 12.684 mm (0.4983 - 0.4994 in)
    Service limit .... 12.650 mm (0.4980 in)
    1000 P models onward .... 17.417 - 17.444 mm (0.6857 - 0.6868 in)
    Service limit .... 17.405 mm (0.6852 in)
Secondary master cylinder - 1000 P models onward:
  Bore ID .... 12.700 - 12.743 mm (0.5000 - 0.5017 in)
  Service limit .... 12.76 mm (0.502 in)
  Piston OD .... 12.657 - 12.684 mm (0.4983 - 0.4994 in)
  Service limit .... 12.65 mm (0.498 in)

Tyres

Size:	Front	Rear
600 models	110/80V17 - V240	130/80V17 - V240
1000 H and J models	110/80V17 - V270	140/80V17 - V270
1000 K models onward	120/70VR17 - V270	170/60VR17 - V270
Tyre pressures and tread depth	see Chapter 1	

Torque settings

	kgf m	lbf ft
Front axle bolt	6.0	43.0
Front axle pinch bolts	2.2	16.0
Front brake caliper bracket mounting bolts*	2.7	20.0
*Left caliper lower mounting bracket - 1000 H, J and all		
600 models	1.2	9.0
Secondary master cylinder mounting bolts - 1000 P models onward . .	1.2	9.0
Secondary master cylinder bracket bolts - 1000 P models onward . . .	2.7	20.0
Front brake/clutch master cylinder clamp bolts - 1000 only	1.2	9.0
Brake caliper bleed nipples:		
All 600 models and 1000 P onward	0.55	4.0
1000 H, J, K, L, M, N models	0.6	4.3
Clutch slave cylinder bleed nipple - 1000 only:		
1000 H, J, K, L, M, N models	0.9	7.0
1000 P models onward	0.8	6.0
Clutch hose union bolts - 1000 only:		
H and J models	3.0	22.0
K models onward	3.5	25.0
Brake caliper backing plate bolts - 1000 P models onward	3.2	23.0
Brake hose 2-way joint union bolts - 600 only	3.5	25.0
Brake hose union bolts:		
H and J models	3.0	22.0
K models onward	3.5	25.0
Front brake lever adjuster arm pivot screw - 1000 only	0.4	2.9
Front brake lever pivot bolt nut	0.6	4.3
Brake disc mounting bolts:		
1000 K models onward	4.3	31.0
All other models	4.0	29.0
Rear axle nut:		
600 models	9.0	65.0
1000 H, J, K, L, M, N models	9.5	69.0
1000 P models onward	9.3	67.0
Rear wheel sprocket retaining nuts:		
600 models	6.5	47.0
1000 H, J, K, L, M, N, M models	9.0	65.0
1000 P models onward	11.0	78.0
Rear master cylinder mounting bolts	1.2	9.0
Rear master cylinder reservoir mounting bolt - 1000 only:		
1000 H, J, K, L, M, N models	0.9	7.0
1000 P models onward	1.2	9.0
Right footrest bracket bolts:		
All 600 models and 1000 H, J, K, L, M, N models	2.7	20.0
1000 P models onward	3.3	24.0

1 General description

All models are fitted with cast alloy wheels designed to accept tubeless tyres. Both front and rear brakes are hydraulically-operated disc brakes, the front using a twin disc set up and the rear a single disc. The brake calipers on all 600 models and on the 1000 H, J, K, L, M, N models are of the dual piston type. The 1000 P models onward use three-piston brake calipers.

The 1000 P models onward are fitted with Honda's dual combined brake system (Dual CBS). The system simultaneously applies front and rear brakes when just the front or rear brake is applied by the rider. When the front brake is applied, the two outer pistons of

each front brake caliper apply pressure to the pads. As braking force increases, the left front caliper actuates the secondary master cylinder which applies pressure to the two outer pistons of the rear caliper via the proportional control valve. When the rider operates the rear brake pedal, pressure is applied equally to the centre piston of all three calipers.

 Warning: Dust created by the brake system contains asbestos, which is harmful to your health. Never blow it out with compressed air and do not inhale any of it. An approved filtering mask should be worn when working on the brakes. Do not, under any circumstances, use petroleum or gasoline-based solvents to clean brake parts - use brake system cleaner or denatured alcohol only.

2 Wheels, brakes and tyres - general information

1 Refer to other parts of this manual for information on the following operations.

a) Checking the tyre pressures - Daily (pre-ride) checks.

b) Checking tyre wear - Daily (pre-ride) checks.

c) Checking the brake fluid level - Daily (pre-ride) checks.

d) Removing and installing the brake pads - Chapter 1.

e) Checking brake pad wear - Chapter 1.

f) Inspection and renovation of the wheels - Chapter 1.

7

3.2 On 1000 models release the brake hoses from the fork sliders before removing the calipers

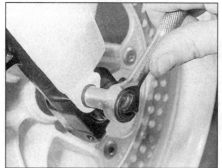

3.4a If necessary, slacken fender mounting bolts . . .

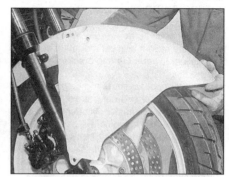

3.4b . . . and remove it for improved access

3 Front wheel -
removal and installation

Caution: Whilst the wheel is removed from the machine, insert a wooden wedge between the brake pads of each caliper. This will prevent the pistons being expelled should the brake lever (or pedal on P models onward) be accidentally operated. Do not allow either caliper to hang from its hose(s) once detached from its mountings. Support the calipers so that there is no strain placed on either the brake hoses or pipe.

1 Place the machine on its centre stand and raise the front wheel clear of the ground by placing a support or stand beneath the engine.
2 On all 1000 H, J, K, L, M, N models remove the bolts which secure both brake hoses to the fork sliders, and on all 600 models free the brake hoses from their guides **(see illustration)**. On all models remove the mounting bolts from both brake calipers. Slide the calipers off the discs and tie them up out of the way of the wheel, taking care not to bend the brake pipe (1000 models only). On all 600 and 1000 H and J models, remove the screw which retains the speedometer drive cable and disconnect the cable from its drive gearbox. Also note the collar fitted to the upper left caliper mounting on the fork slider (lower leg) and remove it for safekeeping.
3 On 1000 P models onward, remove the two bolts which retain the secondary master cylinder link brackets to the left fork slider **(see illustration 11.2)**. Remove the left caliper lower mounting bolt and ease the caliper off the disc; take great care not to place any strain on the hydraulic hoses or secondary master cylinder pushrod. Remove both mounting bolts from the right caliper and ease the caliper off the disc.
4 On all models, slacken the axle pinch bolts at the bottom of each fork slider (lower leg) and remove the axle bolt from the right side. Withdraw the axle from the left side and manoeuvre the front wheel out of the forks. Note that on some models, it may prove necessary to remove the front mudguard to gain the necessary clearance to remove the wheel. Remove the spacer(s) and/or the speedometer drive gearbox from the hub, having first taken note of their correct positions as a guide to installation **(see illustrations)**.
5 Installation is the reverse of the removal procedure. Ensure the axle is straight and free from corrosion and smear its shaft with high melting-point grease to aid future dismantling. Apply a thin coat of grease to the oil seal lips and refit the spacer(s) and/or speedometer

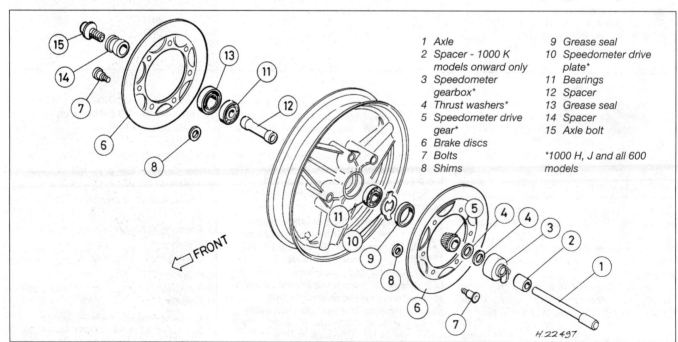

1 Axle	9 Grease seal
2 Spacer - 1000 K models onward only	10 Speedometer drive plate*
3 Speedometer gearbox*	11 Bearings
4 Thrust washers*	12 Spacer
5 Speedometer drive gear*	13 Grease seal
6 Brake discs	14 Spacer
7 Bolts	15 Axle bolt
8 Shims	

1000 H, J and all 600 models

3.4c Front wheel

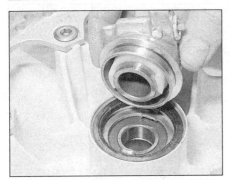

3.5a On 1000 H, J and all 600 models refit the speedometer gearbox ensuring that it is correctly located

3.5b Grease the oil seal lips and install the spacer(s)

3.6a Offer up the wheel and insert the axle

gearbox to the hub **(see illustrations)**. **Note:** *When refitting the speedometer gearbox (where fitted), ensure that the slots in the gearbox are correctly aligned with the drive plate tangs in the hub.*

6 Offer up the front wheel and insert the axle from the left-hand side **(see illustration)**. Align the index line around the axle's head with the outside face of the fork slider and tighten the left axle pinch bolts to the specified torque setting **(see illustration)**. Where fitted, position the speedometer gearbox so that the projection on the gearbox is in contact with the rear of the lug on the slider, then refit the axle bolt and tighten it to the specified torque setting **(see illustrations)**. Insert the brake caliper collar (where fitted) in the left slider (lower leg) and install both calipers **(see illustrations)**. Tighten the caliper mounting bolts to their specified torque settings **(see illustration)**. Note that the left caliper's lower mounting bolt on 1000 H, J and all 600 models is also the anti-dive pin and should only be tightened to a torque setting of 1.2 kgf m (9 lbf ft).

7 Remove the support from under the engine and rest the front wheel on the ground. Pump the front forks a few times to settle all components in position and tighten the right axle pinch bolts to their specified torque setting. Using a 0.7 mm (0.028 in) feeler gauge, check the clearance between the left caliper mounting bracket and disc, on both sides of the disc **(see illustration)**. If the feeler

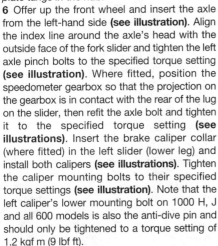

3.6b Position the axle as described in text (axle's index line arrowed)

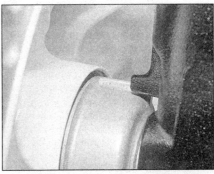

3.6c Ensure speedometer gearbox lug is correctly positioned (where fitted) . . .

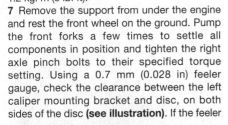

3.6d . . . then refit the axle bolt

3.6e Install the left caliper collar (where fitted) . . .

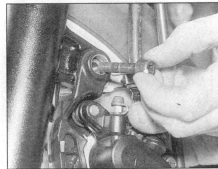

3.6f . . . and refit the brake calipers to the fork legs

3.6g Tighten all caliper mounting bolts to their specified torque setting

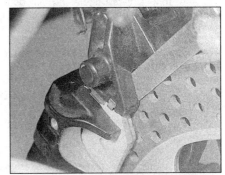

3.7 Check the left caliper mounting bracket to disc clearance as described in text

7

4.2 Rear wheel - 1000 models (600 similar)

1 Axle
2 Spacer
3 Grease seal
4 Sprocket carrier bearing
5 Sprocket
6 Noise damper - 1000 H and J models
7 Nuts
8 Sprocket carrier
9 Studs
10 Spacer
11 Cush drive rubbers
12 Dust seal - 1000 H and J models
13 Bearings
14 O-ring
15 Spacer
16 Grease seal
17 Brake disc
18 Bolts
19 Spacer
20 Washer
21 Nut

H.22498

FRONT

gauge cannot be easily inserted on both sides of the disc, slacken the axle pinch bolts on the left slider (lower leg) and push or pull the left fork slider (lower leg) inwards or outwards until the feeler gauge is a light sliding fit. Retighten the left axle pinch bolts to their specified torque setting. On 1000 P models onward, also check the clearance between the right caliper bracket and disc in the same way.

8 Apply the front brake several times to settle the calipers in position and recheck the left caliper bracket clearance, adjusting it again if necessary.

9 Install the mudguard (if removed) and refit the bolts which secure the brake hose guides to the fork sliders, tightening all bolts securely. Where fitted, refit the speedometer cable to its drive gearbox and tighten its retaining screw securely. Finally, thoroughly check the operation of the front brake before taking the machine on the road.

---

4 Rear wheel -
removal and installation

Caution: Whilst the wheel is removed from the machine, insert a wooden wedge between the brake pads of the caliper. This will prevent the pistons being expelled should the brake pedal (or lever

on 1000 P models onward) be accidentally operated. Also, do not allow the caliper to hang from its hose. Support the caliper so that there is no strain placed on the brake hose.

1 Place the machine on its centre stand on level ground so that the rear wheel is clear of the ground.

2 On 1000 K models onward remove the bolt which secures the brake hose guide to the swingarm and remove the guide. On all models, slacken the rear axle nut and remove it and the washer. Loosen the drive chain adjuster locknuts and slacken the adjuster nuts so that the rear wheel can be pushed fully forwards, the drive chain disengaged from the sprocket and looped over the

swingarm. Tap the wheel axle out of position, using a hammer and suitable drift, and lower the wheel to the ground **(see illustration)**. Tie the rear caliper assembly to the frame, to avoid straining the brake hose. Remove the spacers from the left and right side of the hub having first noted their correct positions.

3 Installation is the reverse of the removal procedure. Refit the spacers to the wheel, having first greased the oil seal lips **(see illustrations)**. Check that the axle is straight, clean and free from corrosion, then smear a liberal quantity of high melting-point grease over it to assist future dismantling. On 1000 K models onward, ensure the boss of the caliper bracket is positioned in the lug of the swingarm. On all models check that the UP

4.3a Grease the oil seal lips and refit the left . . .

4.3b . . . and right spacers to the wheel

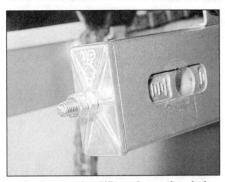

4.3c Ensure that UP marks on the chain adjusters are correctly positioned

4.4a Engage the drive chain with the sprocket . . .

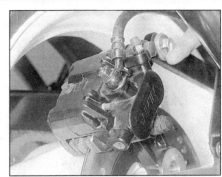

4.4b . . . and slide the caliper onto the disc

mark on the chain adjusters is facing upwards **(see illustration)**.

4 Offer up the wheel, ensuring the disc enters between the brake pads correctly, and insert the axle from the left side. Refit the drive chain to the rear sprocket and the axle nut and washer **(see illustrations)**. Adjust the drive chain tension as described in Chapter 1 and tighten the axle nut to the specified torque setting. On 1000 K models onward, refit the brake hose guide to the swingarm and tighten its retaining bolt securely. On all models thoroughly check the operation of the rear brake before riding the machine.

---

5 Wheel bearings - removal, inspection and installation

Caution: Although not strictly necessary, it is recommended that the brake disc(s) are removed from the wheel. This will prevent damage to them whilst removing and installing the wheel bearings.

Front wheel

1 Remove the wheel as described in Section 3 of this Chapter.

2 Once the wheel has been removed, use a large flat-bladed screwdriver to carefully lever out the grease seal from the left side of the hub and remove the speedometer drive plate (where fitted). Then remove the grease seal from the right side of the hub in a similar

manner. Alternatively, both seals can be driven out of position with the bearings, if desired.

3 Support the wheel firmly on two wooden blocks (placed as close to the hub centre as possible to prevent distortion) and ensure that there is enough space beneath the hub to allow the bearing to drop free. Place the end of a small flat-ended drift against the upper surface of the lower bearing and tap the bearing downwards out of the hub. The spacer located between the two bearings may be moved slightly sideways in order to allow the drift to be positioned against the face of the bearing. Move the drift around the face of the bearing whilst drifting it out of position to ensure that it leaves the hub squarely.

4 With the one bearing removed, the wheel may be lifted and the spacer withdrawn from the hub. Invert the wheel and remove the second bearing, using a similar procedure to that used for the first.

5 If the bearing is of the unsealed type, or is only sealed on one side, wash it thoroughly in a high flash-point solvent to remove all traces of old grease. Check the bearing tracks and balls for wear, pitting or damage to the hardened surfaces. A small amount of side-to-side movement in the bearing is normal but no radial movement should be detectable. Check the bearings for play and roughness when they are spun by hand. All used bearings will emit a small amount of noise when spun but they should not chatter or

4.4c Lift up the wheel and insert the axle from the left side

sound rough. If there is any doubt about the condition of the bearings they should be renewed. Always renew wheel bearings as a pair and never individually.

6 Carefully clean the bearing recesses in the hub and the centre of the cavity. All traces of old grease, which may be contaminated with dirt, must be removed. Inspect the grease seals and renew them if any damage or wear is found.

7 Before installing the bearings pack them with high melting-point grease, noting that this is not necessary on bearings which are sealed on both surfaces. With the wheel hub firmly supported on two wooden blocks, tap the first bearing into place in the hub. Use a hammer and a tubular metal drift or socket which bears only on the outer race of the

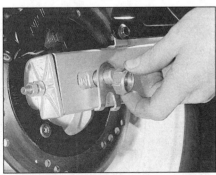

4.4d Fit the axle washer and nut . . .

4.4e . . . and tighten it to the specified torque setting

4.4f On 1000 K models onward, refit the brake hose guides to the swingarm

7

5.7 Drive first wheel bearing into position using a suitable tubular drift . . .

5.8a . . . then invert the wheel and insert central spacer

5.8b Grease the cavity and fit the second bearing

bearing to drive it into position **(see illustration)**. Ensure bearings, if sealed on only one surface, are fitted with their sealed surfaces facing outwards. **Note:** *Install the left wheel bearing first, then the right bearing.*

8 Once the first bearing has been installed, invert the wheel, and fit the central spacer **(see illustration)**. Unless the bearings are sealed on both surfaces, pack the remaining space no more than 2/3 full of high melting-point grease. Once the grease is packed in, fit the second bearing in the same manner as the first **(see illustration)**.

9 Refit the speedometer drive plate (where fitted) to the hub, ensuring that the drive tangs are located in the slots provided for them, and press both the left and right grease seals into position **(see illustrations)**. If necessary, the

seals can be tapped into place using a hammer and tubular drift which bears only on the hard outer edge of the seal.

10 Install the wheel as described in Section 3 of this Chapter.

Rear wheel

11 Remove the wheel as described in Section 4 of this Chapter. Lift out the rear sprocket assembly, noting the spacer fitted to the inside of the sprocket carrier, and remove the cush drive rubbers from the left side of the hub.

12 Due to similarity in design and construction, the procedure for removal, inspection and installation of the rear wheel bearings is exactly the same as those given for the front wheel.

13 Fit the cush drive rubbers to the hub and install the sprocket assembly, ensuring the spacer is fitted to the inside of the sprocket carrier. Install the wheel as described in Section 4 of this Chapter.

5.9a Locate the speedometer drive plate tangs (where fitted) with slots in hub . . .

---

6 Rear sprocket and cush drive assembly - removal, inspection and installation

1 Inspect the teeth of the rear sprocket. If these are hooked, chipped, or otherwise damaged, the sprocket must be renewed. Note that it is considered bad practice to renew just one sprocket or the chain alone; both front and rear sprockets and the chain

should be renewed as a set.

2 Remove the rear wheel from the machine as described in Section 4 of this Chapter. Lift off the sprocket assembly, noting the spacer fitted to the inside of the sprocket carrier, and remove the cush drive rubbers from the hub.

3 To remove the sprocket, clamp one of the sprocket carrier lugs in a vice equipped with soft jaws, and slacken and remove the five (1000 P models onward) or six (all other models) sprocket retaining nuts. Lift off the worn sprocket and install the new one. Refit the sprocket retaining nuts and tighten them to the specified torque setting **(see illustration)**. Note that on 1000 H and J models the sprocket is fitted with a noise damper in the form of a rubber ring fitted to the sprocket flange. On these models do not forget to remove this from the old sprocket and transfer it to the new one.

4 Using a large flat-bladed screwdriver, lever out the grease seal from the centre of the sprocket carrier. Alternatively, the seal can be driven out with the bearing. Remove the spacer from the inside of the sprocket carrier and support the assembly on two pieces of wood, positioned as close to the centre of the sprocket as possible, so that there is enough clearance for the bearing to drop free from its housing. Tap the bearing out of position using hammer and suitable drift, moving the drift around the bearing so that it leaves the housing squarely. Inspect the grease seal for wear or damage, renewing it if necessary.

5.9b . . . and press the left . . .

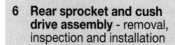

5.9c . . . and right grease seals into position

6.3 Tighten rear sprocket retaining nuts to the specified torque setting

6.6 Renew the cush drive rubbers as a set if perished

6.7a Do not omit the sprocket carrier spacer . . .

6.7b . . . when fitting the carrier to the wheel

Inspect the bearing in the same manner as for the wheel bearings in the previous Section of this Chapter.

5 Install the bearing, using a hammer and tubular drift which bears only on the outer race of the bearing, and fit the grease seal in a similar way. Once the bearing and seal are in position, refit the spacer to the inside of the sprocket carrier.

6 Inspect the cush drive rubbers for signs of wear or compaction **(see illustration)**. If any rubber is suspect, all the cush drive rubbers must be renewed as a set. Also check the condition of the O-ring fitted to the left side of the hub, and renew it if it shows signs of wear or damage.

7 Install the cush drive rubbers in the wheel hub and refit the sprocket and carrier assembly, ensuring that the sprocket carrier spacer is in position **(see illustrations)**. Install the wheel as described in Section 4 of this Chapter.

7 Front brake caliper - removal, overhaul and installation 🔧

Caution: Brake fluid will discolour or remove paint if contact is allowed. If brake fluid comes in contact with any painted or

plastic components it must be washed off immediately with cold water.
Caution: Disassembly, overhaul and reassembly of the brake caliper must be done in a spotlessly clean work area to avoid contamination and possible failure of the hydraulic brake system. If such a work area is not available, have the caliper rebuilt by a Honda dealer. Dismantle the calipers separately to avoid interchanging of components.

1 Have ready a supply of clean rag to catch any hydraulic fluid, then disconnect the union bolt from the brake caliper and drain the fluid into a suitable container **(see illustrations)**. On 1000 P models onward, go on to

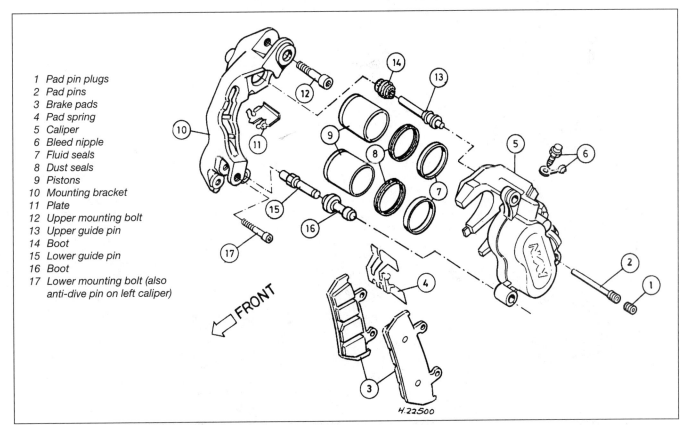

1 Pad pin plugs
2 Pad pins
3 Brake pads
4 Pad spring
5 Caliper
6 Bleed nipple
7 Fluid seals
8 Dust seals
9 Pistons
10 Mounting bracket
11 Plate
12 Upper mounting bolt
13 Upper guide pin
14 Boot
15 Lower guide pin
16 Boot
17 Lower mounting bolt (also anti-dive pin on left caliper)

H.22500

7.1a Front brake caliper - 600 and 1000 H and J models (left caliper shown)

7

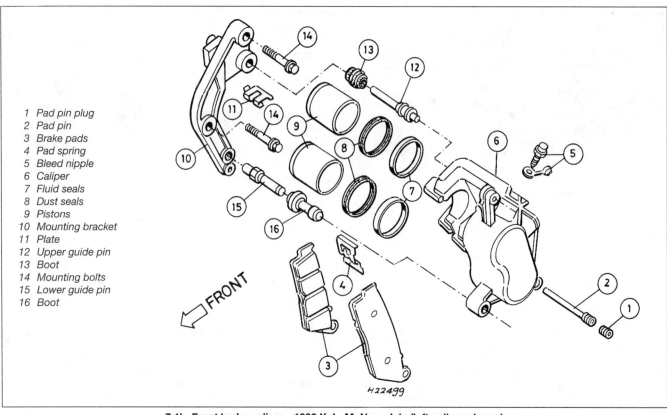

1 Pad pin plug
2 Pad pin
3 Brake pads
4 Pad spring
5 Bleed nipple
6 Caliper
7 Fluid seals
8 Dust seals
9 Pistons
10 Mounting bracket
11 Plate
12 Upper guide pin
13 Boot
14 Mounting bolts
15 Lower guide pin
16 Boot

FRONT

H22499

7.1b Front brake caliper - 1000 K, L, M, N models (left caliper shown)

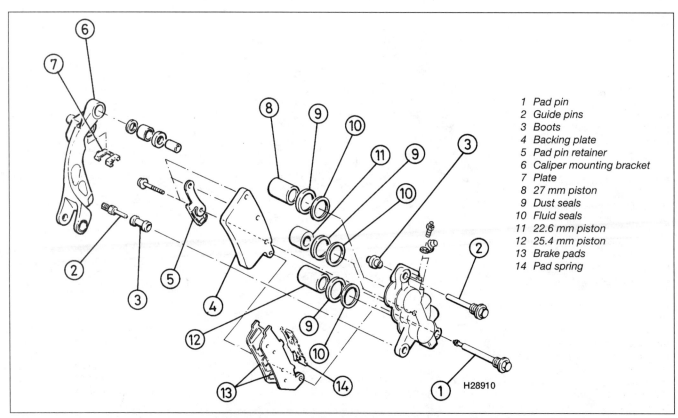

1 Pad pin
2 Guide pins
3 Boots
4 Backing plate
5 Pad pin retainer
6 Caliper mounting bracket
7 Plate
8 27 mm piston
9 Dust seals
10 Fluid seals
11 22.6 mm piston
12 25.4 mm piston
13 Brake pads
14 Pad spring

H28910

7.1c Front brake caliper - 1000 P models onward (left caliper shown)

disconnect the other hydraulic hose having taken note of their exact positions as a guide to installation.

2 When all the fluid has drained from the hose, clean the connections and secure the hose end and fittings inside a polythene bag to await reassembly. This will prevent the ingress of any foreign matter into the hydraulic system.

3 Remove the brake pads as described in Chapter 1. On 1000 K, L, M, N models, then go on to slacken the caliper mounting bolts and remove the calipers from the machine. On 1000 P models onward, if working on the right caliper remove the two caliper bracket mounting bolts and remove the caliper from the fork slider; if working on the left caliper, remove the caliper bracket lower mounting bolt, upper mounting bolt, and the secondary master cylinder bracket bolts, then remove the caliper from the disc. On all models separate the brake caliper from its mounting bracket.

4 On 1000 P models onward, remove the backing plate from the caliper. The backing plate is secured by two bolts, which also clamp the pad pin retainer.

5 The pistons may be driven out of the caliper body by compressed air - an air jet from a foot pump if necessary. Under no circumstances should any attempt be made to lever or prise the pistons out of the caliper. Ensure that both pistons leave the bores at the same time; if one sticks at any time the other piston must be restrained by firm hand pressure so that the pressure can overcome the resistance of the stubborn piston. It is very difficult to extract one piston alone from a caliper without risking damage. If the compressed air method fails, temporarily reconnect the caliper to the brake hose(s) and use hydraulic pressure via the handlebar lever to displace the pistons. Wrap some rag around the caliper to catch the inevitable shower of brake fluid. Once the pistons have been removed, carefully remove the dust and fluid seals from the caliper bores.

6 Label the pistons so that they can be returned to their original bores in the caliper. Note that the pistons on the three-piston caliper fitted to 1000 P models onward all have different diameters.

7 Clean the caliper components thoroughly in new hydraulic fluid. Discard all the seals as a matter of course. The replacement cost is relatively small and does not warrant re-use of components so vital to safety. Check the pistons and caliper bores for scoring, rusting or pitting. If any of these defects are evident it is unlikely that a good fluid seal can be maintained and for this reason the components should be renewed. If measuring equipment is available, compare the dimensions of the caliper bores and pistons to those given in the Specifications Section of this Chapter, renewing any component that is worn beyond the specified service limit.

⚠️ *Warning: On no account use petrol (gasoline), paraffin (kerosene), or oil as these will cause the seals to swell and degrade.*

8 Inspect the shank of each guide pin which the brake caliper slides on for signs of wear or corrosion and clean or renew each one as necessary. Guide pins are a screw fit in either the caliper body or mounting bracket. On refitting apply a few drops of thread-locking compound to their threads and tighten them securely. If the matching bores in the caliper body or mounting bracket are worn or damaged, the body or bracket (as applicable) must be renewed. It is essential that the caliper body can move smoothly and easily on the pins. Inspect the rubber boots which are fitted between the caliper body and mounting bracket and renew any which show signs of damage or deterioration.

9 On reassembly, the components must be clean and dry; cleanliness is essential to prevent the entry of dirt into the system. Dip the new fluid seals in new hydraulic fluid before refitting them to the caliper bores and ensure each one is correctly located in its groove, without being twisted or distorted. Install the new dust seals in the caliper bore grooves, having first smeared them with silicone grease. Smear a liberal quantity of **new** brake fluid over the pistons and caliper bores then carefully insert the pistons using a twisting motion. Wipe any surplus fluid from the piston head areas when they are in position.

10 On 1000 P models onward, install the caliper backing plate and pad pin retainer. Tighten its two bolts to the specified torque setting.

11 Smear the guide pins with silicone grease and refit the caliper body to the bracket, ensuring that the rubber boots are correctly seated.

12 On 1000 H and J models and all 600 models install the pads and mount the caliper on the fork slider as described in Chapter 1. On all other models, mount the caliper on the fork slider and tighten its bolt to the specified torque setting (not forgetting the secondary master cylinder bracket bolts on 1000 P models onward), then install the brake pads as described in Chapter 1.

13 Refit the hydraulic hose to the brake caliper, using new sealing washers on each side of the hose union. Ensure that the neck of the hose union correctly abuts the tab on the caliper, then tighten the union bolt to the specified torque setting. On 1000 P models onward, reconnect the second hydraulic hose.

14 Fill the master cylinder reservoir with the recommended brake fluid and bleed the system as described in Section 13. Thoroughly check the operation of the braking system before riding the machine.

8 Front brake master cylinder - removal, overhaul and installation

Caution: Brake fluid will discolour or remove paint if contact is allowed. If brake fluid comes in contact with any painted or plastic components it must be washed off immediately with cold water.

Caution: Disassembly, overhaul and reassembly of the master cylinder must be done in a spotlessly clean work area to avoid contamination and possible failure of the hydraulic brake system. If such a work area is not available, have the master cylinder overhauled by a Honda dealer.

1 The front brake master cylinder forms a unit with the hydraulic fluid reservoir and front brake lever and is mounted on the right handlebar.

2 The unit must be drained before any dismantling can be undertaken. Place a suitable container below one of the front calipers and run a length of plastic tubing from the bleed nipple to the container. Unscrew the bleed nipple one full turn and proceed to empty the system by pumping the front brake lever. Remove the reservoir cover and check the fluid level; when all the fluid has been expelled tighten the bleed nipple and remove the tube.

3 On models fitted with an adjustable front brake lever, remove the adjuster arm pivot screw and the brake lever pivot bolt, then remove the lever and adjuster arm from the master cylinder; note the small spring fitted in the end of the lever blade. Take care not to lose any of the adjuster components as they are withdrawn. On models fitted with a one-piece lever, remove the pivot bolt and remove the lever.

4 Have ready a supply of clean rag to catch any drops of brake fluid, then slacken the union bolt and free the hydraulic hose from the master cylinder body. Place the union bolt in a polythene bag and tape the bag over the end of the hydraulic hose to prevent the entry of dirt into the system. Disconnect the wires from the stop lamp switch and remove the two bolts which secure the master cylinder clamp half to the body. Lift the master cylinder away from the handlebar, remove the reservoir cover, plate, diaphragm and float (where fitted) and drain any remaining fluid from the reservoir.

5 Carefully remove the rubber boot from the end of the piston bore to expose the piston end and the retaining circlip **(see illustration overleaf)**. Remove the circlip to free the piston. If the piston tends to stick in the bore it can be pulled clear using pointed-nose pliers. As the piston is removed the primary cup and spring will be released. Clean all the disassembled parts with clean brake fluid and inspect them as follows.

6 Check the piston and cups for scoring or wear and renew if necessary. Excessive

7

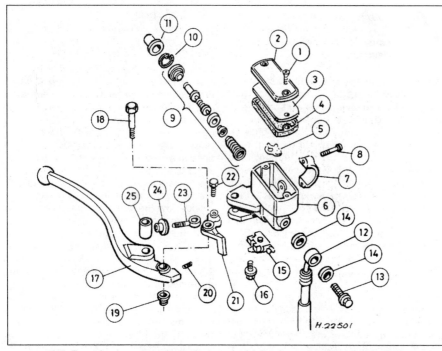

8.5 Front brake master cylinder - typical (clutch master cylinder similar)

1 Screw	9 Piston set	18 Pivot bolt
2 Cover	10 Circlip	19 Nut
3 Plate	11 Boot	20 Spring
4 Diaphragm	12 Brake hose	21 Adjuster arm*
5 Protector	13 Union bolt	22 Pivot screw*
6 Master cylinder body and	14 Sealing washers	23 Adjuster rod*
reservoir	15 Brake light switch	24 Adjuster nut*
7 Clamp	16 Screw	25 Joint pin*
8 Bolts	17 Brake lever	*Where fitted

scoring may be due to contaminated fluid, and if this is suspected, it is probably worth checking the caliper seals and pistons as well. If measuring equipment is available, compare the dimensions of the master cylinder bore and piston with those given in the Specifications Section of this Chapter and renew any component that is worn beyond the specified service limit. It is advisable to renew the piston assembly as a matter of course as the replacement cost is relatively small and does warrant re-use of components vital to safety; the master cylinder piston, cups and spring are supplied as a set - they cannot be obtained individually. Inspect the threads of the union bolt for signs of wear and renew the bolt if in the slightest doubt about its condition. Renew each of the sealing washers located one each side of the hose union as a matter of course.

7 Check before reassembly that all traces of contamination have been removed from inside the reservoir and master cylinder body. Check that the reservoir drilling is clear by directing a jet of compressed air through it.

8 Reassemble the piston assembly in a direct reversal of the removal sequence, noting that the coil spring should be installed with its smaller end against the piston. Use new hydraulic fluid as a lubricant on the piston and cups to aid their installation. Make sure that the circlip is correctly located in its groove and that the rubber boot is correctly fitted.

9 The master cylinder is installed by a reverse of the removal procedure. Refit the master cylinder to the handlebars, ensuring that the UP mark on the clamp faces upwards. Position the assembly so that the punch mark on the handlebar aligns with the left corner of the master cylinder mounting clamp, then tighten the top clamp bolt to the specified torque setting (where given), followed by the bottom bolt. Reconnect the brake hose, positioning a **new** sealing washer on each side of its union, and tighten the union bolt to the specified torque setting.

10 On models with an adjustable front brake lever, refit the adjuster rod to the brake lever joint pin ensuring that the arrow on the pin aligns with the groove on the adjuster nut, and refit the lever assembly and adjuster arm to the master cylinder. Refit the lever pivot bolt and nut, tightening the nut to the specified torque setting (where given). Apply a drop of thread-locking compound to the adjuster arm pivot screw and tighten it securely. On models with a one-piece front brake lever, refit the lever along with the pivot bolt and nut,

tightening the nut to the specified torque setting (where given). On all models, reconnect the wires to the stop lamp switch.

11 Fill the reservoir with the specified brake fluid and bleed the system as described in Section 13 of this Chapter. Finally, thoroughly check the operation of the brake before riding the machine.

9 Rear brake caliper - removal, overhaul and installation

Caution: Brake fluid will discolour or remove paint if contact is allowed. If brake fluid comes in contact with any painted or plastic components it must be washed off immediately with cold water.

1 The rear brake caliper can be dealt with in much the same way as has been described for the front calipers in Section 7, the only differences being in the method of removing the caliper from the machine **(see illustrations)**. Drain the hydraulic fluid as described in paragraphs 1 and 2 of Section 7. On 1000 P models onward, remove the brake hose clamp bolt from the caliper bracket.

2 Remove the brake pads from the caliper as described in Chapter 1. On 1000 K models onward slacken the rear axle nut and remove it along with its washer. Using a hammer and a suitable drift, tap the wheel spindle partially out of position until the brake caliper and mounting bracket assembly can be slid out of the swingarm. Once the caliper assembly has been withdrawn, temporarily push the axle fully home. On all models separate the caliper from its mounting bracket.

3 The caliper can now be dismantled and overhauled using the procedure in Section 7, paragraphs 4 to 11.

4 The rear brake caliper is installed by a reverse of the removal process. On 1000 K models onward, partially withdraw the rear axle until there is enough clearance for the bracket to be installed. Refit the caliper and bracket assembly, ensuring that the boss of the caliper bracket slots into the lug on the swingarm, and push the axle fully home. Refit the axle nut and washer and tighten it to the specified torque setting. On all models refit the brake pads as described in Chapter 1.

5 Refit the brake hose to the caliper, positioning a new sealing washer each side of its union. Ensure that the hose union neck abuts the lug on the caliper (on 1000 P models onward, note that the prongs on the hose unions must abut the caliper body) and tighten the union bolt to the specified torque setting. On 1000 P models onward, bolt the brake hose clamp to the caliper bracket.

6 Fill the master cylinder reservoir with the specified brake fluid and bleed the system as described in Section 13 of this Chapter. Finally, thoroughly check the operation of the rear brake before riding the machine.

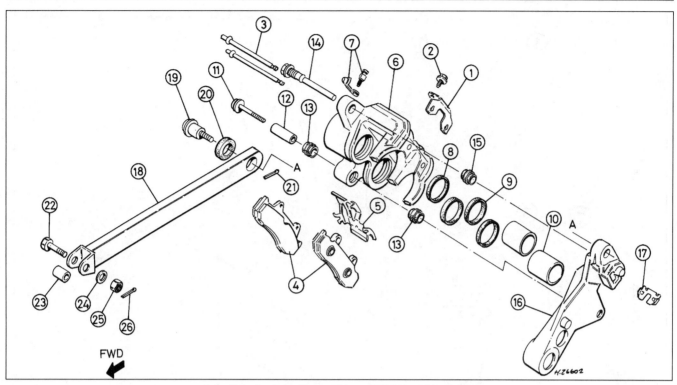

9.1a Rear brake caliper - 600 and 1000 H and J models

1 Pad retaining plate	6 Caliper	11 Lower caliper bolt	15 Boot	19 Bolt	23 Spacer
2 Bolt	7 Bleed nipple	12 Sleeve	16 Mounting bracket	20 Washer	24 Washer
3 Pad pins	8 Fluid seals	13 Boots	17 Plate	21 Split pin	25 Nut
4 Brake pads	9 Dust seals	14 Upper caliper	18 Torque arm	22 Bolt	26 Split pin
5 Pad spring	10 Pistons	bolt			

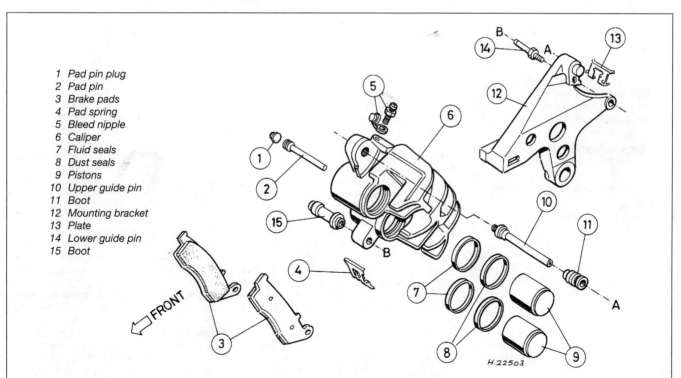

1 Pad pin plug
2 Pad pin
3 Brake pads
4 Pad spring
5 Bleed nipple
6 Caliper
7 Fluid seals
8 Dust seals
9 Pistons
10 Upper guide pin
11 Boot
12 Mounting bracket
13 Plate
14 Lower guide pin
15 Boot

9.1b Rear brake caliper - 1000 K, L, M, N models

7

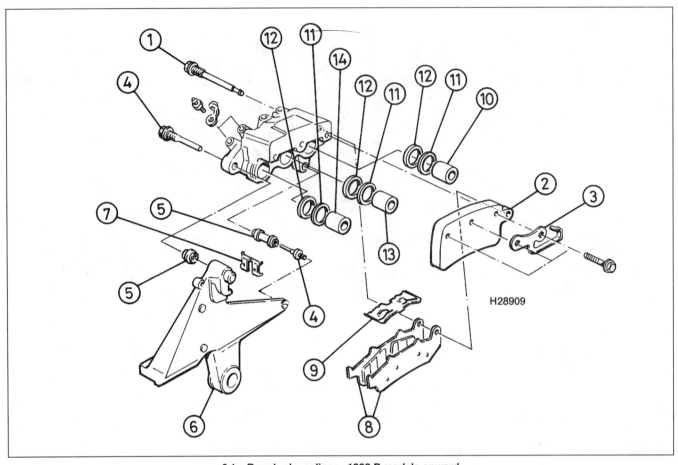

9.1c Rear brake caliper - 1000 P models onward

1 Pad pin	4 Caliper guide pins	bracket	9 Pad spring	12 Fluid seals
2 Backing plate	5 Boots	7 Plate	10 25.4 mm piston	13 22.6 mm piston
3 Pad pin retainer	6 Caliper mounting	8 Brake pads	11 Dust seals	14 27 mm piston

10 Rear brake master cylinder - removal, overhaul and installation

Caution: Brake fluid will discolour or remove paint if contact is allowed. If brake fluid comes in contact with any painted or plastic components it must be washed off immediately with cold water.

Caution: Disassembly, overhaul and reassembly of the master cylinder must be done in a spotlessly clean work area to avoid contamination and possible failure of the hydraulic brake system. If such a work area is not available, have the cylinder overhauled by a Honda dealer.

Removal

1 Remove the right sidepanel and the lower cover (where fitted). Drain the hydraulic system as described in paragraphs 1 and 2 of Section 8.

2 Disconnect the brake hose from the top of the master cylinder. Place the union bolt in a polythene bag and tape the bag over the end of the brake hose to prevent the entry of dirt into the system. Note that there will be two hoses on 1000 P models onward - take note of there fitted position as a guide to installation.

3 Remove the master cylinder mounting bolts, the reservoir mounting bolt and the right footrest bracket mounting bolts. Partially withdraw the footrest bracket then straighten and remove the split pin from the pushrod link pin and remove the pin itself **(see illustration)**. The master cylinder and reservoir assembly can then be removed from the frame.

4 Before disconnecting the reservoir hose from the master cylinder, remove the cap or cover, plate and diaphragm and tip any remaining fluid into the container. Then remove the screw which secures the hose union to the master cylinder and disconnect it noting the O-ring fitted behind the union. Displace the rubber boot from the end of the master cylinder bore to reveal the circlip which retains the pushrod assembly. Remove the circlip and pull out the pushrod. As the pushrod is removed the piston assembly and spring will be released. **Note:** *If the link and locknuts are to be unscrewed from the pushrod, first measure the amount of thread extending from the lower locknut on the underside of the link - this will ensure that the components can be returned to their original position on installation and the pedal height retained.*

5 The master cylinder assembly can be overhauled and reassembled as described in Section 8, paragraphs 6 to 8. Inspect the O-ring which is fitted to the hose union for wear or damage, renewing it if necessary, then refit the hose union and O-ring to the master cylinder, tightening its retaining screw securely.

6 If the link and locknut positions were disturbed, return them to their previously recorded locations on the pushrod. Note that Honda specify a distance of 75 mm (2.95 in) from the eye of the link to the lower mounting hole of the master cylinder body on UK 1000 P models onward and US 1000 L models onward. No settings are available for the other models.

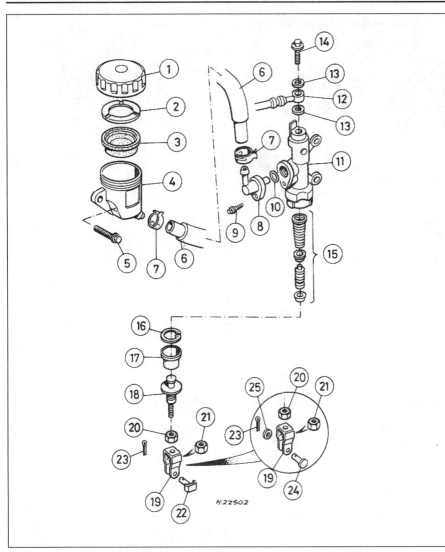

10.3 **Rear brake master cylinder - 1000 models (600 similar)**

1 Reservoir cap	10 O-ring	18 Pushrod
2 Plate	11 Master cylinder	19 Link
3 Diaphragm	12 Brake hose	20 Locknut
4 Reservoir	13 Sealing washers	21 Locknut
5 Bolt	14 Union bolt	22 Link pin - later models
6 Reservoir hose	15 Piston and spring set	23 Split pin
7 Hose clamps	16 Circlip	24 Link pin - early models
8 Hose union	17 Boot	25 Washer - early models
9 Screw		

Installation

7 Installation is a reverse of the removal procedure. Refit the master cylinder to the brake pedal and secure the pushrod pin in position with a new split pin. Secure the footrest bracket to the machine and refit the master cylinder and reservoir mounting bolts, tightening all bolts to the specified torque setting.

8 Refit the brake hose to the master cylinder, positioning a new sealing washer on each side of its union. Ensure that the neck of the hose union(s) abuts the tab on the master cylinder body and tighten the union bolt to the

specified torque setting. Check that the two hoses are installed correctly on 1000 P models onward; install in the order of sealing washer, front caliper union, sealing washer, rear caliper union, sealing washer and union bolt.

9 Fill the reservoir with the specified brake fluid and bleed the brake as described in Section 13 of this Chapter. Finally thoroughly check the operation of the rear brake and stop lamp switch before riding the machine.

10 If adjustment of the brake pedal height or stop lamp switch setting is required, refer to Chapter 1 for details.

11.2 **Link bracket to link bolt (A) and link bracket to fork slider bolts (B)**

11.3 **Unbolt the master cylinder from the fork slider**

11 Secondary master cylinder and proportional control valve - overhaul (1000 P models onward)

Secondary master cylinder

1 Have a supply of clean rags at hand and cover the surrounding area (especially the mudguard and tyre) to prevent damage from brake fluid spills. Take note of the fitted angle of the brake hoses and pipes as a guide to installation, then unscrew each banjo union bolt. Mop up any fluid spills and place the hose/pipe open end in a plastic bag to catch any further drops of fluid and prevent dirt entering the system. Remove the bolt which retains the metal link pipe to the master cylinder.

2 Remove the bolt which retains the triangular link brackets to the caliper link and retrieve the nut and hose guide from the other side of the inner bracket **(see illustration)**. Remove the two bolts which retain the link brackets to the fork slider.

3 Straighten the split pin and slip it out of the clevis pin. Withdraw the clevis pin and separate the clevis from the caliper link. Remove the two bolts (together with reflector on US models) which retain the master cylinder to the fork slider **(see illustration)**.

4 To dismantle the master cylinder, peel back the dust boot from its end and angle the pushrod to one side to access the circlip ears. Remove the circlip and withdraw the pushrod, piston and spring.

7

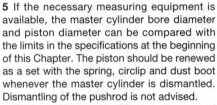

11.8a Remove pivot bolt to separate link from caliper bracket

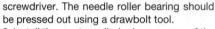

11.8b Slip inner sleeve out to examine needle roller bearing

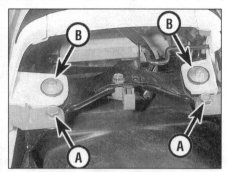

11.10 Grabrail rear mounting bolts (A) and seat cowl bolts (B)

5 If the necessary measuring equipment is available, the master cylinder bore diameter and piston diameter can be compared with the limits in the specifications at the beginning of this Chapter. The piston should be renewed as a set with the spring, circlip and dust boot whenever the master cylinder is dismantled. Dismantling of the pushrod is not advised.

6 Check before reassembly that all traces of contamination have been removed from inside the reservoir and master cylinder body. Check that all internal passages are clear.

7 Install the new spring, piston, circlip and dust boot in the master cylinder noting that the piston seals should be lubricated with new brake fluid before installation. Make sure the circlip properly locates in its groove in the master cylinder and locates in the step of the pushrod stopper plate - when correctly installed, it should be possible to rotate the circlip in its groove and the gap between the circlip ears should be at least 5.2 mm (0.2 in). Slip the dust boot back into place. If the clevis position on the pushrod was disturbed, make sure that the distance from the eye of the clevis to the lower mounting bolt hole of the master cylinder measures 57 mm (2.2 in).

8 The caliper link can be dismantled after removing the pivot bolt to free it from the caliper bracket (see illustration). The pivots in the caliper link and caliper mounting bracket eye consist of an inner sleeve and needle roller bearing (see illustration). Slip the inner sleeve out and pry the grease seal from each side of the pivot using a flat-bladed

screwdriver. The needle roller bearing should be pressed out using a drawbolt tool.

9 Install the master cylinder in a reverse of the removal sequence, noting the following:
a) Tighten the master cylinder mounting bolts to the specified torque setting.
b) Use new bolts on the triangular link bracket and tighten them to the specified torque setting.
c) Use a new split pin to secure the clevis cotter pin and bend its legs to lock it in place.
d) New sealing washers should be used on each side of the hose unions.
e) Check that the neck of the brake hoses abuts the lug on the master cylinder and tighten the hose union bolts to the specified torque setting.

Proportional control valve

10 Remove both side panels and the seat. Remove the four bolts retaining the grabrail to the frame and release the seat link from the lock as it is lifted free (see illustration). Disconnect the taillamp wiring connector, then remove the two bolts retaining the seat cowl (tail fairing) and very carefully manoeuvre the seat cowl away from the frame. Note: Access to the valve is possible with the seat cowl in place, but its removal is advised to improve working space and prevent damage from brake fluid spills.

11 The proportional control valve is held in rubber mountings attached to the frame; remove the air intake duct for access (see

illustrations). Have a supply of clean rags at hand and cover the surrounding area to prevent damage from brake fluid spills. Take note of the fitted angle of the hoses as a guide to installation, then hold the square body of the valve with an open-ended spanner whilst the banjo union bolts are unscrewed. With the hoses detached, work the mounting rubbers off their tabs to free the valve from the frame.

12 Note that the proportional control valve cannot be dismantled; if it fails, it must be renewed. Install the valve in a reverse of the removal procedure, noting that new sealing washers must be used on each side of the hose unions. Tighten the banjo union bolts to the specified torque setting.

13 Bleed the brakes as described in Section 13.

12 Brake discs - inspection and renewal

1 The brake discs can be inspected with the wheels installed. Look for signs of excessive scoring. Some degree of scoring is inevitable, but in severe cases renewal of the disc may prove necessary to restore full braking effect. Check for disc warpage, which can often result from overheating or impact damage and may cause brake judder. This is best checked using a dial gauge mounted on the fork leg or swingarm (as applicable) and should not exceed the specified limit (see illustration).

11.12a Remove bolt (arrowed) to free air duct

11.12b Proportional control valve is held in rubber mountings

12.1 Using a dial indicator to measure disc runout

2 The disc thickness should be measured using a vernier caliper or micrometer in several places around the disc surface **(see illustration)**. If the disc has worn to or beyond the service limit it should be renewed.

3 To remove a disc, first remove the relevant wheel as described in this Chapter, then unscrew the disc mounting bolts evenly and in a diagonal sequence. When removing a front disc, note the shims which are fitted between the disc and the hub. These must not be omitted on reassembly.

4 On installation ensure that the mounting surfaces of the disc and hub are clean and refit the disc to the hub. Note that on some models the front discs are marked with an R or an L. In such cases, the disc marked R must be fitted on the right side, with the R facing outwards, and the one marked L must be fitted on the left side with the L facing outwards. On 1000 P models onward, the rear disc must be installed so that the arrow and DRIVE marking faces outwards. On all models apply a few drops of thread-locking compound to the mounting bolts and tighten them evenly and progressively to the specified torque setting **(see illustration)**.

13 Bleeding the hydraulic brake or clutch system

Caution: Hydraulic fluid will discolour or remove paint if contact is allowed. If brake fluid comes in contact with any painted or plastic components it must be washed off immediately with cold water.

1 If brake (or clutch - 1000 models) action becomes spongy, or any part of the hydraulic system is dismantled (such as when a hose is renewed) it is necessary to bleed the system in order to remove all traces of air. The procedure for bleeding the hydraulic system is best carried out by two people.

Clutch bleeding (all 1000 models), brake bleeding (1000 H, J, K, L, M, N and all 600 models)

2 Check the fluid level in the reservoir and top up with new fluid of the specified type if required. Keep the reservoir at least half full during the bleeding procedure; if the level is allowed to fall too far air will enter the system requiring that the procedure be started again from scratch. Refit the reservoir cap or cover to prevent the ingress of dust or the ejection of a spout of fluid.

3 Remove the dust cap from the caliper (or slave cylinder, if working on the clutch - 1000 models) bleed nipple and clean the area with a rag. Place a clean glass jar below the caliper and connect a pipe from the bleed nipple to the jar **(see illustration)**. A clear plastic pipe should be used so that air bubbles can be more easily seen. When bleeding the front brake do this to both calipers; the calipers

12.2 Using a micrometer to measure disc thickness

should then be bled simultaneously. Pour enough clean hydraulic fluid in the glass jar so that the pipe end is immersed below the fluid surface; ensure that the pipe end remains submerged (to prevent air returning to the system whenever the pressure is released) throughout the operation.

4 If parts of the system have been renewed, and thus the system must be filled, open the bleed nipple about one turn and pump the lever/pedal (as appropriate), until fluid starts to issue from the clear pipe. Tighten the bleed nipple and then continue the normal bleeding operation as described in the following paragraphs. Keep a close check on the reservoir level whilst the system is being filled.

5 Operate the lever/pedal (as appropriate), as far as it will go and hold it in this position against the fluid pressure. If spongy brake operation has occurred it may be necessary to pump the lever/pedal rapidly a number of times until pressure builds up. With pressure applied, loosen the bleed nipple about half a turn, then tighten it as soon as the lever/pedal has reached its full travel and then release the lever/pedal. Repeat this operation until no more air bubbles are expelled with the fluid into the glass jar. When this condition is reached the air bleeding operation should be complete, resulting in a firm feel to the lever/pedal. If sponginess is still evident continue the bleeding operation; it may be that an air bubble trapped at the top of the system has yet to work down through the caliper.

6 When all traces of air have been removed from the system, top up the reservoir and refit the diaphragm, plate and cap or cover. Check the entire system for leaks, and check also that the brake system in general is functioning efficiently before riding the machine.

HAYNES HiNT *If it's not possible to produce a firm feel to the brake lever or pedal the fluid my be aerated. Let the fluid in the system stabilise for a few hours and then repeat the procedure when the tiny bubbles in the system have settled out.*

12.4 Tighten disc mounting bolts to the specified torque setting

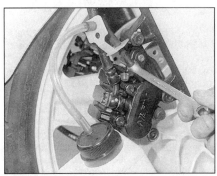
13.3 Connect brake/clutch bleeding kit as shown

Brake bleeding (1000 P models onward)

Note: *Honda utilise a vacuum-type brake bleeder to bleed the brakes which operates by drawing (sucking) air/fluid out of the system, and then bleed the brakes by the conventional pressure method described below. If you find that the conventional method fails to remove air trapped in the brake hoses or pipes, entrust the work to a Honda dealer equipped with the brake bleeder.*

7 It is important to bleed the brake system components as a whole and in the following order:

Right front brake caliper upper bleed nipple - front brake lever pressure.
Left front brake caliper upper bleed nipple - front brake lever pressure.
Right front brake caliper lower bleed nipple - rear brake pedal pressure.
Left front brake caliper lower bleed nipple - rear brake pedal pressure.
Rear brake caliper rearmost bleed nipple - rear brake pedal pressure.
Rear brake caliper foremost bleed nipple - secondary master cylinder pressure.

8 Pry the plug out of the secondary master cylinder body. Using an Allen key, turn the screw anti-clockwise until it seats against the circlip - this is necessary to permit bleeding of the front calipers **(see illustration)**.

9 Adjust the brake lever span adjuster so that the lever is at its furthest position from the handlebar. Remove the two screws which retain the front brake reservoir cover. Lift off

7

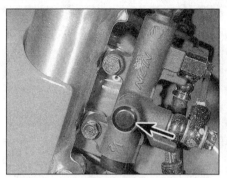

13.8 Remove the plug (arrowed) from the secondary master cylinder to access the Allen screw

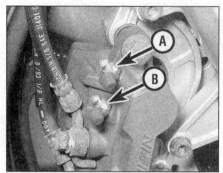

13.10 Right front caliper upper (A) and lower (B) bleed nipples

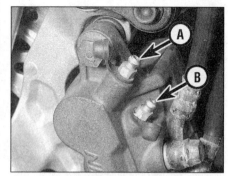

13.13 Left front caliper upper (A) and lower (B) bleed nipples

the cover, plate, diaphragm and float. Check that the fluid level is up to the upper mark, then operate the front brake lever about ten times to bleed air from the reservoir - tiny bubbles will be seen coming up from the bottom of the reservoir.

10 Pull the dust cover off the upper bleed nipple on the right front brake caliper and clean the area with a rag **(see illustration)**. Place a clean glass jar below the caliper and connect a pipe from the bleed nipple to the jar. A clear plastic pipe should be used so that air bubbles can be more easily seen. When bleeding the front brake do this to both calipers; the calipers should then be bled simultaneously. Pour enough clean hydraulic fluid in the glass jar so that the pipe end is immersed below the fluid surface; ensure that the pipe end remains submerged (to prevent air returning to the system whenever the pressure is released) throughout the operation.

11 If parts of the system have been renewed, and thus the system must be filled, open the bleed nipple about one turn and pump the lever until fluid starts to issue from the clear pipe. Tighten the bleed nipple and then continue the normal bleeding operation as described in the following paragraphs. Keep a close check on the reservoir level whilst the system is being filled.

12 Pump the lever rapidly a number of times until pressure builds up, then hold it against the fluid pressure. With pressure applied,

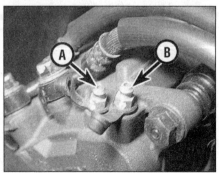

13.18 Rear caliper rearmost (A) and foremost (B) bleed nipples

loosen the bleed nipple a quarter turn, then tighten it as soon as the lever has reached the handlebar. Close the bleed nipple and slowly release the brake lever. Repeat this operation until no more air bubbles are expelled with the fluid into the glass jar. When this condition is reached the air bleeding operation should be complete, resulting in a firm feel to the lever. If sponginess is still evident continue the bleeding operation; it may be that an air bubble trapped at the top of the system has yet to work down through the caliper. Remove the tube from the bleed nipple and wipe off any fluid spills. Tighten it to the specified torque setting and install the dust cap. Check the fluid level in the front brake reservoir, top up and loosely install the cover to prevent spouts of fluid escaping.

13 Repeat steps 10 to 12 on the upper bleed nipple on the left front caliper **(see illustration)**.

14 Remove the right sidepanel to access the rear brake fluid reservoir. To improve access, remove the bolt retaining the air intake duct on that side and slip the duct out of the air intake hose. Unscrew the reservoir cap and lift out the plate and diaphragm. Top up the reservoir if the level is low and pump the brake pedal a few times to bleed air from the master cylinder. Loosely install the cap to prevent spouts of fluid escaping.

15 Connect the bleed tube to the lower bleed nipple on the right front brake caliper **(see illustration 13.10)**. If parts of the system have been renewed, and thus the system must be filled, open the bleed nipple about one turn and pump the rear brake pedal until fluid starts to issue from the clear pipe. Tighten the bleed nipple and then continue the normal bleeding operation as described in the following paragraph. Keep a close check on the rear brake fluid reservoir level whilst the system is being filled.

16 Pump the rear brake pedal five to ten times and hold the pedal down as the bleed valve is loosened a quarter turn. Tighten the bleed valve (do not release the pedal until the valve has been tightened). Repeat this operation until no more air bubbles are expelled with the fluid into the glass jar. When

this condition is reached the air bleeding operation should be complete, resulting in a firm feel to the pedal. If sponginess is still evident continue the bleeding operation; it may be that an air bubble trapped at the top of the system has yet to work down through the caliper. Remove the tube from the bleed nipple and wipe off any fluid spills. Tighten it to the specified torque setting and install the dust cap. Check the fluid level in the rear brake reservoir, top up and loosely install the cap to prevent spouts of fluid.

17 Repeat the procedure described in paragraphs 15 and 16 on the lower bleed nipple on the left front brake caliper **(see illustration 13.13)**.

18 Connect the bleed tube to the rearmost bleed nipple on the rear brake caliper and bleed the line of air as described in paragraphs 15 and 16 **(see illustration)**.

19 Connect the bleed tube to the foremost bleed nipple on the rear brake caliper **(see illustration 13.18)**. Hydraulic fluid supply to the two outer pistons of the rear caliper is via the front brake fluid reservoir, secondary master cylinder and proportional control valve. Using a ring spanner on the secondary master cylinder linkage bolt, crank the bolt clockwise five to ten times and hold it cranked whilst the bleed nipple is loosened a quarter turn. Tighten the bleed nipple and slowly release the crank. Note that you can achieve the same effect by manually grasping the left brake caliper and moving it upwards to operate the secondary master cylinder. Repeat this operation until no more air bubbles are expelled with the fluid into the glass jar. Remove the tube from the bleed nipple and wipe off any fluid spills. Tighten it to the specified torque setting and install the dust cap. Check the fluid level in the front brake reservoir, top up and install the float, diaphragm, plate and cover.

20 The bleeding operation is now complete. Check that all bleed nipples have been tightened, wipe off any fluid spills and install their dust caps. Check the fluid levels in the master cylinder reservoirs and install the float (front only), diaphragm, plate and cover/cap.

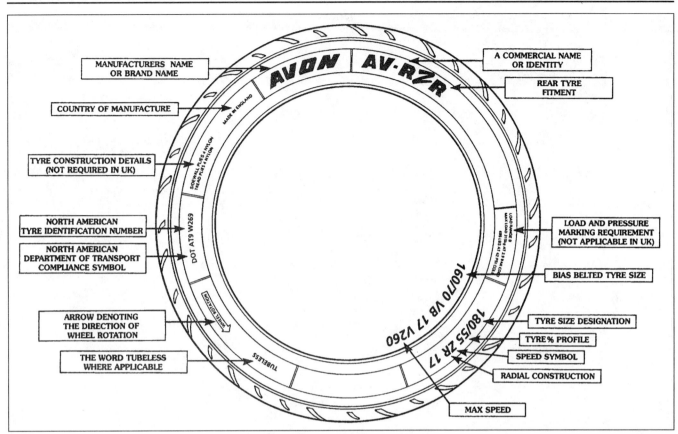

The labels on the tyre diagram read:

MANUFACTURERS NAME OR BRAND NAME

COUNTRY OF MANUFACTURE

TYRE CONSTRUCTION DETAILS (NOT REQUIRED IN UK)

NORTH AMERICAN TYRE IDENTIFICATION NUMBER

NORTH AMERICAN DEPARTMENT OF TRANSPORT COMPLIANCE SYMBOL

ARROW DENOTING THE DIRECTION OF WHEEL ROTATION

THE WORD TUBELESS WHERE APPLICABLE

A COMMERCIAL NAME OR IDENTITY

REAR TYRE FITMENT

LOAD AND PRESSURE MARKING REQUIREMENT (NOT APPLICABLE IN UK)

BIAS BELTED TYRE SIZE

TYRE SIZE DESIGNATION

TYRE % PROFILE

SPEED SYMBOL

RADIAL CONSTRUCTION

MAX SPEED

14.3 Common tyre sidewall markings

21 Using an Allen key, tighten the secondary master cylinder valve. Install the cap.

22 Check the entire system for leaks, and check also that the brake system in general is functioning efficiently before riding the machine.

All models

23 Fluid drained from the system will almost certainly be contaminated, either by foreign matter or more commonly by the absorption of water from the air. All hydraulic fluids are to some degree hygroscopic, that is, they are capable of drawing water from the atmosphere, and thereby degrading their specification. In view of this, and the relative cheapness of the fluid, old fluid should always be discarded.

14 Tyres -
general information and fitting

General information

1 Only tubeless tyres are suitable for fitting on these wheel rims.

2 Refer to the Daily (pre-ride) checks listed at the beginning of this manual, and to the scheduled checks in Chapter 1 for tyre and wheel maintenance.

Fitting new tyres

3 When selecting new tyres, refer to the tyre information label on the motorcycle and the tyre options listed in the owners manual. Ensure that front and rear tyre types are

compatible, the correct size and correct speed rating; if necessary seek advice from a Honda dealer or tyre fitting specialist **(see illustration)**.

4 It is recommended that tyres are fitted by a motorcycle tyre specialist rather than attempted in the home workshop. The force required to break the seal between the wheel rim and tyre bead is substantial, and is usually beyond the capabilities of an individual working with normal tyre levers. Additionally, the specialist will be able to balance the wheels after tyre fitting.

5 Only certain types of puncture repair are suitable for tubeless motorcycle tyres. Refer to a tyre fitting specialist for advice and to your owners manual for details of the reduced speeds advised for a repaired tyre.

7

Notes

Chapter 8
Electrical system

Contents

Degrees of difficulty

Easy, suitable for novice with little experience	**Fairly easy,** suitable for beginner with some experience	**Fairly difficult,** suitable for competent DIY mechanic	**Difficult,** suitable for experienced DIY mechanic	**Very difficult,** suitable for expert DIY or professional

Specifications

Electrical system
Voltage 12
Earth (ground) .... Negative

Battery
Capacity:
  600 models .... 8 Ah
  1000 models .... 14 Ah
Electrolyte specific gravity - 1000 models .... 1.280 @ 20°C (68°F)

Alternator
Type .... Three-phase AC
Output:
  1000 K models onward .... 390 watts @ 5000 rpm
  All other models .... 350 watts @ 5000 rpm
Charging voltage
  600 models and 1000 H, J, K, L, M, N models .... 13.5 - 15.5 volts @ 5000 rpm
  1000 P models onward .... 12.6 - 15.0 volts @ 5000 rpm
Stator coil resistance:
  600 models .... 0.1 - 1.0 ohm
  1000 H, J, K, L, M, N models .... 0.4 - 0.6 ohm
  1000 P models onward .... 0 - 0.1 ohm
Field coil resistance - 1000 H, J, K, L, M, N models .... 2.0 - 2.6 ohms

Starter motor
Standard brush length:
  600 models .... 12.5 mm (0.49 in)
  1000 models .... 12.0 - 13.0 mm (0.47 - 0.51 in)
Service limit:
  600 models .... 8.5 mm (0.33 in)
  1000 models .... 6.5 mm (0.26 in)

8

Fuel level sender unit

Resistance:

Full tank	4 - 10 ohms
Empty tank	90 - 100 ohms

Fuel pump flow rate

600 models	650 cc (22.0 US fl oz/22.8 Imp fl oz) per minute
1000 models	900 cc (30.4 US fl oz/31.7 Imp fl oz) per minute

Fuses

	1000 H, J and all 600 models	1000 K, L, M, N models
Main	30 A	30 A
Fuse A*	10 A	10 A
Fuse B*	10 A	10 A
Fuse C*	10 A	20 A
Fuse D*	10 A	10 A
Fuse E*	10 A	20 A
Fuse F*	15 A	10 A
Fuse G*	10 A	10 A

Refer to the wiring diagrams at the end of this Chapter for fuse identification

Fuses

	1000 P models onward
Main fuse	30 A
Headlamp	20 A
Neutral, oil temperature and tachometer	10 A
Position lamp, meter lights and taillamp	10 A
Turn signals, brake stoplamp, horn, headlamp pass	10A
Ignition, starting and charging	10 A
Fan motor	10 A

Bulbs

	US models	UK models
Headlamp:		
1000 K models onward	12V 45/45W x 2	12V 60/55W x 2
All other models	12V 60/55W	12V 60/55W x 2
Position lamp (where fitted):		
H and J models	12V 2 cp	12V 4W
K models onward	12V 2 cp	12V 5W
Tail/stop lamp	12V 2/32 cp*	12V 5/21V
Turn signal lamps:		
Front (also running lamp on US models)	12V 32/3 cp*	12V 21W
Rear	12V 32 cp	12V 21W
Instrument illuminating lamps:		
600 H and J models	12V 3W	12V 3W
1000 H and J models	12V 3.4W	12V 1.7W
All K models onward	12V 1.7W	12V 1.7W
Warning lamps:		
600 H and J models	12V 3W	12V 3W
600 K and L models	12V 3.4W	12V 3W
1000 models	12V 3.4W	12V 3.4W

Check bulbholder marking

Torque settings

	kgf m	lbf ft
Alternator rotor nut - 1000 H and J models	5.0	36.0
Cooling fan switch - 600 models	1.8	13.0

1 General description

On 600 models the power for the complete electrical system is provided by a three-phase alternator mounted on the right side of the crankshaft. All 1000 models use a brushless field coil type alternator which is mounted on the top left side of the crankcase, behind the cylinder block, and is chain-driven off the crankshaft. On this type of alternator the field coil magnetises the rotor, which then generates power as it passes the stator coil.

On all models the output from the alternator is controlled and rectified by a combined regulator/rectifier unit before being passed to the battery and thence to the main electrical system.

2 Electrical system - general information and preliminary checks

1 In the event of an electrical system fault, always check the physical condition of the wiring and connectors before attempting any of the test procedures described here and in subsequent sections. Look for chafed, trapped

or broken electrical leads and repair or renew them as necessary. Leads which have broken internally are not easily spotted, but may be checked using a multimeter set to the resistance (ohms) scale or a simple battery and bulb circuit as a continuity tester **(see illustration)**. The various multi-pin connectors are generally trouble-free but may corrode if exposed to water. Clean them carefully, scraping off any surface deposits, and pack with silicone grease during assembly to avoid recurrent problems. The same technique can be applied to the handlebar switches.

2 The wiring harness is colour-coded and will correspond with the wiring diagrams at the end of this manual. Where socket connections are used, they are designed so that reconnection can be made only in the correct position.

3 Visual inspection will usually show whether there are any breaks or frayed outer coverings which will give rise to short circuits. Occasionally a wire may become trapped between two components, breaking the inner core but leaving the more resilient outer cover intact. This can give rise to mysterious intermittent or total circuit failure. Another source of trouble may be the snap connectors or sockets, where the connector has not been pushed fully home in the outer housing, or where corrosion has occurred.

4 Intermittent short circuits can often be traced to a chafed wire that passes through or is close to a metal component such as a frame member. Avoid tight bends in the lead or situations where a lead can become trapped between casings.

5 A sound, fully charged battery, is essential to the normal operation of the system. There is no point in attempting to locate a fault if the battery is partly discharged or worn out. Check battery condition and recharge or renew the battery before proceeding further.

6 Many of the test procedures described in this chapter require voltages or resistances to be checked. This necessitates the use of some form of test equipment such as a simple and inexpensive multimeter of the type sold by electronics or automotive accessory shops.

7 If you doubt your ability to check the electrical system, entrust the work to an authorised Honda dealer. In any event have your findings double-checked before consigning expensive components to the scrap bin.

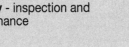

3 Battery - inspection and maintenance

Warning: Batteries can be dangerous if mishandled; read the Safety first! section at the front of this manual before starting work, and always wear overalls or old clothing in case of accidental acid

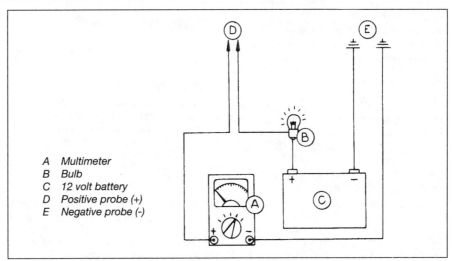

A   Multimeter
B   Bulb
C   12 volt battery
D   Positive probe (+)
E   Negative probe (-)

2.1 Simple testing equipment for checking the wiring

spillage. If acid is ever allowed to splash into your eyes or onto your skin, flush it away with copious quantities of fresh water and seek medical advice immediately.

600 models

1 To gain access to the battery remove both side panels and the seat. Remove the three bolts from the top of the battery box and lift off the lid. The battery is a sealed unit and requires no regular maintenance other than ensuring its terminals are kept clean and its connections are tight.

2 The condition of the battery can be assessed by measuring the voltage present at the battery terminals. When fully charged there should be approximately 13 volts present. If the voltage falls below 12.3 volts the battery must be removed, disconnecting the negative (-) terminal first, and recharged as described below in paragraph 6. On refitting ensure that the terminals are clean and apply a thin smear of petroleum jelly to each to prevent corrosion. Tighten the terminal bolts securely and ensure the rubber cover is correctly installed over the positive (+) terminal.

1000 models

3 Details of the regular checks needed to maintain the battery in good condition are given in Chapter 1, together with instructions on removal and refitting and general battery care.

4 When new, the battery is filled with an electrolyte of dilute sulphuric acid having a specific gravity of 1.280 at 20°C (68°F). Subsequent evaporation, which occurs in normal use, can be compensated for by topping up with distilled or demineralised water only. **Note:** Never use tap water as a substitute and do not add fresh electrolyte unless spillage has occurred.

5 The state of charge of a battery can be checked using an hydrometer to test the specific gravity of the electrolyte. When fully charged this should be 1.280 at 20°C (68°F), and in normal use approximately 1.260 at 20°C (68°F). If the electrolyte falls below 1.260 at 20°C (68°F), the battery must be removed and charged as described in paragraph 6. After charging, top up with distilled water as required, then check the specific gravity and battery voltage. Specific gravity should be above 1.270 and a sound, fully charged battery should produce 12 - 13 volts.

All models

6 The normal charge rate for a battery is 1/10 of its rated capacity, thus for a 14 ampere hour unit charging should take place at 1.4 amp. Exceeding this figure can cause the battery to overheat, buckling the plates and rendering it useless. Few owners will have access to an expensive current-controlled charger, so if a normal domestic charger is used check that after a possible initial peak, the charge rate falls to a safe level. If the battery becomes hot during charging **stop**. Further charging will cause damage. **Note:** On 1000 models the cell caps should be loosened and the vents unobstructed during charging to avoid a build-up of pressure and risk of explosion.

7 If the recharged battery discharges rapidly when left disconnected, it is likely that an internal short caused by physical damage or sulphation has occurred. A new battery will be required. A sound item will tend to lose its charge at about 1% per day.

4 Charging system - checking the output

1 Before checking the charging system a leakage test should be carried out to check that power is not being drained from the battery whilst the machine is not in use.

8

US 600 models

2 Remove the side panels and seat then remove the battery box lid. Check that the ignition switch its turned OFF, then disconnect the lead from the negative (-) battery terminal. Connect a multimeter set to the amps (A) range (select a high scale at first to avoid damage to the meter due to a sudden surge of current, then bring the scale down to suit) between the negative terminal and lead and note the reading obtained. The meter reading should not exceed 0.01 mA.

All 1000 H, J models and UK 1000 K, L, M, N models

3 Remove the seat and left side panel. Check that the ignition switch is turned OFF. Disconnect the regulator/rectifier wiring connectors from the main wiring loom, then disconnect the lead from the negative (-) terminal of the battery. Connect a multimeter set to the voltage range between the lead and negative (-) battery terminal and note the reading obtained. A reading of 0 volts should be shown on the meter.

US 1000 K models onward and UK 1000 P models onward

4 Remove the seat. Check that the ignition switch is turned OFF. Disconnect the lead from the negative (-) terminal of the battery. Set a multimeter to the amps (A) scale (select a high scale at first to avoid damage to the meter due to a sudden surge of current, then bring the scale down to suit) and connect the positive (+) probe to the lead and the negative probe (-) to the battery negative (-) terminal. A reading of 0 amps should be obtained on US models and 0 to 0.1 mA on UK models.

All models

5 If the leakage test fails to provide the above result, the charging system wiring is probably at fault and should be tested as described in Section 2 of this Chapter.

6 If all is well, disconnect the meter and reconnect the lead to the battery's negative (-) terminal.

7 Start the engine and warm it up to normal operating temperature. Stop the engine and connect a multimeter set on the dc volts range across the terminals of the battery, connecting the meter's positive probe to the positive (+) battery terminal, and its negative probe to the negative (-) terminal. Start the engine and allow it to idle, then slowly increase the engine speed to 5000 rpm and note the reading obtained. At this speed the voltage should be 13.5 - 15.5 volts on all 600 and 1000 H, J, K, L, M, N models and 12.6 - 15.0 volts on 1000 P models onward. If the voltage is below this it will be necessary to check the alternator and regulator performance as described in the following Sections. **Note:** *Occasionally the condition may arise where the charging voltage is excessive. This condition is almost certainly due to a faulty regulator/rectifier which should be tested individually.*

5 Alternator - testing

600 models

1 Remove the fuel tank as described in Section 4 of Chapter 4 then disconnect the 3 pin block connector which contains the Yellow wires. Using a multimeter set to the ohms x 1 scale measure the resistance between each of the yellow wires on the alternator side of the connector, taking a total of three readings, then check for continuity between each terminal and earth (ground). If the stator coil windings are in good condition there should be no continuity between any of the terminals and earth (ground) and the three readings should be within the range shown in the Specifications at the start of this Chapter. If not the alternator stator coil assembly is at fault and should be renewed. The coil is bolted to the inside of the right crankcase cover which can be removed as described in Chapter 2 **(see illustration)**.

1000 models

2 Remove the seat and left side panel and disconnect the 6 pin alternator block connector. Using a multimeter set to the ohms x 1 scale measure the resistance between each of the Yellow (stator coil) wires on the alternator side of the connector, taking a total of three measurements, then check for continuity between each wire and earth (ground). Set the meter to the ohms x 10 scale and measure the resistance between the Black and White (field coil) wires.

3 If the readings obtained are not within the limits shown in the Specifications at the start of this Chapter or there is continuity between any of the Yellow wires and earth (ground) the stator assembly is faulty and must be renewed. The stator assembly can be removed as described in the following Section.

All models

4 If the stator assembly is found to be faulty, check first that the fault is not due to a broken

5.1 On 600 models alternator stator coil is bolted to inside of the right crankcase cover

wire or connection to the alternator itself; pinched or broken alternator wires can be easily repaired by the average private owner. Note that if the coil is confirmed faulty it may be worth seeking the advice of an auto electrical specialist, who may well be able to rewind the damaged coil.

6 Stator coil - removal and inspection (1000 models)

1 Remove the seat and left side panel then remove the lower and left side fairing sections (as applicable). Trace the wiring back from the alternator and disconnect the 6-pin block connector from the main wiring loom.

H and J models

2 Slacken the three screws which retain the alternator cover and partially remove the cover. Withdraw the clip which secures the grommet in position then displace the grommet and lift the cover away from the machine.

3 To remove the bearing from the end of the alternator shaft a puller will be required. **Caution: Do not attempt to remove the bearing using any other method as the alternator is easily damaged.** Once the bearing has been removed put the transmission into gear and apply the rear brake hard to prevent the alternator shaft rotating whilst the rotor nut is slackened. Remove the nut and washer then withdraw the rotor and stator windings.

4 The stator windings are installed by reversing the removal sequence. Fit the windings to the alternator body and refit the rotor ensuring that the pin on the alternator shaft engages correctly with the hole in the rotor body. Refit the rotor shaft nut and washer and tighten it to the specified torque setting whilst retaining the shaft using the method described on disassembly. Fit the bearing onto the shaft and tap it into position using a tubular drift which bears only on the inner race of the bearing. Fit the stator grommet to the cover, securing it in position with the clip, then install the cover and tighten its retaining screws securely.

K models onward

5 Remove the three bolts which secure the alternator cover in position and remove the cover, noting its sealing O-ring. The stator windings are fitted inside the cover. On installation, check the condition of the O-ring and renew if necessary, then refit the cover and tighten its retaining bolts securely.

All models

6 Connect the alternator block and refit the left side and lower fairing sections (as applicable). If necessary, check the charging rate as described in Section 4, then refit the side panel and seat.

	Red/White	Green	Yellow
Red/White		∞	∞
Green	1 ~ 20		0·5 ~ 10
Yellow	0·5 ~ 10	10 ~ 200	

Unit: kΩ

H 23724

7.1 Regulator/rectifier test table - 600 models

7.5 On 1000 K models onward the regulator/rectifier is located behind seat cowling

7 Regulator/rectifier unit - testing

Note: *Honda recommend the use of one of the following testers when making the resistance checks on 1000 K models onward and all 600 models, stating that other meters may well produce inaccurate readings. It should, however, be possible to gain an indication of the unit's condition using other meters, but it is advised that your findings are confirmed by a Honda dealer before making a decision on the unit's condition. The recommended meters are: Kowa analogue meter (TH-5H); Kowa digital meter (07411-0020000 or KS-AHM-32-003); Sanwa analogue meter (07308-0020001). The Kowa meter should be set to the x 100 ohms range and the Sanwa to the K ohm range.*

600 models

1 Remove the fuel tank as described in Chapter 4 and disconnect the white (3-pin) and red (4-pin) block connectors. Using a multimeter set to the appropriate resistance scale, check the resistance between the various wires on the regulator/rectifier (rear) side of the connectors. If the readings do not compare closely with those shown in the accompanying table the regulator/rectifier unit can be considered faulty **(see illustration)**.

2 The unit is located behind the carburettors where it is situated between the ignition HT coils. To remove it, first remove the left lower fairing section then remove the two bolts which retain it to the frame.

1000 H and J models

3 Note that there is no internal resistance test provided by the manufacturer for these models. If a fault is suspected, and the output checks specified in Section 4 have proved satisfactory, it is recommended that the machine be taken to a Honda dealer for examination and the temporary substitution of a good known unit.

4 To gain access to the unit, first remove the seat and both side panels then slacken the grab rail and seat cowling mounting bolts and lift the grab rail clear of the machine. Disengage the bulbholders from the back of the stop/tail lamp and carefully remove the seat cowling.

1000 K models onward

5 Remove the seat, side panels and seat cowling. Disconnect the regulator/rectifier connector then slacken the unit's mounting bolts and remove it from the machine **(see illustration)**.

6 Once removed from the machine, the regulator/rectifier unit's internal circuitry can be tested by measuring the resistances present between its various terminals. If the readings do not closely resemble those in the accompanying table the unit can be considered faulty and must be renewed **(see illustrations)**.

7 A test of the unit's wiring can be made with it installed on the machine. Disconnect the main 7-pin block connector and using a multimeter set to the volts function, connect its positive (+) probe to the red/white wire terminal on the wiring harness side of the connector, and its negative (-) probe to earth (ground). Battery voltage should be shown if the wiring is in good condition. Go on to connect the meter's positive probe to the black wire, leaving its negative probe connected to earth (ground). No reading should be shown until the ignition is switched ON, at which point battery voltage should be shown on the meter.

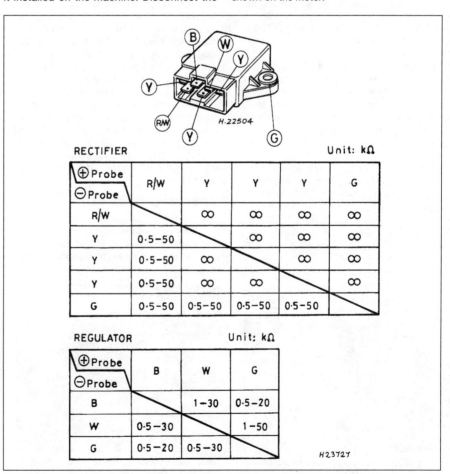

RECTIFIER

Unit: kΩ

⊕ Probe / ⊖ Probe	R/W	Y	Y	Y	G
R/W		∞	∞	∞	∞
Y	0·5-50		∞	∞	∞
Y	0·5-50	∞		∞	∞
Y	0·5-50	∞	∞		∞
G	0·5-50	0·5-50	0·5-50	0·5-50	

REGULATOR

Unit: kΩ

⊕ Probe / ⊖ Probe	B	W	G
B		1-30	0·5-20
W	0·5-30		1-50
G	0·5-20	0·5-30	

H23727

7.6a Regulator/rectifier test table - 1000 K, L, M, N models

+ -	R/W	Y	Y	Y	Bl	W
R/W		∞	∞	∞	∞	∞
Y	0.5 - 50		∞	∞	∞	∞
Y	0.5 - 50	∞		∞	∞	∞.
Y	0.5 - 50	∞	∞		∞	∞
Bl	1 - 70	1 - 70	1 - 70	1 - 70		1 - 30
W	1.5 - 100	1.5 - 100	1.5 - 100	1.5 - 100	0.5 - 30	

Unit: K ohms

7.6b Regulator/rectifier test table - 1000 P models onward

8 Fuses - general

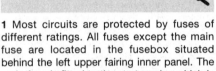

1 Most circuits are protected by fuses of different ratings. All fuses except the main fuse are located in the fusebox situated behind the left upper fairing inner panel. The main fuse is fitted to the starter relay which is behind the right side panel. All fusebox fuses are labelled for easy identification **(see illustrations)**.

2 Blown fuses can be easily recognised by the melted metal strip. Each is clearly marked with its rating and must only be replaced by a fuse of the correct rating.

Caution: Never install a fuse of a higher rating or bridge the terminals with any other substitute, however temporary it may be. Serious damage may be done to the circuit, or a fire may start. Always carry a supply of spare fuses of each rating on the machine.

3 While an isolated fault may occasionally blow a fuse and never occur again, such cases are rare and generally due to faulty connections, although fuses do sometimes blow due to old age or similar factors. However, if the fuse for any circuit blows repeatedly, a more serious fault is indicated which must be traced and remedied as soon as possible.

9 Starter motor - testing

1 In the event of a starter malfunction, always check first that the battery is fully charged. A partially discharged battery may be able to provide enough power for the lighting system, but not the heavy current required for starting the engine. Look also for broken, chafed or corroded wiring before proceeding further. Also ensure that all fuses are in good condition.

2 Remove the right sidepanel to gain access to the starter relay (solenoid). Ensure the transmission is in neutral, the engine kill switch is in the RUN position, and on K and L models that the side stand is up. Turn the ignition switch ON, pull in the clutch lever and operate the starter button whilst listening to the starter relay. As the button is pressed the relay should be heard to click. If the relay clicks as the button is pressed, the fault lies in the starter motor, which should be removed and examined as described in the following Section. If no click is heard the fault lies in the starter circuit components which should be tested as follows.

Starter relay (solenoid)

3 Disconnect the battery terminals, remembering to disconnect the negative (-) terminal first, then disconnect the starter relay wiring connector from the starter relay. Disconnect the starter motor and battery

leads from the relay terminals and remove the relay from the machine **(see illustration)**.

4 Set a multimeter to the ohms x 1 scale and connect it across the relay terminals. Using a fully-charged 12 volt battery and two insulated auxiliary wires, connect the positive (+) terminal of the battery to the yellow/red terminal of the relay, and the negative (-) terminal to the green/red terminal of the relay. At this point the relay should click and the multimeter read 0 ohms (indicating continuity). If this is the case, the relay is proven serviceable and the fault must lie in the starter switch circuit. If the relay is not heard to click, it is proven faulty and must be renewed.

Neutral switch

5 If the neutral switch is not operating correctly, it can be tested as described in Section 6 of Chapter 5.

Ignition and engine kill switches

6 The test procedure is described in Section 5 of Chapter 5.

Starter button

7 Trace the wiring from the right handlebar switch back to its block connectors. Disconnect them and make the following test on the switch side of the wiring. Using a multimeter set to the ohms x 1 scale check for continuity between the yellow/red and black, or yellow/red and black/white (as applicable) terminals. When the button is pressed there should be continuity (low resistance) between the two, and when the button is released there should be an open-circuit (high resistance). On US models also check for continuity between the blue/white and black/red terminals, there should be an open circuit between these two when the button is pressed and continuity when the button is released. If not the starter button is faulty and must either be repaired or the right handlebar switch renewed.

Clutch diode

8 The location of the clutch diode varies depending on the model. On 600 models it is necessary to remove the fuel tank to gain access to the diode which is fitted to the

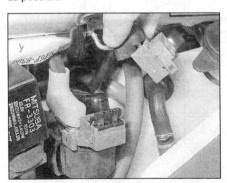

8.1a Main fuse is fitted to the starter relay ...

8.1b ... and all other fuses are situated in fusebox behind left upper fairing inner panel

9.3 Starter relay is located behind right sidepanel - 1000 shown

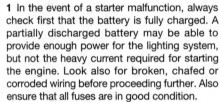

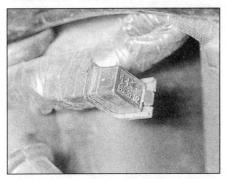

9.8 Test clutch diode as described in text

section of wiring loom running up the left side of the frame. On 1000 H and J models the diode is located behind the upper fairing section (which must first be removed), where it is situated just behind the speedometer cable. On 1000 K models onward, it can be found behind the left sidepanel **(see illustration)**.

9 Remove the diode from the machine and using a multimeter set to the resistance scale check for continuity between the terminals of the diode. Transpose the meter probes and check for continuity in the opposite direction. If the diode is serviceable there should be continuity in one direction (indicated by the arrow on the diode) and an open-circuit in the other. If not, the diode must be renewed.

Clutch lever switch

10 Disconnect the wires from the clutch lever switch and check for continuity between the switch terminals using a multimeter set to the ohms x 1 scale. If the switch is good condition there should be continuity (low resistance) with the clutch lever pulled back to the handlebar and an open-circuit (high resistance) with the lever released. If not, the clutch switch is faulty and must be renewed.

Side stand switch - K models onward only

11 The side stand switch can be tested as described in Section 6 of Chapter 5.

10 Starter motor - removal, overhaul and installation

1 On 600 models remove the left lower fairing section. On 1000 models remove the carburettors as described in Section 7 of Chapter 4 and the lower and right side fairing sections (as applicable). On all models disconnect the battery terminals (negative (-) terminal first) to prevent the risk of a short-circuit.

2 Slacken and remove the nut which secures the starter motor lead and disconnect it from the motor. Release the starter motor bolts and

manoeuvre the motor away from the engine.

3 Wipe clean the splines of the starter shaft pinion teeth then tape over them to protect the oil seal as the cover is removed. Remove the two long retaining screws from the front of the starter motor and carefully lift off the front cover **(see illustrations)**. Note the number of shims fitted to the front of the armature then remove them. Carefully lift off the rear cover, noting that on 600 models the brush plate should come off with the cover. Make a note of the number and position of any shims fitted to the rear of the armature and then remove them. Withdraw the armature from the starter motor body.

4 Disengage the brushes from the brush plate and measure the length of each brush **(see illustration)**. If any brush has worn to or beyond the service limit given in the Specifications, renew the brushes as a set. As the brushes are soldered to either the brush plate (negative brushes) or the terminal bolt (positive brushes), they cannot be renewed separately; both the brush plate and terminal bolt assemblies will be required.

5 If the brush lengths are within the service limits check the brush wiring as follows. Using a multimeter set to the ohms x 1 scale, check for continuity between the positive brush(es) and the terminal bolt. Continuity should be shown; if no continuity (high resistance) is indicated, renewal is required. Repeat the test between the brush plate and negative brush

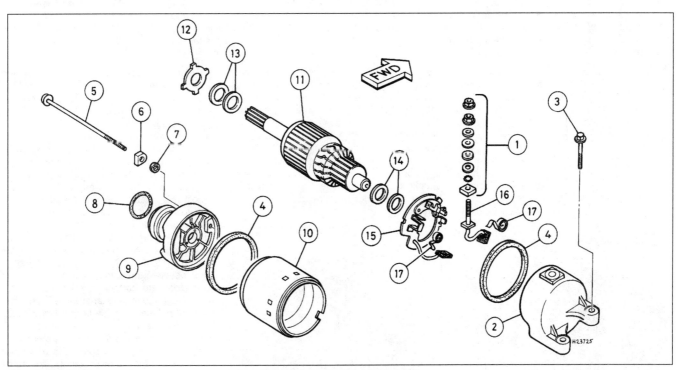

10.3a Starter motor - 600 models

1 Lead terminal	5 Long retaining screws	7 O-rings	10 Motor body	13 Shims	16 Positive brush
2 Rear cover		8 O-ring	11 Armature	14 Shims	17 Brush retaining springs
3 Mounting bolts	6 Washers	9 Front cover	12 Toothed washer	15 Brushplate and negative brush	
4 O-rings					

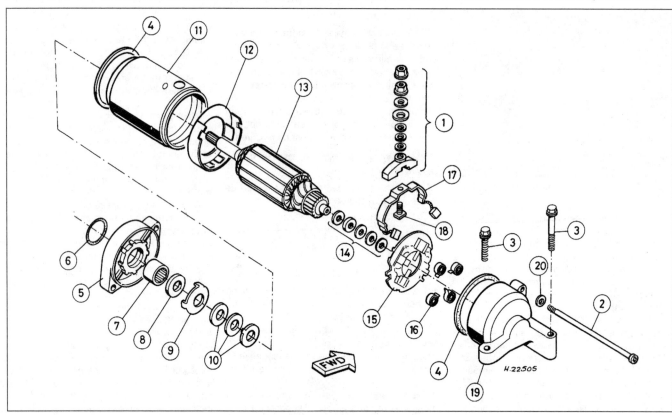

10.3b Starter motor - 1000 models

1 Lead terminal
2 Long retaining screws
3 Mounting bolts
4 O-rings
5 Front cover

6 O-ring
7 Needle roller bearing
8 Oil seal
9 Toothed washer

10 Shims
11 Motor body
12 Shield
13 Armature

14 Shims
15 Brushplate and negative brushes
16 Brush retaining springs

17 Positive brushes
18 Terminal bolt
19 Rear cover
20 Spring washers

tips; renew if no continuity (high resistance) is indicated. Set the meter to the K ohm scale and measure the resistance between the terminal bolt and cover or body (as applicable). If continuity exists, it is likely that the insulation has broken down at some point. If this is the case, remove the terminal bolt retaining nut, followed by all the washers. Make a careful note of how these washers are arranged as a guide to reassembly. Examine the insulating washers for cracks or other damage and renew them if necessary. Note that although they are not listed as being available separately, suitable replacements can be purchased from most automotive suppliers. Also check for continuity between the positive brush holder(s) and brush plate; if continuity exists the brush plate must be renewed.

6 Examine the brush retaining springs for signs of damage. Spring tension can only be checked by comparison with a new item. Renew the springs if in any doubt as to their condition.

7 Clean the commutator segments and grooves with a rag moistened with a high flash-point solvent. If necessary, smooth the surface of the commutator with a piece of fine emery cloth. Check the condition of the armature windings using a multimeter set to the ohms x 1 scale. Check the resistance between various pairs of commutator segments. If a high resistance is shown between any two segments, one of the windings is open-circuit and the starter motor should be renewed. Set the meter to the K ohm scale and measure the resistance between each commutator segment and the armature shaft. No continuity (high resistance) should be shown. Continuity will indicate a short between the commutator and shaft and will necessitate starter motor renewal.

8 If oil is found in the starter motor assembly, the seal pressed into the front cover is faulty and must be renewed **(see illustration)**. However, this seal is not listed as a separate part and is only available as part of the complete starter motor assembly. The same applies to the needle roller bearing fitted behind the seal. To avoid unnecessary expense, it is worth contacting an automotive parts supplier, who may be able to supply a suitable substitute. Ensure that all the relevan

10.4 Measure brush length and renew as a set if any have worn beyond the service limit

10.8 Inspect bearing and oil seal as described in text

10.9a On 600 models ensure the brushplate tab locates with the cover groove

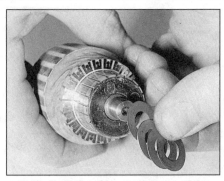

10.9b Refit the shims to the rear of the armature . . .

10.9c . . . and fit the armature to the cover

seal or bearing markings are quoted so that the correct item is selected. If necessary, take the old components along to use as a pattern. Inspect the starter motor O-rings for signs of wear and renew them if necessary.

9 On 600 models refit the brushes to their holders and fit the brushplate to the rear cover, ensuring that its tab is correctly located in the cover groove **(see illustration)**. Refit the shims to the rear of the armature, ensuring they are fitted in their original positions and apply a small amount of grease to the rear cover armature bush **(see illustration)**. Install the armature in the rear cover whilst taking care not to damage the brushes **(see illustration)**.

10 On 1000 models, fit the brushes to the brush plate and refit the plate to the starter body, aligning its tab with the groove in the body. Hook the brush retaining springs over the end of their holders and push the brushes fully into the holders. Install the armature in the body then push all brush springs back into position ensuring that each spring is correctly seated. Apply a small amount of grease to the rear cover bush and refit the shims to the rear of the commutator using the notes made on disassembly for correct positioning.

11 On all models, fit the O-rings to the motor body then refit the body to the rear cover ensuring that its slot aligns with the brush plate pin **(see illustrations)**. Refit the shims to

the front of the armature, ensuring they are correctly positioned, and fit the toothed washer to the front cover so that its teeth locate with the ribs in the cover **(see illustrations)**. Grease the lips of the front cover oil seal and carefully fit the cover making sure that the splines of the starter shaft are still taped over. Check that the O-rings, plate and washers (as applicable) are still fitted to the starter motor screws then rotate the front cover until the line cast on its side aligns with that on the rear cover, install the screws and tighten them securely **(see illustrations)**.

12 Remove the tape from the teeth of the starter motor pinion and apply a small amount

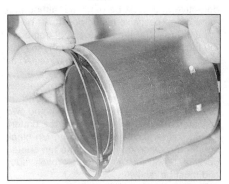

10.11a Do not omit the O-rings from the starter motor body

10.11b Fit the body to the rear cover as described in text

10.11c Ensure shims are fitted in their original positions

10.11d Fit the toothed washer to the front cover . . .

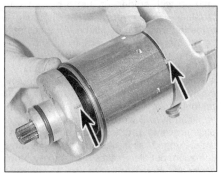

10.11e . . . and fit the cover to the body so that the index marks (arrowed) align

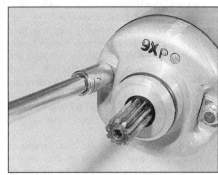

10.11f Install the starter motor screws and tighten them securely

8

10.12 Apply a small amount of oil to the starter motor O-ring and refit it to the engine

13.2 Cooling fan switch is fitted to the left side of the radiator - 600 shown

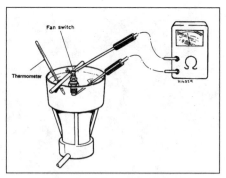

13.5 Fan switch testing apparatus

of oil to the starter motor O-ring. Refit the motor to the engine then install its mounting bolts, tightening them securely **(see illustration)**. Note: *On 600 models do not forget to fit the earth (ground) lead to one of the starter motor mounting bolts.* Refit the lead to the starter motor terminal and tighten its retaining nut securely. Ensure the rubber cap is correctly fitted to the terminal bolt. On 1000 models install the carburettors as described in Chapter 4, and on all models refit the disturbed fairing sections. Reconnect the battery.

11 Oil pressure warning lamp circuit - testing

1 The circuit consists of a pressure switch, which illuminates a warning lamp in the instrument panel whenever the ignition is switched on. As soon as the engine is started, and the oil pressure rises above a certain point, the lamp should go out. On 600 models, the pressure switch is located on the top right of the crankcase, just behind the engine number. On 1000 models it can be found on the right side of the crankcase, just below the crankshaft end cover.

2 If the lamp fails to light when the ignition is switched ON, first suspect a blown bulb. If this fails to cure the fault, remove the necessary fairing sections to gain access to the switch, then disconnect the switch lead and earth (ground) it briefly on the crankcase. If the lamp comes on when the lead is earthed (grounded), the switch is defective and must be renewed. The switch can be removed and installed as described in Section 14 of Chapter 4. If the lamp still fails to come on, the wiring between the switch and warning lamp is at fault and it should be checked with a continuity tester as described in Section 2 to trace the wire breakage.

3 If the lamp lights while the engine is running, pull over and stop the engine immediately. Check first that the engine oil level is correct and top up if necessary. If this does not cure the problem check the oil

pressure as described in Chapter 4, at the earliest opportunity. If the oil pressure is correct the oil pressure switch is likely to be faulty. The switch can only be tested by substitution of a new component.

Caution: Serious engine damage is likely to occur if the engine is run with low oil pressure.

12 Switches - general

1 While the switches should give little trouble, they can be tested using a continuity tester as described in Section 2. Using the information given in the wiring diagrams at the end of this Manual, check that full continuity exists in all switch positions and between the relevant pairs of wires. When checking a particular circuit follow a logical sequence to eliminate the switch concerned.

2 Always disconnect the battery (negative lead first) before removing any of the switches to prevent the possibility of a short-circuit. Most troubles are caused by dirty contacts, which can be cleaned, but in the event of breakage, it will be necessary to renew the complete switch.

3 If a switch is tested and found to be faulty, there is nothing to be lost by attempting a repair. It may be that worn contacts can be built up with solder, or that a broken wire terminal can be repaired, again using a soldering iron. The handlebar switches may be dismantled to a certain extent. It is however up to the owner to decide if they have the skill to carry out this sort of work.

4 While none of the switches require routine maintenance, some regular attention will prolong their life. The regular and constant application of a water-dispersant spray not only prevents problems occurring due to water-logged switches and the resulting corrosion, but also makes the switches much easier and more positive to use. Alternatively, the switch may be packed with a silicone-based grease to achieve the same result.

13 Cooling fan circuit - testing

1 In the event of a cooling fan fault, check first that the fan fuse is intact before proceeding as follows.

2 On 600 models remove the left fairing side cover and on 1000 models remove the left lower or side fairing section (as applicable). On all models disconnect the wire from the fan switch fitted to the left side of the radiator **(see illustration)**. Turn the ignition switch ON and earth (ground) the fan switch wire. As the wire is earthed (grounded) the fan should come on. If this is the case, the fan switch is defective and must be renewed, although a more comprehensive test is described below in paragraph 4. If the fan does not come on, the fault lies in either the cooling fan motor or associated wiring. The wiring can be tested as described in Section 2.

3 To test the cooling fan motor it is necessary to remove the radiator as described in Chapter 3. Using a 12 volt battery and two insulated auxiliary wires, connect the battery across the terminals of the cooling fan block connector. Once connected, the fan should operate. If not, the fan motor is proven faulty and must be renewed.

4 To test the fan switch, first slacken the switch using a suitable spanner. Unscrew the switch as fast as possible, withdraw it from the radiator and plug the opening to prevent the coolant escaping. To test the switch a heatproof container, a small gas-powered stove, a thermometer capable of reading up to 110°C (230°F) and an ohmmeter or multimeter will be required.

5 Fill the container with coolant of the specified type and strength and suspend the switch on some wire so that just the sensing portion and threads are submerged. Connect one probe of the meter to the switch terminal and the other to the body of the switch. Suspend the thermometer so that its bulb is close to the switch **(see illustration)**. **Note:** *No components should be allowed to touch the container.*

14.1 Coolant temperature gauge sender unit is located in the thermostat housing - 1000 K models onward shown

6 Set the meter to the ohms x 1 scale and start to heat the coolant, stirring it gently to evenly distribute the heat.

 Warning: This must be done very carefully to avoid the risk of personal injury.

7 When cold, the switch will be open with no continuity (high resistance) being shown on the meter. Watch the switch and meter as the temperature rises to 100°C (212°F), and take note of the temperature when the switch closes and continuity (low resistance) is shown on the meter. This should occur between 98 - 102°C (208 - 216°F) if the switch is functioning correctly. Turn off the stove, and observe the switch and meter as the temperature falls. When it falls to 98°C (208°F) there should no longer be continuity between the meter probes. If this is not the case the fan switch is defective and must be renewed.

8 On installation, apply sealant to the fan switch threads and tighten it securely (1000 models) or to the specified torque setting (600 models).

14 Coolant temperature gauge circuit - testing

1 The circuit consists of the sender unit mounted in the thermostat housing and the gauge assembly mounted in the instrument panel **(see illustration)**. If the system malfunctions check first that the battery is fully charged and that all fuses are in good condition.

2 To test the circuit, disconnect the wire from the temperature sender unit, then turn the ignition ON and earth (ground) the sender unit wire for one or two seconds. When the wire is earthed the needle should swing immediately over to the H on the gauge. If the needle moves as described, the sender unit is proven defective and must be renewed, although a more comprehensive test is described below. If the needle's movement is still faulty, or if it does not move at all, the fault lies in the wiring or the gauge. The wiring can be checked with a continuity tester as described in Section 2,

but the gauge can only be tested by substitution - see paragraph 5.
Caution: Do not earth (ground) the wire for any longer than is necessary to take the reading, or the gauge will be damaged.

3 Slacken the temperature sender unit and unscrew it as quickly as possible, plugging its hole in the thermostat housing to prevent the coolant escaping. The sender unit is tested in the same way as the fan switch, referring to paragraphs 4 and 5 Section 13, noting that the container should be filled with oil rather than coolant and that a thermometer capable of reading up to 120°C (248°F) will be required. Heat the oil gently, stirring it slowly to keep a uniform temperature throughout, whilst noting the resistance readings of the sender unit. A serviceable sender unit should give the following readings at the specified temperatures.

All 600 and 1000 H, J, K, L, M, N models:
  104 ohms @ 60°C (140°F)
  44 ohms @ 85°C (185°F)
  20 ohms @ 110°C (230°F)
  16 ohms @ 120°C (248°F)
1000 P models onward:
  130-180 ohms @ 50°C (122°F)
  45-60 ohms @ 80°C (176°F)
  10-20 ohms @ 120°C (248°F)

4 If the sender unit does not give the specified resistances at the stated temperatures it must be renewed. On installation, apply a sealant to the threads of the sender unit and tighten it securely.

5 If the sender unit and circuit wiring are proven sound, the gauge must be at fault. Remove the instrument panel as described in Section 16 of Chapter 6, to gain access to the gauge unit. The gauge can only be checked by the substitution of a new unit; no repairs are possible.

15 Fuel gauge circuit - testing (1000 models)

 Warning: Petrol (gasoline) is extremely flammable, especially when in the form of vapour. Take all precautions to prevent the risk of fire and read through the Safety first! Section of this Manual before carrying out the following operation.

1 The fuel gauge circuit consists of the sender unit inside the fuel tank, and the gauge assembly mounted in the instrument panel. If the system malfunctions check first that the battery is fully charged and that all fuses are in good condition before testing the circuit as follows.

2 Remove the fuel tank as described in Section 4 of Chapter 4 and turn the ignition switch ON. The fuel gauge should point to RES on the gauge. Using an insulated auxiliary wire, join the two terminals of the fuel

level sender on the wiring side of the block connector. As the terminals are joined the needle on the gauge should swing immediately over to the F on the gauge.
Caution: Do not join the terminals for any longer than is necessary to take the reading or the gauge will be damaged.

If the needle moves as described above, a sender unit fault is indicated and it should be removed and tested as described in paragraph 3 below. If the needle's movement is still thought to be faulty, or it does not move at all, the fault lies in the wiring or the gauge itself. If this is the case, proceed as described in paragraph 4.

3 Drain the contents of the fuel tank into a clean metal container marked as being suitable for holding petrol (gasoline), taking great care to avoid the risk of fire. Place the tank on its side on some soft cloth. Remove the sender unit retaining nuts which secure it to the underside of the tank and carefully manoeuvre the sender out of the tank **(see illustration)**.

4 Check that the float moves up and down smoothly without any sign of binding, and that it always returns to the empty position under its own weight. Also check the sender unit wires for signs of damage as they can easily get trapped if the fuel tank is fitted carelessly. If all is well, check the operation of the sender unit using a multimeter set to the resistance (ohms) scale. Connect the meter probes to the sender unit block connector terminals and measure the resistance of the sender in both the full and empty positions. If the readings obtained are not within the limits given in the Specifications, or the readings do not change smoothly as the float is moved up and down, the sender unit is defective and must be renewed.

5 On installation, check the sender unit O-ring for signs of wear or damage and renew it if necessary. Carefully install the unit into the tank and tighten its retaining nuts evenly and securely.

6 If a fault with the gauge itself is indicated, remove the instrument panel as described in Section 16 of Chapter 6 and inspect all the relevant wiring for broken, chafed or corroded wires as described in Section 2 of this Chapter. Note that the gauge can only be tested by the substitution of a new unit.

15.3 Fuel level sender unit is retained by four nuts

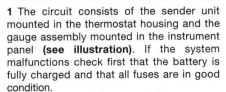

8

16.1a Fuel pump is located behind the left sidepanel - 600 shown

16 Fuel pump and relay - testing (1000 H, J and all 600 models)

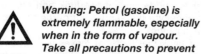

> ⚠ Warning: Petrol (gasoline) is extremely flammable, especially when in the form of vapour. Take all precautions to prevent the risk of fire and read through the Safety first! Section of this Manual before carrying out the following operation.

1 On 600 models the fuel pump is situated behind the left side panel and the relay is located beneath the fuel tank **(see illustrations)**. On 1000 H and J models the pump and relay can be found behind the left side panel. If the system malfunctions, first ensure that the battery is fully charged and that all fuses are in good condition. Check all relevant wiring for signs of broken or chafed wires and corroded connections as described in Section 2 before carrying out the following procedure.

2 Ensure the ignition switch is turned OFF and disconnect the fuel pump outlet pipe from the fuel tap or joint (as appropriate). Disconnect the fuel pump relay from the wiring loom and use an insulated auxiliary wire to connect the black and black/blue (600 models) or black and brown/red (1000 models) of the relay block connector. Hold the fuel outlet pipe over a suitable container and turn the fuel tap and then the ignition switch ON for a short while. When the ignition switch is ON fuel should be pumped out of the outlet pipe and into the container. If this is the case, the fuel pump is operating correctly and the relay is proven faulty. If the fuel does not flow from the outlet pipe, then the pump is defective and must be renewed.

3 It is also necessary to check that the pump is supplying a sufficient quantity of fuel to the carburettors. To do this place a graduated container of at least 200 cc beneath the disconnected outlet pipe and turn the fuel tap and ignition switch ON for 5 seconds and then OFF again. Measure the quantity of fuel collected in the container then multiply that amount by 12 to obtain the fuel pump flow rate per minute. If the pump flow rate is less

16.1b Fuel pump relay can be tested as described in text

than the service limit shown in the Specifications at the start of this Chapter the pump is defective and must be renewed.

17 Tachometer - testing

1 All models use an electronic tachometer operated off the ignition system. If the tachometer malfunctions, yet the ignition system is still operating correctly, first check that all fuses are in good condition before proceeding further.

2 On all 600 models and 1000 H, J models, remove the instrument panel as described in Section 16 of Chapter 6 then disconnect the instrument block connectors. Connect a multimeter set to the volts range between the black/brown (positive) and green (ground/earth) tachometer terminals on the harness side of the wiring, and turn the ignition ON. If battery voltage is shown this indicates that the power supply to the unit is correct. Using a multimeter set to the resistance (ohms) range, check the yellow/blue wire from the tachometer terminal to the connector of the spark unit for continuity. If continuity exists, the tachometer is proved defective and must be renewed.

3 On 1000 K models onward, disconnect the wire connectors from the instrument panel and ignition spark unit. Using a multimeter set to the resistance (ohms) range, check the yellow/green wire from the spark unit to the

18.1a Turn signal relay location - 600 models

instrument panel for continuity. If the wiring is sound, the fault must lie in the spark unit or tachometer.

18 Turn signal relay - location and testing

1 On 600 models the turn signal relay is located behind the right side panel, behind the starter relay **(see illustration)**. On 1000 models the relay is situated underneath the seat cowling, on the right side of the machine behind the spark unit on 1000 H and J models, and on the left side of the machine on K models onward **(see illustration)**.

2 If the turn signal lamps cease to function correctly, there may be several possible causes before the relay is suspected. First check that the fuses are intact and that the battery is fully charged. Check that the turn signal lamps are securely mounted and that their connections are clean and tight. Check that the bulbs are all of the correct wattage and that corrosion has not developed on the bulbs or in their holders. Any such corrosion must be thoroughly cleaned off to ensure proper bulb contact. Also check that the turn signal switch is functioning correctly and that the wiring is in good order.

3 Faults in any of the above items will produce symptoms for which the turn signal relay may be unfairly blamed. If the fault persists even after the preliminary checks have been made the relay is at fault and must be renewed. The condition of the relay can only be assessed by substitution, no test details being available.

19 Horn - location and testing

1 The horn is either mounted onto the bottom triple clamp (yoke) or onto one of the radiator mounting bolts, depending on the model.

2 If the horn fails to work, first check that the fuses are intact. Check that power is reaching the horns by disconnecting the wires and connecting them to a 12 volt bulb. Switch on

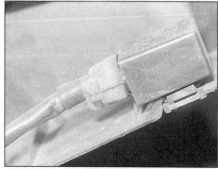

18.1b Turn signal relay location - 1000 K models onward

20.3a Secure headlamp bulb in position with the spring clip . . .

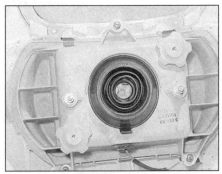

20.3b . . . and install bulb cover as described in text

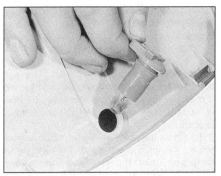

20.4 On UK models position lamp bulb-holder is a push fit in headlamp assembly

the ignition and press the horn button. If the bulb lights, the horn circuit is proven good and the horn is at fault. If not there is a fault in either the wiring or the horn button.

3 To test a horn, connect a fully-charged 12 volt battery directly to the horn itself using two insulated auxiliary wires. If the horn does not sound, a gentle tap on the outside of the horn may free the internal contacts. If this fails, the horn must be renewed; repairs are not possible.

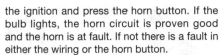

20 Bulbs - renewal

Headlamp and position lamp

Note: *The headlamp bulb is of the quartz-halogen type with a conventional H4 fitting. Do not touch the bulb's glass envelope as skin acids will shorten its service life. If the bulb is accidentally touched, it should be wiped carefully when cold with a rag moistened with methylated spirit (stoddard solvent) and dried before refitting.*

1 On 600 models it will probably be necessary to remove the fairing to renew the headlamp bulb, however, some owners may find it possible to renew the bulb with the fairing in place by simply removing the inner covers. Due to the amount of work necessary

to remove the fairing it is therefore recommended that an attempt be made to carry out the operation with the fairing on the machine. This applies equally to the parking lamp bulb in the case of UK models.

2 On 1000 H and J models access to the bulb can be gained once the right upper fairing inner cover has been renewed. The 1000 K models onward are fitted with twin headlamp bulbs which can be reached once the instrument panel has been removed as described in Section 16 of Chapter 6.

3 On all models, to renew the bulb, disconnect the headlamp bulb connector and remove the rubber bulb cover, noting its correct position. Disengage the retaining spring clip from the headlamp unit and carefully withdraw the bulb. On installation, note that the bulb can only be fitted one way. Secure the bulb in position with the spring clip and fit the rubber bulb cover ensuring that it is fitted with the TOP mark uppermost and that it is correctly seated **(see illustrations)**. Refit the headlamp connector. Check the headlamp beam setting as described in Chapter 1 before riding the machine.

4 The position lamp bulbholder, fitted to UK models, is a push fit in the headlamp assembly **(see illustration)**. The bulb is a bayonet fit in the holder and can be removed by pressing it in and turning it anticlockwise.

Stop/tail lamp

5 All models are fitted with twin stop/tail lamp bulbs which can be accessed from inside the seat cowling once the seat has been removed. Remove the bulbholders from the back of the tail lamp assembly by turning anticlockwise (counterclockwise). The bulbs are a bayonet fit and can be removed by pressing in and turning them anticlockwise (counterclockwise). The bulbs are installed by a reversal of the removal procedure noting that the pins on each bulb are offset to prevent incorrect installation **(see illustration)**.

> **HAYNES HINT**
> *If the socket contacts are dirty or corroded, scrape them clean and spray them with electrical contact cleaner before a new bulb is installed.*

Turn signal lamps

6 On 600 models the front turn signal bulbs can be accessed from beneath the upper fairing section **(see illustration)**. On 1000 H and J models it will be necessary to remove the upper fairing inner covers, and on K, L, M, N models the instrument panel must first be removed as described in Section 16 of Chapter 6. On 1000 P models onward, remove the maintenance cover from the upper

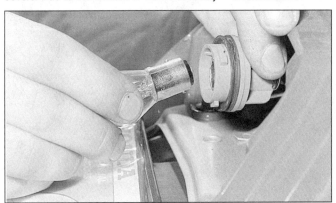

20.5 Note offset pins when installing stop/tail lamp bulbs

20.6 On 600 models front turn signal bulbs can be accessed from below the fairing

8

fairing **(see illustration 19.24a in Chapter 6)**; reach inside the fairing for access to the turn signals.

7 On all models, remove the bulbholder from the back of the lamp by turning it anticlockwise (counterclockwise). The can then be removed by pressing it in and turning it anticlockwise (counterclockwise). The bulb is installed by a reversal of the removal procedure.

8 To renew the rear turn signal bulbs, remove the screw from the back of the turn signal lamp and lift off the lens **(see illustration)**. The bulb can then be removed from the lamp by pressing it in and turning it anticlockwise (counterclockwise) **(see illustration)**. On installation ensure that the rubber lens gasket is correctly positioned and refit the lens. Avoid overtightening the lens retaining screw as the lenses are easily damaged.

Instrument panel bulbs

9 Remove the instrument panel from the machine as described in Section 16 of Chapter 6. All instrument panel bulbs are of the capless type, being pressed into their holders, which are also a push fit in the underside of the instrument panel **(see illustrations)**. Be careful not to damage the bulbs' delicate wire terminals when removing or installing.

20.8a Rear turn signal lenses are retained by a single screw . . .

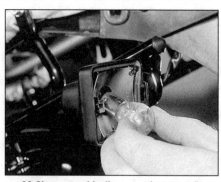
20.8b . . . and bulbs are a bayonet fit

20.9a Instrument panel bulbholders are a push fit in the panel . . .

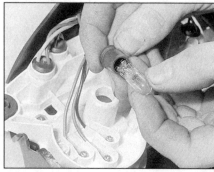
20.9b . . . and the bulbs are of the capless type

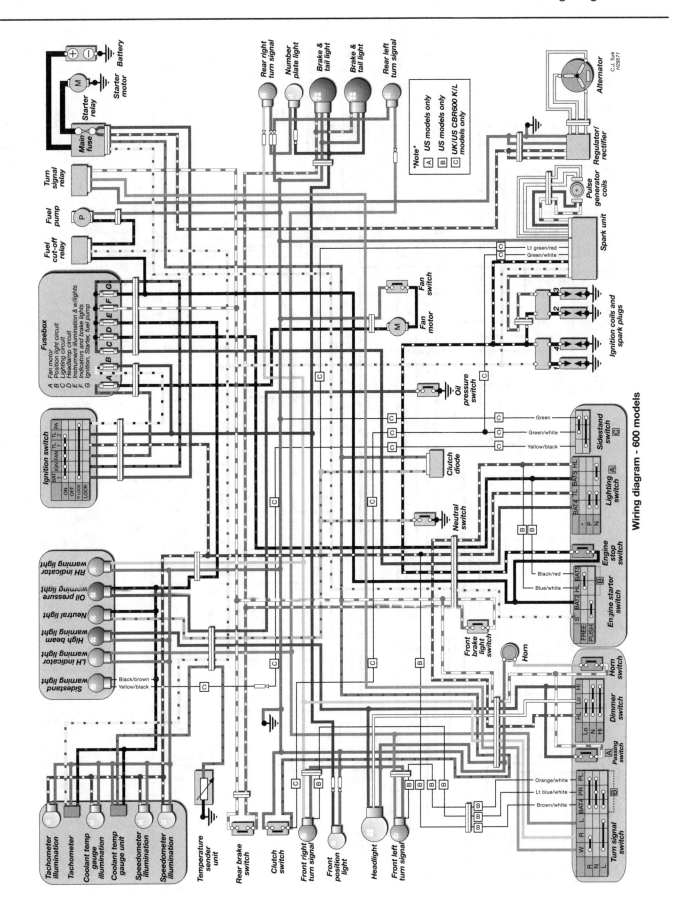

Wiring diagram - 600 models

8

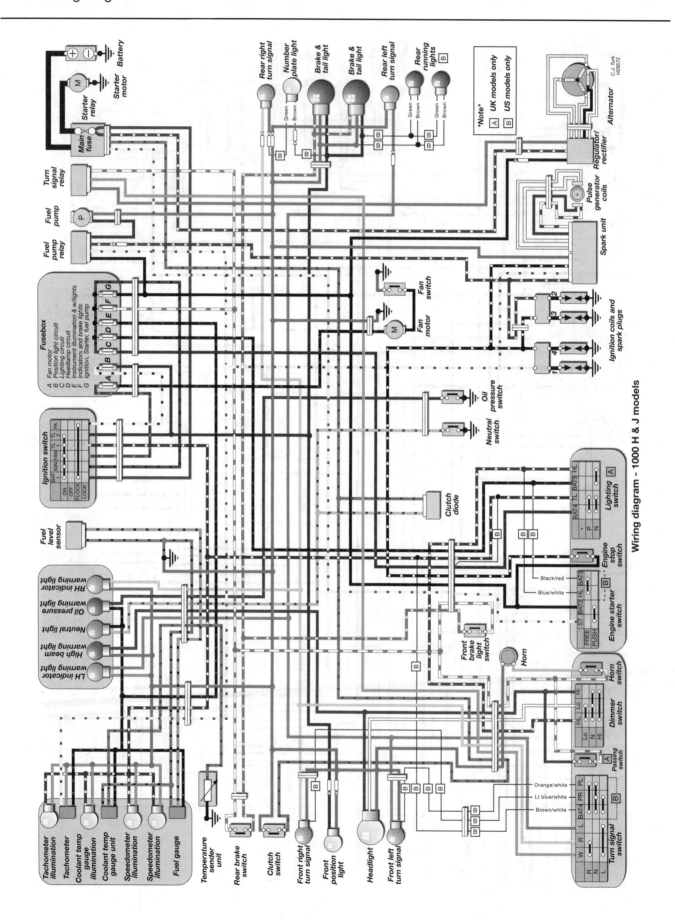

Wiring diagram - 1000 H & J models

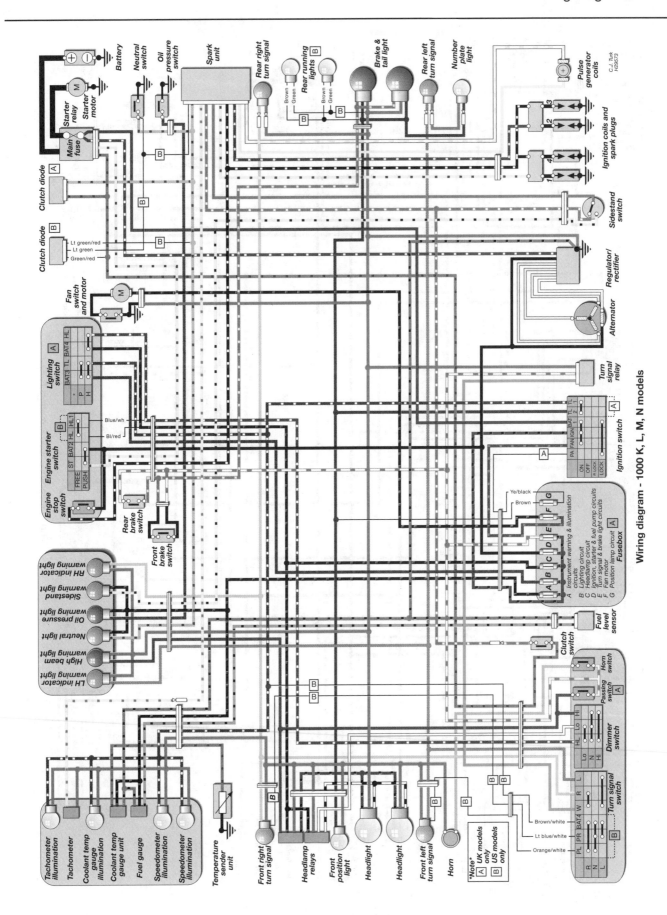

Wiring diagram - 1000 K, L, M, N models

8

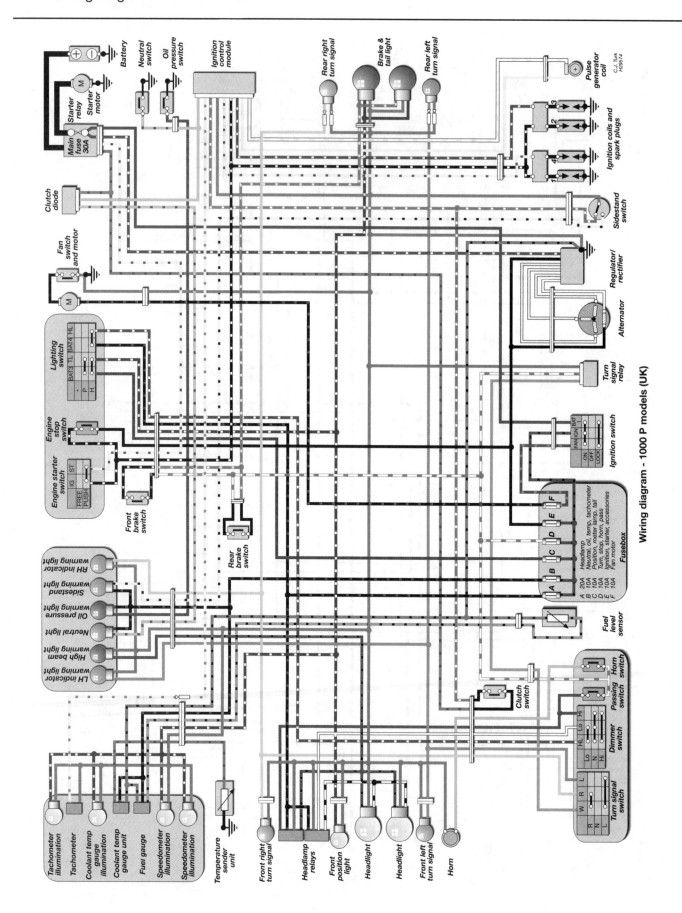

Wiring diagram - 1000 P models (UK)

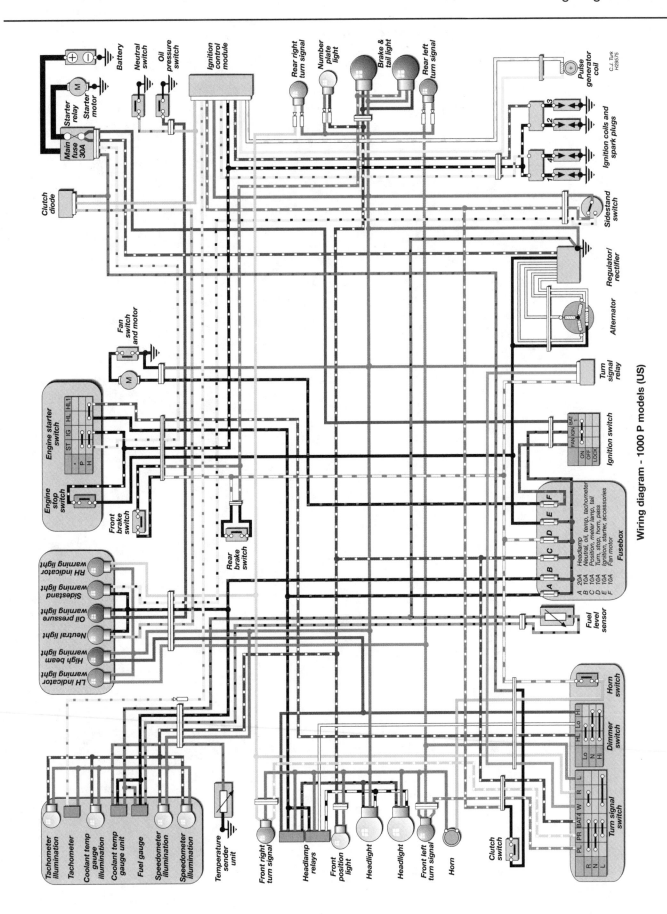

Wiring diagram - 1000 P models (US)

C.J. Turk
H29575

Battery
Neutral switch
Oil pressure switch
Ignition control module
Rear right turn signal
Number plate light
Brake & tail light
Rear left turn signal
Pulse generator coil

Starter relay
Starter motor
Ignition coils and spark plugs

Main fuse 30A
Clutch diode
Sidestand switch
Regulator/rectifier
Alternator

Fan switch and motor
Turn signal relay

Engine starter switch
ST IG HL HL1

Ignition switch
FAN IGN BAT
ON
OFF
LOCK

Engine stop switch
Front brake switch
Rear brake switch

Fusebox
A B C D E F
A 20A Headlamp
B 10A Neutral, oil, temp, tachometer
C 10A Position, meter lamp, tail
D 10A Turn stop, horn, pass
E 10A Ignition, starter, accessories
F 10A Fan motor

RH indicator warning light
Sidestand warning light
Oil pressure warning light
Neutral warning light
High beam warning light
LH indicator warning light

Fuel level sensor

Horn switch
Dimmer switch
HL Lo Hi
Lo N Hi

Turn signal switch
PL PR BAT4 W R L
R
N
L

Tachometer illumination
Tachometer
Coolant temp gauge illumination
Coolant temp gauge unit
Fuel gauge
Speedometer illumination
Speedometer illumination
Temperature sender unit
Front right turn signal
Headlamp relays
Front position light
Headlight
Headlight
Front left turn signal
Horn
Clutch switch

8

Notes

Reference REF•1

Dimensions and Weights

CBR600 models

Length - US H, J, K models	2050 mm (80.7 in)	
Length - US L model	2080 mm (81.9 in)	
Length - UK models	2130 mm (83.9 in)	
Width	685 mm (27.0 in)	
Height - US H, J, K models	1110 mm (43.7 in)	
Height - US L and all UK models	1115 mm (43.9 in)	
Wheelbase	1410 mm (55.5 in)	
Ground clearance	140 mm (5.5 in)	
Weights:	**Dry weight**	**Kerb weight**
US H, J, K models*	180 kg (397 lb)	199 kg (439 lb)
US L model*	188 kg (414 lb)	204 kg (450 lb)
UK H, J models	182 kg (401 lb)	201 kg (443 lb)
UK K, L models	186 kg (410 lb)	205 kg (452 lb)

Weights increase by 1 - 3 kg (2.2 - 6.6 lb) on California models

CBR1000

	H and J models	K, L, M, N models
Length - US models	2200 mm (86.6 in)	2235 mm (88.0 in)
Length - UK models	2245 mm (88.4 in)	2235 mm (88.0 in)
Width	725 mm (28.5 in)	740 mm (29.1 in)
Height	1185 mm (46.7 in)	1200 mm (47.2 in)
Wheelbase	1505 mm (59.3 in)	1500 mm (59.1 in)
Ground clearance	135 mm (5.3 in)	135 mm (5.3 in)
Dry weight - US models*	224 kg (494 lb)	246 kg (542 lb)
Dry weight - UK models	222 kg (489 lb)	230 kg (507 lb)
Kerb weight - US models*	250 kg (551 lb)	269 kg (593 lb)
Kerb weight - UK models	248 kg (548 lb)	264 kg (582 lb)

Weights increase by 1 - 3 kg (2.2 - 6.6 lb) on California models

CBR1000

	P models onward
Length	2235 mm (88.0 in)
Width	740 mm (29.1 in)
Height	1215 mm (47.8 in)
Wheelbase	1500 mm (59.1 in)
Ground clearance	140 mm (5.5 in)
Dry weight - US models*	249 kg (549 lb)
Dry weight - UK models	235 kg (518 lb)
Kerb weight - US models*	273 kg (602 lb)
Kerb weight - UK models	271 kg (597 lb)

Weights increase by 1 - 3 kg (2.2 - 6.6 lb) on California models

Maximum vehicle loading

Figures include total weight of rider(s), luggage and any additional accessories

US 600 models	157 kg (346 lb)
UK 600 H and J models	157 kg (346 lb)
UK 600 K and L models	175 kg (386 lb)
US 1000 H and J models	166 kg (366 lb)
UK 1000 H and J models	180 kg (397 lb)
US 1000 L models onward	174 kg (384 lb)
UK 1000 K, L, M, N models	192 kg (423 lb)
UK 1000 P models onward	185 kg (408 lb)

Buying tools

A toolkit is a fundamental requirement for servicing and repairing a motorcycle. Although there will be an initial expense in building up enough tools for servicing, this will soon be offset by the savings made by doing the job yourself. As experience and confidence grow, additional tools can be added to enable the repair and overhaul of the motorcycle. Many of the specialist tools are expensive and not often used so it may be preferable to hire them, or for a group of friends or motorcycle club to join in the purchase.

As a rule, it is better to buy more expensive, good quality tools. Cheaper tools are likely to wear out faster and need to be renewed more often, nullifying the original saving.

> **Warning: To avoid the risk of a poor quality tool breaking in use, causing injury or damage to the component being worked on, always aim to purchase tools which meet the relevant national safety standards.**

The following lists of tools do not represent the manufacturer's service tools, but serve as a guide to help the owner decide which tools are needed for this level of work. In addition, items such as an electric drill, hacksaw, files, soldering iron and a workbench equipped with a vice, may be needed. Although not classed as tools, a selection of bolts, screws, nuts, washers and pieces of tubing always come in useful.

For more information about tools, refer to the Haynes *Motorcycle Workshop Practice TechBook* (Bk. No. 3470).

Manufacturer's service tools

Inevitably certain tasks require the use of a service tool. Where possible an alternative tool or method of approach is recommended, but sometimes there is no option if personal injury or damage to the component is to be avoided. Where required, service tools are referred to in the relevant procedure.

Service tools can usually only be purchased from a motorcycle dealer and are identified by a part number. Some of the commonly-used tools, such as rotor pullers, are available in aftermarket form from mail-order motorcycle tool and accessory suppliers.

Maintenance and minor repair tools

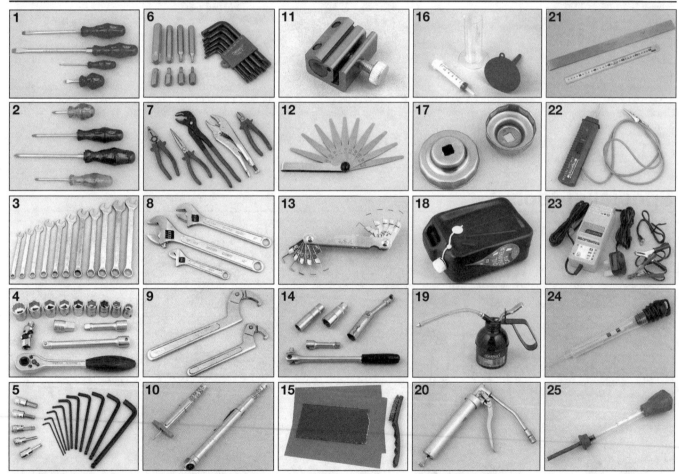

1 Set of flat-bladed screwdrivers
2 Set of Phillips head screwdrivers
3 Combination open-end and ring spanners
4 Socket set (3/8 inch or 1/2 inch drive)
5 Set of Allen keys or bits
6 Set of Torx keys or bits
7 Pliers, cutters and self-locking grips (Mole grips)
8 Adjustable spanners
9 C-spanners
10 Tread depth gauge and tyre pressure gauge
11 Cable oiler clamp
12 Feeler gauges
13 Spark plug gap measuring tool
14 Spark plug spanner or deep plug sockets
15 Wire brush and emery paper
16 Calibrated syringe, measuring vessel and funnel
17 Oil filter adapters
18 Oil drainer can or tray
19 Pump type oil can
20 Grease gun
21 Straight-edge and steel rule
22 Continuity tester
23 Battery charger
24 Hydrometer (for battery specific gravity check)
25 Anti-freeze tester (for liquid-cooled engines)

Repair and overhaul tools

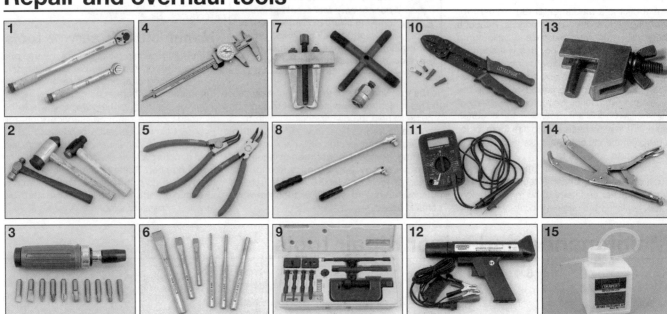

1 *Torque wrench
(small and mid-ranges)*
2 *Conventional, plastic or
soft-faced hammers*
3 *Impact driver set*

4 *Vernier gauge*
5 *Circlip pliers (internal and
external, or combination)*
6 *Set of cold chisels
and punches*

7 *Selection of pullers*
8 *Breaker bars*
9 *Chain breaking/
riveting tool set*

10 *Wire stripper and
crimper tool*
11 *Multimeter (measures
amps, volts and ohms)*
12 *Stroboscope (for
dynamic timing checks)*

13 *Hose clamp
(wingnut type shown)*
14 *Clutch holding tool*
15 *One-man brake/clutch
bleeder kit*

Specialist tools

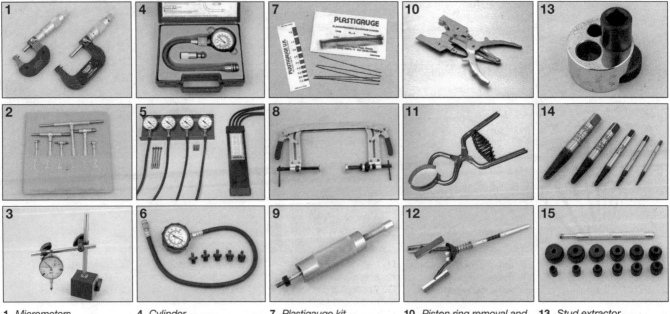

1 *Micrometers
(external type)*
2 *Telescoping gauges*
3 *Dial gauge*

4 *Cylinder
compression gauge*
5 *Vacuum gauges (left) or
manometer (right)*
6 *Oil pressure gauge*

7 *Plastigauge kit*
8 *Valve spring compressor
(4-stroke engines)*
9 *Piston pin drawbolt tool*

10 *Piston ring removal and
installation tool*
11 *Piston ring clamp*
12 *Cylinder bore hone
(stone type shown)*

13 *Stud extractor*
14 *Screw extractor set*
15 *Bearing driver set*

1 Workshop equipment and facilities

The workbench

● Work is made much easier by raising the bike up on a ramp - components are much more accessible if raised to waist level. The hydraulic or pneumatic types seen in the dealer's workshop are a sound investment if you undertake a lot of repairs or overhauls **(see illustration 1.1)**.

1.1 Hydraulic motorcycle ramp

● If raised off ground level, the bike must be supported on the ramp to avoid it falling. Most ramps incorporate a front wheel locating clamp which can be adjusted to suit different diameter wheels. When tightening the clamp, take care not to mark the wheel rim or damage the tyre - use wood blocks on each side to prevent this.
● Secure the bike to the ramp using tie-downs **(see illustration 1.2)**. If the bike has only a sidestand, and hence leans at a dangerous angle when raised, support the bike on an auxiliary stand.

1.2 Tie-downs are used around the passenger footrests to secure the bike

● Auxiliary (paddock) stands are widely available from mail order companies or motorcycle dealers and attach either to the wheel axle or swingarm pivot **(see illustration 1.3)**. If the motorcycle has a centrestand, you can support it under the crankcase to prevent it toppling whilst either wheel is removed **(see illustration 1.4)**.

1.3 This auxiliary stand attaches to the swingarm pivot

1.4 Always use a block of wood between the engine and jack head when supporting the engine in this way

Fumes and fire

● Refer to the Safety first! page at the beginning of the manual for full details. Make sure your workshop is equipped with a fire extinguisher suitable for fuel-related fires (Class B fire - flammable liquids) - it is not sufficient to have a water-filled extinguisher.
● Always ensure adequate ventilation is available. Unless an exhaust gas extraction system is available for use, ensure that the engine is run outside of the workshop.
● If working on the fuel system, make sure the workshop is ventilated to avoid a build-up of fumes. This applies equally to fume build-up when charging a battery. Do not smoke or allow anyone else to smoke in the workshop.

Fluids

● If you need to drain fuel from the tank, store it in an approved container marked as suitable for the storage of petrol (gasoline) **(see illustration 1.5)**. Do not store fuel in glass jars or bottles.

1.5 Use an approved can only for storing petrol (gasoline)

● Use proprietary engine degreasers or solvents which have a high flash-point, such as paraffin (kerosene), for cleaning off oil, grease and dirt - never use petrol (gasoline) for cleaning. Wear rubber gloves when handling solvent and engine degreaser. The fumes from certain solvents can be dangerous - always work in a well-ventilated area.

Dust, eye and hand protection

● Protect your lungs from inhalation of dust particles by wearing a filtering mask over the nose and mouth. Many frictional materials still contain asbestos which is dangerous to your health. Protect your eyes from spouts of liquid and sprung components by wearing a pair of protective goggles **(see illustration 1.6)**.

1.6 A fire extinguisher, goggles, mask and protective gloves should be at hand in the workshop

● Protect your hands from contact with solvents, fuel and oils by wearing rubber gloves. Alternatively apply a barrier cream to your hands before starting work. If handling hot components or fluids, wear suitable gloves to protect your hands from scalding and burns.

What to do with old fluids

● Old cleaning solvent, fuel, coolant and oils should not be poured down domestic drains or onto the ground. Package the fluid up in old oil containers, label it accordingly, and take it to a garage or disposal facility. Contact your local authority for location of such sites or ring the oil care hotline.

OIL CARE
FOLLOW THE CODE
OIL BANK LINE
0800 66 33 66

Note: It is antisocial and illegal to dump oil down the drain. To find the location of your local oil recycling bank, call this number free.

In the USA, note that any oil supplier must accept used oil for recycling.

2 Fasteners -
screws, bolts and nuts

Fastener types and applications

Bolts and screws

● Fastener head types are either of hexagonal, Torx or splined design, with internal and external versions of each type **(see illustrations 2.1 and 2.2)**; splined head fasteners are not in common use on motorcycles. The conventional slotted or Phillips head design is used for certain screws. Bolt or screw length is always measured from the underside of the head to the end of the item **(see illustration 2.11)**.

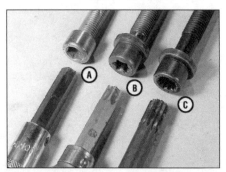

2.1 Internal hexagon/Allen (A), Torx (B) and splined (C) fasteners, with corresponding bits

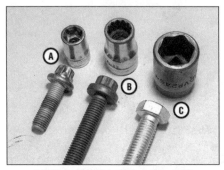

2.2 External Torx (A), splined (B) and hexagon (C) fasteners, with corresponding sockets

● Certain fasteners on the motorcycle have a tensile marking on their heads, the higher the marking the stronger the fastener. High tensile fasteners generally carry a 10 or higher marking. Never replace a high tensile fastener with one of a lower tensile strength.

Washers (see illustration 2.3)

● Plain washers are used between a fastener head and a component to prevent damage to the component or to spread the load when torque is applied. Plain washers can also be used as spacers or shims in certain assemblies. Copper or aluminium plain washers are often used as sealing washers on drain plugs.

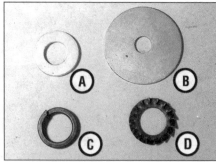

2.3 Plain washer (A), penny washer (B), spring washer (C) and serrated washer (D)

● The split-ring spring washer works by applying axial tension between the fastener head and component. If flattened, it is fatigued and must be renewed. If a plain (flat) washer is used on the fastener, position the spring washer between the fastener and the plain washer.

● Serrated star type washers dig into the fastener and component faces, preventing loosening. They are often used on electrical earth (ground) connections to the frame.

● Cone type washers (sometimes called Belleville) are conical and when tightened apply axial tension between the fastener head and component. They must be installed with the dished side against the component and often carry an OUTSIDE marking on their outer face. If flattened, they are fatigued and must be renewed.

● Tab washers are used to lock plain nuts or bolts on a shaft. A portion of the tab washer is bent up hard against one flat of the nut or bolt to prevent it loosening. Due to the tab washer being deformed in use, a new tab washer should be used every time it is disturbed.

● Wave washers are used to take up endfloat on a shaft. They provide light springing and prevent excessive side-to-side play of a component. Can be found on rocker arm shafts.

Nuts and split pins

● Conventional plain nuts are usually six-sided **(see illustration 2.4)**. They are sized by thread diameter and pitch. High tensile nuts carry a number on one end to denote their tensile strength.

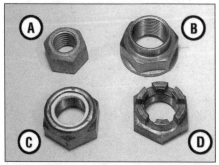

2.4 Plain nut (A), shouldered locknut (B), nylon insert nut (C) and castellated nut (D)

● Self-locking nuts either have a nylon insert, or two spring metal tabs, or a shoulder which is staked into a groove in the shaft - their advantage over conventional plain nuts is a resistance to loosening due to vibration. The nylon insert type can be used a number of times, but must be renewed when the friction of the nylon insert is reduced, ie when the nut spins freely on the shaft. The spring tab type can be reused unless the tabs are damaged. The shouldered type must be renewed every time it is disturbed.

● Split pins (cotter pins) are used to lock a castellated nut to a shaft or to prevent slackening of a plain nut. Common applications are wheel axles and brake torque arms. Because the split pin arms are deformed to lock around the nut a new split pin must always be used on installation - always fit the correct size split pin which will fit snugly in the shaft hole. Make sure the split pin arms are correctly located around the nut **(see illustrations 2.5 and 2.6)**.

2.5 Bend split pin (cotter pin) arms as shown (arrows) to secure a castellated nut

2.6 Bend split pin (cotter pin) arms as shown to secure a plain nut

Caution: If the castellated nut slots do not align with the shaft hole after tightening to the torque setting, tighten the nut until the next slot aligns with the hole - never slacken the nut to align its slot.

● R-pins (shaped like the letter R), or slip pins as they are sometimes called, are sprung and can be reused if they are otherwise in good condition. Always install R-pins with their closed end facing forwards **(see illustration 2.7)**.

2.7 Correct fitting of R-pin. Arrow indicates forward direction

Circlips (see illustration 2.8)

● Circlips (sometimes called snap-rings) are used to retain components on a shaft or in a housing and have corresponding external or internal ears to permit removal. Parallel-sided (machined) circlips can be installed either way round in their groove, whereas stamped circlips (which have a chamfered edge on one face) must be installed with the chamfer facing away from the direction of thrust load **(see illustration 2.9)**.

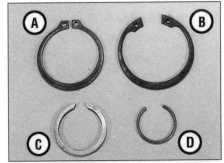

2.8 External stamped circlip (A), internal stamped circlip (B), machined circlip (C) and wire circlip (D)

● Always use circlip pliers to remove and install circlips; expand or compress them just enough to remove them. After installation, rotate the circlip in its groove to ensure it is securely seated. If installing a circlip on a splined shaft, always align its opening with a shaft channel to ensure the circlip ends are well supported and unlikely to catch **(see illustration 2.10)**.

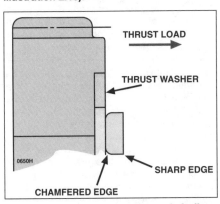

2.9 Correct fitting of a stamped circlip

THRUST LOAD

THRUST WASHER

SHARP EDGE

CHAMFERED EDGE

0650H

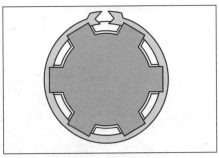

2.10 Align circlip opening with shaft channel

● Circlips can wear due to the thrust of components and become loose in their grooves, with the subsequent danger of becoming dislodged in operation. For this reason, renewal is advised every time a circlip is disturbed.

● Wire circlips are commonly used as piston pin retaining clips. If a removal tang is provided, long-nosed pliers can be used to dislodge them, otherwise careful use of a small flat-bladed screwdriver is necessary. Wire circlips should be renewed every time they are disturbed.

Thread diameter and pitch

● Diameter of a male thread (screw, bolt or stud) is the outside diameter of the threaded portion **(see illustration 2.11)**. Most motorcycle manufacturers use the ISO (International Standards Organisation) metric system expressed in millimetres, eg M6 refers to a 6 mm diameter thread. Sizing is the same for nuts, except that the thread diameter is measured across the valleys of the nut.

● Pitch is the distance between the peaks of the thread **(see illustration 2.11)**. It is expressed in millimetres, thus a common bolt size may be expressed as 6.0 x 1.0 mm (6 mm thread diameter and 1 mm pitch). Generally pitch increases in proportion to thread diameter, although there are always exceptions.

● Thread diameter and pitch are related for conventional fastener applications and the accompanying table can be used as a guide. Additionally, the AF (Across Flats), spanner or socket size dimension of the bolt or nut **(see illustration 2.11)** is linked to thread and pitch specification. Thread pitch can be measured with a thread gauge **(see illustration 2.12)**.

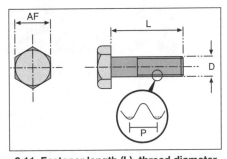

2.11 Fastener length (L), thread diameter (D), thread pitch (P) and head size (AF)

AF

L

D

P

2.12 Using a thread gauge to measure pitch

AF size	Thread diameter x pitch (mm)
8 mm	M5 x 0.8
8 mm	M6 x 1.0
10 mm	M6 x 1.0
12 mm	M8 x 1.25
14 mm	M10 x 1.25
17 mm	M12 x 1.25

● The threads of most fasteners are of the right-hand type, ie they are turned clockwise to tighten and anti-clockwise to loosen. The reverse situation applies to left-hand thread fasteners, which are turned anti-clockwise to tighten and clockwise to loosen. Left-hand threads are used where rotation of a component might loosen a conventional right-hand thread fastener.

Seized fasteners

● Corrosion of external fasteners due to water or reaction between two dissimilar metals can occur over a period of time. It will build up sooner in wet conditions or in countries where salt is used on the roads during the winter. If a fastener is severely corroded it is likely that normal methods of removal will fail and result in its head being ruined. When you attempt removal, the fastener thread should be heard to crack free and unscrew easily - if it doesn't, stop there before damaging something.

● A smart tap on the head of the fastener will often succeed in breaking free corrosion which has occurred in the threads **(see illustration 2.13)**.

● An aerosol penetrating fluid (such as WD-40) applied the night beforehand may work its way down into the thread and ease removal. Depending on the location, you may be able to make up a Plasticine well around the fastener head and fill it with penetrating fluid.

2.13 A sharp tap on the head of a fastener will often break free a corroded thread

● If you are working on an engine internal component, corrosion will most likely not be a problem due to the well lubricated environment. However, components can be very tight and an impact driver is a useful tool in freeing them **(see illustration 2.14)**.

**2.14 Using an impact driver
to free a fastener**

● Where corrosion has occurred between dissimilar metals (eg steel and aluminium alloy), the application of heat to the fastener head will create a disproportionate expansion rate between the two metals and break the seizure caused by the corrosion. Whether heat can be applied depends on the location of the fastener - any surrounding components likely to be damaged must first be removed **(see illustration 2.15)**. Heat can be applied using a paint stripper heat gun or clothes iron, or by immersing the component in boiling water - wear protective gloves to prevent scalding or burns to the hands.

2.15 Using heat to free a seized fastener

● As a last resort, it is possible to use a hammer and cold chisel to work the fastener head unscrewed **(see illustration 2.16)**. This will damage the fastener, but more importantly extreme care must be taken not to damage the surrounding component.

Caution: Remember that the component being secured is generally of more value than the bolt, nut or screw - when the fastener is freed, do not unscrew it with force, instead work the fastener back and forth when resistance is felt to prevent thread damage.

**2.16 Using a hammer and chisel
to free a seized fastener**

Broken fasteners and damaged heads

● If the shank of a broken bolt or screw is accessible you can grip it with self-locking grips. The knurled wheel type stud extractor tool or self-gripping stud puller tool is particularly useful for removing the long studs which screw into the cylinder mouth surface of the crankcase or bolts and screws from which the head has broken off **(see illustration 2.17)**. Studs can also be removed by locking two nuts together on the threaded end of the stud and using a spanner on the lower nut **(see illustration 2.18)**.

2.17 Using a stud extractor tool to remove a broken crankcase stud

2.18 Two nuts can be locked together to unscrew a stud from a component

● A bolt or screw which has broken off below or level with the casing must be extracted using a screw extractor set. Centre punch the fastener to centralise the drill bit, then drill a hole in the fastener **(see illustration 2.19)**. Select a drill bit which is approximately half to three-quarters the

**2.19 When using a screw extractor,
first drill a hole in the fastener . . .**

diameter of the fastener and drill to a depth which will accommodate the extractor. Use the largest size extractor possible, but avoid leaving too small a wall thickness otherwise the extractor will merely force the fastener walls outwards wedging it in the casing thread.

● If a spiral type extractor is used, thread it anti-clockwise into the fastener. As it is screwed in, it will grip the fastener and unscrew it from the casing **(see illustration 2.20)**.

**2.20 . . . then thread the extractor
anti-clockwise into the fastener**

● If a taper type extractor is used, tap it into the fastener so that it is firmly wedged in place. Unscrew the extractor (anti-clockwise) to draw the fastener out.

⚠ *Warning: Stud extractors are very hard and may break off in the fastener if care is not taken - ask an engineer about spark erosion if this happens.*

● Alternatively, the broken bolt/screw can be drilled out and the hole retapped for an oversize bolt/screw or a diamond-section thread insert. It is essential that the drilling is carried out squarely and to the correct depth, otherwise the casing may be ruined - if in doubt, entrust the work to an engineer.

● Bolts and nuts with rounded corners cause the correct size spanner or socket to slip when force is applied. Of the types of spanner/socket available always use a six-point type rather than an eight or twelve-point type - better grip

2.21 Comparison of surface drive ring spanner (left) with 12-point type (right)

is obtained. Surface drive spanners grip the middle of the hex flats, rather than the corners, and are thus good in cases of damaged heads **(see illustration 2.21)**.

● Slotted-head or Phillips-head screws are often damaged by the use of the wrong size screwdriver. Allen-head and Torx-head screws are much less likely to sustain damage. If enough of the screw head is exposed you can use a hacksaw to cut a slot in its head and then use a conventional flat-bladed screwdriver to remove it. Alternatively use a hammer and cold chisel to tap the head of the fastener around to slacken it. Always replace damaged fasteners with new ones, preferably Torx or Allen-head type.

HAYNES HiNT

A dab of valve grinding compound between the screw head and screw-driver tip will often give a good grip.

Thread repair

● Threads (particularly those in aluminium alloy components) can be damaged by overtightening, being assembled with dirt in the threads, or from a component working loose and vibrating. Eventually the thread will fail completely, and it will be impossible to tighten the fastener.

● If a thread is damaged or clogged with old locking compound it can be renovated with a thread repair tool (thread chaser) **(see illustrations 2.22 and 2.23)**; special thread

2.22 A thread repair tool being used to correct an internal thread

2.23 A thread repair tool being used to correct an external thread

chasers are available for spark plug hole threads. The tool will not cut a new thread, but clean and true the original thread. Make sure that you use the correct diameter and pitch tool. Similarly, external threads can be cleaned up with a die or a thread restorer file **(see illustration 2.24)**.

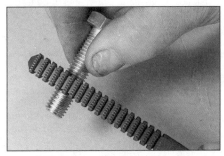

2.24 Using a thread restorer file

● It is possible to drill out the old thread and retap the component to the next thread size. This will work where there is enough surrounding material and a new bolt or screw can be obtained. Sometimes, however, this is not possible - such as where the bolt/screw passes through another component which must also be suitably modified, also in cases where a spark plug or oil drain plug cannot be obtained in a larger diameter thread size.

● The diamond-section thread insert (often known by its popular trade name of Heli-Coil) is a simple and effective method of renewing the thread and retaining the original size. A kit can be purchased which contains the tap, insert and installing tool **(see illustration 2.25)**. Drill out the damaged thread with the size drill specified **(see illustration 2.26)**. Carefully retap the thread **(see illustration 2.27)**. Install the

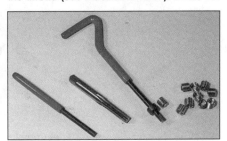

2.25 Obtain a thread insert kit to suit the thread diameter and pitch required

2.26 To install a thread insert, first drill out the original thread . . .

2.27 . . . tap a new thread . . .

2.28 . . . fit insert on the installing tool . . .

2.29 . . . and thread into the component . . .

2.30 . . . break off the tang when complete

insert on the installing tool and thread it slowly into place using a light downward pressure **(see illustrations 2.28 and 2.29)**. When positioned between a 1/4 and 1/2 turn below the surface withdraw the installing tool and use the break-off tool to press down on the tang, breaking it off **(see illustration 2.30)**.

● There are epoxy thread repair kits on the market which can rebuild stripped internal threads, although this repair should not be used on high load-bearing components.

Thread locking and sealing compounds

● Locking compounds are used in locations where the fastener is prone to loosening due to vibration or on important safety-related items which might cause loss of control of the motorcycle if they fail. It is also used where important fasteners cannot be secured by other means such as lockwashers or split pins.

● Before applying locking compound, make sure that the threads (internal and external) are clean and dry with all old compound removed. Select a compound to suit the component being secured - a non-permanent general locking and sealing type is suitable for most applications, but a high strength type is needed for permanent fixing of studs in castings. Apply a drop or two of the compound to the first few threads of the fastener, then thread it into place and tighten to the specified torque. Do not apply excessive thread locking compound otherwise the thread may be damaged on subsequent removal.

● Certain fasteners are impregnated with a dry film type coating of locking compound on their threads. Always renew this type of fastener if disturbed.

● Anti-seize compounds, such as copper-based greases, can be applied to protect threads from seizure due to extreme heat and corrosion. A common instance is spark plug threads and exhaust system fasteners.

3 Measuring tools and gauges

Feeler gauges

● Feeler gauges (or blades) are used for measuring small gaps and clearances (see illustration 3.1). They can also be used to measure endfloat (sideplay) of a component on a shaft where access is not possible with a dial gauge.

● Feeler gauge sets should be treated with care and not bent or damaged. They are etched with their size on one face. Keep them clean and very lightly oiled to prevent corrosion build-up.

3.1 Feeler gauges are used for measuring small gaps and clearances - thickness is marked on one face of gauge

● When measuring a clearance, select a gauge which is a light sliding fit between the two components. You may need to use two gauges together to measure the clearance accurately.

Micrometers

● A micrometer is a precision tool capable of measuring to 0.01 or 0.001 of a millimetre. It should always be stored in its case and not in the general toolbox. It must be kept clean and never dropped, otherwise its frame or measuring anvils could be distorted resulting in inaccurate readings.

● External micrometers are used for measuring outside diameters of components and have many more applications than internal micrometers. Micrometers are available in different size ranges, eg 0 to 25 mm, 25 to 50 mm, and upwards in 25 mm steps; some large micrometers have interchangeable anvils to allow a range of measurements to be taken. Generally the largest precision measurement you are likely to take on a motorcycle is the piston diameter.

● Internal micrometers (or bore micrometers) are used for measuring inside diameters, such as valve guides and cylinder bores. Telescoping gauges and small hole gauges are used in conjunction with an external micrometer, whereas the more expensive internal micrometers have their own measuring device.

External micrometer

Note: *The conventional analogue type instrument is described. Although much easier to read, digital micrometers are considerably more expensive.*

● Always check the calibration of the micrometer before use. With the anvils closed (0 to 25 mm type) or set over a test gauge (for

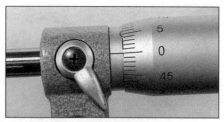

3.2 Check micrometer calibration before use

the larger types) the scale should read zero (see illustration 3.2); make sure that the anvils (and test piece) are clean first. Any discrepancy can be adjusted by referring to the instructions supplied with the tool. Remember that the micrometer is a precision measuring tool - don't force the anvils closed, use the ratchet (4) on the end of the micrometer to close it. In this way, a measured force is always applied.

● To use, first make sure that the item being measured is clean. Place the anvil of the micrometer (1) against the item and use the thimble (2) to bring the spindle (3) lightly into contact with the other side of the item (see illustration 3.3). Don't tighten the thimble down because this will damage the micrometer - instead use the ratchet (4) on the end of the micrometer. The ratchet mechanism applies a measured force preventing damage to the instrument.

● The micrometer is read by referring to the linear scale on the sleeve and the annular scale on the thimble. Read off the sleeve first to obtain the base measurement, then add the fine measurement from the thimble to obtain the overall reading. The linear scale on the sleeve represents the measuring range of the micrometer (eg 0 to 25 mm). The annular scale

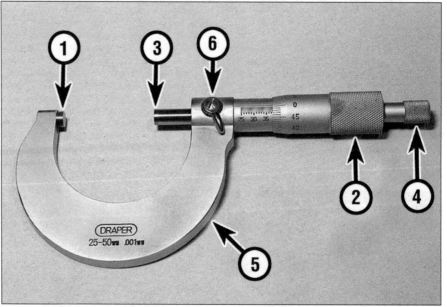

3.3 Micrometer component parts

1 Anvil	3 Spindle	5 Frame
2 Thimble	4 Ratchet	6 Locking lever

on the thimble will be in graduations of 0.01 mm (or as marked on the frame) - one full revolution of the thimble will move 0.5 mm on the linear scale. Take the reading where the datum line on the sleeve intersects the thimble's scale. Always position the eye directly above the scale otherwise an inaccurate reading will result.

In the example shown the item measures 2.95 mm (see illustration 3.4):

Linear scale	2.00 mm
Linear scale	0.50 mm
Annular scale	0.45 mm
Total figure	**2.95 mm**

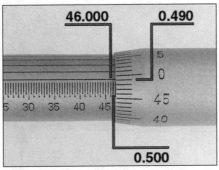

3.5 Micrometer reading of 46.99 mm on linear and annular scales . . .

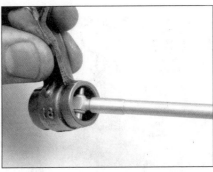

3.7 Expand the telescoping gauge in the bore, lock its position . . .

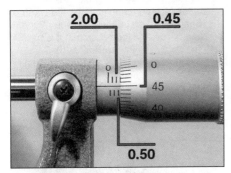

3.4 Micrometer reading of 2.95 mm

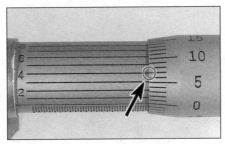

3.6 . . . and 0.004 mm on vernier scale

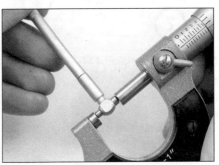

3.8 . . . then measure the gauge with a micrometer

Most micrometers have a locking lever (6) on the frame to hold the setting in place, allowing the item to be removed from the micrometer.

● Some micrometers have a vernier scale on their sleeve, providing an even finer measurement to be taken, in 0.001 increments of a millimetre. Take the sleeve and thimble measurement as described above, then check which graduation on the vernier scale aligns with that of the annular scale on the thimble **Note:** *The eye must be perpendicular to the scale when taking the vernier reading - if necessary rotate the body of the micrometer to ensure this.* Multiply the vernier scale figure by 0.001 and add it to the base and fine measurement figures.

In the example shown the item measures 46.994 mm (see illustrations 3.5 and 3.6):

Linear scale (base)	46.000 mm
Linear scale (base)	00.500 mm
Annular scale (fine)	00.490 mm
Vernier scale	00.004 mm
Total figure	**46.994 mm**

Internal micrometer

● Internal micrometers are available for measuring bore diameters, but are expensive and unlikely to be available for home use. It is suggested that a set of telescoping gauges and small hole gauges, both of which must be used with an external micrometer, will suffice for taking internal measurements on a motorcycle.

● Telescoping gauges can be used to measure internal diameters of components. Select a gauge with the correct size range, make sure its ends are clean and insert it into the bore. Expand the gauge, then lock its position and withdraw it from the bore (see illustration 3.7). Measure across the gauge ends with a micrometer (see illustration 3.8).

● Very small diameter bores (such as valve guides) are measured with a small hole gauge. Once adjusted to a slip-fit inside the component, its position is locked and the gauge withdrawn for measurement with a micrometer (see illustrations 3.9 and 3.10).

Vernier caliper

Note: *The conventional linear and dial gauge type instruments are described. Digital types are easier to read, but are far more expensive.*

● The vernier caliper does not provide the precision of a micrometer, but is versatile in being able to measure internal and external diameters. Some types also incorporate a depth gauge. It is ideal for measuring clutch plate friction material and spring free lengths.

● To use the conventional linear scale vernier, slacken off the vernier clamp screws (1) and set its jaws over (2), or inside (3), the item to be measured (see illustration 3.11). Slide the jaw into contact, using the thumb-wheel (4) for fine movement of the sliding scale (5) then tighten the clamp screws (1). Read off the main scale (6) where the zero on the sliding scale (5) intersects it, taking the whole number to the left of the zero; this provides the base measurement. View along the sliding scale and select the division which

3.9 Expand the small hole gauge in the bore, lock its position . . .

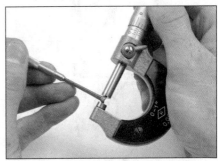

3.10 . . . then measure the gauge with a micrometer

lines up exactly with any of the divisions on the main scale, noting that the divisions usually represents 0.02 of a millimetre. Add this fine measurement to the base measurement to obtain the total reading.

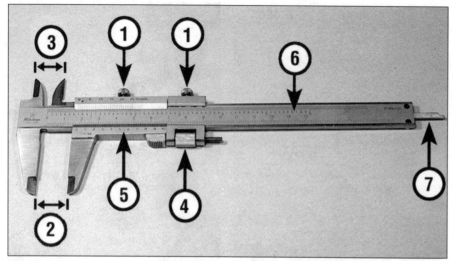

3.11 Vernier component parts (linear gauge)

1 Clamp screws	3 Internal jaws	5 Sliding scale	7 Depth gauge
2 External jaws	4 Thumbwheel	6 Main scale	

In the example shown the item measures 55.92 mm **(see illustration 3.12)**:

Base measurement	55.00 mm
Fine measurement	00.92 mm
Total figure	**55.92 mm**

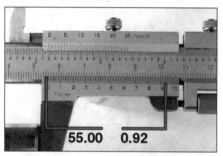

3.12 Vernier gauge reading of 55.92 mm

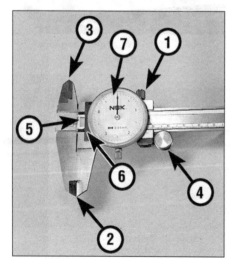

3.13 Vernier component parts (dial gauge)

1 Clamp screw	5 Main scale
2 External jaws	6 Sliding scale
3 Internal jaws	7 Dial gauge
4 Thumbwheel	

● Some vernier calipers are equipped with a dial gauge for fine measurement. Before use, check that the jaws are clean, then close them fully and check that the dial gauge reads zero. If necessary adjust the gauge ring accordingly. Slacken the vernier clamp screw (1) and set its jaws over (2), or inside (3), the item to be measured **(see illustration 3.13)**. Slide the jaws into contact, using the thumbwheel (4) for fine movement. Read off the main scale (5) where the edge of the sliding scale (6) intersects it, taking the whole number to the left of the zero; this provides the base measurement. Read off the needle position on the dial gauge (7) scale to provide the fine measurement; each division represents 0.05 of a millimetre. Add this fine measurement to the base measurement to obtain the total reading.

In the example shown the item measures 55.95 mm **(see illustration 3.14)**:

Base measurement	55.00 mm
Fine measurement	00.95 mm
Total figure	**55.95 mm**

3.14 Vernier gauge reading of 55.95 mm

Plastigauge

● Plastigauge is a plastic material which can be compressed between two surfaces to measure the oil clearance between them. The width of the compressed Plastigauge is measured against a calibrated scale to determine the clearance.

● Common uses of Plastigauge are for measuring the clearance between crankshaft journal and main bearing inserts, between crankshaft journal and big-end bearing inserts, and between camshaft and bearing surfaces. The following example describes big-end oil clearance measurement.

● Handle the Plastigauge material carefully to prevent distortion. Using a sharp knife, cut a length which corresponds with the width of the bearing being measured and place it carefully across the journal so that it is parallel with the shaft **(see illustration 3.15)**. Carefully install both bearing shells and the connecting rod. Without rotating the rod on the journal tighten its bolts or nuts (as applicable) to the specified torque. The connecting rod and bearings are then disassembled and the crushed Plastigauge examined.

3.15 Plastigauge placed across shaft journal

● Using the scale provided in the Plastigauge kit, measure the width of the material to determine the oil clearance **(see illustration 3.16)**. Always remove all traces of Plastigauge after use using your fingernails.

Caution: Arriving at the correct clearance demands that the assembly is torqued correctly, according to the settings and sequence (where applicable) provided by the motorcycle manufacturer.

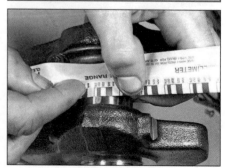

**3.16 Measuring the width
of the crushed Plastigauge**

Dial gauge or DTI (Dial Test Indicator)

● A dial gauge can be used to accurately measure small amounts of movement. Typical uses are measuring shaft runout or shaft endfloat (sideplay) and setting piston position for ignition timing on two-strokes. A dial gauge set usually comes with a range of different probes and adapters and mounting equipment.
● The gauge needle must point to zero when at rest. Rotate the ring around its periphery to zero the gauge.
● Check that the gauge is capable of reading the extent of movement in the work. Most gauges have a small dial set in the face which records whole millimetres of movement as well as the fine scale around the face periphery which is calibrated in 0.01 mm divisions. Read off the small dial first to obtain the base measurement, then add the measurement from the fine scale to obtain the total reading.

In the example shown the gauge reads 1.48 mm (see illustration 3.17):

Base measurement	1.00 mm
Fine measurement	0.48 mm
Total figure	**1.48 mm**

3.17 Dial gauge reading of 1.48 mm

● If measuring shaft runout, the shaft must be supported in vee-blocks and the gauge mounted on a stand perpendicular to the shaft. Rest the tip of the gauge against the centre of the shaft and rotate the shaft slowly whilst watching the gauge reading (see illustration 3.18). Take several measurements along the length of the shaft and record the

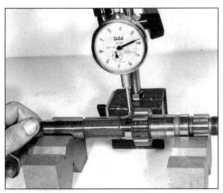

3.18 Using a dial gauge to measure shaft runout

maximum gauge reading as the amount of runout in the shaft. **Note:** *The reading obtained will be total runout at that point - some manufacturers specify that the runout figure is halved to compare with their specified runout limit.*
● Endfloat (sideplay) measurement requires that the gauge is mounted securely to the surrounding component with its probe touching the end of the shaft. Using hand pressure, push and pull on the shaft noting the maximum endfloat recorded on the gauge (see illustration 3.19).

3.19 Using a dial gauge to measure shaft endfloat

● A dial gauge with suitable adapters can be used to determine piston position BTDC on two-stroke engines for the purposes of ignition timing. The gauge, adapter and suitable length probe are installed in the place of the spark plug and the gauge zeroed at TDC. If the piston position is specified as 1.14 mm BTDC, rotate the engine back to 2.00 mm BTDC, then slowly forwards to 1.14 mm BTDC.

Cylinder compression gauges

● A compression gauge is used for measuring cylinder compression. Either the rubber-cone type or the threaded adapter type can be used. The latter is preferred to ensure a perfect seal against the cylinder head. A 0 to 300 psi (0 to 20 Bar) type gauge (for petrol/gasoline engines) will be suitable for motorcycles.
● The spark plug is removed and the gauge either held hard against the cylinder head (cone type) or the gauge adapter screwed into the cylinder head (threaded type) (see illustration 3.20). Cylinder compression is measured with the engine turning over, but not running - carry out the compression test as described in

3.20 Using a rubber-cone type cylinder compression gauge

Fault Finding Equipment. The gauge will hold the reading until manually released.

Oil pressure gauge

● An oil pressure gauge is used for measuring engine oil pressure. Most gauges come with a set of adapters to fit the thread of the take-off point (see illustration 3.21). If the take-off point specified by the motorcycle manufacturer is an external oil pipe union, make sure that the specified replacement union is used to prevent oil starvation.

3.21 Oil pressure gauge and take-off point adapter (arrow)

● Oil pressure is measured with the engine running (at a specific rpm) and often the manufacturer will specify pressure limits for a cold and hot engine.

Straight-edge and surface plate

● If checking the gasket face of a component for warpage, place a steel rule or precision straight-edge across the gasket face and measure any gap between the straight-edge and component with feeler gauges (see illustration 3.22). Check diagonally across the component and between mounting holes (see illustration 3.23).

3.22 Use a straight-edge and feeler gauges to check for warpage

3.23 Check for warpage in these directions

● Checking individual components for warpage, such as clutch plain (metal) plates, requires a perfectly flat plate or piece or plate glass and feeler gauges.

4 Torque and leverage

What is torque?

● Torque describes the twisting force about a shaft. The amount of torque applied is determined by the distance from the centre of the shaft to the end of the lever and the amount of force being applied to the end of the lever; distance multiplied by force equals torque.

● The manufacturer applies a measured torque to a bolt or nut to ensure that it will not slacken in use and to hold two components securely together without movement in the joint. The actual torque setting depends on the thread size, bolt or nut material and the composition of the components being held.

● Too little torque may cause the fastener to loosen due to vibration, whereas too much torque will distort the joint faces of the component or cause the fastener to shear off. Always stick to the specified torque setting.

Using a torque wrench

● Check the calibration of the torque wrench and make sure it has a suitable range for the job. Torque wrenches are available in Nm (Newton-metres), kgf m (kilograms-force metre), lbf ft (pounds-feet), lbf in (inch-pounds). Do not confuse lbf ft with lbf in.

● Adjust the tool to the desired torque on the scale **(see illustration 4.1)**. If your torque wrench is not calibrated in the units specified, carefully convert the figure (see *Conversion Factors*). A manufacturer sometimes gives a torque setting as a range (8 to 10 Nm) rather than a single figure - in this case set the tool midway between the two settings. The same torque may be expressed as 9 Nm ± 1 Nm. Some torque wrenches have a method of locking the setting so that it isn't inadvertently altered during use.

4.1 Set the torque wrench index mark to the setting required, in this case 12 Nm

● Install the bolts/nuts in their correct location and secure them lightly. Their threads must be clean and free of any old locking compound. Unless specified the threads and flange should be dry - oiled threads are necessary in certain circumstances and the manufacturer will take this into account in the specified torque figure. Similarly, the manufacturer may also specify the application of thread-locking compound.

● Tighten the fasteners in the specified sequence until the torque wrench clicks, indicating that the torque setting has been reached. Apply the torque again to double-check the setting. Where different thread diameter fasteners secure the component, as a rule tighten the larger diameter ones first.

● When the torque wrench has been finished with, release the lock (where applicable) and fully back off its setting to zero - do not leave the torque wrench tensioned. Also, do not use a torque wrench for slackening a fastener.

Angle-tightening

● Manufacturers often specify a figure in degrees for final tightening of a fastener. This usually follows tightening to a specific torque setting.

● A degree disc can be set and attached to the socket **(see illustration 4.2)** or a protractor can be used to mark the angle of movement on the bolt/nut head and the surrounding casting **(see illustration 4.3)**.

4.2 Angle tightening can be accomplished with a torque-angle gauge . . .

4.3 . . . or by marking the angle on the surrounding component

Loosening sequences

● Where more than one bolt/nut secures a component, loosen each fastener evenly a little at a time. In this way, not all the stress of the joint is held by one fastener and the components are not likely to distort.

● If a tightening sequence is provided, work in the REVERSE of this, but if not, work from the outside in, in a criss-cross sequence **(see illustration 4.4)**.

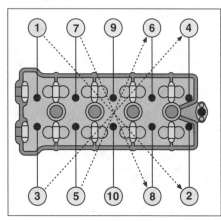

4.4 When slackening, work from the outside inwards

Tightening sequences

● If a component is held by more than one fastener it is important that the retaining bolts/nuts are tightened evenly to prevent uneven stress build-up and distortion of sealing faces. This is especially important on high-compression joints such as the cylinder head.

● A sequence is usually provided by the manufacturer, either in a diagram or actually marked in the casting. If not, always start in the centre and work outwards in a criss-cross pattern **(see illustration 4.5)**. Start off by securing all bolts/nuts finger-tight, then set the torque wrench and tighten each fastener by a small amount in sequence until the final torque is reached. By following this practice,

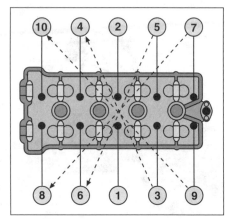

4.5 When tightening, work from the inside outwards

the joint will be held evenly and will not be distorted. Important joints, such as the cylinder head and big-end fasteners often have two- or three-stage torque settings.

Applying leverage

● Use tools at the correct angle. Position a socket wrench or spanner on the bolt/nut so that you pull it towards you when loosening. If this can't be done, push the spanner without curling your fingers around it **(see illustration 4.6)** - the spanner may slip or the fastener loosen suddenly, resulting in your fingers being crushed against a component.

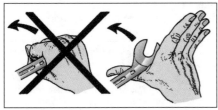

4.6 If you can't pull on the spanner to loosen a fastener, push with your hand open

● Additional leverage is gained by extending the length of the lever. The best way to do this is to use a breaker bar instead of the regular length tool, or to slip a length of tubing over the end of the spanner or socket wrench.
● If additional leverage will not work, the fastener head is either damaged or firmly corroded in place (see *Fasteners*).

5 Bearings

Bearing removal and installation

Drivers and sockets

● Before removing a bearing, always inspect the casing to see which way it must be driven out - some casings will have retaining plates or a cast step. Also check for any identifying markings on the bearing and if installed to a certain depth, measure this at this stage. Some roller bearings are sealed on one side - take note of the original fitted position.
● Bearings can be driven out of a casing using a bearing driver tool (with the correct size head) or a socket of the correct diameter. Select the driver head or socket so that it contacts the outer race of the bearing, not the balls/rollers or inner race. Always support the casing around the bearing housing with wood blocks, otherwise there is a risk of fracture. The bearing is driven out with a few blows on the driver or socket from a heavy mallet. Unless access is severely restricted (as with wheel bearings), a pin-punch is not recommended unless it is moved around the bearing to keep it square in its housing.

● The same equipment can be used to install bearings. Make sure the bearing housing is supported on wood blocks and line up the bearing in its housing. Fit the bearing as noted on removal - generally they are installed with their marked side facing outwards. Tap the bearing squarely into its housing using a driver or socket which bears only on the bearing's outer race - contact with the bearing balls/rollers or inner race will destroy it **(see illustrations 5.1 and 5.2)**.
● Check that the bearing inner race and balls/rollers rotate freely.

5.1 Using a bearing driver against the bearing's outer race

5.2 Using a large socket against the bearing's outer race

Pullers and slide-hammers

● Where a bearing is pressed on a shaft a puller will be required to extract it **(see illustration 5.3)**. Make sure that the puller clamp or legs fit securely behind the bearing and are unlikely to slip out. If pulling a bearing

5.3 This bearing puller clamps behind the bearing and pressure is applied to the shaft end to draw the bearing off

off a gear shaft for example, you may have to locate the puller behind a gear pinion if there is no access to the race and draw the gear pinion off the shaft as well **(see illustration 5.4)**.

> *Caution: Ensure that the puller's centre bolt locates securely against the end of the shaft and will not slip when pressure is applied. Also ensure that puller does not damage the shaft end.*

5.4 Where no access is available to the rear of the bearing, it is sometimes possible to draw off the adjacent component

● Operate the puller so that its centre bolt exerts pressure on the shaft end and draws the bearing off the shaft.
● When installing the bearing on the shaft, tap only on the bearing's inner race - contact with the balls/rollers or outer race with destroy the bearing. Use a socket or length of tubing as a drift which fits over the shaft end **(see illustration 5.5)**.

5.5 When installing a bearing on a shaft use a piece of tubing which bears only on the bearing's inner race

● Where a bearing locates in a blind hole in a casing, it cannot be driven or pulled out as described above. A slide-hammer with knife-edged bearing puller attachment will be required. The puller attachment passes through the bearing and when tightened expands to fit firmly behind the bearing **(see illustration 5.6)**. By operating the slide-hammer part of the tool the bearing is jarred out of its housing **(see illustration 5.7)**.
● It is possible, if the bearing is of reasonable weight, for it to drop out of its housing if the casing is heated as described opposite. If this

5.6 Expand the bearing puller so that it locks behind the bearing . . .

5.7 . . . attach the slide hammer to the bearing puller

method is attempted, first prepare a work surface which will enable the casing to be tapped face down to help dislodge the bearing - a wood surface is ideal since it will not damage the casing's gasket surface. Wearing protective gloves, tap the heated casing several times against the work surface to dislodge the bearing under its own weight **(see illustration 5.8)**.

5.8 Tapping a casing face down on wood blocks can often dislodge a bearing

● Bearings can be installed in blind holes using the driver or socket method described above.

Drawbolts

● Where a bearing or bush is set in the eye of a component, such as a suspension linkage arm or connecting rod small-end, removal by drift may damage the component. Furthermore, a rubber bushing in a shock absorber eye cannot successfully be driven out of position. If access is available to a engineering press, the task is straightforward. If not, a drawbolt can be fabricated to extract the bearing or bush.

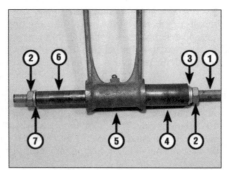

5.9 Drawbolt component parts assembled on a suspension arm

1 Bolt or length of threaded bar
2 Nuts
3 Washer (external diameter greater than tubing internal diameter)
4 Tubing (internal diameter sufficient to accommodate bearing)
5 Suspension arm with bearing
6 Tubing (external diameter slightly smaller than bearing)
7 Washer (external diameter slightly smaller than bearing)

5.10 Drawing the bearing out of the suspension arm

● To extract the bearing/bush you will need a long bolt with nut (or piece of threaded bar with two nuts), a piece of tubing which has an internal diameter larger than the bearing/bush, another piece of tubing which has an external diameter slightly smaller than the bearing/ bush, and a selection of washers **(see illustrations 5.9 and 5.10)**. Note that the pieces of tubing must be of the same length, or longer, than the bearing/bush.

● The same kit (without the pieces of tubing) can be used to draw the new bearing/bush back into place **(see illustration 5.11)**.

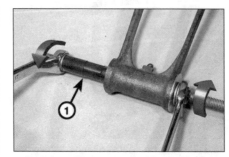

5.11 Installing a new bearing (1) in the suspension arm

Temperature change

● If the bearing's outer race is a tight fit in the casing, the aluminium casing can be heated to release its grip on the bearing. Aluminium will expand at a greater rate than the steel bearing outer race. There are several ways to do this, but avoid any localised extreme heat (such as a blow torch) - aluminium alloy has a low melting point.

● Approved methods of heating a casing are using a domestic oven (heated to 100°C) or immersing the casing in boiling water **(see illustration 5.12)**. Low temperature range localised heat sources such as a paint stripper heat gun or clothes iron can also be used **(see illustration 5.13)**. Alternatively, soak a rag in boiling water, wring it out and wrap it around the bearing housing.

> ⚠ **Warning: All of these methods require care in use to prevent scalding and burns to the hands. Wear protective gloves when handling hot components.**

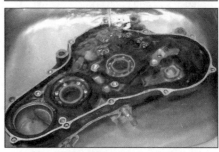

5.12 A casing can be immersed in a sink of boiling water to aid bearing removal

5.13 Using a localised heat source to aid bearing removal

● If heating the whole casing note that plastic components, such as the neutral switch, may suffer - remove them beforehand.

● After heating, remove the bearing as described above. You may find that the expansion is sufficient for the bearing to fall out of the casing under its own weight or with a light tap on the driver or socket.

● If necessary, the casing can be heated to aid bearing installation, and this is sometimes the recommended procedure if the motorcycle manufacturer has designed the housing and bearing fit with this intention.

● Installation of bearings can be eased by placing them in a freezer the night before installation. The steel bearing will contract slightly, allowing easy insertion in its housing. This is often useful when installing steering head outer races in the frame.

Bearing types and markings

● Plain shell bearings, ball bearings, needle roller bearings and tapered roller bearings will all be found on motorcycles **(see illustrations 5.14 and 5.15)**. The ball and roller types are usually caged between an inner and outer race, but uncaged variations may be found.

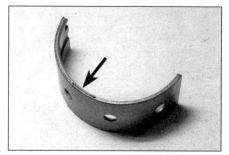

5.14 Shell bearings are either plain or grooved. They are usually identified by colour code (arrow)

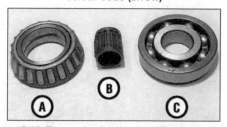

5.15 Tapered roller bearing (A), needle roller bearing (B) and ball journal bearing (C)

● Shell bearings (often called inserts) are usually found at the crankshaft main and connecting rod big-end where they are good at coping with high loads. They are made of a phosphor-bronze material and are impregnated with self-lubricating properties.
● Ball bearings and needle roller bearings consist of a steel inner and outer race with the balls or rollers between the races. They require constant lubrication by oil or grease and are good at coping with axial loads. Taper roller bearings consist of rollers set in a tapered cage set on the inner race; the outer race is separate. They are good at coping with axial loads and prevent movement along the shaft - a typical application is in the steering head.
● Bearing manufacturers produce bearings to ISO size standards and stamp one face of the bearing to indicate its internal and external diameter, load capacity and type **(see illustration 5.16)**.
● Metal bushes are usually of phosphor-bronze material. Rubber bushes are used in suspension mounting eyes. Fibre bushes have also been used in suspension pivots.

5.16 Typical bearing marking

Bearing fault finding

● If a bearing outer race has spun in its housing, the housing material will be damaged. You can use a bearing locking compound to bond the outer race in place if damage is not too severe.
● Shell bearings will fail due to damage of their working surface, as a result of lack of lubrication, corrosion or abrasive particles in the oil **(see illustration 5.17)**. Small particles of dirt in the oil may embed in the bearing material whereas larger particles will score the bearing and shaft journal. If a number of short journeys are made, insufficient heat will be generated to drive off condensation which has built up on the bearings.

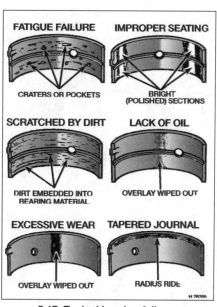

5.17 Typical bearing failures

● Ball and roller bearings will fail due to lack of lubrication or damage to the balls or rollers. Tapered-roller bearings can be damaged by overloading them. Unless the bearing is sealed on both sides, wash it in paraffin (kerosene) to remove all old grease then allow it to dry. Make a visual inspection looking to dented balls or rollers, damaged cages and worn or pitted races **(see illustration 5.18)**.
● A ball bearing can be checked for wear by listening to it when spun. Apply a film of light oil to the bearing and hold it close to the ear - hold the outer race with one hand and spin the inner

5.18 Example of ball journal bearing with damaged balls and cages

5.19 Hold outer race and listen to inner race when spun

race with the other hand **(see illustration 5.19)**. The bearing should be almost silent when spun; if it grates or rattles it is worn.

6 Oil seals

Oil seal removal and installation

● Oil seals should be renewed every time a component is dismantled. This is because the seal lips will become set to the sealing surface and will not necessarily reseal.
● Oil seals can be prised out of position using a large flat-bladed screwdriver **(see illustration 6.1)**. In the case of crankcase seals, check first that the seal is not lipped on the inside, preventing its removal with the crankcases joined.

6.1 Prise out oil seals with a large flat-bladed screwdriver

● New seals are usually installed with their marked face (containing the seal reference code) outwards and the spring side towards the fluid being retained. In certain cases, such as a two-stroke engine crankshaft seal, a double lipped seal may be used due to there being fluid or gas on each side of the joint.

● Use a bearing driver or socket which bears only on the outer hard edge of the seal to install it in the casing - tapping on the inner edge will damage the sealing lip.

Oil seal types and markings

● Oil seals are usually of the single-lipped type. Double-lipped seals are found where a liquid or gas is on both sides of the joint.

● Oil seals can harden and lose their sealing ability if the motorcycle has been in storage for a long period - renewal is the only solution.

● Oil seal manufacturers also conform to the ISO markings for seal size - these are moulded into the outer face of the seal **(see illustration 6.2)**.

6.2 These oil seal markings indicate inside diameter, outside diameter and seal thickness

7 Gaskets and sealants

Types of gasket and sealant

● Gaskets are used to seal the mating surfaces between components and keep lubricants, fluids, vacuum or pressure contained within the assembly. Aluminium gaskets are sometimes found at the cylinder joints, but most gaskets are paper-based. If the mating surfaces of the components being joined are undamaged the gasket can be installed dry, although a dab of sealant or grease will be useful to hold it in place during assembly.

● RTV (Room Temperature Vulcanising) silicone rubber sealants cure when exposed to moisture in the atmosphere. These sealants are good at filling pits or irregular gasket faces, but will tend to be forced out of the joint under very high torque. They can be used to replace a paper gasket, but first make sure that the width of the paper gasket is not essential to the shimming of internal components. RTV sealants should not be used on components containing petrol (gasoline).

● Non-hardening, semi-hardening and hard setting liquid gasket compounds can be used with a gasket or between a metal-to-metal joint. Select the sealant to suit the application: universal non-hardening sealant can be used on virtually all joints; semi-hardening on joint faces which are rough or damaged; hard setting sealant on joints which require a permanent bond and are subjected to high temperature and pressure. **Note:** *Check first if the paper gasket has a bead of sealant*

impregnated in its surface before applying additional sealant.

● When choosing a sealant, make sure it is suitable for the application, particularly if being applied in a high-temperature area or in the vicinity of fuel. Certain manufacturers produce sealants in either clear, silver or black colours to match the finish of the engine. This has a particular application on motorcycles where much of the engine is exposed.

● Do not over-apply sealant. That which is squeezed out on the outside of the joint can be wiped off, whereas an excess of sealant on the inside can break off and clog oilways.

Breaking a sealed joint

● Age, heat, pressure and the use of hard setting sealant can cause two components to stick together so tightly that they are difficult to separate using finger pressure alone. Do not resort to using levers unless there is a pry point provided for this purpose **(see illustration 7.1)** or else the gasket surfaces will be damaged.

● Use a soft-faced hammer **(see illustration 7.2)** or a wood block and conventional hammer to strike the component near the mating surface. Avoid hammering against cast extremities since they may break off. If this method fails, try using a wood wedge between the two components.

Caution: If the joint will not separate, double-check that you have removed all the fasteners.

7.1 If a pry point is provided, apply gently pressure with a flat-bladed screwdriver

7.2 Tap around the joint with a soft-faced mallet if necessary - don't strike cooling fins

Removal of old gasket and sealant

● Paper gaskets will most likely come away complete, leaving only a few traces stuck on

Most components have one or two hollow locating dowels between the two gasket faces. If a dowel cannot be removed, do not resort to gripping it with pliers - it will almost certainly be distorted. Install a close-fitting socket or Phillips screwdriver into the dowel and then grip the outer edge of the dowel to free it.

the sealing faces of the components. It is imperative that all traces are removed to ensure correct sealing of the new gasket.

● Very carefully scrape all traces of gasket away making sure that the sealing surfaces are not gouged or scored by the scraper **(see illustrations 7.3, 7.4 and 7.5)**. Stubborn deposits can be removed by spraying with an aerosol gasket remover. Final preparation of

7.3 Paper gaskets can be scraped off with a gasket scraper tool . . .

7.4 . . . a knife blade . . .

7.5 . . . or a household scraper

7.6 Fine abrasive paper is wrapped around a flat file to clean up the gasket face

7.7 A kitchen scourer can be used on stubborn deposits

the gasket surface can be made with very fine abrasive paper or a plastic kitchen scourer **(see illustrations 7.6 and 7.7)**.
● Old sealant can be scraped or peeled off components, depending on the type originally used. Note that gasket removal compounds are available to avoid scraping the components clean; make sure the gasket remover suits the type of sealant used.

8 Chains

Breaking and joining final drive chains

● Drive chains for all but small bikes are continuous and do not have a clip-type connecting link. The chain must be broken using a chain breaker tool and the new chain securely riveted together using a new soft rivet-type link. Never use a clip-type connecting link instead of a rivet-type link, except in an emergency. Various chain breaking and riveting tools are available, either as separate tools or combined as illustrated in the accompanying photographs - read the instructions supplied with the tool carefully.

> ⚠️ *Warning: The need to rivet the new link pins correctly cannot be overstressed - loss of control of the motorcycle is very likely to result if the chain breaks in use.*

● Rotate the chain and look for the soft link. The soft link pins look like they have been

8.1 Tighten the chain breaker to push the pin out of the link . . .

8.2 . . . withdraw the pin, remove the tool . . .

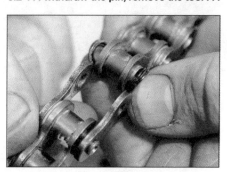

8.3 . . . and separate the chain link

deeply centre-punched instead of peened over like all the other pins **(see illustration 8.9)** and its sideplate may be a different colour. Position the soft link midway between the sprockets and assemble the chain breaker tool over one of the soft link pins **(see illustration 8.1)**. Operate the tool to push the pin out through the chain **(see illustration 8.2)**. On an O-ring chain, remove the O-rings **(see illustration 8.3)**. Carry out the same procedure on the other soft link pin.

> *Caution: Certain soft link pins (particularly on the larger chains) may require their ends to be filed or ground off before they can be pressed out using the tool.*

● Check that you have the correct size and strength (standard or heavy duty) new soft link - do not reuse the old link. Look for the size marking on the chain sideplates **(see illustration 8.10)**.
● Position the chain ends so that they are engaged over the rear sprocket. On an O-ring

8.4 Insert the new soft link, with O-rings, through the chain ends . . .

8.5 . . . install the O-rings over the pin ends . . .

8.6 . . . followed by the sideplate

chain, install a new O-ring over each pin of the link and insert the link through the two chain ends **(see illustration 8.4)**. Install a new O-ring over the end of each pin, followed by the sideplate (with the chain manufacturer's marking facing outwards) **(see illustrations 8.5 and 8.6)**. On an unsealed chain, insert the link through the two chain ends, then install the sideplate with the chain manufacturer's marking facing outwards.
● Note that it may not be possible to install the sideplate using finger pressure alone. If using a joining tool, assemble it so that the plates of the tool clamp the link and press the sideplate over the pins **(see illustration 8.7)**. Otherwise, use two small sockets placed over

8.7 Push the sideplate into position using a clamp

8.8 Assemble the chain riveting tool over one pin at a time and tighten it fully

8.9 Pin end correctly riveted (A), pin end unriveted (B)

the rivet ends and two pieces of the wood between a G-clamp. Operate the clamp to press the sideplate over the pins.

● Assemble the joining tool over one pin (following the maker's instructions) and tighten the tool down to spread the pin end securely **(see illustrations 8.8 and 8.9)**. Do the same on the other pin.

Warning: Check that the pin ends are secure and that there is no danger of the sideplate coming loose. If the pin ends are cracked the soft link must be renewed.

Final drive chain sizing

● Chains are sized using a three digit number, followed by a suffix to denote the chain type **(see illustration 8.10)**. Chain type is either standard or heavy duty (thicker sideplates), and also unsealed or O-ring/X-ring type.
● The first digit of the number relates to the pitch of the chain, ie the distance from the centre of one pin to the centre of the next pin **(see illustration 8.11)**. Pitch is expressed in eighths of an inch, as follows:

8.10 Typical chain size and type marking

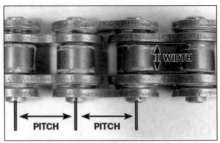

8.11 Chain dimensions

Sizes commencing with a 4 (eg 428) have a pitch of 1/2 inch (12.7 mm)

Sizes commencing with a 5 (eg 520) have a pitch of 5/8 inch (15.9 mm)

Sizes commencing with a 6 (eg 630) have a pitch of 3/4 inch (19.1 mm)

● The second and third digits of the chain size relate to the width of the rollers, again in imperial units, eg the 525 shown has 5/16 inch (7.94 mm) rollers **(see illustration 8.11)**.

9 Hoses

Clamping to prevent flow

● Small-bore flexible hoses can be clamped to prevent fluid flow whilst a component is worked on. Whichever method is used, ensure that the hose material is not permanently distorted or damaged by the clamp.
  a) A brake hose clamp available from auto accessory shops **(see illustration 9.1)**.
  b) A wingnut type hose clamp **(see illustration 9.2)**.

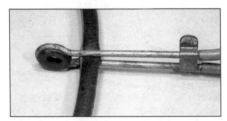

9.1 Hoses can be clamped with an automotive brake hose clamp . . .

9.2 . . . a wingnut type hose clamp . . .

  c) Two sockets placed each side of the hose and held with straight-jawed self-locking grips **(see illustration 9.3)**.
  d) Thick card each side of the hose held between straight-jawed self-locking grips **(see illustration 9.4)**.

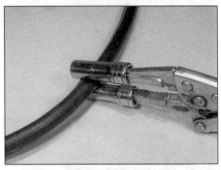

9.3 . . . two sockets and a pair of self-locking grips . . .

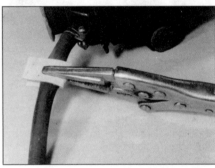

9.4 . . . or thick card and self-locking grips

Freeing and fitting hoses

● Always make sure the hose clamp is moved well clear of the hose end. Grip the hose with your hand and rotate it whilst pulling it off the union. If the hose has hardened due to age and will not move, slit it with a sharp knife and peel its ends off the union **(see illustration 9.5)**.
● Resist the temptation to use grease or soap on the unions to aid installation; although it helps the hose slip over the union it will equally aid the escape of fluid from the joint. It is preferable to soften the hose ends in hot water and wet the inside surface of the hose with water or a fluid which will evaporate.

9.5 Cutting a coolant hose free with a sharp knife

Length (distance)

Inches (in)	x 25.4	= Millimetres (mm)	x 0.0394	= Inches (in)
Feet (ft)	x 0.305	= Metres (m)	x 3.281	= Feet (ft)
Miles	x 1.609	= Kilometres (km)	x 0.621	= Miles

Volume (capacity)

Cubic inches (cu in; in³)	x 16.387	= Cubic centimetres (cc; cm³)	x 0.061	= Cubic inches (cu in; in³)
Imperial pints (Imp pt)	x 0.568	= Litres (l)	x 1.76	= Imperial pints (Imp pt)
Imperial quarts (Imp qt)	x 1.137	= Litres (l)	x 0.88	= Imperial quarts (Imp qt)
Imperial quarts (Imp qt)	x 1.201	= US quarts (US qt)	x 0.833	= Imperial quarts (Imp qt)
US quarts (US qt)	x 0.946	= Litres (l)	x 1.057	= US quarts (US qt)
Imperial gallons (Imp gal)	x 4.546	= Litres (l)	x 0.22	= Imperial gallons (Imp gal)
Imperial gallons (Imp gal)	x 1.201	= US gallons (US gal)	x 0.833	= Imperial gallons (Imp gal)
US gallons (US gal)	x 3.785	= Litres (l)	x 0.264	= US gallons (US gal)

Mass (weight)

Ounces (oz)	x 28.35	= Grams (g)	x 0.035	= Ounces (oz)
Pounds (lb)	x 0.454	= Kilograms (kg)	x 2.205	= Pounds (lb)

Force

Ounces-force (ozf; oz)	x 0.278	= Newtons (N)	x 3.6	= Ounces-force (ozf; oz)
Pounds-force (lbf; lb)	x 4.448	= Newtons (N)	x 0.225	= Pounds-force (lbf; lb)
Newtons (N)	x 0.1	= Kilograms-force (kgf; kg)	x 9.81	= Newtons (N)

Pressure

Pounds-force per square inch (psi; lbf/in²; lb/in²)	x 0.070	= Kilograms-force per square centimetre (kgf/cm²; kg/cm²)	x 14.223	= Pounds-force per square inch (psi; lbf/in²; lb/in²)
Pounds-force per square inch (psi; lbf/in²; lb/in²)	x 0.068	= Atmospheres (atm)	x 14.696	= Pounds-force per square inch (psi; lbf/in²; lb/in²)
Pounds-force per square inch (psi; lbf/in²; lb/in²)	x 0.069	= Bars	x 14.5	= Pounds-force per square inch (psi; lbf/in²; lb/in²)
Pounds-force per square inch (psi; lbf/in²; lb/in²)	x 6.895	= Kilopascals (kPa)	x 0.145	= Pounds-force per square inch (psi; lbf/in²; lb/in²)
Kilopascals (kPa)	x 0.01	= Kilograms-force per square centimetre (kgf/cm²; kg/cm²)	x 98.1	= Kilopascals (kPa)
Millibar (mbar)	x 100	= Pascals (Pa)	x 0.01	= Millibar (mbar)
Millibar (mbar)	x 0.0145	= Pounds-force per square inch (psi; lbf/in²; lb/in²)	x 68.947	= Millibar (mbar)
Millibar (mbar)	x 0.75	= Millimetres of mercury (mmHg)	x 1.333	= Millibar (mbar)
Millibar (mbar)	x 0.401	= Inches of water (inH₂O)	x 2.491	= Millibar (mbar)
Millimetres of mercury (mmHg)	x 0.535	= Inches of water (inH₂O)	x 1.868	= Millimetres of mercury (mmHg)
Inches of water (inH₂O)	x 0.036	= Pounds-force per square inch (psi; lbf/in²; lb/in²)	x 27.68	= Inches of water (inH₂O)

Torque (moment of force)

Pounds-force inches (lbf in; lb in)	x 1.152	= Kilograms-force centimetre (kgf cm; kg cm)	x 0.868	= Pounds-force inches (lbf in; lb in)
Pounds-force inches (lbf in; lb in)	x 0.113	= Newton metres (Nm)	x 8.85	= Pounds-force inches (lbf in; lb in)
Pounds-force inches (lbf in; lb in)	x 0.083	= Pounds-force feet (lbf ft; lb ft)	x 12	= Pounds-force inches (lbf in; lb in)
Pounds-force feet (lbf ft; lb ft)	x 0.138	= Kilograms-force metres (kgf m; kg m)	x 7.233	= Pounds-force feet (lbf ft; lb ft)
Pounds-force feet (lbf ft; lb ft)	x 1.356	= Newton metres (Nm)	x 0.738	= Pounds-force feet (lbf ft; lb ft)
Newton metres (Nm)	x 0.102	= Kilograms-force metres (kgf m; kg m)	x 9.804	= Newton metres (Nm)

Power

Horsepower (hp)	x 745.7	= Watts (W)	x 0.0013	= Horsepower (hp)

Velocity (speed)

Miles per hour (miles/hr; mph)	x 1.609	= Kilometres per hour (km/hr; kph)	x 0.621	= Miles per hour (miles/hr; mph)

Fuel consumption*

Miles per gallon (mpg)	x 0.354	= Kilometres per litre (km/l)	x 2.825	= Miles per gallon (mpg)

Temperature

Degrees Fahrenheit = (°C x 1.8) + 32   Degrees Celsius (Degrees Centigrade; °C) = (°F - 32) x 0.56

It is common practice to convert from miles per gallon (mpg) to litres/100 kilometres (l/100km), where mpg x l/100 km = 282

A number of chemicals and lubricants are available for use in motorcycle maintenance and repair. They include a wide variety of products ranging from cleaning solvents and degreasers to lubricants and protective sprays for rubber, plastic and vinyl.

● **Contact point/spark plug cleaner** is a solvent used to clean oily film and dirt from points, grime from electrical connectors and oil deposits from spark plugs. It is oil free and leaves no residue. It can also be used to remove gum and varnish from carburettor jets and other orifices.

● **Carburettor cleaner** is similar to contact point/spark plug cleaner but it usually has a stronger solvent and may leave a slight oily reside. It is not recommended for cleaning electrical components or connections.

● **Brake system cleaner** is used to remove grease or brake fluid from brake system components (where clean surfaces are absolutely necessary and petroleum-based solvents cannot be used); it also leaves no residue.

● **Silicone-based lubricants** are used to protect rubber parts such as hoses and grommets, and are used as lubricants for hinges and locks.

● **Multi-purpose grease** is an all purpose lubricant used wherever grease is more practical than a liquid lubricant such as oil. Some multi-purpose grease is coloured white and specially formulated to be more resistant to water than ordinary grease.

● **Gear oil** (sometimes called gear lube) is a specially designed oil used in transmissions and final drive units, as well as other areas where high friction, high temperature lubrication is required. It is available in a number of viscosities (weights) for various applications.

● **Motor oil**, of course, is the lubricant specially formulated for use in the engine. It normally contains a wide variety of additives to prevent corrosion and reduce foaming and wear. Motor oil comes in various weights (viscosity ratings) of from 5 to 80. The recommended weight of the oil depends on the seasonal temperature and the demands on the engine. Light oil is used in cold climates and under light load conditions; heavy oil is used in hot climates and where high loads are encountered. Multi-viscosity oils are designed to have characteristics of both light and heavy oils and are available in a number of weights from 5W-20 to 20W-50.

● **Petrol additives** perform several functions, depending on their chemical makeup. They usually contain solvents that help dissolve gum and varnish that build up on carburettor and inlet parts. They also serve to break down carbon deposits that form on the inside surfaces of the combustion chambers. Some additives contain upper cylinder lubricants for valves and piston rings.

● **Brake and clutch fluid** is a specially formulated hydraulic fluid that can withstand the heat and pressure encountered in brake/clutch systems. Care must be taken that this fluid does not come in contact with painted surfaces or plastics. An opened container should always be resealed to prevent contamination by water or dirt.

● **Chain lubricants** are formulated especially for use on motorcycle final drive chains. A good chain lube should adhere well and have good penetrating qualities to be effective as a lubricant inside the chain and on the side plates, pins and rollers. Most chain lubes are either the foaming type or quick drying type and are usually marketed as sprays. Take care to use a lubricant marked as being suitable for O-ring chains.

● **Degreasers** are heavy duty solvents used to remove grease and grime that may accumulate on engine and frame components. They can be sprayed or brushed on and, depending on the type, are rinsed with either water or solvent.

● **Solvents** are used alone or in combination with degreasers to clean parts and assemblies during repair and overhaul. The home mechanic should use only solvents that are non-flammable and that do not produce irritating fumes.

● **Gasket sealing compounds** may be used in conjunction with gaskets, to improve their sealing capabilities, or alone, to seal metal-to-metal joints. Many gasket sealers can withstand extreme heat, some are impervious to petrol and lubricants, while others are capable of filling and sealing large cavities. Depending on the intended use, gasket sealers either dry hard or stay relatively soft and pliable. They are usually applied by hand, with a brush, or are sprayed on the gasket sealing surfaces.

● **Thread locking compound** is an adhesive locking compound that prevents threaded fasteners from loosening because of vibration. It is available in a variety of types for different applications.

● **Moisture dispersants** are usually sprays that can be used to dry out electrical components such as the fuse block and wiring connectors. Some types can also be used as treatment for rubber and as a lubricant for hinges, cables and locks.

● **Waxes and polishes** are used to help protect painted and plated surfaces from the weather. Different types of paint may require the use of different types of wax polish. Some polishes utilise a chemical or abrasive cleaner to help remove the top layer of oxidised (dull) paint on older vehicles. In recent years, many non-wax polishes (that contain a wide variety of chemicals such as polymers and silicones) have been introduced. These non-wax polishes are usually easier to apply and last longer than conventional waxes and polishes.

About the MOT Test

In the UK, all vehicles more than three years old are subject to an annual test to ensure that they meet minimum safety requirements. A current test certificate must be issued before a machine can be used on public roads, and is required before a road fund licence can be issued. Riding without a current test certificate will also invalidate your insurance.

For most owners, the MOT test is an annual cause for anxiety, and this is largely due to owners not being sure what needs to be checked prior to submitting the motorcycle for testing. The simple answer is that a fully roadworthy motorcycle will have no difficulty in passing the test.

This is a guide to getting your motorcycle through the MOT test. Obviously it will not be possible to examine the motorcycle to the same standard as the professional MOT tester, particularly in view of the equipment required for some of the checks. However, working through the following procedures will enable you to identify any problem areas before submitting the motorcycle for the test.

It has only been possible to summarise the test requirements here, based on the regulations in force at the time of printing. Test standards are becoming increasingly stringent, although there are some exemptions for older vehicles. More information about the MOT test can be obtained from the TSO publications, *How Safe is your Motorcycle* and *The MOT Inspection Manual for Motorcycle Testing*.

Many of the checks require that one of the wheels is raised off the ground. If the motorcycle doesn't have a centre stand, note that an auxiliary stand will be required. Additionally, the help of an assistant may prove useful.

Certain exceptions apply to machines under 50 cc, machines without a lighting system, and Classic bikes - if in doubt about any of the requirements listed below seek confirmation from an MOT tester prior to submitting the motorcycle for the test.

Check that the frame number is clearly visible.

> **HAYNES HiNT**
>
> *If a component is in borderline condition, the tester has discretion in deciding whether to pass or fail it. If the motorcycle presented is clean and evidently well cared for, the tester may be more inclined to pass a borderline component than if the motorcycle is scruffy and apparently neglected.*

Electrical System

Lights, turn signals, horn and reflector

✔ With the ignition on, check the operation of the following electrical components. **Note:** *The electrical components on certain small-capacity machines are powered by the generator, requiring that the engine is run for this check.*

a) Headlight and tail light. Check that both illuminate in the low and high beam switch positions.

b) Position lights. Check that the front position (or sidelight) and tail light illuminate in this switch position.

c) Turn signals. Check that all flash at the correct rate, and that the warning light(s) function correctly. Check that the turn signal switch works correctly.

d) Hazard warning system (where fitted). Check that all four turn signals flash in this switch position.

e) Brake stop light. Check that the light comes on when the front and rear brakes are independently applied. Models first used on or after 1st April 1986 must have a brake light switch on each brake.

f) Horn. Check that the sound is continuous and of reasonable volume.

✔ Check that there is a red reflector on the rear of the machine, either mounted separately or as part of the tail light lens.

✔ Check the condition of the headlight, tail light and turn signal lenses.

Headlight beam height

✔ The MOT tester will perform a headlight beam height check using specialised beam setting equipment **(see illustration 1)**. This equipment will not be available to the home mechanic, but if you suspect that the headlight is incorrectly set or may have been maladjusted in the past, you can perform a rough test as follows.

✔ Position the bike in a straight line facing a brick wall. The bike must be off its stand, upright and with a rider seated. Measure the height from the ground to the centre of the headlight and mark a horizontal line on the wall at this height. Position the motorcycle 3.8 metres from the wall and draw a vertical

Headlight beam height checking equipment

line up the wall central to the centreline of the motorcycle. Switch to dipped beam and check that the beam pattern falls slightly lower than the horizontal line and to the left of the vertical line **(see illustration 2)**.

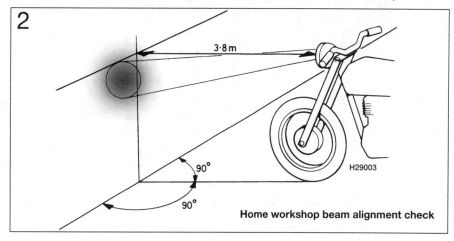

3·8 m

90°

90°

H29003

Home workshop beam alignment check

Exhaust System and Final Drive

Exhaust

✔ Check that the exhaust mountings are secure and that the system does not foul any of the rear suspension components.
✔ Start the motorcycle. When the revs are increased, check that the exhaust is neither holed nor leaking from any of its joints. On a linked system, check that the collector box is not leaking due to corrosion.

✔ Note that the exhaust decibel level ("loudness" of the exhaust) is assessed at the discretion of the tester. If the motorcycle was first used on or after 1st January 1985 the silencer must carry the BSAU 193 stamp, or a marking relating to its make and model, or be of OE (original equipment) manufacture. If the silencer is marked NOT FOR ROAD USE, RACING USE ONLY or similar, it will fail the MOT.

Final drive

✔ On chain or belt drive machines, check that the chain/belt is in good condition and does not have excessive slack. Also check that the sprocket is securely mounted on the rear wheel hub. Check that the chain/belt guard is in place.
✔ On shaft drive bikes, check for oil leaking from the drive unit and fouling the rear tyre.

Steering and Suspension

Steering

✔ With the front wheel raised off the ground, rotate the steering from lock to lock. The handlebar or switches must not contact the fuel tank or be close enough to trap the rider's hand. Problems can be caused by damaged lock stops on the lower yoke and frame, or by the fitting of non-standard handlebars.
✔ When performing the lock to lock check, also ensure that the steering moves freely without drag or notchiness. Steering movement can be impaired by poorly routed cables, or by overtight head bearings or worn bearings. The tester will perform a check of the steering head bearing lower race by mounting the front wheel on a surface plate, then performing a lock to lock check with the weight of the machine on the lower bearing (see illustration 3).
✔ Grasp the fork sliders (lower legs) and attempt to push and pull on the forks (see

Front wheel mounted on a surface plate for steering head bearing lower race check

illustration 4). Any play in the steering head bearings will be felt. Note that in extreme cases, wear of the front fork bushes can be misinterpreted for head bearing play.
✔ Check that the handlebars are securely mounted.
✔ Check that the handlebar grip rubbers are secure. They should by bonded to the bar left end and to the throttle cable pulley on the right end.

Front suspension

✔ With the motorcycle off the stand, hold the front brake on and pump the front forks up and down (see illustration 5). Check that they are adequately damped.

Checking the steering head bearings for freeplay

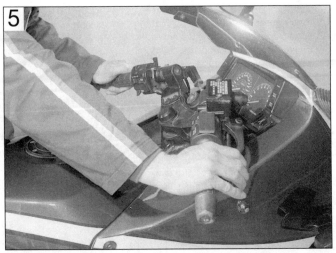

Hold the front brake on and pump the front forks up and down to check operation

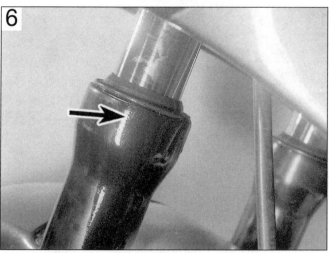

Inspect the area around the fork dust seal for oil leakage (arrow)

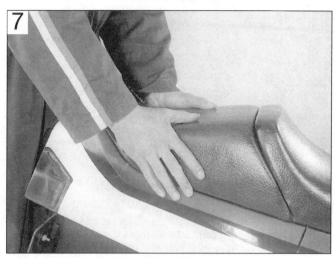

Bounce the rear of the motorcycle to check rear suspension operation

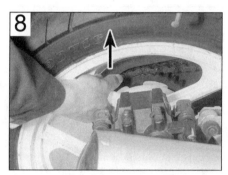

Checking for rear suspension linkage play

✔ Inspect the area above and around the front fork oil seals **(see illustration 6)**. There should be no sign of oil on the fork tube (stanchion) nor leaking down the slider (lower

leg). On models so equipped, check that there is no oil leaking from the anti-dive units.

✔ On models with swingarm front suspension, check that there is no freeplay in the linkage when moved from side to side.

Rear suspension

✔ With the motorcycle off the stand and an assistant supporting the motorcycle by its handlebars, bounce the rear suspension **(see illustration 7)**. Check that the suspension components do not foul on any of the cycle parts and check that the shock absorber(s) provide adequate damping.

✔ Visually inspect the shock absorber(s) and

check that there is no sign of oil leakage from its damper. This is somewhat restricted on certain single shock models due to the location of the shock absorber.

✔ With the rear wheel raised off the ground, grasp the wheel at the highest point and attempt to pull it up **(see illustration 8)**. Any play in the swingarm pivot or suspension linkage bearings will be felt as movement. **Note:** *Do not confuse play with actual suspension movement.* Failure to lubricate suspension linkage bearings can lead to bearing failure **(see illustration 9)**.

✔ With the rear wheel raised off the ground, grasp the swingarm ends and attempt to move the swingarm from side to side and forwards and backwards - any play indicates wear of the swingarm pivot bearings **(see illustration 10)**.

Worn suspension linkage pivots (arrows) are usually the cause of play in the rear suspension

Grasp the swingarm at the ends to check for play in its pivot bearings

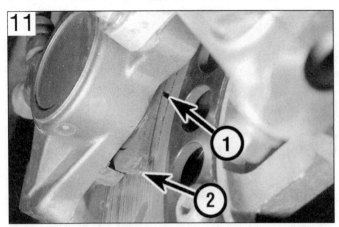

Brake pad wear can usually be viewed without removing the caliper. Most pads have wear indicator grooves (1) and some also have indicator tangs (2)

On drum brakes, check the angle of the operating lever with the brake fully applied. Most drum brakes have a wear indicator pointer and scale.

Brakes, Wheels and Tyres

Brakes

✔ With the wheel raised off the ground, apply the brake then free it off, and check that the wheel is about to revolve freely without brake drag.

✔ On disc brakes, examine the disc itself. Check that it is securely mounted and not cracked.

✔ On disc brakes, view the pad material through the caliper mouth and check that the pads are not worn down beyond the limit **(see illustration 11)**.

✔ On drum brakes, check that when the brake is applied the angle between the operating lever and cable or rod is not too great **(see illustration 12)**. Check also that the operating lever doesn't foul any other components.

✔ On disc brakes, examine the flexible hoses from top to bottom. Have an assistant hold the brake on so that the fluid in the hose is under pressure, and check that there is no sign of fluid leakage, bulges or cracking. If there are any metal brake pipes or unions, check that these are free from corrosion and damage. Where a brake-linked anti-dive system is fitted, check the hoses to the anti-dive in a similar manner.

✔ Check that the rear brake torque arm is secure and that its fasteners are secured by self-locking nuts or castellated nuts with split-pins or R-pins **(see illustration 13)**.

✔ On models with ABS, check that the self-check warning light in the instrument panel works.

✔ The MOT tester will perform a test of the motorcycle's braking efficiency based on a calculation of rider and motorcycle weight. Although this cannot be carried out at home, you can at least ensure that the braking systems are properly maintained. For hydraulic disc brakes, check the fluid level, lever/pedal feel (bleed of air if its spongy) and pad material. For drum brakes, check adjustment, cable or rod operation and shoe lining thickness.

Wheels and tyres

✔ Check the wheel condition. Cast wheels should be free from cracks and if of the built-up design, all fasteners should be secure. Spoked wheels should be checked for broken, corroded, loose or bent spokes.

✔ With the wheel raised off the ground, spin the wheel and visually check that the tyre and wheel run true. Check that the tyre does not foul the suspension or mudguards.

✔ With the wheel raised off the ground, grasp the wheel and attempt to move it about the axle (spindle) **(see illustration 14)**. Any play felt here indicates wheel bearing failure.

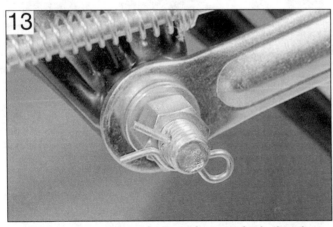

Brake torque arm must be properly secured at both ends

Check for wheel bearing play by trying to move the wheel about the axle (spindle)

Checking the tyre tread depth

Tyre direction of rotation arrow can be found on tyre sidewall

Castellated type wheel axle (spindle) nut must be secured by a split pin or R-pin

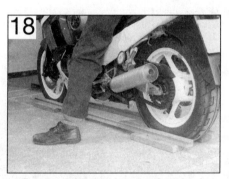

Two straightedges are used to check wheel alignment

✔ Check the tyre tread depth, tread condition and sidewall condition **(see illustration 15)**.
✔ Check the tyre type. Front and rear tyre types must be compatible and be suitable for road use. Tyres marked NOT FOR ROAD USE, COMPETITION USE ONLY or similar, will fail the MOT.

✔ If the tyre sidewall carries a direction of rotation arrow, this must be pointing in the direction of normal wheel rotation **(see illustration 16)**.
✔ Check that the wheel axle (spindle) nuts (where applicable) are properly secured. A self-locking nut or castellated nut with a split-pin or R-pin can be used **(see illustration 17)**.
✔ Wheel alignment is checked with the motorcycle off the stand and a rider seated. With the front wheel pointing straight ahead, two perfectly straight lengths of metal or wood and placed against the sidewalls of both tyres **(see illustration 18)**. The gap each side of the front tyre must be equidistant on both sides. Incorrect wheel alignment may be due to a cocked rear wheel (often as the result of poor chain adjustment) or in extreme cases, a bent frame.

General checks and condition

✔ Check the security of all major fasteners, bodypanels, seat, fairings (where fitted) and mudguards.

✔ Check that the rider and pillion footrests, handlebar levers and brake pedal are securely mounted.

✔ Check for corrosion on the frame or any load-bearing components. If severe, this may affect the structure, particularly under stress.

Sidecars

A motorcycle fitted with a sidecar requires additional checks relating to the stability of the machine and security of attachment and swivel joints, plus specific wheel alignment (toe-in) requirements. Additionally, tyre and lighting requirements differ from conventional motorcycle use. Owners are advised to check MOT test requirements with an official test centre.

Preparing for storage

Before you start

If repairs or an overhaul is needed, see that this is carried out now rather than left until you want to ride the bike again.

Give the bike a good wash and scrub all dirt from its underside. Make sure the bike dries completely before preparing for storage.

Engine

● Remove the spark plug(s) and lubricate the cylinder bores with approximately a teaspoon of motor oil using a spout-type oil can **(see illustration 1)**. Reinstall the spark plug(s). Crank the engine over a couple of times to coat the piston rings and bores with oil. If the bike has a kickstart, use this to turn the engine over. If not, flick the kill switch to the OFF position and crank the engine over on the starter **(see illustration 2)**. If the nature on the ignition system prevents the starter operating with the kill switch in the OFF position,

remove the spark plugs and fit them back in their caps; ensure that the plugs are earthed (grounded) against the cylinder head when the starter is operated **(see illustration 3)**.

> ⚠️ **Warning: It is important that the plugs are earthed (grounded) away from the spark plug holes otherwise there is a risk of atomised fuel from the cylinders igniting.**

> **HAYNES HiNT** *On a single cylinder four-stroke engine, you can seal the combustion chamber completely by positioning the piston at TDC on the compression stroke.*

● Drain the carburettor(s) otherwise there is a risk of jets becoming blocked by gum deposits from the fuel **(see illustration 4)**.

● If the bike is going into long-term storage, consider adding a fuel stabiliser to the fuel in the tank. If the tank is drained completely, corrosion of its internal surfaces may occur if left unprotected for a long period. The tank can be treated with a rust preventative especially for this purpose. Alternatively, remove the tank and pour half a litre of motor oil into it, install the filler cap and shake the tank to coat its internals with oil before draining off the excess. The same effect can also be achieved by spraying WD40 or a similar water-dispersant around the inside of the tank via its flexible nozzle.

● Make sure the cooling system contains the correct mix of antifreeze. Antifreeze also contains important corrosion inhibitors.

● The air intakes and exhaust can be sealed off by covering or plugging the openings. Ensure that you do not seal in any condensation; run the engine until it is hot,

Squirt a drop of motor oil into each cylinder

Flick the kill switch to OFF . . .

. . . and ensure that the metal bodies of the plugs (arrows) are earthed against the cylinder head

Connect a hose to the carburettor float chamber drain stub (arrow) and unscrew the drain screw

Exhausts can be sealed off with a plastic bag

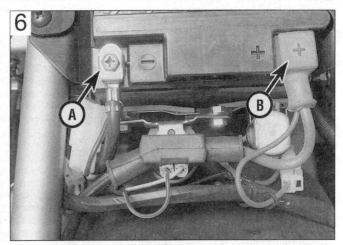

Disconnect the negative lead (A) first, followed by the positive lead (B)

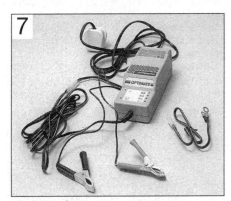

Use a suitable battery charger - this kit also assess battery condition

then switch off and allow to cool. Tape a piece of thick plastic over the silencer end(s) **(see illustration 5)**. Note that some advocate pouring a tablespoon of motor oil into the silencer(s) before sealing them off.

Battery

● Remove it from the bike - in extreme cases of cold the battery may freeze and crack its case **(see illustration 6)**.

● Check the electrolyte level and top up if necessary (conventional refillable batteries). Clean the terminals.
● Store the battery off the motorcycle and away from any sources of fire. Position a wooden block under the battery if it is to sit on the ground.
● Give the battery a trickle charge for a few hours every month **(see illustration 7)**.

Tyres

● Place the bike on its centrestand or an auxiliary stand which will support the motorcycle in an upright position. Position wood blocks under the tyres to keep them off the ground and to provide insulation from damp. If the bike is being put into long-term storage, ideally both tyres should be off the ground; not only will this protect the tyres, but will also ensure that no load is placed on the steering head or wheel bearings.
● Deflate each tyre by 5 to 10 psi, no more or the beads may unseat from the rim, making subsequent inflation difficult on tubeless tyres.

Pivots and controls

● Lubricate all lever, pedal, stand and footrest pivot points. If grease nipples are fitted to the rear suspension components, apply lubricant to the pivots.
● Lubricate all control cables.

Cycle components

● Apply a wax protectant to all painted and plastic components. Wipe off any excess, but don't polish to a shine. Where fitted, clean the screen with soap and water.
● Coat metal parts with Vaseline (petroleum jelly). When applying this to the fork tubes, do not compress the forks otherwise the seals will rot from contact with the Vaseline.
● Apply a vinyl cleaner to the seat.

Storage conditions

● Aim to store the bike in a shed or garage which does not leak and is free from damp.
● Drape an old blanket or bedspread over the bike to protect it from dust and direct contact with sunlight (which will fade paint). This also hides the bike from prying eyes. Beware of tight-fitting plastic covers which may allow condensation to form and settle on the bike.

Getting back on the road

Engine and transmission

● Change the oil and replace the oil filter. If this was done prior to storage, check that the oil hasn't emulsified - a thick whitish substance which occurs through condensation.
● Remove the spark plugs. Using a spout-type oil can, squirt a few drops of oil into the cylinder(s). This will provide initial lubrication as the piston rings and bores comes back into contact. Service the spark plugs, or fit new ones, and install them in the engine.

● Check that the clutch isn't stuck on. The plates can stick together if left standing for some time, preventing clutch operation. Engage a gear and try rocking the bike back and forth with the clutch lever held against the handlebar. If this doesn't work on cable-operated clutches, hold the clutch lever back against the handlebar with a strong elastic band or cable tie for a couple of hours **(see illustration 8)**.
● If the air intakes or silencer end(s) were blocked off, remove the bung or cover used.
● If the fuel tank was coated with a rust

Hold clutch lever back against the handlebar with elastic bands or a cable tie

preventative, oil or a stabiliser added to the fuel, drain and flush the tank and dispose of the fuel sensibly. If no action was taken with the fuel tank prior to storage, it is advised that the old fuel is disposed of since it will go off over a period of time. Refill the fuel tank with fresh fuel.

Frame and running gear

● Oil all pivot points and cables.

● Check the tyre pressures. They will definitely need inflating if pressures were reduced for storage.

● Lubricate the final drive chain (where applicable).

● Remove any protective coating applied to the fork tubes (stanchions) since this may well destroy the fork seals. If the fork tubes weren't protected and have picked up rust spots, remove them with very fine abrasive paper and refinish with metal polish.

● Check that both brakes operate correctly. Apply each brake hard and check that it's not possible to move the motorcycle forwards, then check that the brake frees off again once released. Brake caliper pistons can stick due to corrosion around the piston head, or on the sliding caliper types, due to corrosion of the slider pins. If the brake doesn't free after repeated operation, take the caliper off for examination. Similarly drum brakes can stick due to a seized operating cam, cable or rod linkage.

● If the motorcycle has been in long-term storage, renew the brake fluid and clutch fluid (where applicable).

● Depending on where the bike has been stored, the wiring, cables and hoses may have been nibbled by rodents. Make a visual check and investigate disturbed wiring loom tape.

Battery

● If the battery has been previously removal and given top up charges it can simply be reconnected. Remember to connect the positive cable first and the negative cable last.

● On conventional refillable batteries, if the battery has not received any attention, remove it from the motorcycle and check its electrolyte level. Top up if necessary then charge the battery. If the battery fails to hold a charge and a visual checks show heavy white sulphation of the plates, the battery is probably defective and must be renewed. This is particularly likely if the battery is old. Confirm battery condition with a specific gravity check.

● On sealed (MF) batteries, if the battery has not received any attention, remove it from the motorcycle and charge it according to the information on the battery case - if the battery fails to hold a charge it must be renewed.

Starting procedure

● If a kickstart is fitted, turn the engine over a couple of times with the ignition OFF to distribute oil around the engine. If no kickstart is fitted, flick the engine kill switch OFF and the ignition ON and crank the engine over a couple of times to work oil around the upper cylinder components. If the nature of the ignition system is such that the starter won't work with the kill switch OFF, remove the spark plugs, fit them back into their caps and earth (ground) their bodies on the cylinder head. Reinstall the spark plugs afterwards.

● Switch the kill switch to RUN, operate the choke and start the engine. If the engine won't start don't continue cranking the engine - not only will this flatten the battery, but the starter motor will overheat. Switch the ignition off and try again later. If the engine refuses to start, go through the fault finding procedures in this manual. **Note:** *If the bike has been in storage for a long time, old fuel or a carburettor blockage may be the problem. Gum deposits in carburettors can block jets - if a carburettor cleaner doesn't prove successful the carburettors must be dismantled for cleaning.*

● Once the engine has started, check that the lights, turn signals and horn work properly.

● Treat the bike gently for the first ride and check all fluid levels on completion. Settle the bike back into the maintenance schedule.

This Section provides an easy reference-guide to the more common faults that are likely to afflict your machine. Obviously, the opportunities are almost limitless for faults to occur as a result of obscure failures, and to try and cover all eventualities would require a book. Indeed, a number have been written on the subject.

Successful troubleshooting is not a mysterious 'black art' but the application of a bit of knowledge combined with a systematic and logical approach to the problem. Approach any troubleshooting by first accurately identifying the symptom and then checking through the list of possible causes, starting with the simplest or most obvious and progressing in stages to the most complex.

Take nothing for granted, but above all apply liberal quantities of common sense.

The main symptom of a fault is given in the text as a major heading below which are listed the various systems or areas which may contain the fault. Details of each possible cause for a fault and the remedial action to be taken are given, in brief, in the paragraphs below each heading. Further information should be sought in the relevant Chapter.

1 Starter motor problems

☐ Starter motor not rotating
☐ Starter motor rotates but engine does not turn over
☐ Starter motor and clutch function but engine will not turn over

2 Engine does not start when turned over

☐ No fuel flow to carburetor
☐ Fuel not reaching cylinder
☐ Engine flooding
☐ No spark at plug
☐ Weak spark at plug
☐ Compression low

3 Engine stalls after starting

☐ General causes

4 Poor running at idle and low speed

☐ Weak spark at plug or erratic firing
☐ Fuel/air mixture incorrect
☐ Compression low

5 Acceleration poor

☐ General causes

6 Poor running or lack of power at high speeds

☐ Weak spark at plug or erratic firing
☐ Fuel/air mixture incorrect
☐ Compression low

7 Knocking or pinking

☐ General causes

8 Overheating

☐ Firing incorrect
☐ Fuel/air mixture incorrect
☐ Lubrication inadequate
☐ Miscellaneous causes

9 Clutch operating problems

☐ Clutch slip
☐ Clutch drag

10 Gear selection problems

☐ Gear lever does not return
☐ Gear selection difficult or impossible
☐ Jumping out of gear
☐ Overselection

11 Abnormal engine noise

☐ Knocking or pinking
☐ Piston slap or rattling from cylinder
☐ Valve noise or tapping from cylinder head
☐ Other noises

12 Abnormal transmission noise

☐ Clutch noise
☐ Transmission noise

13 Exhaust smokes excessively

☐ White/blue smoke (caused by oil burning)
☐ Black smoke (caused by over-rich mixture)

14 Oil pressure warning light comes on

☐ Engine lubrication system failure
☐ Electrical system failure

15 Poor handling or roadholding

☐ Directional instability
☐ Steering bias to left or right
☐ Handlebar vibrates or oscillates
☐ Poor front fork performance
☐ Front fork judder when braking
☐ Poor rear suspension performance

16 Abnormal frame and suspension noise

☐ Front end noise
☐ Rear suspension noise

17 Brake problems

☐ Brakes are spongy or ineffective
☐ Brakes drag
☐ Brake lever or pedal pulsates in operation
☐ Disc brake noise
☐ Brake induced fork judder

18 Electrical problems

☐ Battery dead or weak
☐ Battery overcharged
☐ Total electrical failure
☐ Circuit failure
☐ Bulbs blowing repeatedly

1 Starter motor problems

Starter motor not rotating

☐ Engine stop switch off.

☐ Fuse blown. Check the main fuse located on the starter relay.

☐ Battery voltage low. Switching on the headlamp and operating the horn will give a good indication of the charge level. If necessary recharge the battery from an external source.

☐ Neutral gear not selected.

☐ Faulty neutral indicator switch, clutch interlock switch or sidestand switch. Check the switch wiring and switches for correct operation.

☐ Ignition switch defective. Check switch for continuity and connections for security.

☐ Engine stop switch defective. Check switch for continuity in 'Run' position. Fault will be caused by broken, wet or corroded switch contacts. Clean or renew as necessary.

☐ Starter button switch faulty. Check continuity of switch. Faults as for engine stop switch.

☐ Starter relay (solenoid) faulty. If the switch is functioning correctly a pronounced click should be heard when the starter button is depressed. This presupposes that current is flowing to the solenoid when the button is depressed.

☐ Wiring open or shorted. Check first that the battery terminal connections are tight and corrosion free. Follow this by checking that all wiring connections are dry, tight and corrosion free. Check also for frayed or broken wiring. Occasionally a wire may become trapped between two moving components, particularly in the vicinity of the steering head, leading to breakage of the internal core but leaving the softer but more resilient outer cover intact. This can cause mysterious intermittent or total power loss.

☐ Starter motor defective. A badly worn starter motor may cause high current drain from a battery without the motor rotating. If current is found to be reaching the motor, after checking the starter button and starter relay, suspect a damaged motor. The motor should be removed for inspection.

Starter motor rotates but engine does not turn over

☐ Starter motor clutch defective. Suspect jammed or worn engagement rollers.

☐ Damaged starter motor drive train. Inspect and renew component where necessary. Failure in this area is unlikely.

Starter motor and clutch function but engine will not turn over

☐ Engine seized. Seizure of the engine is always a result of damage to internal components due to lubrication failure, or component breakage resulting from abuse, neglect or old age. A seizing or partially seized component may go un-noticed until the engine has cooled down and an attempt is made to restart the engine. Suspect first seizure of the valves, valve gear and the pistons. Instantaneous seizure whilst the engine is running indicates component breakage. In either case major dismantling and inspection will be required.

2 Engine does not start when turned over

No fuel flow to carburetor

☐ No fuel or insufficient fuel in tank.

☐ Fuel tap lever position incorrectly selected.

☐ Faulty fuel pump (where fitted). Inspect as described in Chapter 8.

☐ Float chambers require priming after running dry.

☐ Tank filler cap air vent obstructed. Usually caused by dirt or water. Clean the vent orifice.

☐ Fuel tap or filter blocked. Blockage may be due to accumulation of rust or paint flakes from the tank's inner surface or of foreign matter from contaminated fuel. Remove the tap and clean it and the filter. Look also for water droplets in the fuel.

☐ Fuel pipe blocked. Blockage of the fuel line is more likely to result from a kink in the line rather than the accumulation of debris.

Fuel not reaching cylinder

☐ Float chamber not filling. Caused by float needle or floats sticking in up position. This may occur after the machine has been left standing for an extended length of time allowing the fuel to evaporate. When this occurs a gummy residue is often left which hardens to a varnish-like substance. This condition may be worsened by corrosion and crystalline deposits produced prior to the total evaporation of contaminated fuel. Sticking of the float needle may also be caused by wear. In any case removal of the float chamber will be necessary for inspection and cleaning.

☐ Blockage in starting circuit, slow running circuit or jets. Blockage of these items may be attributable to debris from the fuel tank by-passing the filter system or to gumming up as described in paragraph 1. Water droplets in the fuel will also lock jets and passages. The carburetor should be dismantled for cleaning.

☐ Fuel level too low. The fuel level in the float chamber is controlled by float height. The float height may increase with wear or damage but will never reduce, thus a low float height is an inherent rather than developing condition. Check the float height and make any necessary adjustment.

Engine flooding

☐ Float valve needle worn or stuck open. A piece of rust or other debris can prevent correct seating of the needle against the valve seat thereby permitting an uncontrolled flow of fuel. Similarly, a worn needle or needle seat will prevent valve closure. Dismantle the carburetor float bowl for cleaning and, if necessary, renewal of the worn components.

☐ Fuel level too high. The fuel level is controlled by the float height which may increase due to wear of the float needle, pivot pin or operating tang. Check the float height, and make any necessary adjustment. A leaking float will cause an increase in fuel level, and thus should be renewed.

☐ Cold starting mechanism. Check the choke (starter mechanism) for correct operation. If the mechanism jams in the 'On' position subsequent starting of a hot engine will be difficult.

☐ Blocked air filter. A badly restricted air filter will cause flooding. Check the filter and clean or renew as required. A collapsed inlet hose will have a similar effect.

No spark at plug

- [ ] Ignition switch not on.
- [ ] Engine stop switch off.
- [ ] Fuse blown. Check fuse for ignition circuit. See wiring diagram.
- [ ] Battery voltage low. The current draw required by a starter motor is sufficiently high that an under-charged battery may not have enough spare capacity to provide power for the ignition circuit during starting.
- [ ] Starter motor inefficient. A starter motor with worn brushes and a worn or dirty commutator will draw excessive amounts of current causing power starvation in the ignition system. See the preceding paragraph. Starter motor overhaul will be required.
- [ ] Spark plug failure. Clean the spark plugs thoroughly and reset their electrode gaps. Refer to the spark plug section in Chapter 1. If the spark plug shorts internally or has sustained visible damage to the electrodes, core or ceramic insulator it should be renewed. On rare occasions a plug that appears to spark vigorously will fail to do so when refitted to the engine and subjected to the compression pressure in the cylinder.
- [ ] Spark plug cap or high tension (HT) lead faulty. Check condition and security. Replace if deterioration is evident.
- [ ] Spark plug cap loose. Check that the spark plug cap fits securely over the plug and, where fitted, the screwed terminal on the plug end is secure.
- [ ] Shorting due to moisture. Certain parts of the ignition system are susceptible to shorting when the machine is ridden or parked in wet weather. Check particularly the area from the spark plug cap back to the ignition coil. A water dispersant spray may be used to dry out waterlogged components. Recurrence of the problem can be prevented by using an ignition sealant spray after drying out and cleaning.
- [ ] Ignition or stop switch shorted. May be caused by water, corrosion or wear. Water dispersant and contact cleaning sprays may be used. If this fails to overcome the problem dismantling and visual inspection of the switches will be required.
- [ ] Shorting or open-circuit in wiring. Failure in any wire connecting any of the ignition components will cause ignition malfunction. Check also that all connections are clean, dry and tight.
- [ ] Ignition HT coil failure. Check the coil, referring to Chapter 5.
- [ ] Faulty pulser coil(s). Check the coil(s), referring to Chapter 5.
- [ ] Faulty spark unit. Check the spark unit as described in Chapter 5.

Weak spark at plug

- [ ] Feeble sparking at the plug may be caused by any of the faults mentioned in the preceding Section other than those items in the first 3 paragraphs. Check first the spark plugs, these being the most likely culprits.

Compression low

- [ ] Spark plug loose. This will be self-evident on inspection, and may be accompanied by a hissing noise when the engine is turned over. Remove the plug and check that the threads in the cylinder head are not damaged. Check also that the plug sealing washer is in good condition.
- [ ] Cylinder head gasket leaking. This condition is often accompanied by a high pitched squeak from around the cylinder head and oil loss, and may be caused by insufficiently tightened cylinder head fasteners, a warped cylinder head or mechanical failure of the gasket material. Re-torqueing the fasteners to the correct specification may seal the leak in some instances but if damage has occurred this course of action will provide, at best, only a temporary cure.
- [ ] Valve not seating correctly. The failure of a valve to seat may be caused by insufficient valve clearance, pitting of the valve seat or face, carbon deposits on the valve seat or seizure of the valve stem or valve gear components. Valve spring breakage will also prevent correct valve closure. The valve clearances should be checked first and then, if these are found to be in order, further dismantling will be required to inspect the relevant components for failure.
- [ ] Cylinder, piston and ring wear. Compression pressure will be lost if any of these components are badly worn. Wear in one component is invariably accompanied by wear in another. A top-end overhaul will be required.
- [ ] Piston rings sticking or broken. Sticking of the piston rings may be caused by seizure due to lack of lubrication or heating as a result of poor carburation or incorrect fuel type. Gumming of the rings may result from lack of use, or carbon deposits in the ring grooves. Broken rings result from over-revving, overheating or general wear. In either case a top-end overhaul will be required.

3 Engine stalls after starting

General causes

- [ ] Improper cold start mechanism (choke) operation. Check that the operating controls function smoothly and are correctly adjusted. A cold engine may not require application of an enriched mixture to start initially but may baulk without choke once firing. Likewise a hot engine may start with an enriched mixture but will stop almost immediately if the choke is inadvertently in operation.
- [ ] Ignition malfunction. See Section 2, 'Weak spark at plug'.
- [ ] Carburetor incorrectly adjusted. Maladjustment of the mixture strength or idle speed may cause the engine to stop immediately after starting. See Chapter 4.
- [ ] Intake air leak. Check for security of the carburetor mounting and hose connections, and for cracks or splits in the hoses. Check also that the carburetor tops are secure and that the vacuum gauge adaptor plugs are tight.
- [ ] Fuel contamination. Check for filter blockage by debris or water which reduces, but does not completely stop, fuel flow or blockage of the slow speed circuit in the carburetor by the same agents. If water is present it can often be seen as droplets in the bottom of the float chamber. Clean the filter and, where water is in evidence, drain and flush the fuel tank and float chamber.
- [ ] Air filter blocked or omitted. A blocked filter will cause an over-rich mixture; the omission of a filter will cause an excessively weak mixture. Both conditions will have a detrimental effect on carburation. Clean or renew the filter as necessary.
- [ ] Fuel filler cap air vent blocked - clean the vent orifice (except California models).
- [ ] Blocked or malfunctioning Evaporative emission control system component - California models.

4 Poor running at idle and low speed

Weak spark at plug or erratic firing

☐ Battery voltage low. In certain conditions low battery charge, especially when coupled with a badly sulphated battery, may result in misfiring. If the battery is in good general condition it should be recharged; an old battery suffering from sulphated plates should be renewed.

☐ Spark plugs fouled, faulty or incorrectly adjusted. See Section 2 or refer to Chapter 1.

☐ Spark plug cap or high tension lead shorting. Check the condition of both these items ensuring that they are in good condition and dry and that the cap is fitted correctly.

☐ Spark plug type incorrect. Fit plugs of correct type and heat range as given in Specifications. In certain conditions a plug of hotter or colder type may be required for normal running.

☐ Ignition timing incorrect. Check the ignition timing statically and dynamically, ensuring that the advance is functioning correctly.

☐ Faulty ignition HT coil. Partial failure of the coil internal insulation will diminish the performance of the coil. No repair is possible, a new component must be fitted.

☐ Faulty pulser coil(s). Check the coil(s), referring to Chapter 5.

☐ Faulty spark unit. Check the spark unit as described in Chapter 5.

Fuel/air mixture incorrect

☐ Intake air leak. See Section 3 'General causes'.

☐ Mixture strength incorrect. Adjust slow running mixture strength using pilot adjustment screw.

☐ Carburetor synchronisation.

☐ Pilot jet or slow running circuit blocked. The carburetors should be removed and dismantled for thorough cleaning. Blow through all jets and air passages with compressed air to clear obstructions.

☐ Air cleaner clogged or omitted. Clean or fit air cleaner element as necessary. Check also that the element and air filter cover are correctly seated.

☐ Cold start mechanism (choke) in operation. Check that the choke has not been left on inadvertently and the operation is correct. Also check the operating cable freeplay.

☐ Fuel level too high or too low. Check the float height and adjust as necessary. See Section 2 'Engine flooding'.

☐ Fuel tank air vent obstructed - clean vent orifice (except California models).

☐ Malfunctioning Evaporative emission control system component - California models.

☐ Valve clearance incorrect. Check, and if necessary, adjust the clearances.

Compression low

☐ See Section 2.

5 Acceleration poor

General causes

☐ All items as for previous Section.
☐ Sticking carburetor piston.

☐ Brakes binding. Usually caused by sticking caliper piston(s). A bent wheel axle or warped brake disc can produce similar symptoms.

6 Poor running or lack of power at high speeds

Weak spark at plug or erratic firing

☐ See Section 4.

☐ HT lead insulation failure. Insulation failure of the HT lead and spark plug cap due to old age or damage can cause shorting when the engine is driven hard. This condition may be less noticeable, or not noticeable at all at lower engine speeds.

Fuel/air mixture incorrect

☐ All items as for Section 4, with the exception of items 2 and 4.

☐ Main jet blocked. Debris from contaminated fuel, or from the fuel tank, and water in the fuel can block the main jet. Clean the fuel filter, the float chamber area, and if water is present, flush and refill the fuel tank.

☐ Main jet is the wrong size. The standard carburetor jetting is for sea level atmospheric pressure. For high altitudes, usually above 5000 ft, a smaller main jet will be required.

☐ Jet needle and needle jet worn. These can be renewed individually but should be renewed as a pair. Renewal of both items requires partial dismantling of the carburetors.

☐ Air bleed holes blocked. Dismantle carburetor and use compressed air to blow out all air passages.

☐ Reduced fuel flow. A reduction in the maximum fuel flow from the fuel tank to the carburetor will cause fuel starvation, proportionate to the engine speed. Check for blockages through debris or a kinked fuel pipe.

☐ Vacuum diaphragm split. Renew.

Compression low

☐ See Section 2.

7 Knocking or pinking

General causes

☐ Carbon build-up in combustion chamber. After a high mileage has been covered large accumulation of carbon may occur. This may glow red hot and cause premature ignition of the fuel/air mixture, in advance of normal firing by the spark plug. Cylinder head removal will be required to allow inspection and cleaning.

☐ Fuel incorrect. A low grade fuel, or one of poor quality may result in compression induced detonation of the fuel resulting in knocking and pingink (pinging) noises. Old fuel can cause similar problems. A too highly leaded fuel will reduce detonation but will accelerate deposit formation in the combustion chamber and may lead to early pre-ignition as described in the previous paragraph.

☐ Spark plug heat range incorrect. Uncontrolled pre-ignition can result from the use of spark plugs with too hot a heat range.

☐ Weak mixture. Overheating of the engine due to a weak mixture can result in pre-ignition occurring where it would not occur when engine temperature was within normal limits. Maladjustment, blocked jets or passages and air leaks can cause this condition.

8 Overheating

Firing incorrect

☐ Spark plugs fouled, defective or maladjusted. See Section 2 *'No spark at plug'*.
☐ Spark plug type incorrect. Refer to the Specifications and ensure that the correct plug type is fitted.
☐ Incorrect ignition timing. Timing that is far too much advanced or far too much retarded will cause overheating. Check the ignition timing is correct.

Fuel/air mixture incorrect

☐ Slow speed mixture strength incorrect. Adjust pilot air screw.
☐ Main jet wrong size. The carburetor is jetted for sea level atmospheric conditions. For high altitudes, usually above 5000 ft, a smaller main jet will be required.
☐ Air filter badly fitted or omitted. Check that the filter element is in place and that it and the air filter casing cover are sealing correctly. Any leaks will cause a weak mixture.
☐ Induction air leaks. Check the security of the carburetor mountings and hose connections, and for cracks and splits in the hoses. Check also that the carburetor tops are secure and that the vacuum gauge adaptor plugs are tight.

☐ Fuel level too low. See Section 2 *'Fuel not reaching cylinder'*.
☐ Fuel tank filler cap air vent obstructed. Clear blockage.

Lubrication inadequate

☐ Engine oil too low. Not only does the oil serve as a lubricant by preventing friction between moving components, but it also acts as a coolant. Check the oil level and replenish.
☐ Engine oil overworked. The lubricating properties of oil are lost slowly during use as a result of changes resulting from heat and also contamination. Always change the oil at the recommended interval.
☐ Engine oil of incorrect viscosity or poor quality. Always use the recommended viscosity and type of oil.
☐ Oil filter and relief valve blocked. Renew filter and clean the relief valve.

Miscellaneous causes

☐ Radiator fins clogged. A build-up of mud in the radiator matrix will decrease the cooling capabilities of the fins. Clean the radiator as required.

9 Clutch operating problems

Clutch slip

☐ No clutch lever freeplay (600 models). Adjust the clutch lever freeplay according to the procedure given in Chapter 1.
☐ Clutch inner cable snagging (600 models). Caused by a frayed or kinked outer cable. Replace the cable with a new one. Repair of a frayed cable is not recommended.
☐ Clutch operating mechanism defective (600 models). Worn or damaged parts in the clutch lifting mechanism could include the operating arm, return spring, pushrod or bearings. Renew the worn components.
☐ Excess fluid in the reservoir (1000 models). Check the fluid level as described in *Daily (pre-ride) checks*.
☐ Friction plates worn or warped. Overhaul clutch assembly, renewing plates as a set if any are worn to or beyond the service limit.
☐ Plain plates warped. Overhaul clutch assembly renewing plates as a set if any exceed the service limit.
☐ Clutch springs broken or worn. Old or heat damaged (from slipping clutch) springs must be renewed. Renew the springs as a set.
☐ Clutch centre and outer drum worn. Severe indentations by the clutch plate tangs of the channels in the center and drum will cause snagging of the plates preventing correct engagement. If this damage occurs, renewal of the worn components will be required.
☐ Lubricant incorrect. Use of an engine/transmission oil other than that specified may allow the plates to slip.

Clutch drag

☐ Clutch lever freeplay excessive (600 models). Adjust the lever freeplay as described in Chapter 1.
☐ Clutch operating mechanism defective (600 models). Worn or damaged lifting mechanism components can stick and fail to provide leverage. Overhaul clutch components.

☐ Insufficient fluid in reservoir (1000 models). Top up as described in *Daily (pre-ride) checks*.
☐ Air in hydraulic fluid (1000 models). Bleed the system as described in Chapter 7.
☐ Clutch slave cylinder defective (1000 models). A worn or damaged piston can stick and fail to return correctly. Overhaul clutch cylinder clutch components as described in Chapter 2.
☐ Clutch spring tension uneven. Usually caused by a sagged or broken spring. Check and replace springs as a set.
☐ Engine oil deteriorated. Badly contaminated oil and a heavy deposit of oil sludge and carbon on the plates will cause plate sticking. The oil recommended for this machine is of the detergent type, therefore it is unlikely that this problem will arise unless regular oil changes are neglected.
☐ Engine oil viscosity too high. Drag on the plates will result from the use of an oil with too high a viscosity. In very cold weather clutch drag may occur until the engine has reached normal operating temperature.
☐ Clutch centre and outer drum worn. Indentation by the clutch plate tangs of the channels in the centre and drum will prevent easy plate disengagement. If the damage is light the affected areas may be dressed with a fine file. More pronounced damage will necessitate the renewal of the components.
☐ Clutch outer drum seized to the shaft. Lack of lubrication, severe wear or damage can cause the drum to seize to the shaft. Overhaul of the clutch, and perhaps the transmission, may be necessary to repair the damage.
☐ Loose clutch nut. Causes drum and center misalignment, putting a drag on the engine. Engagement adjustment continually varies. Overhaul the clutch assembly.

10 Gear selection problems

Gear lever does not return

☐ Weak or broken return spring. Renew the spring.
☐ Gearshift shaft bent or seized. Distortion of the gearshift shaft often occurs if the machine is dropped heavily on the gear lever. Provided that damage is not severe, straightening of the shaft is permissible.

Gear selection difficult or impossible

☐ Clutch not disengaging fully. See Section 9.
☐ Gearshift shaft bent. This often occurs if the machine is dropped heavily on the gear lever. Straightening of the shaft is permissible if the damage is not too great.
☐ Gearshift mechanism worn or damaged. Wear or breakage of any component may cause difficulty in selecting one or more gears. Overhaul the shift mechanism.
☐ Gearshift drum detent arm damaged. Failure, rather than wear, may jam the drum thereby preventing gearshifting.
☐ Shift forks bent or seized. This can be caused by dropping the machine heavily on the gearchange lever or as a result of lack of lubrication. Though rare, bending of a shaft can result from a missed gearshift or false selection at high speed.
☐ Shift fork end and pin wear. Pronounced wear of these items and the grooves in the gearshift drum can lead to imprecise selection and, eventually, no selection. Renewal of the worn components will be required.
☐ Structural failure. Failure of any one component of the gearshift mechanism will result in improper or fouled gear selection.

Jumping out of gear

☐ Detent arm assembly worn or damaged. Wear of the arm and the cam with which it locates and breakage of the detent spring can cause imprecise gear selection resulting in jumping out of gear. Renew the damaged components.
☐ Gear pinion dogs worn or damaged. Rounding off the dog edges and the mating recesses in adjacent pinion can lead to jumping out of gear when under load. The gears should be inspected and renewed. Attempting to reprofile the dogs is not recommended.
☐ Shift forks, gearshift drum and pinion grooves worn. Extreme wear of these interconnected items can occur after high mileages especially when lubrication has been neglected. The worn components must be renewed.
☐ Gear pinions, bushes and shafts worn. Renew the worn components.
☐ Bent gearshift shaft. Often caused by dropping the machine on the gear lever.
☐ Gear pinion tooth broken. Chipped teeth are unlikely to cause jumping out of gear once the gear has been selected fully; a tooth which is completely broken off, however, may cause problems in this respect and in any event will cause transmission noise.

Overselection

☐ Detent arm worn or broken. Renew if damaged.

11 Abnormal engine noise

Knocking or pinking

☐ See Section 7.

Piston slap or rattling from cylinder

☐ Cylinder bore/piston clearance excessive. Resulting from wear, partial seizure or improper boring during overhaul. This condition can often be heard as a high, rapid tapping noise when the engine is under little or no load, particularly when power is just beginning to be applied. Reboring to the next correct oversize should be carried out and a new oversize piston fitted.
☐ Connecting rod bent. This can be caused by over-revving, trying to start a very badly flooded engine (resulting in a hydraulic lock in the cylinder) or by earlier mechanical failure such as a dropped valve. Attempts at straightening a bent connecting rod are not recommended. Careful inspection of the crankshaft should be made before renewing the damaged connecting rod.
☐ Piston pin, piston boss bore or small-end bearing wear or seizure. Excess clearance or partial seizure between normal moving parts of these items can cause continuous or intermittent tapping noises. Rapid wear or seizure is caused by lubrication starvation resulting from an insufficient engine oil level or oilway blockage.
☐ Piston rings worn, broken or sticking. Renew the rings after careful inspection of the piston and bore.

Valve noise or tapping from the cylinder head

☐ Valve clearance incorrect. Adjust the clearances with the engine cold.
☐ Valve spring broken or weak. Renew the spring set.
☐ Camshaft or cylinder head worn or damaged. The camshaft lobes are the most highly stressed of all components in the engine and are subject to high wear if lubrication becomes inadequate. The bearing surfaces on the camshaft and cylinder head are also sensitive to a lack of lubrication. Lubrication failure due to blocked oilways can occur, but over-enthusiastic revving before engine warm-up is complete is the usual cause.
☐ Cam follower wear. Rapid wear of a follower, and the resulting need for frequent valve clearance adjustment, indicates breakthrough or failure of the surface hardening on the follower surface. Similar wear in the cam lobes can be expected. Renew the worn components after checking for lubrication failure.
☐ Worn camshaft drive components. A rustling noise or light tapping can be emitted by a worn cam chain or worn sprockets and chain. If uncorrected, subsequent cam chain breakage may cause extensive damage. The worn components must be renewed before wear becomes too far advanced.

Other noises

☐ Big-end bearing wear. A pronounced knock from within the crankcase which worsens rapidly is indicative of big-end bearing failure as a result of extreme normal wear or lubrication failure. Remedial action in the form of a bottom end overhaul should be taken; continuing to run the engine will lead to further damage including the possibility of connecting rod breakage.
☐ Main bearing failure. Extreme normal wear or failure of the main bearings is characteristically accompanied by a rumble from the crankcase and vibration felt through the frame and footrests. Renew the worn bearings and carry out a very careful examination of the crankshaft.
☐ Crankshaft excessively out of true. A bent crank may result from over-revving or damage from an upper cylinder component or gearbox failure. Damage can also result from dropping the machine on either crankshaft end. Straightening of the crankshaft is not possible in normal circumstances; a replacement item should be fitted.
☐ Engine mounting loose. Tighten all the engine mounting nuts and bolts.

11 Abnormal engine noise

☐ Cylinder head gasket leaking. The noise most often associated with a leaking head gasket is a high pitched squeaking, although any other noise consistent with gas being forced out under pressure from a small orifice can also be emitted. Gasket leakage is often accompanied by oil seepage from around the mating joint or from the cylinder head nuts. Leakage into the cam chain tunnel or oil return passages will increase crankcase pressure and may cause oil leakage at joints and oil seals. Also, oil contamination will be accelerated. Leakage results from insufficient or uneven tightening of the cylinder head fasteners, or from random mechanical failure. Retightening to the correct torque figure will, at best, only provide a temporary cure. The gasket should be renewed at the earliest opportunity.

☐ Exhaust system leakage. Popping or crackling in the exhaust system, particularly when it occurs with the engine on the overrun, indicates a poor joint either at the cylinder port or at the header/muffler connection. Failure of the gasket or looseness of the clamp should be looked for.

12 Abnormal transmission noise

Clutch noise

☐ Clutch outer drum/friction plate tang clearance excessive.
☐ Clutch outer drum/spacer clearance excessive.
☐ Clutch outer drum/thrust washer clearance excessive.
☐ Primary drive gear teeth worn or damaged.

Transmission noise

☐ Bearings or bushes worn or damaged. Renew the affected components.
☐ Gear pinions worn or chipped. Renew the gear pinions.
☐ Metal chips jammed in gear teeth. This can occur when pieces of metal from any failed component are picked up by a meshing pinion. The condition will lead to rapid bearing wear or early gear failure.

☐ Engine/transmission oil level too low. Top up immediately to prevent damage to gearbox and engine.
☐ Gearshift mechanism worn or damaged. Wear or failure of certain items in the selection and change components can induce mis-selection of gears (see Section 10) where incipient engagement of more than one gear set is promoted. Remedial action, by the overhaul of the transmission, should be taken without delay.
☐ Loose drive chain sprocket. Remove the sprocket and check for impact damage to the splines of the sprocket and shaft. Excessive slack between the splines will promote loosening of the securing nut; renewal of the worn components is required. When retightening the nut ensure that it is tightened fully to its specified torque setting.
☐ Chain snagging on cases or cycle parts. A badly worn chain or one that is excessively loose may snag or smack against adjacent components.

13 Exhaust smokes excessively

White/blue smoke (caused by oil burning)

☐ Piston rings worn or broken. Breakage or wear of any ring, but particularly the oil control ring, will allow engine oil past the piston into the combustion chamber. Overhaul the cylinder barrel and piston.
☐ Cylinder cracked, worn or scored. These conditions may be caused by overheating, lack of lubrication, component failure or advanced normal wear. The cylinder barrel should be renewed or rebored and the next oversize piston fitted.
☐ Valve oil seal damaged or worn. This can occur as a result of valve guide failure or old age. The emission of smoke is likely to occur when the throttle is closed rapidly after acceleration, for instance, when changing gear. Renew the valve oil seals and, if necessary, the valve guides.
☐ Valve guides worn. See the preceding paragraph.
☐ Engine oil level too high. This increases the crankcase pressure and allows oil to be forced past the piston rings. Often accompanied by seepage of oil at joints and oil seals.
☐ Cylinder head gasket blown between cam chain tunnel or oil return passage. Renew the cylinder head gasket.
☐ Abnormal crankcase pressure. This may be caused by blocked breather passages or hoses causing back-pressure at high engine revolutions.

Black smoke (caused by over-rich mixture)

☐ Air filter element clogged. Clean or renew the element.
☐ Main jet loose or too large. Remove the float chambers to check for tightness of the jets. If the machine is used at high altitudes rejetting will be required to compensate for the lower atmospheric pressure.
☐ Cold start mechanism (choke) jammed on. Check that the mechanism works smoothly and correctly and that the operating cable is lubricated and not snagged.
☐ Fuel level too high. The fuel level is controlled by the float height which can increase as a result of wear or damage. Remove the float bowl and check the float height. Check also that floats have not punctured; a punctured float will loose buoyancy and allow an increased fuel level.
☐ Float valve needle stuck open. Caused by dirt or a worn valve. Clean the float chamber or renew the needle and, if necessary, the valve seat.

14 Oil pressure warning light comes on

Engine lubrication system failure

☐ Engine oil defective. Oil pump shaft or locating pin sheared off from ingesting debris or seizing from lack of lubrication (low oil level).

☐ Engine oil strainer clogged. Change oil and filter and clean strainer gauze.

☐ Engine oil level too low. Inspect for leak or other problem causing low oil level and add recommended lubricant.

☐ Engine oil viscosity too low. Very old, thin oil, or an improper weight of oil used in engine. Change to correct lubricant.

☐ Camshaft or journals worn. High wear causing drop in oil pressure. Replace camshaft and/or head. Abnormal wear could be caused by oil starvation at high rpm from low oil level, improper oil weight or type, or loose oil fitting on upper cylinder oil line.

☐ Crankshaft and/or bearings worn. Same problems as previous paragraph. Overhaul lower end.

☐ Relief valve stuck open. This causes the oil to be dumped back into the sump. Repair or renew.

Electrical system failure

☐ Oil pressure switch defective. Check switch operation. Renew if defective.

☐ Oil pressure warning lamp wiring circuit defective. Check for pinched, shorted, disconnected or damaged wiring.

15 Poor handling or roadholding

Directional instability

☐ Steering head bearing adjustment too tight. This will cause rolling or weaving at low speeds. Re-adjust the bearings.

☐ Steering head bearings worn or damaged. Correct adjustment of the bearing will prove impossible to achieve if wear or damage has occurred. Inconsistent handling will occur including rolling or weaving at low speed and poor directional control at indeterminate higher speeds. The steering head bearing should be dismantled for inspection and renewed if required. Lubrication should also be carried out.

☐ Bearing races pitted or dented. Impact damage caused, perhaps, by an accident or riding over a pot-hole can cause indentation of the bearing, usually in one position. This should be noted as notchiness when the handlebars are turned. Renew and lubricate the bearings.

☐ Steering stem bent. This will occur only if the machine is subjected to a high impact such as hitting a kerb or a pot-hole. The lower triple clamp/stem should be renewed; do not attempt to straighten the stem.

☐ Front or rear tyre pressures too low.

☐ Front or rear tyre worn. General instability, high speed wobbles and skipping over white lines indicates that tyre renewal may be required. Tyre induced problems, in some machine/tyre combinations, can occur even when the tyre in question is by no means fully worn.

☐ Swingarm bearings worn. Difficulty in holding line, particularly when cornering or when changing power settings indicates wear in the swingarm bearings. The swingarm should be removed from the machine and the bearings renewed.

☐ Swingarm flexing. The symptoms given in the preceding paragraph will also occur if the swinging arm fork flexes badly. This can be caused by structural weakness as a result of corrosion, fatigue or impact damage, or because the rear wheel spindle is slack.

☐ Wheel bearings worn. Renew the worn bearings.

☐ Tyres unsuitable for machine. Not all available tyres will suit the characteristics of the frame and suspension, indeed, some tyres or tyre combinations may cause a transformation in the handling characteristics. If handling problems occur immediately after changing to a new tyre type or make, revert to the original tyres to see whether an improvement can be noted. In some instances a change to what are, in fact, suitable tyres may give rise to handling deficiencies. In this case a thorough check should be made of all frame and suspension items which affect stability.

Steering bias to left or right

☐ Rear wheel out of alignment. Caused by uneven adjustment of chain tensioner adjusters allowing the wheel to be askew in the fork ends. A bent rear wheel axle will also misalign the wheel in the swinging arm.

☐ Wheels out of alignment. This can be caused by impact damage to the frame, swingarm, wheel axles or front forks. Although occasionally a result of material failure or corrosion it is usually as a result of a crash.

☐ Front forks twisted in the triple clamps. A light impact, for instance with a pot-hole or low curb, can twist the fork legs in the triple clamps without causing structural damage to the fork legs or the triple clamps themselves. Re-alignment can be made by loosening the triple clamp pinch bolts, wheel axle and mudguard bolts. Re-align the wheel with the handlebars and tighten the bolts working upwards from the wheel axle. This action should be carried out only when there is no chance that structural damage has occurred.

Handlebar vibrates or oscillates

☐ Tyres worn or out of balance. Either condition, particularly in the front tyre, will promote shaking of the fork assembly and thus the handlebars. A sudden onset of shaking can result if a balance weight is displaced during use.

☐ Tyres badly positioned on the wheel rims. A moulded line on each wall of a tyre is provided to allow visual verification that the tyre is correctly positioned on the rim. A check can be made by rotating the tyre; any misalignment will be immediately obvious.

☐ Wheel rims warped or damaged. Inspect the wheels for runout.

☐ Swingarm bearings worn. Renew the bearings.

☐ Wheel bearings worn. Renew the bearings.

☐ Steering head bearings incorrectly adjusted. Vibration is more likely to result from bearings which are too loose rather than too tight. Re-adjust the bearings.

☐ Loose fork component fasteners. Loose nuts and bolts holding the fork legs, wheel axle, mudguards or steering stem can promote shaking at the handlebars. Fasteners on running gear such as the forks and suspension should be check tightened occasionally to prevent dangerous looseness of components occurring.

☐ Engine mounting bolts loose. Tighten all fasteners.

Poor front fork performance

☐ Damping fluid level incorrect. If the fluid level is too low poor suspension control will occur resulting in a general impairment of roadholding and early loss of tyre adhesion when cornering and braking. Too much oil is unlikely to change the fork characteristics unless severe overfilling occurs when the fork action will become stiffer and oil seal failure may occur.

☐ Damping oil viscosity incorrect. The damping action of the fork is directly related to the viscosity of the damping oil. The lighter the oil used, the less will be the damping action imparted. For general use, use the recommended viscosity of oil, changing to a slightly higher or heavier oil only when a change in damping characteristic is required. Overworked oil, or oil contaminated with water which has found its way past the seals, should be renewed to restore the correct damping performance and to prevent bottoming of the forks.

15 Poor handling or roadholding (continued)

☐ Damping components worn or corroded. Advanced normal wear of the fork internals is unlikely to occur until a very high mileage has been covered. Continual use of the machine with damaged oil seals which allows the ingress of water, or neglect, will lead to rapid corrosion and wear. Dismantle the forks for inspection and overhaul.

☐ Weak fork springs. Progressive fatigue of the fork springs, resulting in a reduced spring free length, will occur after extensive use. This condition will promote excessive fork dive under braking, and in its advanced form will reduce the at-rest extended length of the forks and thus the fork geometry. Renewal of the springs as a pair is the only satisfactory course of action.

☐ Bent or corroded tubes. Both conditions will prevent correct telescoping of the fork legs, and in an advanced state can cause sticking of the fork in one position. In a mild form corrosion will cause stiction of the fork thereby increasing the time the suspension takes to react to an uneven road surface. Bent fork tubes should be attended to immediately because they indicate that impact damage has occurred, and there is a danger that the forks will fail with disastrous consequences.

☐ Faulty anti-dive mechanism - 1000 H, J and all 600 models. Overhaul as described in Chapter 6.

Front fork judder when braking (see also Section 17)

☐ Wear between the fork tubes and the fork sliders. Renewal of the affected components is required.

☐ Slack steering head bearings. Re-adjust the bearings.

☐ Warped brake disc. If irregular braking action occurs fork judder can be induced in what are normally serviceable forks. Renew the damaged brake components.

Poor rear suspension performance

☐ Rear shock absorber damper worn out or leaking. The damping performance of most rear suspension units falls off with age. This is a gradual process, and thus may not be immediately obvious. Indications of poor damping include hopping of the rear end when cornering or braking, and a general loss of positive stability. See Chapter 4.

☐ Weak shock absorber spring. If the spring fatigues it will promote excessive pitching of the machine and reduce the ground clearance when cornering. Although replacement springs are available separately from the rear suspension damper unit it is probable that if spring fatigue has occurred the damper unit will also require renewal.

☐ Swingarm flexing or bearings worn. See *Directional instability*.

☐ Bent shock absorber damper rod. This is likely to occur only if the machine is dropped or if seizure of the piston occurs.

16 Abnormal frame and suspension noise

Front end noise

☐ Oil level low or too thin. This can cause a 'spurting' sound and is usually accompanied by irregular fork action.

☐ Spring weak or broken. Makes a clicking or scraping sound. Fork oil will have a lot of metal particles in it.

☐ Steering head bearings loose or damaged. Clicks when braking. Check, adjust or renew.

☐ Fork clamps loose. Make sure all triple clamp pinch bolts are tight.

☐ Fork tubes. Good possibility if machine has been dropped. Repair or renew tube.

Rear suspension noise

☐ Fluid level too low. Leakage of the shock absorber is usually evident by oil on the outer surfaces, can cause a spurting noise.

☐ Defective shock absorber with internal damage.

17 Brake problems

Brakes are spongy or ineffective

☐ Air in brake circuit. This is only likely to happen in service due to neglect in checking the fluid level or because a leak has developed. The problem should be identified and the brake system bled of air.

☐ Pads worn. Check the pad wear against the wear indicators provided and renew the pads if necessary.

☐ Contaminated pads. Cleaning pads which have been contaminated with oil, grease or brake fluid is unlikely to prove successful; the pads should be renewed.

☐ Pads glazed. This is usually caused by overheating. The surface of the pads may be roughened using glass-paper or a fine file.

☐ Brake fluid deterioration. A brake which on initial operation is firm but rapidly becomes spongy in use may be failing due to water contamination of the fluid. The fluid should be drained and then the system refilled and bled.

☐ Master cylinder seal failure. Wear or damage of master cylinder internal parts will prevent pressurisation of the brake fluid. Overhaul the master cylinder unit.

☐ Caliper seal failure. This will almost certainly be obvious by loss of fluid, a lowering of fluid in the master cylinder reservoir and contamination of the brake pads and caliper.

☐ Overhaul the caliper assembly.

☐ Brake lever or pedal improperly adjusted. Adjust as described in Chapter 1.

Brakes drag

☐ Disc warped. The disc must be renewed.

☐ Caliper piston, caliper or pads corroded. The brake caliper assembly is vulnerable to corrosion due to water and dirt, and unless cleaned at regular intervals and lubricated in the recommended manner, will become sticky in operation.

☐ Piston seal deteriorated. The seal is designed to return the piston in the caliper to the retracted position when the brake is released. Wear or old age can affect this function. The caliper should be overhauled if this occurs.

☐ Brake pad damaged. Pad material separating from the backing plate due to wear or faulty manufacture. Renew the pads. Faulty installation of a pad also will cause dragging.

☐ Wheel axle bent. The axle may be straightened if no structural damage has occurred.

☐ Brake lever or pedal not returning. Check that the lever or pedal works smoothly throughout its operating range and does not snag on any adjacent cycle parts. Lubricate the pivot if necessary.

☐ Twisted caliper mounting bracket. This is likely to occur only after impact in an accident. No attempt should be made to re-align the caliper; the bracket should be renewed.

☐ Secondary master cylinder failure or incorrect pushrod lengh (1000 P models onward).

17 Brake problems (continued)

Brake lever or pedal pulsates in operation

☐ Disc warped or irregularly worn. The disc must be renewed.

☐ Wheel axle bent. The axle may be straightened provided no structural damage has occurred.

Disc brake noise

☐ Brake squeal. Squealing can be caused by dust on the pads, usually in combination with glazed pads, or other contamination from oil, grease, brake fluid or corrosion. Persistent squealing which cannot be traced to any of the normal causes can often be cured by applying a thin layer of high temperature silicone grease to the rear of the pads. Make absolutely certain that no grease is allowed to contaminate the braking surface of the pads.

☐ Glazed pads. This is usually caused by high temperatures or contamination. The pad surfaces may be roughened using glass-paper or a fine file. If this approach does not effect a cure the pads should be renewed.

☐ Disc warped. This can cause a chattering, clicking or intermittent squeal and is usually accompanied by a pulsating brake lever or pedal or uneven braking. The disc must be renewed.

☐ Brake pads fitted incorrectly or undersize. Longitudinal play in the pads due to omission of the pad springs or because pads of the wrong size have been fitted will cause a single tapping noise every time the brake is operated. Inspect the pads for correct installation and security.

Brake induced fork judder

☐ Worn front fork tubes and legs, or worn or badly adjusted steering head bearings. These conditions, combined with uneven or pulsating braking will induce more or less judder when the brakes are applied, dependent on the degree of wear and poor brake operation.

☐ Attention should be given to both areas of malfunction. See the relevant Sections.

18 Electrical problems

Battery dead or weak

☐ Battery faulty. Battery life should not be expected to exceed 3 to 4 years, particularly where a starter motor is used regularly. Gradual sulphation of the plates and sediment deposits will reduce the battery performance. Plate and insulator damage can often occur as a result of vibration. Complete power failure, or intermittent failure, may be due to a broken battery terminal. Lack of electrolyte will prevent the battery maintaining charge. Refer to *Fault Finding Equipment* for battery voltage and specific gravity checks.

☐ Battery leads making poor contact. Remove the battery leads and clean them and the terminals, removing all traces of corrosion and tarnish. Reconnect the leads and apply a coating of petroleum jelly to the terminals.

☐ Load excessive. If additional items such as spot lamps, are fitted, which increase the total electrical load above the maximum alternator output, the battery will fail to maintain full charge. Reduce the electrical load to suit the electrical capacity.

☐ Regulator/rectifier failure.

☐ Alternator coils open-circuit or shorted.

☐ Charging circuit shorting or open-circuit. This may be caused by frayed or broken wiring, dirty connectors or a faulty ignition switch. The system should be tested in a logical manner.

Battery overcharged

☐ Rectifier/regulator faulty. Overcharging is indicated if the battery becomes hot or it is noticed that the electrolyte level falls repeatedly between checks. In extreme cases the battery will boil causing corrosive gases and electrolyte to be emitted through the vent pipes.

☐ Battery wrongly matched to the electrical circuit. Ensure that the specified battery is fitted to the machine.

Total electrical failure

☐ Fuse blown. Check the main fuse. If a fault has occurred, it must be rectified before a new fuse is fitted.

☐ Battery faulty. Refer to *Fault Finding Equipment* for battery condition checks

☐ Earth (ground) failure. Check that the negative (-) lead from the battery is securely affixed to the frame and is making a good contact. Refer to *Fault Finding Equipment* for earth circuit checks.

☐ Ignition switch or power circuit failure. Check for current flow through the battery positive lead (red) to the ignition switch. Check the ignition switch for continuity. Refer to *Fault Finding Equipment* for voltage checks

Circuit failure

☐ Wiring failure. Refer to the machine's wiring diagram and check the circuit for continuity. Open-circuits are a result of loose or corroded connections, either at terminals or in-line connectors, or because of broken wires. Occasionally, the core of a wire will break without there being any apparent damage to the outer plastic cover. Refer to *Fault Finding Equipment* for continuity checks

☐ Switch failure. All switches may be checked for continuity in each switch position, after referring to the switch position boxes incorporated in the wiring diagram for the machine. Switch failure may be a result of mechanical breakage, corrosion or water. Refer to *Fault Finding Equipment* for continuity checks.

☐ Fuse blown. Refer to the wiring diagram to check whether or not a circuit fuse is fitted. Replace the fuse, if blown, only after the fault has been identified and rectified. Refer to *Fault Finding Equipment* for short-circuit checks.

Bulbs blowing repeatedly

☐ Vibration failure. This is often an inherent fault related to the natural vibration characteristics of the engine and frame and is, thus, difficult to resolve. Modifications of the lamp mounting, to change the damping characteristics may help.

☐ Intermittent earth. Repeated failure of one bulb, particularly where the bulb is fed directly from the generator, indicates that a poor earth exists somewhere in the circuit. Check that a good contact is available at each earthing point in the circuit. Refer to *Fault Finding Equipment* for earth circuit checks

☐ Reduced voltage. Voltage to the quartz halogen headlamp bulb(s) should be maintained or early failure of the bulb(s) will occur. Do not overload the system with additional electrical equipment in excess of the system's power capacity and ensure that all circuit connections are maintained clean and tight.

Checking engine compression

● Low compression will result in exhaust smoke, heavy oil consumption, poor starting and poor performance. A compression test will provide useful information about an engine's condition and if performed regularly, can give warning of trouble before any other symptoms become apparent.

● A compression gauge will be required, along with an adapter to suit the spark plug hole thread size. Note that the screw-in type gauge/adapter set up is preferable to the rubber cone type.

● Before carrying out the test, first check the valve clearances as described in Chapter 1.

1 Run the engine until it reaches normal operating temperature, then stop it and remove the spark plug(s), taking care not to scald your hands on the hot components.

2 Install the gauge adapter and compression gauge in No. 1 cylinder spark plug hole (see illustration 1).

Screw the compression gauge adapter into the spark plug hole, then screw the gauge into the adapter

3 On kickstart-equipped motorcycles, make sure the ignition switch is OFF, then open the throttle fully and kick the engine over a couple of times until the gauge reading stabilises.

4 On motorcycles with electric start only, the procedure will differ depending on the nature of the ignition system. Flick the engine kill switch (engine stop switch) to OFF and turn the ignition switch ON; open the throttle fully and crank the engine over on the starter motor for a couple of revolutions until the gauge reading stabilises. If the starter will not operate with the kill switch OFF, turn the ignition switch OFF and refer to the next paragraph.

5 Install the spark plugs back into their suppressor caps and arrange the plug electrodes so that their metal bodies are earthed (grounded) against the cylinder head; this is essential to prevent damage to the ignition system as the engine is spun over (see illustration 2). Position the plugs well

All spark plugs must be earthed (grounded) against the cylinder head

away from the plug holes otherwise there is a risk of atomised fuel escaping from the combustion chambers and igniting. As a safety precaution, cover the top of the valve cover with rag. Now turn the ignition switch ON and kill switch ON, open the throttle fully and crank the engine over on the starter motor for a couple of revolutions until the gauge reading stabilises.

6 After one or two revolutions the pressure should build up to a maximum figure and then stabilise. Take a note of this reading and on multi-cylinder engines repeat the test on the remaining cylinders.

7 The correct pressures are given in Chapter 2 Specifications. If the results fall within the specified range and on multi-cylinder engines all are relatively equal, the engine is in good condition. If there is a marked difference between the readings, or if the readings are lower than specified, inspection of the top-end components will be required.

8 Low compression pressure may be due to worn cylinder bores, pistons or rings, failure of the cylinder head gasket, worn valve seals, or poor valve seating.

9 To distinguish between cylinder/piston wear and valve leakage, pour a small quantity of oil into the bore to temporarily seal the piston rings, then repeat the compression tests (see illustration 3). If the readings show

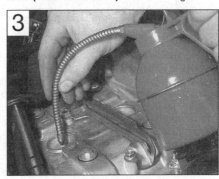

Bores can be temporarily sealed with a squirt of motor oil

a noticeable increase in pressure this confirms that the cylinder bore, piston, or rings are worn. If, however, no change is indicated, the cylinder head gasket or valves should be examined.

10 High compression pressure indicates excessive carbon build-up in the combustion chamber and on the piston crown. If this is the case the cylinder head should be removed and the deposits removed. Note that excessive carbon build-up is less likely with the used on modern fuels.

Checking battery open-circuit voltage

 Warning: The gases produced by the battery are explosive - never smoke or create any sparks in the vicinity of the battery. Never allow the electrolyte to contact your skin or clothing - if it does, wash it off and seek immediate medical attention.

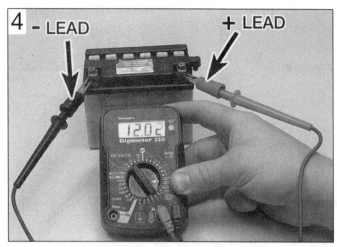

Measuring open-circuit battery voltage

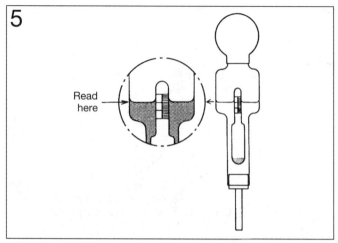

Float-type hydrometer for measuring battery specific gravity

● Before any electrical fault is investigated the battery should be checked.

● You'll need a dc voltmeter or multimeter to check battery voltage. Check that the leads are inserted in the correct terminals on the meter, red lead to positive (+ve), black lead to negative (-ve). Incorrect connections can damage the meter.

● A sound fully-charged 12 volt battery should produce between 12.3 and 12.6 volts across its terminals (12.8 volts for a maintenance-free battery). On machines with a 6 volt battery, voltage should be between 6.1 and 6.3 volts.

1 Set a multimeter to the 0 to 20 volts dc range and connect its probes across the battery terminals. Connect the meter's positive (+ve) probe, usually red, to the battery positive (+ve) terminal, followed by the meter's negative (-ve) probe, usually black, to the battery negative terminal (-ve) **(see illustration 4)**.

2 If battery voltage is low (below 10 volts on a 12 volt battery or below 4 volts on a six volt battery), charge the battery and test the voltage again. If the battery repeatedly goes flat, investigate the motorcycle's charging system.

Checking battery specific gravity (SG)

⚠️ **Warning: The gases produced by the battery are explosive - never smoke or create any sparks in the vicinity of the battery. Never allow the electrolyte to contact your skin or clothing - if it does, wash it off and seek immediate medical attention.**

● The specific gravity check gives an indication of a battery's state of charge.

● A hydrometer is used for measuring specific gravity. Make sure you purchase one

which has a small enough hose to insert in the aperture of a motorcycle battery.

● Specific gravity is simply a measure of the electrolyte's density compared with that of water. Water has an SG of 1.000 and fully-charged battery electrolyte is about 26% heavier, at 1.260.

● Specific gravity checks are not possible on maintenance-free batteries. Testing the open-circuit voltage is the only means of determining their state of charge.

1 To measure SG, remove the battery from the motorcycle and remove the first cell cap. Draw

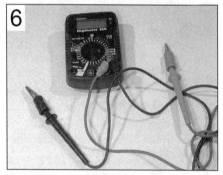

Digital multimeter can be used for all electrical tests

some electrolyte into the hydrometer and note the reading **(see illustration 5)**. Return the electrolyte to the cell and install the cap.

2 The reading should be in the region of 1.260 to 1.280. If SG is below 1.200 the battery needs charging. Note that SG will vary with temperature; it should be measured at 20°C (68°F). Add 0.007 to the reading for every 10°C above 20°C, and subtract 0.007 from the reading for every 10°C below 20°C. Add 0.004 to the reading for every 10°F above 68°F, and subtract 0.004 from the reading for every 10°F below 68°F.

3 When the check is complete, rinse the hydrometer thoroughly with clean water.

Checking for continuity

● The term continuity describes the uninterrupted flow of electricity through an electrical circuit. A continuity check will determine whether an **open-circuit** situation exists.

● Continuity can be checked with an ohmmeter, multimeter, continuity tester or battery and bulb test circuit **(see illustrations 6, 7 and 8)**.

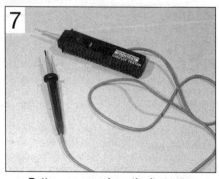

Battery-powered continuity tester

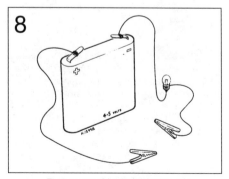

Battery and bulb test circuit

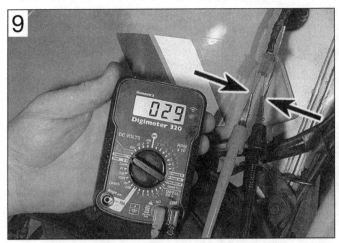

Continuity check of front brake light switch using a meter - note split pins used to access connector terminals

Continuity check of rear brake light switch using a continuity tester

● All of these instruments are self-powered by a battery, therefore the checks are made with the ignition OFF.

● As a safety precaution, always disconnect the battery negative (-ve) lead before making checks, particularly if ignition switch checks are being made.

● If using a meter, select the appropriate ohms scale and check that the meter reads infinity (∞). Touch the meter probes together and check that meter reads zero; where necessary adjust the meter so that it reads zero.

● After using a meter, always switch it OFF to conserve its battery.

Switch checks

1 If a switch is at fault, trace its wiring up to the wiring connectors. Separate the wire connectors and inspect them for security and condition. A build-up of dirt or corrosion here will most likely be the cause of the problem - clean up and apply a water dispersant such as WD40.

2 If using a test meter, set the meter to the ohms x 10 scale and connect its probes across the wires from the switch **(see illustration 9)**. Simple ON/OFF type switches, such as brake light switches, only have two

wires whereas combination switches, like the ignition switch, have many internal links. Study the wiring diagram to ensure that you are connecting across the correct pair of wires. Continuity (low or no measurable resistance - 0 ohms) should be indicated with the switch ON and no continuity (high resistance) with it OFF.

3 Note that the polarity of the test probes doesn't matter for continuity checks, although care should be taken to follow specific test procedures if a diode or solid-state component is being checked.

4 A continuity tester or battery and bulb circuit can be used in the same way. Connect its probes as described above **(see illustration 10)**. The light should come on to indicate continuity in the ON switch position, but should extinguish in the OFF position.

Wiring checks

● Many electrical faults are caused by damaged wiring, often due to incorrect routing or chaffing on frame components.

● Loose, wet or corroded wire connectors can also be the cause of electrical problems, especially in exposed locations.

1 A continuity check can be made on a single length of wire by disconnecting it at each end

and connecting a meter or continuity tester across both ends of the wire **(see illustration 11)**.

2 Continuity (low or no resistance - 0 ohms) should be indicated if the wire is good. If no continuity (high resistance) is shown, suspect a broken wire.

Checking for voltage

● A voltage check can determine whether current is reaching a component.

● Voltage can be checked with a dc voltmeter, multimeter set on the dc volts scale, test light or buzzer **(see illustrations 12 and 13)**. A meter has the advantage of being able to measure actual voltage.

● When using a meter, check that its leads are inserted in the correct terminals on the meter, red to positive (+ve), black to negative (-ve). Incorrect connections can damage the meter.

● A voltmeter (or multimeter set to the dc volts scale) should always be connected in parallel (across the load). Connecting it in series will destroy the meter.

● Voltage checks are made with the ignition ON.

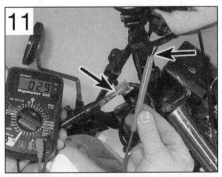

Continuity check of front brake light switch sub-harness

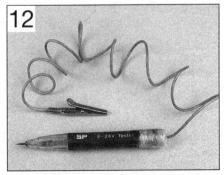

A simple test light can be used for voltage checks

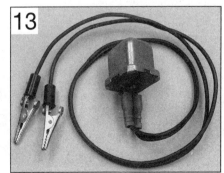

A buzzer is useful for voltage checks

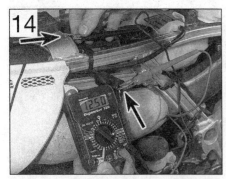

Checking for voltage at the rear brake light power supply wire using a meter . . .

1 First identify the relevant wiring circuit by referring to the wiring diagram at the end of this manual. If other electrical components share the same power supply (ie are fed from the same fuse), take note whether they are working correctly - this is useful information in deciding where to start checking the circuit.
2 If using a meter, check first that the meter leads are plugged into the correct terminals on the meter (see above). Set the meter to the dc volts function, at a range suitable for the battery voltage. Connect the meter red probe (+ve) to the power supply wire and the black probe to a good metal earth (ground) on the motorcycle's frame or directly to the battery negative (-ve) terminal **(see illustration 14)**. Battery voltage should be shown on the meter

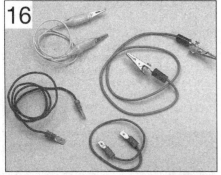

A selection of jumper wires for making earth (ground) checks

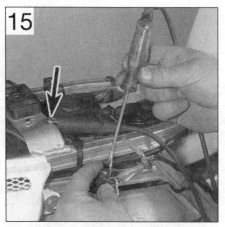

. . . or a test light - note the earth connection to the frame (arrow)

with the ignition switched ON.
3 If using a test light or buzzer, connect its positive (+ve) probe to the power supply terminal and its negative (-ve) probe to a good earth (ground) on the motorcycle's frame or directly to the battery negative (-ve) terminal **(see illustration 15)**. With the ignition ON, the test light should illuminate or the buzzer sound.
4 If no voltage is indicated, work back towards the fuse continuing to check for voltage. When you reach a point where there is voltage, you know the problem lies between that point and your last check point.

Checking the earth (ground)

● Earth connections are made either directly to the engine or frame (such as sensors, neutral switch etc. which only have a positive feed) or by a separate wire into the earth circuit of the wiring harness. Alternatively a short earth wire is sometimes run directly from the component to the motorcycle's frame.
● Corrosion is often the cause of a poor earth connection.
● If total failure is experienced, check the security of the main earth lead from the

negative (-ve) terminal of the battery and also the main earth (ground) point on the wiring harness. If corroded, dismantle the connection and clean all surfaces back to bare metal.
1 To check the earth on a component, use an insulated jumper wire to temporarily bypass its earth connection **(see illustration 16)**. Connect one end of the jumper wire between the earth terminal or metal body of the component and the other end to the motorcycle's frame.
2 If the circuit works with the jumper wire installed, the original earth circuit is faulty. Check the wiring for open-circuits or poor connections. Clean up direct earth connections, removing all traces of corrosion and remake the joint. Apply petroleum jelly to the joint to prevent future corrosion.

Tracing a short-circuit

● A short-circuit occurs where current shorts to earth (ground) bypassing the circuit components. This usually results in a blown fuse.

● A short-circuit is most likely to occur where the insulation has worn through due to wiring chafing on a component, allowing a direct path to earth (ground) on the frame.

1 Remove any bodypanels necessary to access the circuit wiring.
2 Check that all electrical switches in the circuit are OFF, then remove the circuit fuse and connect a test light, buzzer or voltmeter (set to the dc scale) across the fuse terminals. No voltage should be shown.
3 Move the wiring from side to side whilst observing the test light or meter. When the test light comes on, buzzer sounds or meter shows voltage, you have found the cause of the short. It will usually shown up as damaged or burned insulation.
4 Note that the same test can be performed on each component in the circuit, even the switch.

A

ABS (Anti-lock braking system) A system, usually electronically controlled, that senses incipient wheel lockup during braking and relieves hydraulic pressure at wheel which is about to skid.

Aftermarket Components suitable for the motorcycle, but not produced by the motorcycle manufacturer.

Allen key A hexagonal wrench which fits into a recessed hexagonal hole.

Alternating current (ac) Current produced by an alternator. Requires converting to direct current by a rectifier for charging purposes.

Alternator Converts mechanical energy from the engine into electrical energy to charge the battery and power the electrical system.

Ampere (amp) A unit of measurement for the flow of electrical current. Current = Volts ÷ Ohms.

Ampere-hour (Ah) Measure of battery capacity.

Angle-tightening A torque expressed in degrees. Often follows a conventional tightening torque for cylinder head or main bearing fasteners **(see illustration)**.

Angle-tightening cylinder head bolts

Antifreeze A substance (usually ethylene glycol) mixed with water, and added to the cooling system, to prevent freezing of the coolant in winter. Antifreeze also contains chemicals to inhibit corrosion and the formation of rust and other deposits that would tend to clog the radiator and coolant passages and reduce cooling efficiency.

Anti-dive System attached to the fork lower leg (slider) to prevent fork dive when braking hard.

Anti-seize compound A coating that reduces the risk of seizing on fasteners that are subjected to high temperatures, such as exhaust clamp bolts and nuts.

API American Petroleum Institute. A quality standard for 4-stroke motor oils.

Asbestos A natural fibrous mineral with great heat resistance, commonly used in the composition of brake friction materials. Asbestos is a health hazard and the dust created by brake systems should never be inhaled or ingested.

ATF Automatic Transmission Fluid. Often used in front forks.

ATU Automatic Timing Unit. Mechanical device for advancing the ignition timing on early engines.

ATV All Terrain Vehicle. Often called a Quad.

Axial play Side-to-side movement.

Axle A shaft on which a wheel revolves. Also known as a spindle.

B

Backlash The amount of movement between meshed components when one component is held still. Usually applies to gear teeth.

Ball bearing A bearing consisting of a hardened inner and outer race with hardened steel balls between the two races.

Bearings Used between two working surfaces to prevent wear of the components and a build-up of heat. Four types of bearing are commonly used on motorcycles: plain shell bearings, ball bearings, tapered roller bearings and needle roller bearings.

Bevel gears Used to turn the drive through 90°. Typical applications are shaft final drive and camshaft drive **(see illustration)**.

Bevel gears are used to turn the drive through 90°

BHP Brake Horsepower. The British measurement for engine power output. Power output is now usually expressed in kilowatts (kW).

Bias-belted tyre Similar construction to radial tyre, but with outer belt running at an angle to the wheel rim.

Big-end bearing The bearing in the end of the connecting rod that's attached to the crankshaft.

Bleeding The process of removing air from an hydraulic system via a bleed nipple or bleed screw.

Bottom-end A description of an engine's crankcase components and all components contained there-in.

BTDC Before Top Dead Centre in terms of piston position. Ignition timing is often expressed in terms of degrees or millimetres BTDC.

Bush A cylindrical metal or rubber component used between two moving parts.

Burr Rough edge left on a component after machining or as a result of excessive wear.

C

Cam chain The chain which takes drive from the crankshaft to the camshaft(s).

Canister The main component in an evaporative emission control system (California market only); contains activated charcoal granules to trap vapours from the fuel system rather than allowing them to vent to the atmosphere.

Castellated Resembling the parapets along the top of a castle wall. For example, a castellated wheel axle or spindle nut.

Catalytic converter A device in the exhaust system of some machines which converts certain pollutants in the exhaust gases into less harmful substances.

Charging system Description of the components which charge the battery, ie the alternator, rectifer and regulator.

Circlip A ring-shaped clip used to prevent endwise movement of cylindrical parts and shafts. An internal circlip is installed in a groove in a housing; an external circlip fits into a groove on the outside of a cylindrical piece such as a shaft. Also known as a snap-ring.

Clearance The amount of space between two parts. For example, between a piston and a cylinder, between a bearing and a journal, etc.

Coil spring A spiral of elastic steel found in various sizes throughout a vehicle, for example as a springing medium in the suspension and in the valve train.

Compression Reduction in volume, and increase in pressure and temperature, of a gas, caused by squeezing it into a smaller space.

Compression damping Controls the speed the suspension compresses when hitting a bump.

Compression ratio The relationship between cylinder volume when the piston is at top dead centre and cylinder volume when the piston is at bottom dead centre.

Continuity The uninterrupted path in the flow of electricity. Little or no measurable resistance.

Continuity tester Self-powered bleeper or test light which indicates continuity.

Cp Candlepower. Bulb rating commonly found on US motorcycles.

Crossply tyre Tyre plies arranged in a criss-cross pattern. Usually four or six plies used, hence 4PR or 6PR in tyre size codes.

Cush drive Rubber damper segments fitted between the rear wheel and final drive sprocket to absorb transmission shocks **(see illustration)**.

Cush drive rubbers dampen out transmission shocks

D

Degree disc Calibrated disc for measuring piston position. Expressed in degrees.

Dial gauge Clock-type gauge with adapters for measuring runout and piston position. Expressed in mm or inches.

Diaphragm The rubber membrane in a master cylinder or carburettor which seals the upper chamber.

Diaphragm spring A single sprung plate often used in clutches.

Direct current (dc) Current produced by a dc generator.

Decarbonisation The process of removing carbon deposits - typically from the combustion chamber, valves and exhaust port/system.

Detonation Destructive and damaging explosion of fuel/air mixture in combustion chamber instead of controlled burning.

Diode An electrical valve which only allows current to flow in one direction. Commonly used in rectifiers and starter interlock systems.

Disc valve (or rotary valve) A induction system used on some two-stroke engines.

Double-overhead camshaft (DOHC) An engine that uses two overhead camshafts, one for the intake valves and one for the exhaust valves.

Drivebelt A toothed belt used to transmit drive to the rear wheel on some motorcycles. A drivebelt has also been used to drive the camshafts. Drivebelts are usually made of Kevlar.

Driveshaft Any shaft used to transmit motion. Commonly used when referring to the final driveshaft on shaft drive motorcycles.

E

Earth return The return path of an electrical circuit, utilising the motorcycle's frame.

ECU (Electronic Control Unit) A computer which controls (for instance) an ignition system, or an anti-lock braking system.

EGO Exhaust Gas Oxygen sensor. Sometimes called a Lambda sensor.

Electrolyte The fluid in a lead-acid battery.

EMS (Engine Management System) A computer controlled system which manages the fuel injection and the ignition systems in an integrated fashion.

Endfloat The amount of lengthways movement between two parts. As applied to a crankshaft, the distance that the crankshaft can move side-to-side in the crankcase.

Endless chain A chain having no joining link. Common use for cam chains and final drive chains.

EP (Extreme Pressure) Oil type used in locations where high loads are applied, such as between gear teeth.

Evaporative emission control system Describes a charcoal filled canister which stores fuel vapours from the tank rather than allowing them to vent to the atmosphere. Usually only fitted to California models and referred to as an EVAP system.

Expansion chamber Section of two-stroke engine exhaust system so designed to improve engine efficiency and boost power.

F

Feeler blade or gauge A thin strip or blade of hardened steel, ground to an exact thickness, used to check or measure clearances between parts.

Final drive Description of the drive from the transmission to the rear wheel. Usually by chain or shaft, but sometimes by belt.

Firing order The order in which the engine cylinders fire, or deliver their power strokes, beginning with the number one cylinder.

Flooding Term used to describe a high fuel level in the carburettor float chambers, leading to fuel overflow. Also refers to excess fuel in the combustion chamber due to incorrect starting technique.

Free length The no-load state of a component when measured. Clutch, valve and fork spring lengths are measured at rest, without any preload.

Freeplay The amount of travel before any action takes place. The looseness in a linkage, or an assembly of parts, between the initial application of force and actual movement. For example, the distance the rear brake pedal moves before the rear brake is actuated.

Fuel injection The fuel/air mixture is metered electronically and directed into the engine intake ports (indirect injection) or into the cylinders (direct injection). Sensors supply information on engine speed and conditions.

Fuel/air mixture The charge of fuel and air going into the engine. See **Stoichiometric ratio**.

Fuse An electrical device which protects a circuit against accidental overload. The typical fuse contains a soft piece of metal which is calibrated to melt at a predetermined current flow (expressed as amps) and break the circuit.

G

Gap The distance the spark must travel in jumping from the centre electrode to the side electrode in a spark plug. Also refers to the distance between the ignition rotor and the pickup coil in an electronic ignition system.

Gasket Any thin, soft material - usually cork, cardboard, asbestos or soft metal - installed between two metal surfaces to ensure a good seal. For instance, the cylinder head gasket seals the joint between the block and the cylinder head.

Gauge An instrument panel display used to monitor engine conditions. A gauge with a movable pointer on a dial or a fixed scale is an analogue gauge. A gauge with a numerical readout is called a digital gauge.

Gear ratios The drive ratio of a pair of gears in a gearbox, calculated on their number of teeth.

Glaze-busting see **Honing**

Grinding Process for renovating the valve face and valve seat contact area in the cylinder head.

Gudgeon pin The shaft which connects the connecting rod small-end with the piston. Often called a piston pin or wrist pin.

H

Helical gears Gear teeth are slightly curved and produce less gear noise that straight-cut gears. Often used for primary drives.

Installing a Helicoil thread insert in a cylinder head

Helicoil A thread insert repair system. Commonly used as a repair for stripped spark plug threads **(see illustration)**.

Honing A process used to break down the glaze on a cylinder bore (also called glaze-busting). Can also be carried out to roughen a rebored cylinder to aid ring bedding-in.

HT (High Tension) Description of the electrical circuit from the secondary winding of the ignition coil to the spark plug.

Hydraulic A liquid filled system used to transmit pressure from one component to another. Common uses on motorcycles are brakes and clutches.

Hydrometer An instrument for measuring the specific gravity of a lead-acid battery.

Hygroscopic Water absorbing. In motorcycle applications, braking efficiency will be reduced if DOT 3 or 4 hydraulic fluid absorbs water from the air - care must be taken to keep new brake fluid in tightly sealed containers.

I

lbf ft Pounds-force feet. An imperial unit of torque. Sometimes written as ft-lbs.

lbf in Pound-force inch. An imperial unit of torque, applied to components where a very low torque is required. Sometimes written as in-lbs.

IC Abbreviation for Integrated Circuit.

Ignition advance Means of increasing the timing of the spark at higher engine speeds. Done by mechanical means (ATU) on early engines or electronically by the ignition control unit on later engines.

Ignition timing The moment at which the spark plug fires, expressed in the number of crankshaft degrees before the piston reaches the top of its stroke, or in the number of millimetres before the piston reaches the top of its stroke.

Infinity (∞) Description of an open-circuit electrical state, where no continuity exists.

Inverted forks (upside down forks) The sliders or lower legs are held in the yokes and the fork tubes or stanchions are connected to the wheel axle (spindle). Less unsprung weight and stiffer construction than conventional forks.

J

JASO Quality standard for 2-stroke oils.

Joule The unit of electrical energy.

Journal The bearing surface of a shaft.

K

Kickstart Mechanical means of turning the engine over for starting purposes. Only usually fitted to mopeds, small capacity motorcycles and off-road motorcycles.

Kill switch Handebar-mounted switch for emergency ignition cut-out. Cuts the ignition circuit on all models, and additionally prevent starter motor operation on others.

km Symbol for kilometre.

kmh Abbreviation for kilometres per hour.

L

Lambda (λ) sensor A sensor fitted in the exhaust system to measure the exhaust gas oxygen content (excess air factor).

Lapping see **Grinding**.
LCD Abbreviation for Liquid Crystal Display.
LED Abbreviation for Light Emitting Diode.
Liner A steel cylinder liner inserted in a aluminium alloy cylinder block.
Locknut A nut used to lock an adjustment nut, or other threaded component, in place.
Lockstops The lugs on the lower triple clamp (yoke) which abut those on the frame, preventing handlebar-to-fuel tank contact.
Lockwasher A form of washer designed to prevent an attaching nut from working loose.
LT Low Tension Description of the electrical circuit from the power supply to the primary winding of the ignition coil.

M

Main bearings The bearings between the crankshaft and crankcase.
Maintenance-free (MF) battery A sealed battery which cannot be topped up.
Manometer Mercury-filled calibrated tubes used to measure intake tract vacuum. Used to synchronise carburettors on multi-cylinder engines.
Micrometer A precision measuring instrument that measures component outside diameters (see illustration).

Tappet shims are measured with a micrometer

MON (Motor Octane Number) A measure of a fuel's resistance to knock.
Monograde oil An oil with a single viscosity, eg SAE80W.
Monoshock A single suspension unit linking the swingarm or suspension linkage to the frame.
mph Abbreviation for miles per hour.
Multigrade oil Having a wide viscosity range (eg 10W40). The W stands for Winter, thus the viscosity ranges from SAE10 when cold to SAE40 when hot.
Multimeter An electrical test instrument with the capability to measure voltage, current and resistance. Some meters also incorporate a continuity tester and buzzer.

N

Needle roller bearing Inner race of caged needle rollers and hardened outer race. Examples of uncaged needle rollers can be found on some engines. Commonly used in rear suspension applications and in two-stroke engines.
Nm Newton metres.
NOx Oxides of Nitrogen. A common toxic pollutant emitted by petrol engines at higher temperatures.

O

Octane The measure of a fuel's resistance to knock.
OE (Original Equipment) Relates to components fitted to a motorcycle as standard or replacement parts supplied by the motorcycle manufacturer.
Ohm The unit of electrical resistance. Ohms = Volts ÷ Current.
Ohmmeter An instrument for measuring electrical resistance.
Oil cooler System for diverting engine oil outside of the engine to a radiator for cooling purposes.
Oil injection A system of two-stroke engine lubrication where oil is pump-fed to the engine in accordance with throttle position.
Open-circuit An electrical condition where there is a break in the flow of electricity - no continuity (high resistance).
O-ring A type of sealing ring made of a special rubber-like material; in use, the O-ring is compressed into a groove to provide the sealing action.
Oversize (OS) Term used for piston and ring size options fitted to a rebored cylinder.
Overhead cam (sohc) engine An engine with single camshaft located on top of the cylinder head.
Overhead valve (ohv) engine An engine with the valves located in the cylinder head, but with the camshaft located in the engine block or crankcase.
Oxygen sensor A device installed in the exhaust system which senses the oxygen content in the exhaust and converts this information into an electric current. Also called a Lambda sensor.

P

Plastigauge A thin strip of plastic thread, available in different sizes, used for measuring clearances. For example, a strip of Plastigauge is laid across a bearing journal. The parts are assembled and dismantled; the width of the crushed strip indicates the clearance between journal and bearing.
Polarity Either negative or positive earth (ground), determined by which battery lead is connected to the frame (earth return). Modern motorcycles are usually negative earth.
Pre-ignition A situation where the fuel/air mixture ignites before the spark plug fires. Often due to a hot spot in the combustion chamber caused by carbon build-up. Engine has a tendency to 'run-on'.
Pre-load (suspension) The amount a spring is compressed when in the unloaded state. Preload can be applied by gas, spacer or mechanical adjuster.
Premix The method of engine lubrication on older two-stroke engines. Engine oil is mixed with the petrol in the fuel tank in a specific ratio. The fuel/oil mix is sometimes referred to as "petroil".
Primary drive Description of the drive from the crankshaft to the clutch. Usually by gear or chain.
PS Pfedestärke - a German interpretation of BHP.
PSI Pounds-force per square inch. Imperial measurement of tyre pressure and cylinder pressure measurement.
PTFE Polytetrafluoroethylene. A low friction substance.

Pulse secondary air injection system A process of promoting the burning of excess fuel present in the exhaust gases by routing fresh air into the exhaust ports.

Q

Quartz halogen bulb Tungsten filament surrounded by a halogen gas. Typically used for the headlight (see illustration).

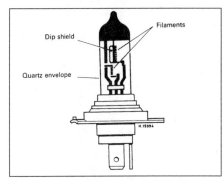

Quartz halogen headlight bulb construction

R

Rack-and-pinion A pinion gear on the end of a shaft that mates with a rack (think of a geared wheel opened up and laid flat). Sometimes used in clutch operating systems.
Radial play Up and down movement about a shaft.
Radial ply tyres Tyre plies run across the tyre (from bead to bead) and around the circumference of the tyre. Less resistant to tread distortion than other tyre types.
Radiator A liquid-to-air heat transfer device designed to reduce the temperature of the coolant in a liquid cooled engine.
Rake A feature of steering geometry - the angle of the steering head in relation to the vertical (see illustration).

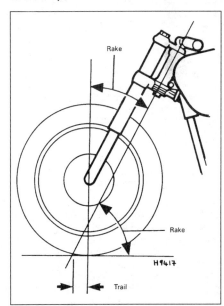

Steering geometry

Rebore Providing a new working surface to the cylinder bore by boring out the old surface. Necessitates the use of oversize piston and rings.

Rebound damping A means of controlling the oscillation of a suspension unit spring after it has been compressed. Resists the spring's natural tendency to bounce back after being compressed.

Rectifier Device for converting the ac output of an alternator into dc for battery charging.

Reed valve An induction system commonly used on two-stroke engines.

Regulator Device for maintaining the charging voltage from the generator or alternator within a specified range.

Relay A electrical device used to switch heavy current on and off by using a low current auxiliary circuit.

Resistance Measured in ohms. An electrical component's ability to pass electrical current.

RON (Research Octane Number) A measure of a fuel's resistance to knock.

rpm revolutions per minute.

Runout The amount of wobble (in-and-out movement) of a wheel or shaft as it's rotated. The amount a shaft rotates 'out-of-true'. The out-of-round condition of a rotating part.

S

SAE (Society of Automotive Engineers) A standard for the viscosity of a fluid.

Sealant A liquid or paste used to prevent leakage at a joint. Sometimes used in conjunction with a gasket.

Service limit Term for the point where a component is no longer useable and must be renewed.

Shaft drive A method of transmitting drive from the transmission to the rear wheel.

Shell bearings Plain bearings consisting of two shell halves. Most often used as big-end and main bearings in a four-stroke engine. Often called bearing inserts.

Shim Thin spacer, commonly used to adjust the clearance or relative positions between two parts. For example, shims inserted into or under tappets or followers to control valve clearances. Clearance is adjusted by changing the thickness of the shim.

Short-circuit An electrical condition where current shorts to earth (ground) bypassing the circuit components.

Skimming Process to correct warpage or repair a damaged surface, eg on brake discs or drums.

Slide-hammer A special puller that screws into or hooks onto a component such as a shaft or bearing; a heavy sliding handle on the shaft bottoms against the end of the shaft to knock the component free.

Small-end bearing The bearing in the upper end of the connecting rod at its joint with the gudgeon pin.

Spalling Damage to camshaft lobes or bearing journals shown as pitting of the working surface.

Specific gravity (SG) The state of charge of the electrolyte in a lead-acid battery. A measure of the electrolyte's density compared with water.

Straight-cut gears Common type gear used on gearbox shafts and for oil pump and water pump drives.

Stanchion The inner sliding part of the front forks, held by the yokes. Often called a fork tube.

Stoichiometric ratio The optimum chemical air/fuel ratio for a petrol engine, said to be 14.7 parts of air to 1 part of fuel.

Sulphuric acid The liquid (electrolyte) used in a lead-acid battery. Poisonous and extremely corrosive.

Surface grinding (lapping) Process to correct a warped gasket face, commonly used on cylinder heads.

T

Tapered-roller bearing Tapered inner race of caged needle rollers and separate tapered outer race. Examples of taper roller bearings can be found on steering heads.

Tappet A cylindrical component which transmits motion from the cam to the valve stem, either directly or via a pushrod and rocker arm. Also called a cam follower.

TCS Traction Control System. An electronically-controlled system which senses wheel spin and reduces engine speed accordingly.

TDC Top Dead Centre denotes that the piston is at its highest point in the cylinder.

Thread-locking compound Solution applied to fastener threads to prevent slackening. Select type to suit application.

Thrust washer A washer positioned between two moving components on a shaft. For example, between gear pinions on gearshaft.

Timing chain See **Cam Chain.**

Timing light Stroboscopic lamp for carrying out ignition timing checks with the engine running.

Top-end A description of an engine's cylinder block, head and valve gear components.

Torque Turning or twisting force about a shaft.

Torque setting A prescribed tightness specified by the motorcycle manufacturer to ensure that the bolt or nut is secured correctly. Undertightening can result in the bolt or nut coming loose or a surface not being sealed. Overtightening can result in stripped threads, distortion or damage to the component being retained.

Torx key A six-point wrench.

Tracer A stripe of a second colour applied to a wire insulator to distinguish that wire from another one with the same colour insulator. For example, Br/W is often used to denote a brown insulator with a white tracer.

Trail A feature of steering geometry. Distance from the steering head axis to the tyre's central contact point.

Triple clamps The cast components which extend from the steering head and support the fork stanchions or tubes. Often called fork yokes.

Turbocharger A centrifugal device, driven by exhaust gases, that pressurises the intake air. Normally used to increase the power output from a given engine displacement.

TWI Abbreviation for Tyre Wear Indicator. Indicates the location of the tread depth indicator bars on tyres.

U

Universal joint or U-joint (UJ) A double-pivoted connection for transmitting power from a driving to a driven shaft through an angle. Typically found in shaft drive assemblies.

Unsprung weight Anything not supported by the bike's suspension (ie the wheel, tyres, brakes, final drive and bottom (moving) part of the suspension).

V

Vacuum gauges Clock-type gauges for measuring intake tract vacuum. Used for carburettor synchronisation on multi-cylinder engines.

Valve A device through which the flow of liquid, gas or vacuum may be stopped, started or regulated by a moveable part that opens, shuts or partially obstructs one or more ports or passageways. The intake and exhaust valves in the cylinder head are of the poppet type.

Valve clearance The clearance between the valve tip (the end of the valve stem) and the rocker arm or tappet/follower. The valve clearance is measured when the valve is closed. The correct clearance is important - if too small the valve won't close fully and will burn out, whereas if too large noisy operation will result.

Valve lift The amount a valve is lifted off its seat by the camshaft lobe.

Valve timing The exact setting for the opening and closing of the valves in relation to piston position.

Vernier caliper A precision measuring instrument that measures inside and outside dimensions. Not quite as accurate as a micrometer, but more convenient.

VIN Vehicle Identification Number. Term for the bike's engine and frame numbers.

Viscosity The thickness of a liquid or its resistance to flow.

Volt A unit for expressing electrical "pressure" in a circuit. Volts = current x ohms.

W

Water pump A mechanically-driven device for moving coolant around the engine.

Watt A unit for expressing electrical power. Watts = volts x current.

Wear limit see **Service limit**

Wet liner A liquid-cooled engine design where the pistons run in liners which are directly surrounded by coolant **(see illustration).**

Wet liner arrangement

Wheelbase Distance from the centre of the front wheel to the centre of the rear wheel.

Wiring harness or loom Describes the electrical wires running the length of the motorcycle and enclosed in tape or plastic sheathing. Wiring coming off the main harness is usually referred to as a sub harness.

Woodruff key A key of semi-circular or square section used to locate a gear to a shaft. Often used to locate the alternator rotor on the crankshaft.

Wrist pin Another name for gudgeon or piston pin.

Note: References throughout this index are in the form – "Chapter number" • "page number"

Haynes Motorcycle Manuals – The Complete List

Title	Book No
BMW	
BMW 2-valve Twins (70 - 96)	0249
BMW K100 & 75 2-valve Models (83 - 96)	1373
BMW R850 & R1100 4-valve Twins (93 - 97)	3466
BSA	
BSA Bantam (48 - 71)	0117
BSA Unit Singles (58 - 72)	0127
BSA Pre-unit Singles (54 - 61)	0326
BSA A7 & A10 Twins (47 - 62)	0121
BSA A50 & A65 Twins (62 - 73)	0155
DUCATI	
Ducati 600, 750 & 900 2-valve V-Twins (91 - 96)	3290
Ducati 748, 916 & 996 4-valve V-Twins (94 - 01)	3756
HARLEY-DAVIDSON	
Harley-Davidson Sportsters (70 - 01)	0702
Harley-Davidson Big Twins (70 - 99)	0703
HONDA	
Honda NB, ND, NP & NS50 Melody (81 - 85)	◊ 0622
Honda NE/NB50 Vision & SA50 Vision Met-in (85 - 95)	◊ 1278
Honda MB, MBX, MT & MTX50 (80 - 93)	0731
Honda C50, C70 & C90 (67 - 99)	0324
Honda XR80R & XR100R (85 - 96)	2218
Honda XL/XR 80, 100, 125, 185 & 200 2-valve Models (78 - 87)	0566
Honda H100 & H100S Singles (80 - 92)	◊ 0734
Honda CB/CD125T & CM125C Twins (77 - 88)	◊ 0571
Honda CG125 (76 - 00)	◊ 0433
Honda NS125 (86 - 93)	◊ 3056
Honda MBX/MTX125 & MTX200 (83 - 93)	◊ 1132
Honda CD/CM185 200T & CM250C 2-valve Twins (77 - 85)	0572
Honda XL/XR 250 & 500 (78 - 84)	0567
Honda XR250L, XR250R & XR400R (86 - 01)	2219
Honda CB250 & CB400N Super Dreams (78 - 84)	◊ 0540
Honda CR Motocross Bikes (86 - 01)	2222
Honda Elsinore 250 (73 - 75)	0217
Honda CBR400RR Fours (88 - 99)	3552
Honda VFR400 (NC30) & RVF400 (NC35) V-Fours (89 - 98)	3496
Honda CB500 (93 - 01)	3753
Honda CB400 & CB550 Fours (73 - 77)	0262
Honda CX/GL500 & 650 V-Twins (78 - 86)	0442
Honda CBX550 Four (82 - 86)	◊ 0940
Honda XL600R & XR600R (83 - 00)	2183
Honda XL600/650V Transalp & XRV750 Africa Twin (87 - 02)	3919
Honda CBR600F1 & 1000F Fours (87 - 96)	1730
Honda CBR600F2 & F3 Fours (91 - 98)	2070
Honda CBR600F4 (99 - 02)	3911
Honda CB600F Hornet (98 - 02)	3915
Honda CB650 sohc Fours (78 - 84)	0665
Honda NTV600/650/Deauville V-Twins (88 - 01)	3243
Honda Shadow VT600 & 750 (USA) (88 - 99)	2312
Honda CB750 sohc Four (69 - 79)	0131
Honda V45/65 Sabre & Magna (82 - 88)	0820
Honda VFR750 & 700 V-Fours (86 - 97)	2101
Honda VFR800 V-Fours (97 - 99)	3703
Honda VTR1000 (FireStorm, Super Hawk) & XL1000V (Varadero) (97 - 00)	3744
Honda CB750 & CB900 dohc Fours (78 - 84)	0535
Honda CBR900RR FireBlade (92 - 99)	2161
Honda CBR1100XX Super Blackbird (97 - 02)	3901
Honda ST1100 Pan European V-Fours (90 - 01)	3384

Title	Book No
Honda Shadow VT1100 (USA) (85 - 98)	2313
Honda GL1000 Gold Wing (75 - 79)	0309
Honda GL1100 Gold Wing (79 - 81)	0669
Honda Gold Wing 1200 (USA) (84 - 87)	2199
Honda Gold Wing 1500 (USA) (88 - 00)	2225
KAWASAKI	
Kawasaki AE/AR 50 & 80 (81 - 95)	1007
Kawasaki KC, KE & KH100 (75 - 99)	1371
Kawasaki KMX125 & 200 (86 - 96)	◊ 3046
Kawasaki 250, 350 & 400 Triples (72 - 79)	0134
Kawasaki 400 & 440 Twins (74 - 81)	0281
Kawasaki 400, 500 & 550 Fours (79 - 91)	0910
Kawasaki EN450 & 500 Twins (Ltd/Vulcan) (85 - 93)	2053
Kawasaki EX & ER500 (GPZ500S & ER-5) Twins (87 - 99)	2052
Kawasaki ZX600 (Ninja ZX-6, ZZ-R600) Fours (90 - 00)	2146
Kawasaki ZX-6R Ninja Fours (95 - 98)	3541
Kawasaki ZX600 (GPZ600R, GPX600R, Ninja 600R & RX) & ZX750 (GPX750R, Ninja 750R) Fours (85 - 97)	1780
Kawasaki 650 Four (76 - 78)	0373
Kawasaki 750 Air-cooled Fours (80 - 91)	0574
Kawasaki ZR550 & 750 Zephyr Fours (90 - 97)	3382
Kawasaki ZX750 (Ninja ZX-7 & ZXR750) Fours (89 - 96)	2054
Kawasaki Ninja ZX-7R & ZX-9R (ZX750P, ZX900B/C/D/E) (94 - 00)	3721
Kawasaki 900 & 1000 Fours (73 - 77)	0222
Kawasaki ZX900, 1000 & 1100 Liquid-cooled Fours (83 - 97)	1681
MOTO GUZZI	
Moto Guzzi 750, 850 & 1000 V-Twins (74 - 78)	0339
MZ	
MZ ETZ Models (81 - 95)	◊ 1680
NORTON	
Norton 500, 600, 650 & 750 Twins (57 - 70)	0187
Norton Commando (68 - 77)	0125
PIAGGIO	
Piaggio (Vespa) Scooters (91 - 98)	3492
SUZUKI	
Suzuki GT, ZR & TS50 (77 - 90)	◊ 0799
Suzuki TS50X (84 - 00)	◊ 1599
Suzuki 100, 125, 185 & 250 Air-cooled Trail bikes (79 - 89)	0797
Suzuki GP100 & 125 Singles (78 - 93)	◊ 0576
Suzuki GS, GN, GZ & DR125 Singles (82 - 99)	◊ 0888
Suzuki GT250X7, GT200X5 & SB200 Twins (78 - 83)	◊ 0469
Suzuki GS/GSX250, 400 & 450 Twins (79 - 85)	0736
Suzuki GS500E Twin (89 - 97)	3238
Suzuki GS550 (77 - 82) & GS750 Fours (76 - 79)	0363
Suzuki GS/GSX550 4-valve Fours (83 - 88)	1133
Suzuki GSX-R600 & 750 (96 - 99)	3553
Suzuki GSF600 & 1200 Bandit Fours (95 - 01)	3367
Suzuki GS850 Fours (78 - 88)	0536
Suzuki GS1000 Four (77 - 79)	0484
Suzuki GSX-R750, GSX-R1100 (85 - 92), GSX600F, GSX750F, GSX1100F (Katana) Fours (88 - 96)	2055
Suzuki GS/GSX1000, 1100 & 1150 4-valve Fours (79 - 88)	0737
TRIUMPH	
Triumph 350 & 500 Unit Twins (58 - 73)	0137
Triumph Pre-Unit Twins (47 - 62)	0251
Triumph 650 & 750 2-valve Unit Twins (63 - 83)	0122
Triumph Trident & BSA Rocket 3 (69 - 75)	0136
Triumph Fuel Injected Triples (97 - 00)	3755
Triumph Triples & Fours (carburettor engines) (91 - 99)	2162

Title	Book No
VESPA	
Vespa P/PX125, 150 & 200 Scooters (78 - 95)	0707
Vespa Scooters (59 - 78)	0126
YAMAHA	
Yamaha DT50 & 80 Trail Bikes (78 - 95)	◊ 0800
Yamaha T50 & 80 Townmate (83 - 95)	◊ 1247
Yamaha YB100 Singles (73 - 91)	◊ 0474
Yamaha RS/RXS100 & 125 Singles (74 - 95)	0331
Yamaha RD & DT125LC (82 - 87)	◊ 0887
Yamaha TZR125 (87 - 93) & DT125R (88 - 95)	◊ 1655
Yamaha TY50, 80, 125 & 175 (74 - 84)	◊ 0464
Yamaha XT & SR125 (82 - 96)	1021
Yamaha Trail Bikes (81 - 00)	2350
Yamaha 250 & 350 Twins (70 - 79)	0040
Yamaha XS250, 360 & 400 sohc Twins (75 - 84)	0378
Yamaha RD250 & 350LC Twins (80 - 82)	0803
Yamaha RD350 YPVS Twins (83 - 95)	1158
Yamaha RD400 Twin (75 - 79)	0333
Yamaha XT, TT & SR500 Singles (75 - 83)	0342
Yamaha XZ550 Vision V-Twins (82 - 85)	0821
Yamaha FJ, FZ, XJ & YX600 Radian (84 - 92)	2100
Yamaha XJ600S (Diversion, Seca II) & XJ600N Fours (92 - 99)	2145
Yamaha YZF600R Thundercat & FZS600 Fazer (96 - 00)	3702
Yamaha YZF-R6 (98 - 02)	3900
Yamaha 650 Twins (70 - 83)	0341
Yamaha XJ650 & 750 Fours (80 - 84)	0738
Yamaha XS750 & 850 Triples (76 - 85)	0340
Yamaha TDM850, TRX850 & XTZ750 (89 - 99)	3540
Yamaha YZF750R & YZF1000R Thunderace (93 - 00)	3720
Yamaha FZR600, 750 & 1000 Fours (87 - 96)	2056
Yamaha XV V-Twins (81 - 96)	0802
Yamaha XJ900F Fours (83 - 94)	3239
Yamaha XJ900S Diversion (94 - 01)	3739
Yamaha YZF-R1 (98 - 01)	3754
Yamaha FJ1100 & 1200 Fours (84 - 96)	2057
ATVs	
Honda ATC70, 90, 110, 185 & 200 (71 - 85)	0565
Honda TRX300 Shaft Drive ATVs (88 - 00)	2125
Honda TRX300EX & TRX400EX ATVs (93 - 99)	2318
Kawasaki Bayou 220/300 & Prairie 300 ATVs (86 - 01)	2351
Polaris ATVs (85 to 97)	2302
Yamaha YT, YFM, YTM & YTZ ATVs (80 - 85)	1154
Yamaha YFS200 Blaster ATV (88 - 98)	2317
Yamaha YFB250 Timberwolf ATV (92 - 96)	2217
Yamaha YFM350 (ER and Big Bear) ATVs (87 - 99)	2126
Yamaha Warrior and Banshee ATVs (87 - 99)	2314
ATV Basics	10450
MOTORCYCLE TECHBOOKS	
Motorcycle Basics TechBook (2nd Edition)	3515
Motorcycle Electrical TechBook (3rd Edition)	3471
Motorcycle Fuel Systems TechBook	3514
Motorcycle Workshop Practice TechBook (2nd Edition)	3470

◊ = not available in the USA   **Bold type** = *Superbike*

The manuals on this page are available through good motorcycle dealers and accessory shops. In case of difficulty, contact: **Haynes Publishing** (UK) +44 1963 442030   (USA) +1 805 4986703 (FR) +33 1 47 78 50 50   (SV) +46 18 124016 (Australia/New Zealand) +61 3 9763 8100

MCL13.4/02

Preserving Our Motoring Heritage

<
The Model J Duesenberg Derham Tourster. Only eight of these magnificent cars were ever built – this is the only example to be found outside the United States of America

Almost every car you've ever loved, loathed or desired is gathered under one roof at the Haynes Motor Museum. Over 300 immaculately presented cars and motorbikes represent every aspect of our motoring heritage, from elegant reminders of bygone days, such as the superb Model J Duesenberg to curiosities like the bug-eyed BMW Isetta. There are also many old friends and flames. Perhaps you remember the 1959 Ford Popular that you did your courting in? The magnificent 'Red Collection' is a spectacle of classic sports cars including AC, Alfa Romeo, Austin Healey, Ferrari, Lamborghini, Maserati, MG, Riley, Porsche and Triumph.

A Perfect Day Out

Each and every vehicle at the Haynes Motor Museum has played its part in the history and culture of Motoring. Today, they make a wonderful spectacle and a great day out for all the family. Bring the kids, bring Mum and Dad, but above all bring your camera to capture those golden memories for ever. You will also find an impressive array of motoring memorabilia, a comfortable 70 seat video cinema and one of the most extensive transport book shops in Britain. The Pit Stop Cafe serves everything from a cup of tea to wholesome, home-made meals or, if you prefer, you can enjoy the large picnic area nestled in the beautiful rural surroundings of Somerset.

John Haynes O.B.E., Founder and Chairman of the museum at the wheel of a Haynes Light 12.

<
The 1936 490cc sohc-engined International Norton – well known for its racing success

The Museum is situated on the A359 Yeovil to Frome road at Sparkford, just off the A303 in Somerset. It is about 40 miles south of Bristol, and 25 minutes drive from the M5 intersection at Taunton.

Open 9.30am - 5.30pm (10.00am - 4.00pm Winter) 7 days a week, *except Christmas Day, Boxing Day and New Years Day*
Special rates available for schools, coach parties and outings Charitable Trust No. 292048